...MES...

DAREDEVIL

THE MAN WITHOUT FEAR!

a

MARVEL
KNIGHTS

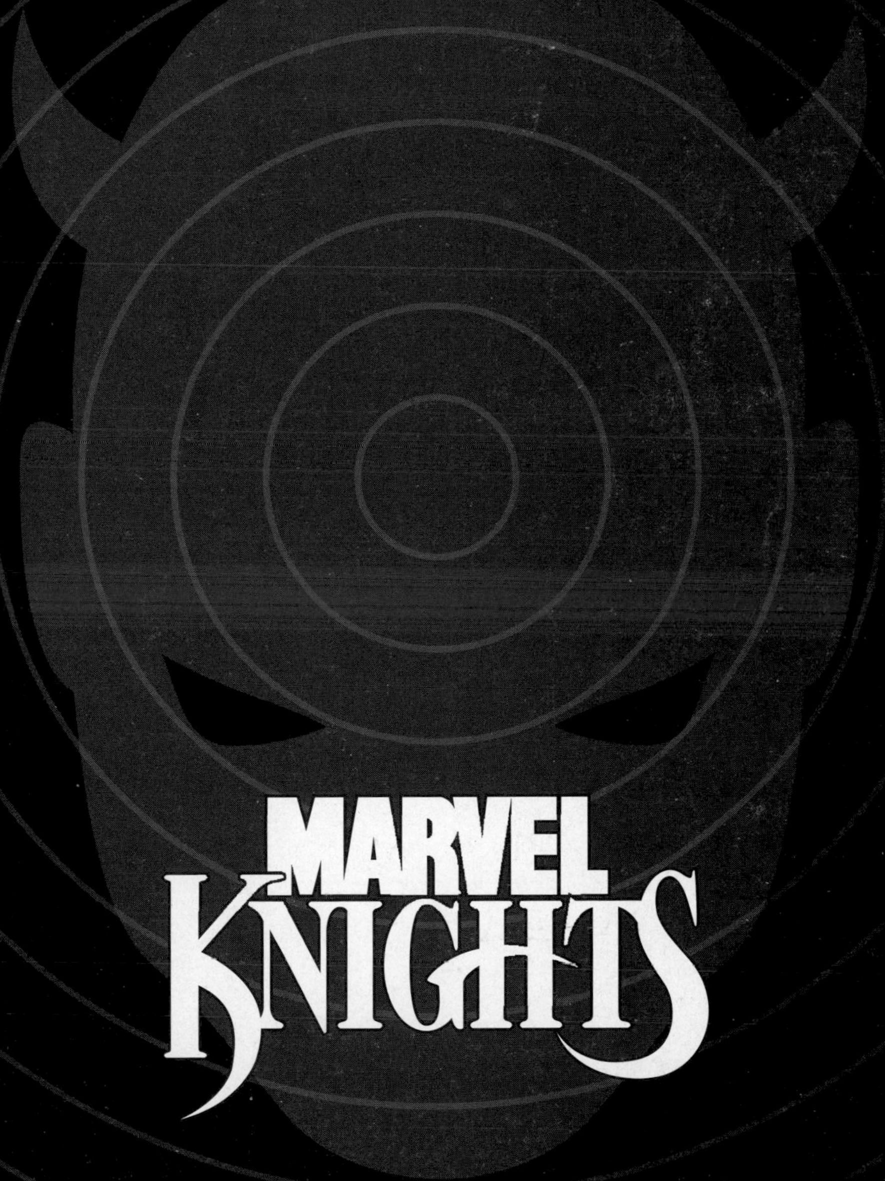

DAREDEVIL
THE MAN WITHOUT FEAR!

PARTS OF A HOLE

Writer: **David Mack**

Penciler: **Joe Quesada**
with **David Ross**

Inks: **Jimmy Palmiotti & Mark Morales**

Letters: **Richard Starkings & Comicraft**

Colors: **Richard Isanove**

Cover art: **Joe Quesada & David Mack**

Editor in Chief: **Joe Quesada**

President: **Bill Jemas**

DAREDEVIL® PARTS OF A HOLE. Contains material originally published in magazine form as Daredevil Vol. II, #9-15. First printing, January 2002. ISBN # 0-7851-0808-4. Published by MARVEL COMICS, a division of MARVEL ENTERTAINMENT GROUP, INC. OFFICE OF PUBLICATION: 10 EAST 40th STREET, NEW YORK, NY 10016. Copyright © 2001, 2002 Marvel Characters, Inc. All rights reserved. Price $17.95 in the U.S. and $28.75 in Canada (GST #R127032852). No similarity between any of the names, characters, persons, and/or institutions in this publication with those of any living or dead person or institutions is intended, and any such similarity which may exist is purely coincidental. This publication may not be sold except by authorized dealers and is sold subject to the conditions that it shall not be sold or distributed with any part of its cover or markings removed, nor in a mutilated condition. DAREDEVIL (including prominent characters featured in this publication and the distinctive likenesses thereof) is a trademark of MARVEL CHARACTERS, INC. Printed in Canada. PETER CUNEO, Chief Executive Officer; AVI ARAD, Chief Creative Officer; GUI KARYO, Chief Information Officer; STAN LEE, Chairman Emeritus.

10 9 8 7 6 5 4 3 2 1

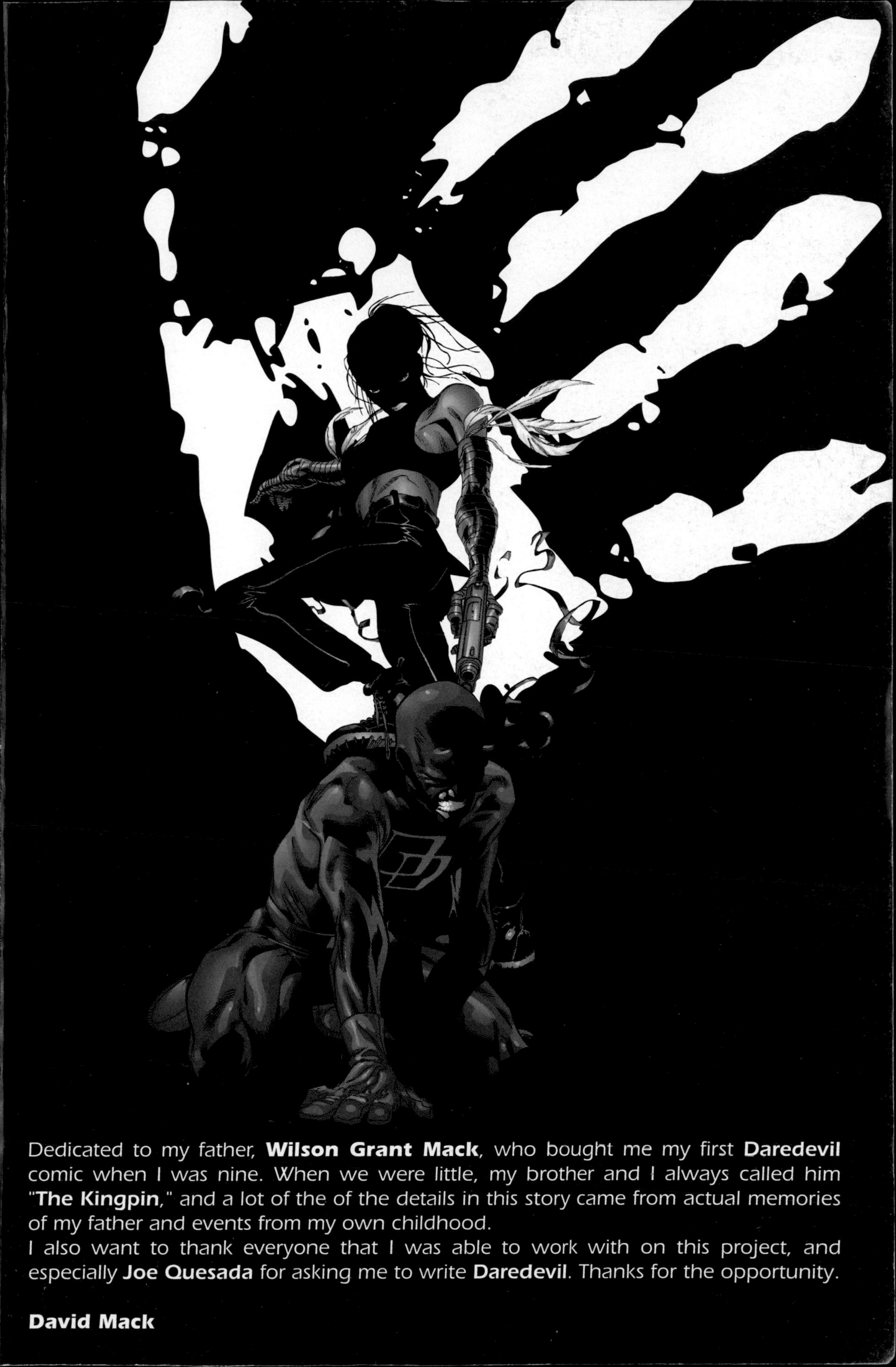

Dedicated to my father, **Wilson Grant Mack**, who bought me my first **Daredevil** comic when I was nine. When we were little, my brother and I always called him "**The Kingpin**," and a lot of the of the details in this story came from actual memories of my father and events from my own childhood.
I also want to thank everyone that I was able to work with on this project, and especially **Joe Quesada** for asking me to write **Daredevil**. Thanks for the opportunity.

David Mack

INTRODUCTION

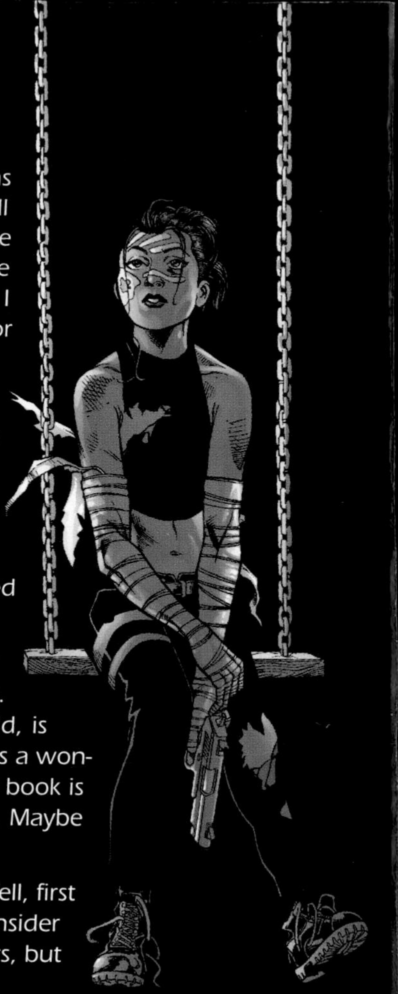

When I was nine years old, I read Daredevil for the first time. It was one of the Frank Miller issues from 1982 (DD #183 to be exact). To tell you the truth, I was a little unsettled by it. The story was an edgy tale of inner city crime fiction that dealt with the dangers of drug use. The story (and the storytelling) was more sophisticated than anything I had seen or read before. It wasn't something that I was prepared for and it left my little nine-year-old brain on overdrive and thinking about things in a new way.

Years later, I would read these old books again, and see even more in them that I did not pick up the first time. I think it was these early Frank Miller Daredevils that first had me thinking about telling a story with pictures. I believe they were also responsible for giving me the desire to read books that educated as well as entertained. Comics broadened my understanding of the world, and strengthened my passion for learning and for creating.

The book you now hold in your hand is very important to me for many reasons. It marks the first work that I ever did for Marvel Comics. To have the opportunity to write Daredevil, after reading it as a child, is a nine-year-old kid's dream come true. This book also marks what was a wonderful and fantastic collaboration with Joe Quesada. I think that this book is the finest collection of Joe's art and storytelling to ever be compiled. Maybe I'm biased, but I think this is Joe's richest and strongest work ***ever***.

When Joe first asked me to write Daredevil, I was a little conflicted. Well, first I was stunned. Then I was flattered. But then I had to seriously consider the challenge. I had written *Kabuki* (my creator owned book) for years, but I had never written a character that I had not created myself.

I've always felt that my writing is felt most powerfully if I am able to write it from a personal context. I need to be able to emotionally imbue the character with my own personal experience. The challenge was to find a way to do this, bring something of my own to the main characters (and to my new characters), but to also write the book in a way that respected the rich history of Daredevil, and all that the previous writers have brought to the character. Otherwise there really was no point in doing it.

It wasn't until I saw Joe's first penciled pages of my script that I truly felt that the story succeeded at meeting those challenges. Joe's artwork brought the story to life, and made it breathe in a way that I could not have imagined. Joe's work ranges in style, composition, and pacing all based on the subtle changes in the tone of the story and character development. His art in this story knows when to whisper, and it knows when to scream. He shows such a range in the application of his art in the characters of this story that many people thought that I was drawing and painting some of the pages.

Joe took the best parts of my storytelling and composition suggestions and married that to his own unique art style to such a degree that sometimes it seems to have created some kind of a hybrid. Joe's work (and the rest of the art team, especially colorist Richard Isanove) made the finished puzzle so much better than the sum of its parts that the collaboration of this story was like a kind of magic. That is why it is very important to me that this story is finally collected in one volume. All of the chapters of this book were written at one time, as one story, and I think that it reads best in one sitting. What's even better is that it can be re-read and I think you will enjoy it more the second time. Try it. Joe's art tells the direct story in a dynamic way, but it is also subtle enough to encode the subtext.

This book will be someone's first introduction to Daredevil, and even some readers' first introduction to comic books. I hope this book gives you the same kind of magic that my first Daredevil comics gave to me. If it does, then pass the book on to a friend. That's how I started.

David Mack
December 2001

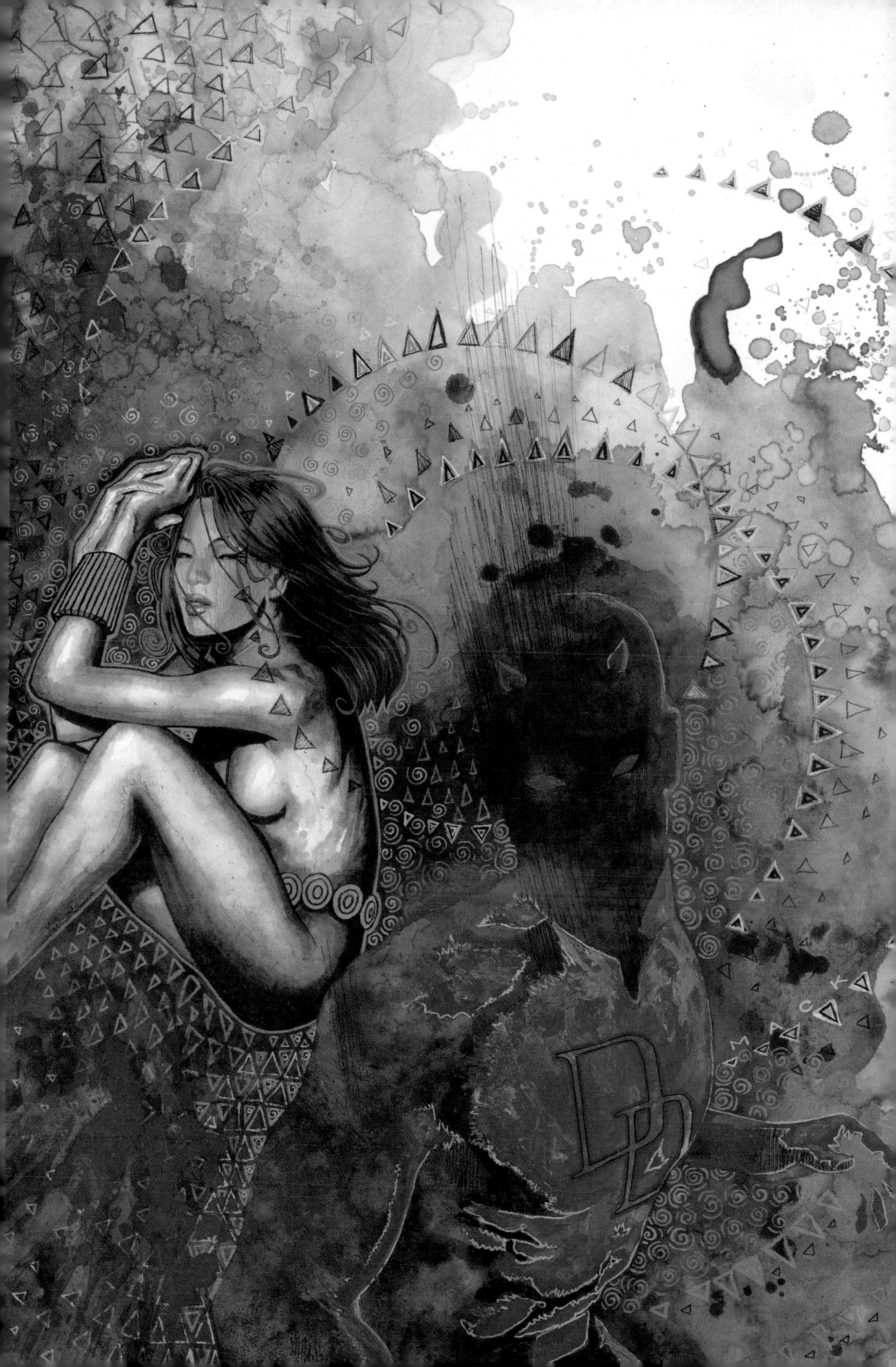

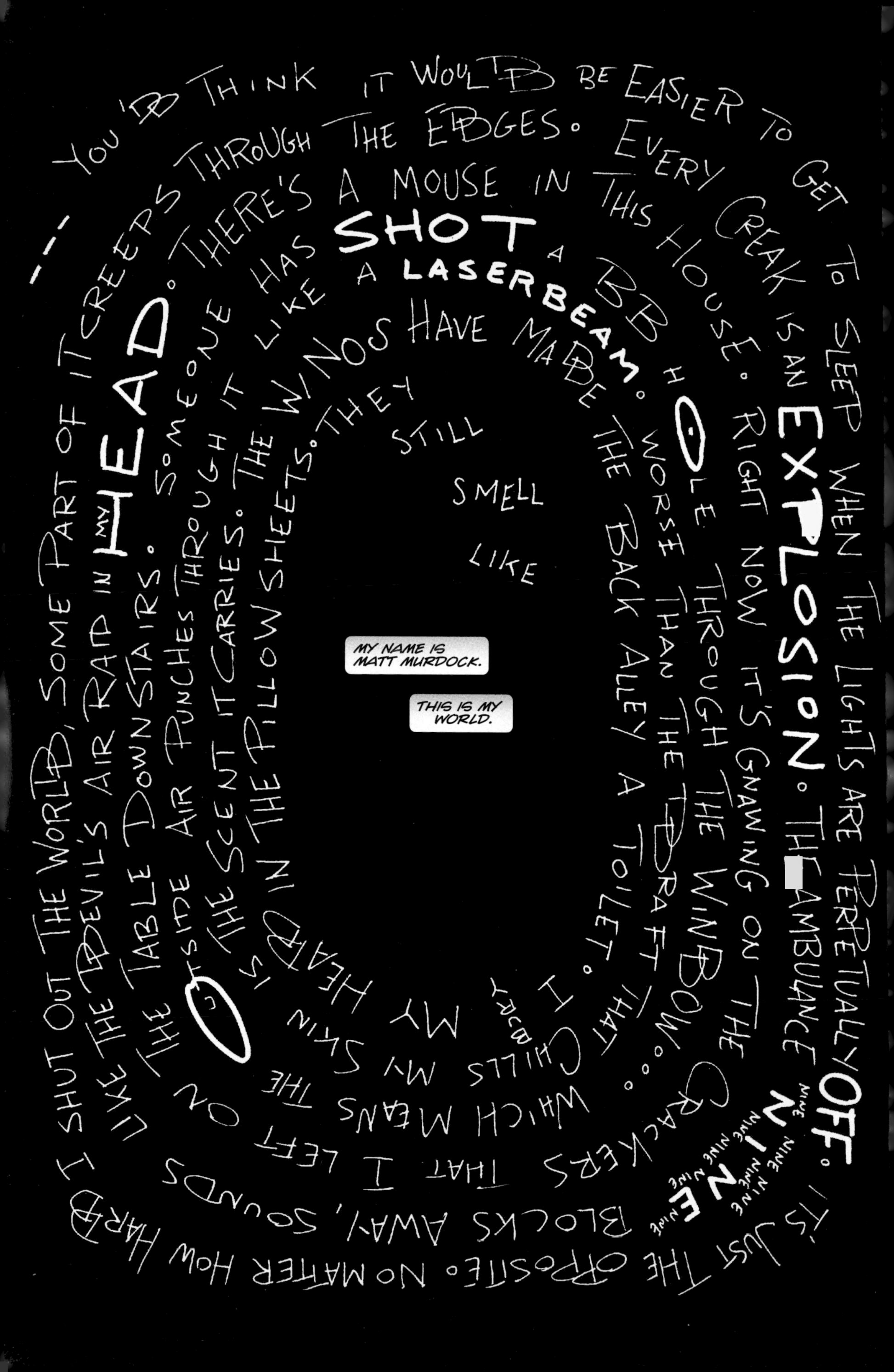

...YOU'D THINK IT WOULD BE EASIER TO GET TO SLEEP WHEN THE LIGHTS ARE PERPETUALLY OFF. IT'S JUST THE OPPOSITE. NO MATTER HOW HARD I SHUT OUT THE WORLD, SOME PART OF IT CREEPS THROUGH THE EDGES. EVERY CREAK IS AN EXPLOSION. THE AMBULANCE NINE NINE NINE NINE NINE NINE NINE BLOCKS AWAY, SOUNDS LIKE THE DEVIL'S AIR RAID IN MY HEAD. THERE'S A MOUSE IN THIS HOUSE. RIGHT NOW IT'S GNAWING ON THE CRACKERS THAT I LEFT ON THE TABLE DOWNSTAIRS. SOMEONE HAS SHOT A BB HOLE THROUGH THE WINDOW.. WHICH MEANS THE OUTSIDE AIR PUNCHES THROUGH IT LIKE A LASERBEAM. WORSE THAN THE DRAFT THAT CHILLS MY SKIN IS THE SCENT IT CARRIES. THE WINOS HAVE MADE THE BACK ALLEY A TOILET. I BURY MY HEAD IN THE PILLOWSHEETS. THEY STILL SMELL LIKE
MY NAME IS MATT MURDOCK.
THIS IS MY WORLD.

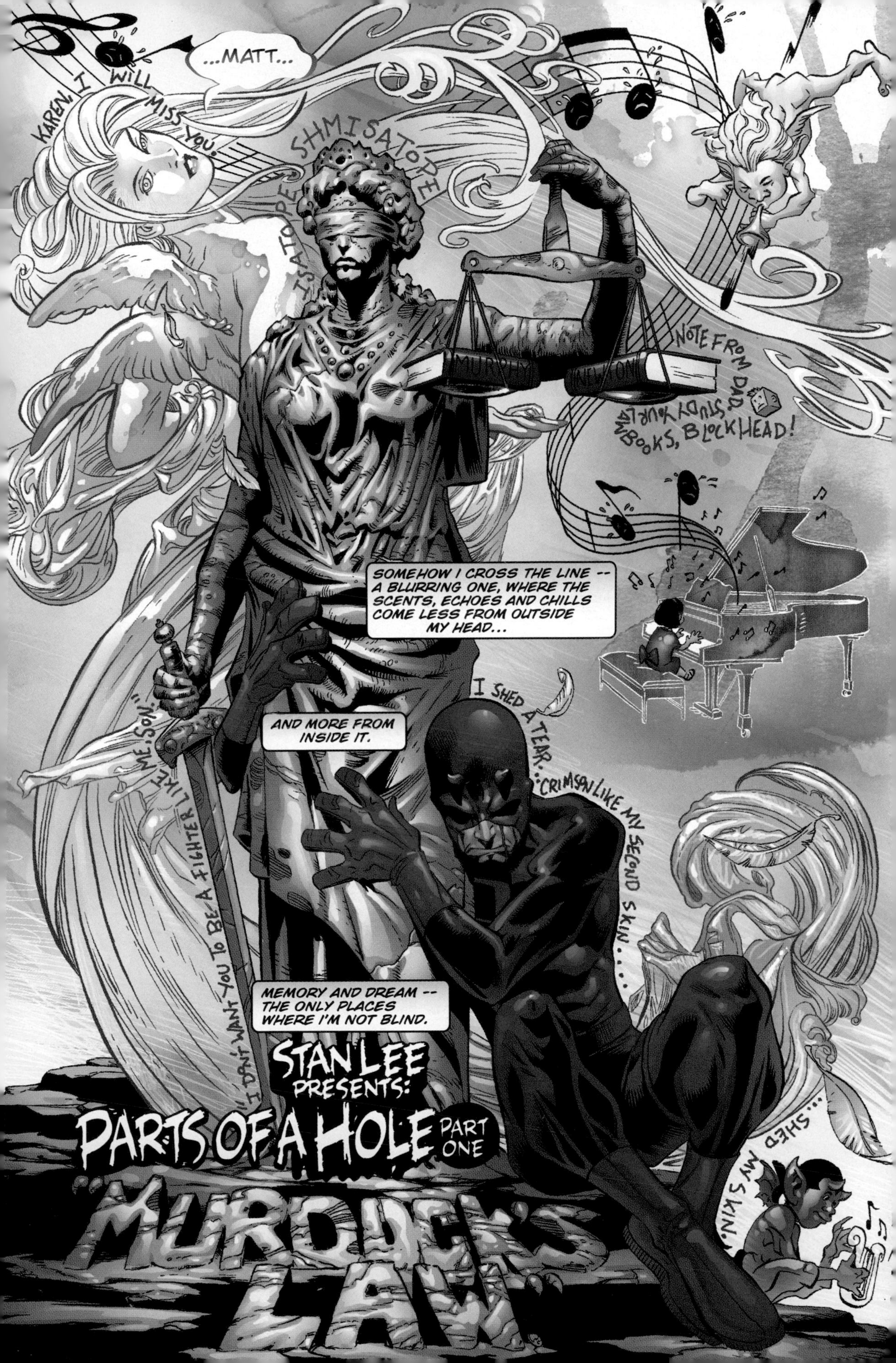
...MATT...
KAREN, I WILL MISS YOU.
ISATOPE SHMISATOPE
NOTE FROM DAD: STUDY YOUR LAW BOOKS, BLOCKHEAD!
MURPHY
NEWTON
SOMEHOW I CROSS THE LINE -- A BLURRING ONE, WHERE THE SCENTS, ECHOES AND CHILLS COME LESS FROM OUTSIDE MY HEAD...
AND MORE FROM INSIDE IT.
I SHED A TEAR...CRIMSON LIKE MY SECOND SKIN...
SHED MY SKIN...
I DON'T WANT YOU TO BE A FIGHTER LIKE ME, SON.
MEMORY AND DREAM -- THE ONLY PLACES WHERE I'M NOT BLIND.
STAN LEE PRESENTS:
PARTS OF A HOLE PART ONE
"MURDOCK'S LAW"

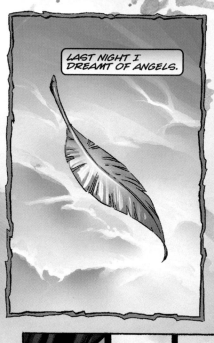

LAST NIGHT I DREAMT OF ANGELS.
FROM THE OUTSIDE WINDOW, THE AIR IS BRISK.
THOUGH IT SHOULD BE COLD, IT'S ONE OF THOSE TEMPORARY SPRING DAYS. INDIAN SUMMER. THE KIND THAT MAKES ME THINK I SHOULD BE OUTSIDE--AS IF I'M MISSING SOMETHING.
AND THE SMELL OF THE DAY AT THE EDGE OF DUSK IS THE SMELL OF NOSTALGIA. LIKE I'M REMEMBERING AN IMPORTANT EVENT THAT HASN'T YET HAPPENED.
WHEN I FIND MY WORLD IN CHAOS--
--I REMEMBER THAT THE NOTES ARE IN ORDER.
THE CHROMATIC SCALE IS MAPPED OUT, LIKE MY LAW BOOKS, IN SIMPLE BLACK AND WHITE.
THERE IS ORDER IN THAT.
THE SHEET MUSIC HAS A RAISED TEXTURE FOR MY FINGERS TO READ.
DAVID MACK STORY
JOE QUESADA ART
JIMMY PALMIOTTI INKS
RICHARD ISANOVE COLORS
COMICRAFT'S RICH + LIZ LETTERING
NANCI DAKESIAN EDITOR
KELLY LAMY ASSISTANT
BOB HARRAS • CHIEF
IT WAS A CHRISTMAS PRESENT FROM AN OLD GIRLFRIEND.
GIVE ME JUST A LITTLE MORE TIME

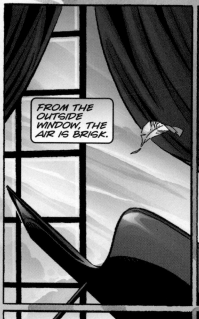

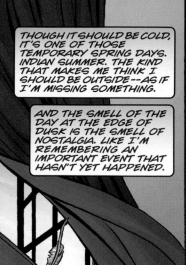

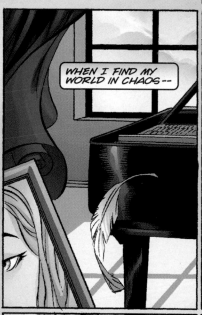

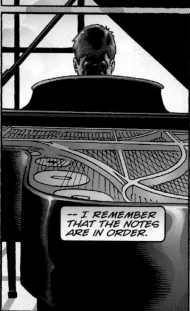

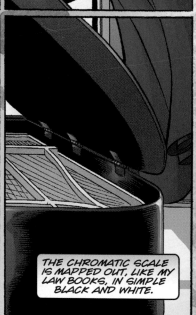

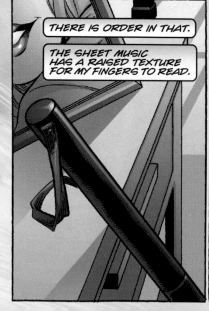

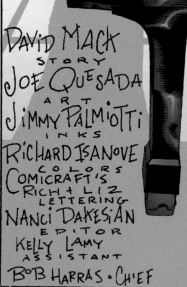

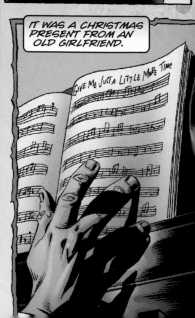

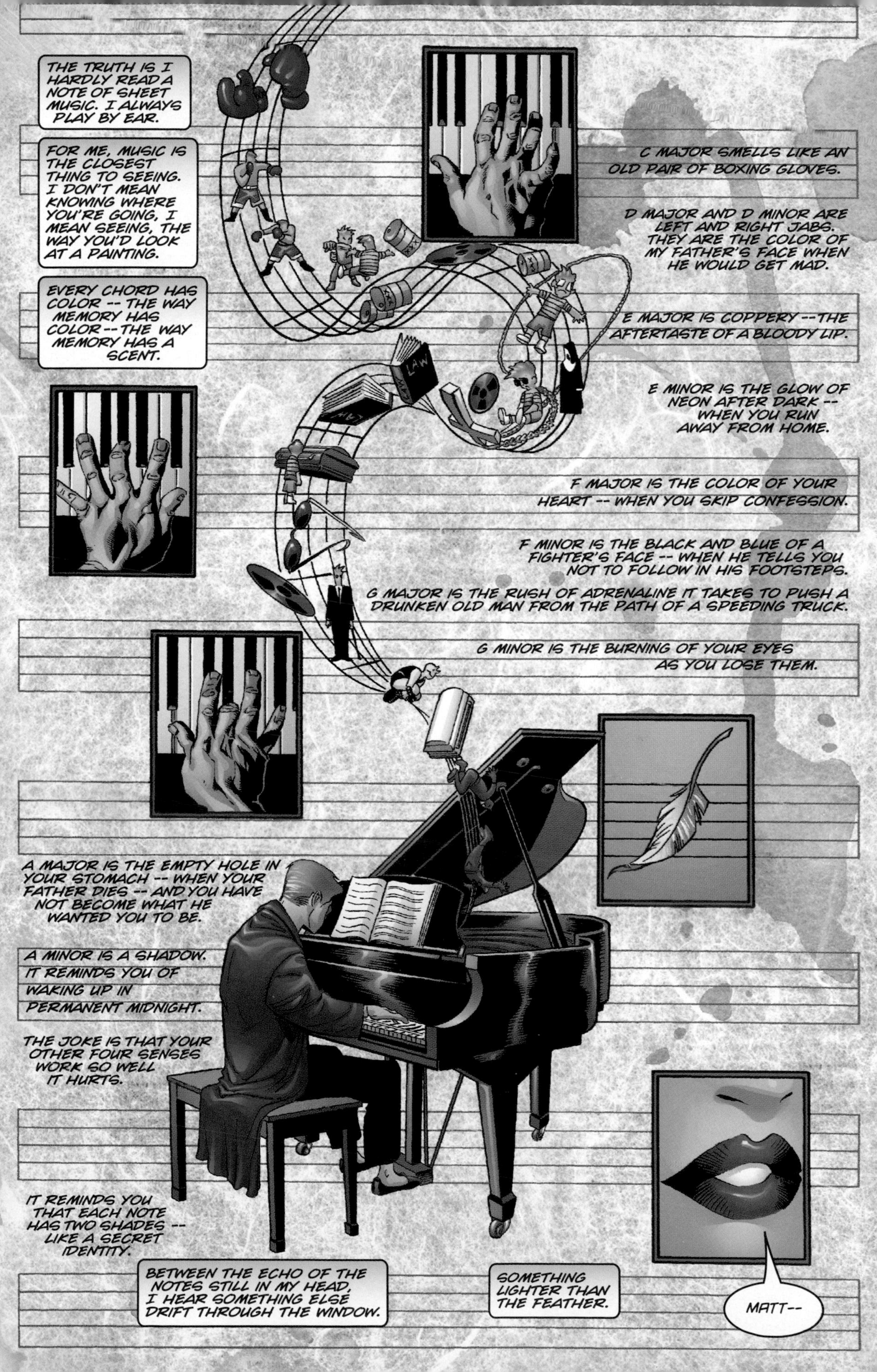
THE TRUTH IS I HARDLY READ A NOTE OF SHEET MUSIC. I ALWAYS PLAY BY EAR.
FOR ME, MUSIC IS THE CLOSEST THING TO SEEING. I DON'T MEAN KNOWING WHERE YOU'RE GOING, I MEAN SEEING, THE WAY YOU'D LOOK AT A PAINTING.
EVERY CHORD HAS COLOR -- THE WAY MEMORY HAS COLOR -- THE WAY MEMORY HAS A SCENT.
C MAJOR SMELLS LIKE AN OLD PAIR OF BOXING GLOVES.
D MAJOR AND D MINOR ARE LEFT AND RIGHT JABS. THEY ARE THE COLOR OF MY FATHER'S FACE WHEN HE WOULD GET MAD.
E MAJOR IS COPPERY -- THE AFTERTASTE OF A BLOODY LIP.
E MINOR IS THE GLOW OF NEON AFTER DARK -- WHEN YOU RUN AWAY FROM HOME.
F MAJOR IS THE COLOR OF YOUR HEART -- WHEN YOU SKIP CONFESSION.
F MINOR IS THE BLACK AND BLUE OF A FIGHTER'S FACE -- WHEN HE TELLS YOU NOT TO FOLLOW IN HIS FOOTSTEPS.
G MAJOR IS THE RUSH OF ADRENALINE IT TAKES TO PUSH A DRUNKEN OLD MAN FROM THE PATH OF A SPEEDING TRUCK.
G MINOR IS THE BURNING OF YOUR EYES AS YOU LOSE THEM.
A MAJOR IS THE EMPTY HOLE IN YOUR STOMACH -- WHEN YOUR FATHER DIES -- AND YOU HAVE NOT BECOME WHAT HE WANTED YOU TO BE.
A MINOR IS A SHADOW. IT REMINDS YOU OF WAKING UP IN PERMANENT MIDNIGHT.
THE JOKE IS THAT YOUR OTHER FOUR SENSES WORK SO WELL IT HURTS.
IT REMINDS YOU THAT EACH NOTE HAS TWO SHADES -- LIKE A SECRET IDENTITY.
BETWEEN THE ECHO OF THE NOTES STILL IN MY HEAD, I HEAR SOMETHING ELSE DRIFT THROUGH THE WINDOW.
SOMETHING LIGHTER THAN THE FEATHER.
MATT--

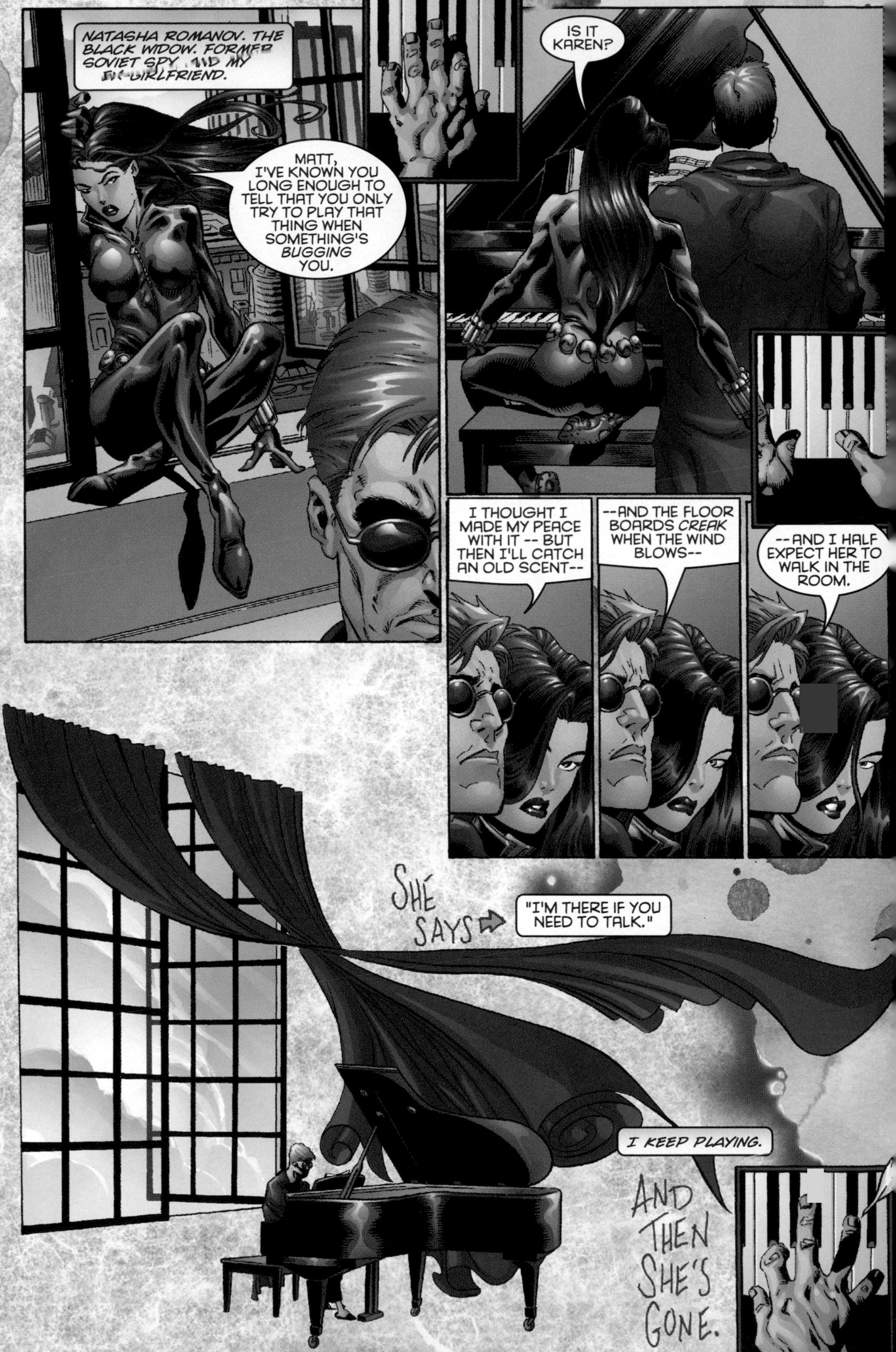
NATASHA ROMANOV. THE BLACK WIDOW. FORMER SOVIET SPY AND MY GIRLFRIEND.
MATT, I'VE KNOWN YOU LONG ENOUGH TO TELL THAT YOU ONLY TRY TO PLAY THAT THING WHEN SOMETHING'S BUGGING YOU.
IS IT KAREN?
I THOUGHT I MADE MY PEACE WITH IT -- BUT THEN I'LL CATCH AN OLD SCENT--
--AND THE FLOOR BOARDS CREAK WHEN THE WIND BLOWS--
--AND I HALF EXPECT HER TO WALK IN THE ROOM.
SHE SAYS
"I'M THERE IF YOU NEED TO TALK."
I KEEP PLAYING.
AND THEN SHE'S GONE.

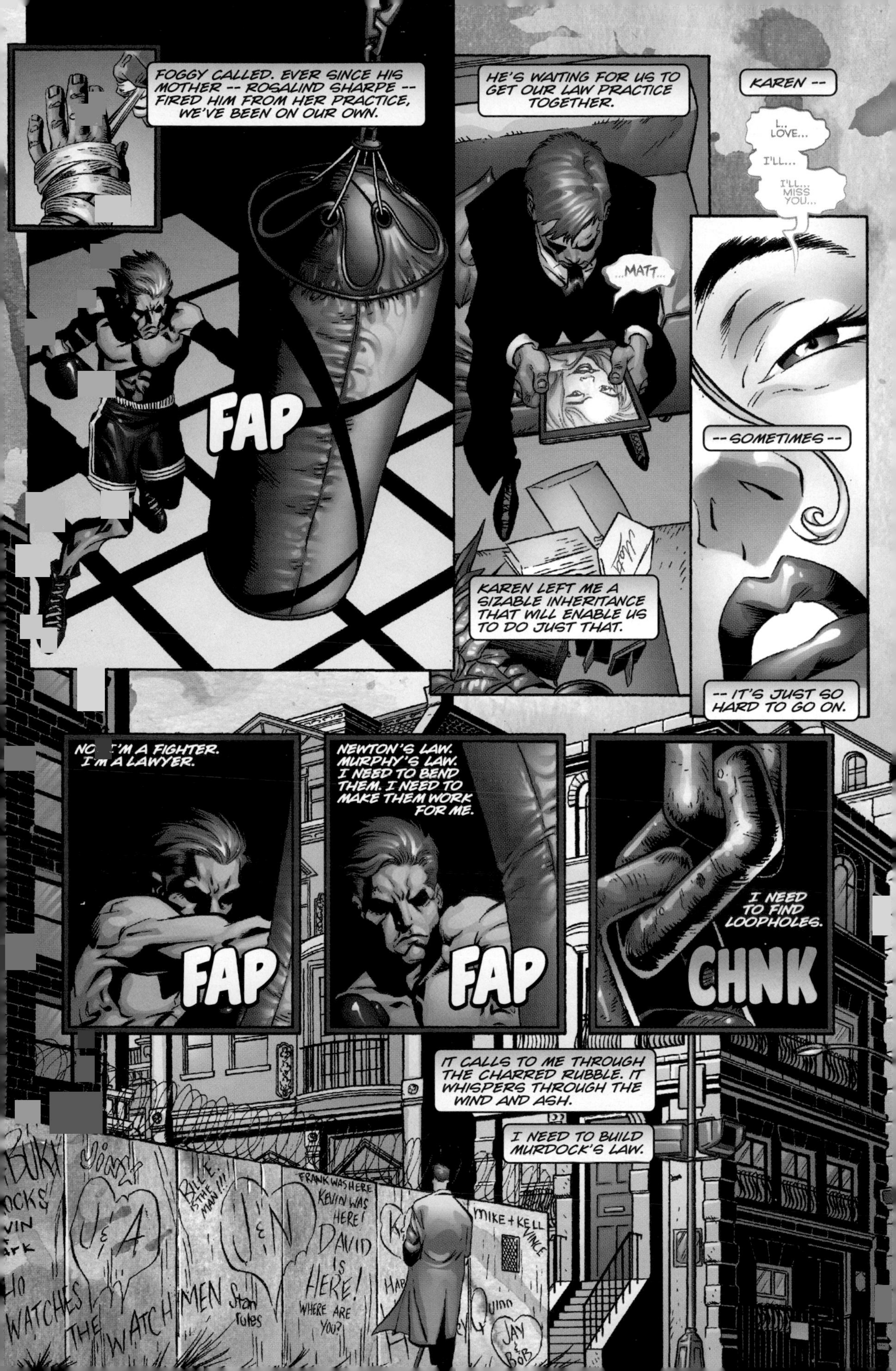
FOGGY CALLED. EVER SINCE HIS MOTHER -- ROSALIND SHARPE -- FIRED HIM FROM HER PRACTICE, WE'VE BEEN ON OUR OWN.
FAP
HE'S WAITING FOR US TO GET OUR LAW PRACTICE TOGETHER.
...MATT...
KAREN LEFT ME A SIZABLE INHERITANCE THAT WILL ENABLE US TO DO JUST THAT.
KAREN --
L... LOVE... I'LL... I'LL... MISS YOU...
-- SOMETIMES --
-- IT'S JUST SO HARD TO GO ON.
NO… I'M A FIGHTER. I'M A LAWYER.
FAP
NEWTON'S LAW. MURPHY'S LAW. I NEED TO BEND THEM. I NEED TO MAKE THEM WORK FOR ME.
FAP
I NEED TO FIND LOOPHOLES.
CHNK
IT CALLS TO ME THROUGH THE CHARRED RUBBLE. IT WHISPERS THROUGH THE WIND AND ASH.
I NEED TO BUILD MURDOCK'S LAW.
BILL E. IS THE MAN!!!
FRANK WAS HERE
KEVIN WAS HERE!
DAVID IS HERE! WHERE ARE YOU?
MIKE + KELL
VINCE
WHO WATCHES THE WATCHMEN
Stan rules
JAY & BOB

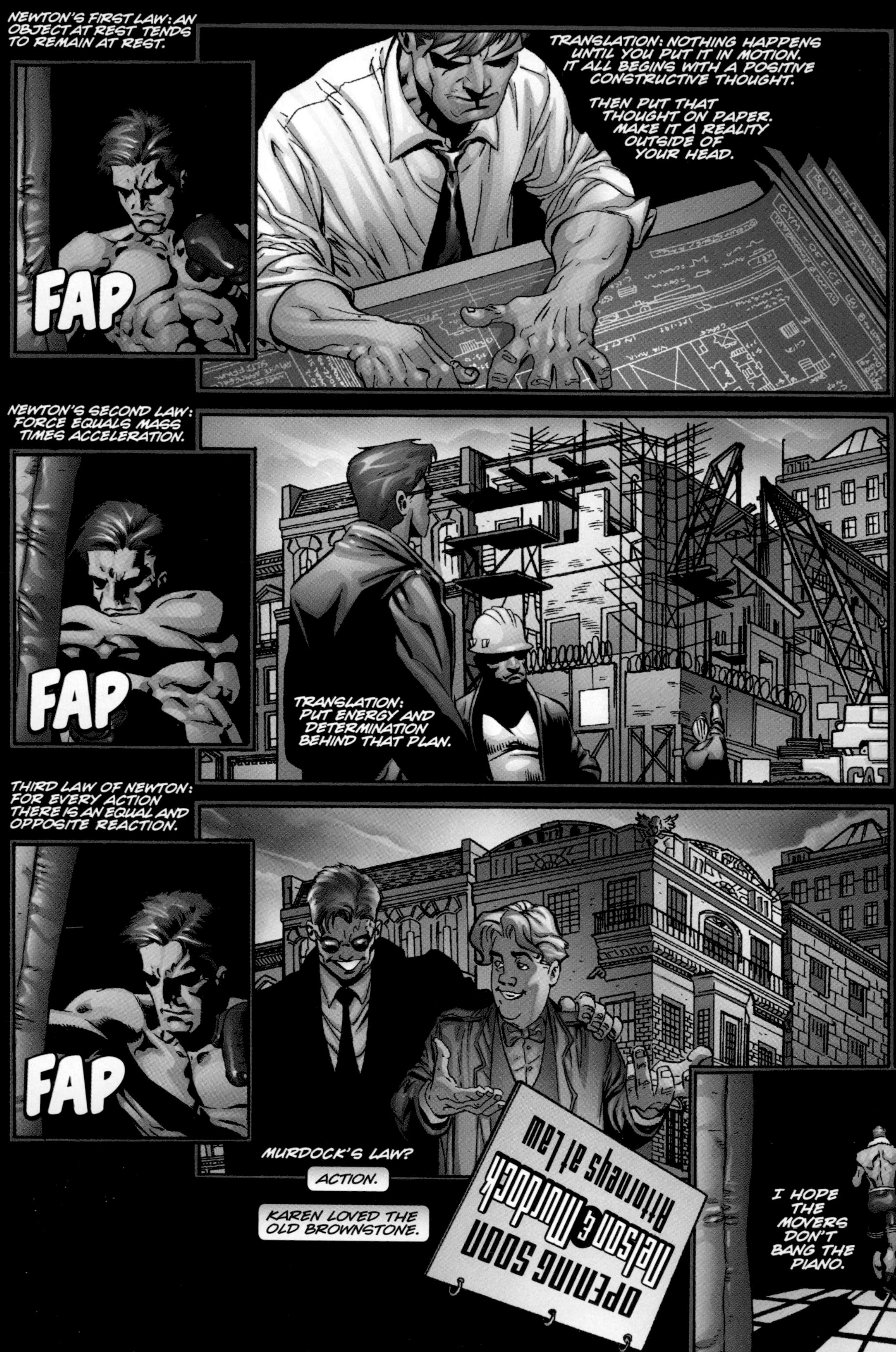
NEWTON'S FIRST LAW: AN OBJECT AT REST TENDS TO REMAIN AT REST.
TRANSLATION: NOTHING HAPPENS UNTIL YOU PUT IT IN MOTION. IT ALL BEGINS WITH A POSITIVE CONSTRUCTIVE THOUGHT.
THEN PUT THAT THOUGHT ON PAPER. MAKE IT A REALITY OUTSIDE OF YOUR HEAD.
FAP
NEWTON'S SECOND LAW: FORCE EQUALS MASS TIMES ACCELERATION.
FAP
TRANSLATION: PUT ENERGY AND DETERMINATION BEHIND THAT PLAN.
THIRD LAW OF NEWTON: FOR EVERY ACTION THERE IS AN EQUAL AND OPPOSITE REACTION.
FAP
OPENING SOON
Nelson & Murdock
Attorneys at Law
MURDOCK'S LAW?
ACTION.
KAREN LOVED THE OLD BROWNSTONE.
I HOPE THE MOVERS DON'T BANG THE PIANO.

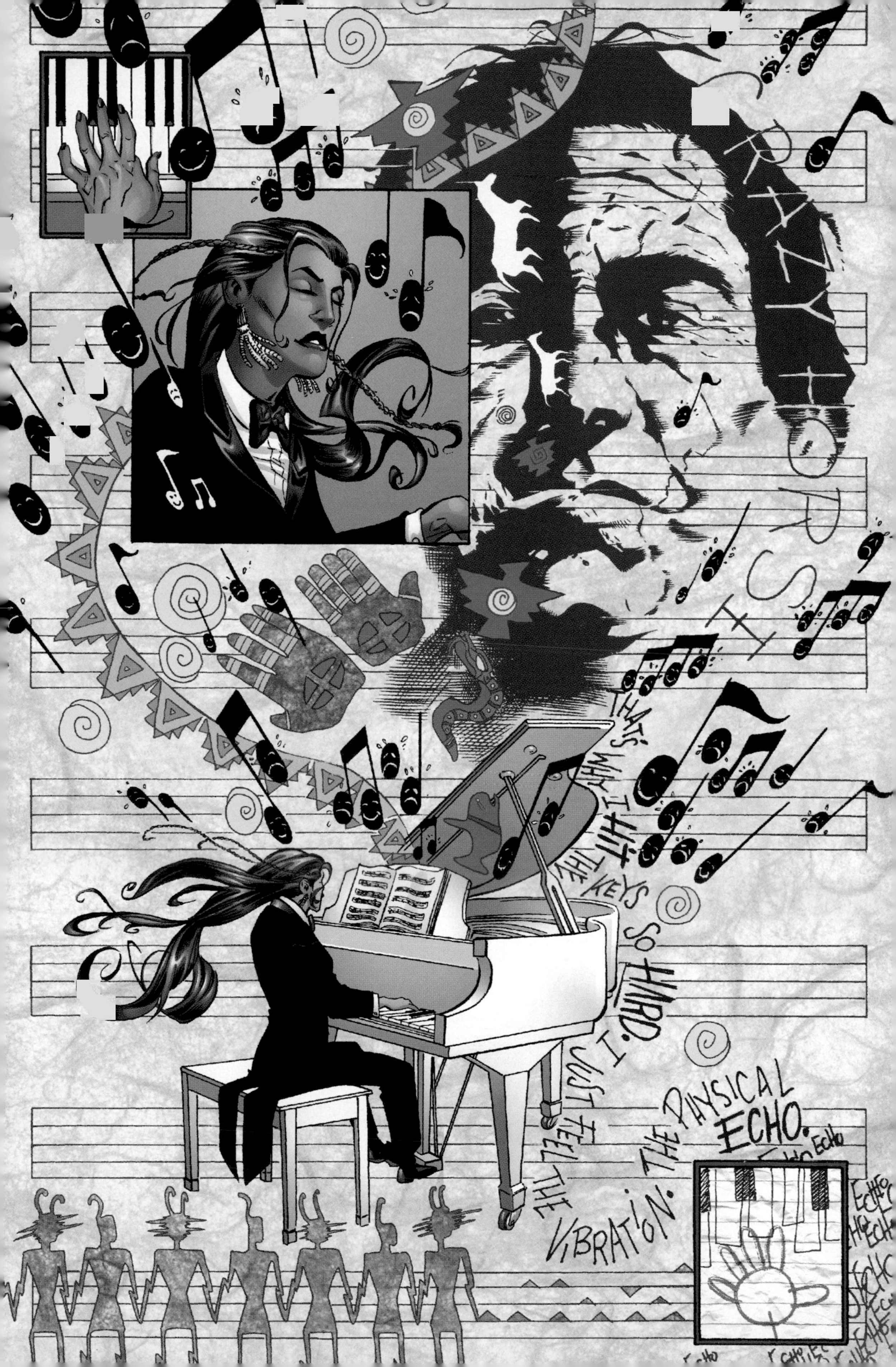
THAT'S WHY I HIT THE KEYS SO HARD. I JUST FEEL THE VIBRATION. THE PHYSICAL ECHO.
ECHO ECHO
ECHO ECHO ECHO

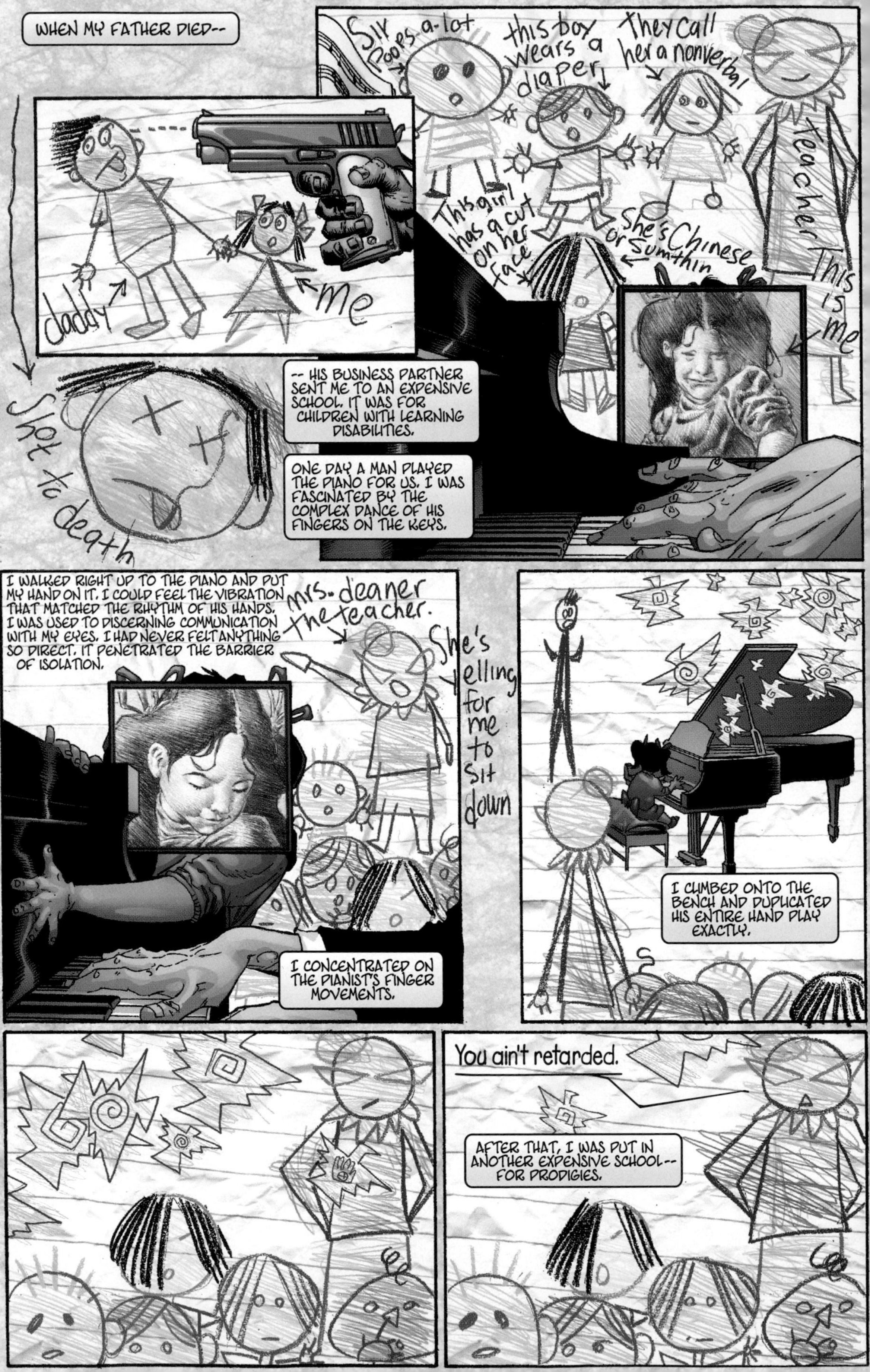
WHEN MY FATHER DIED--
daddy
me
Shot to death
Sir Poops-a-lot
this boy wears a diaper
They call her a nonverbal
Teacher
This girl has a cut on her face
She's Chinese or Sumthin
This is me
-- HIS BUSINESS PARTNER SENT ME TO AN EXPENSIVE SCHOOL. IT WAS FOR CHILDREN WITH LEARNING DISABILITIES.
ONE DAY A MAN PLAYED THE PIANO FOR US. I WAS FASCINATED BY THE COMPLEX DANCE OF HIS FINGERS ON THE KEYS.
I WALKED RIGHT UP TO THE PIANO AND PUT MY HAND ON IT. I COULD FEEL THE VIBRATION THAT MATCHED THE RHYTHM OF HIS HANDS. I WAS USED TO DISCERNING COMMUNICATION WITH MY EYES. I HAD NEVER FELT ANYTHING SO DIRECT. IT PENETRATED THE BARRIER OF ISOLATION.
mrs. deaner the teacher.
She's yelling for me to sit down
I CONCENTRATED ON THE PIANIST'S FINGER MOVEMENTS.
I CLIMBED ONTO THE BENCH AND DUPLICATED HIS ENTIRE HAND PLAY EXACTLY.
You ain't retarded.
AFTER THAT, I WAS PUT IN ANOTHER EXPENSIVE SCHOOL-- FOR PRODIGIES.

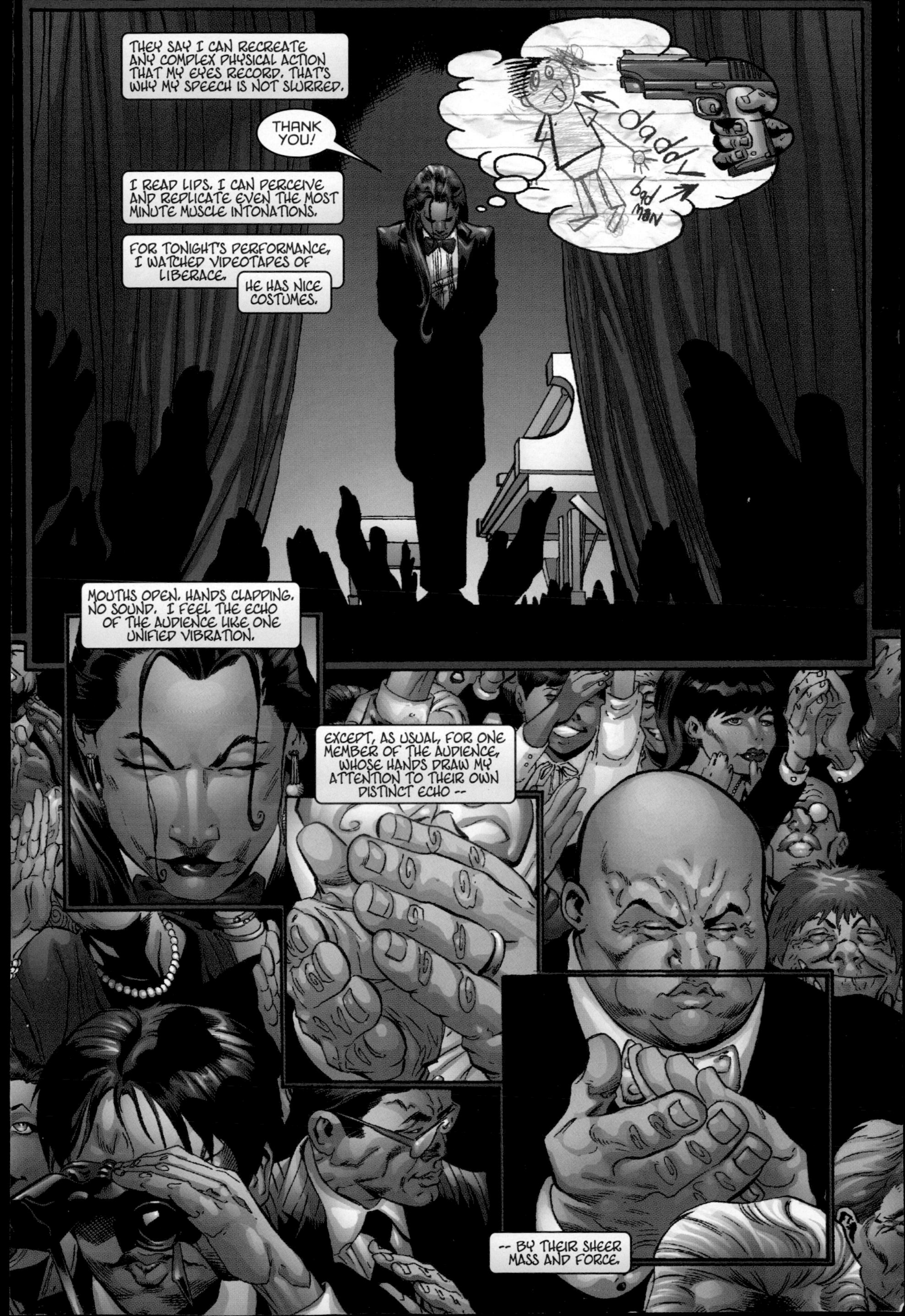
THEY SAY I CAN RECREATE ANY COMPLEX PHYSICAL ACTION THAT MY EYES RECORD. THAT'S WHY MY SPEECH IS NOT SLURRED.
THANK YOU!
daddy
bad man
I READ LIPS. I CAN PERCEIVE AND REPLICATE EVEN THE MOST MINUTE MUSCLE INTONATIONS.
FOR TONIGHT'S PERFORMANCE, I WATCHED VIDEOTAPES OF LIBERACE.
HE HAS NICE COSTUMES.
MOUTHS OPEN. HANDS CLAPPING. NO SOUND. I FEEL THE ECHO OF THE AUDIENCE LIKE ONE UNIFIED VIBRATION.
EXCEPT, AS USUAL, FOR ONE MEMBER OF THE AUDIENCE, WHOSE HANDS DRAW MY ATTENTION TO THEIR OWN DISTINCT ECHO --
-- BY THEIR SHEER MASS AND FORCE.

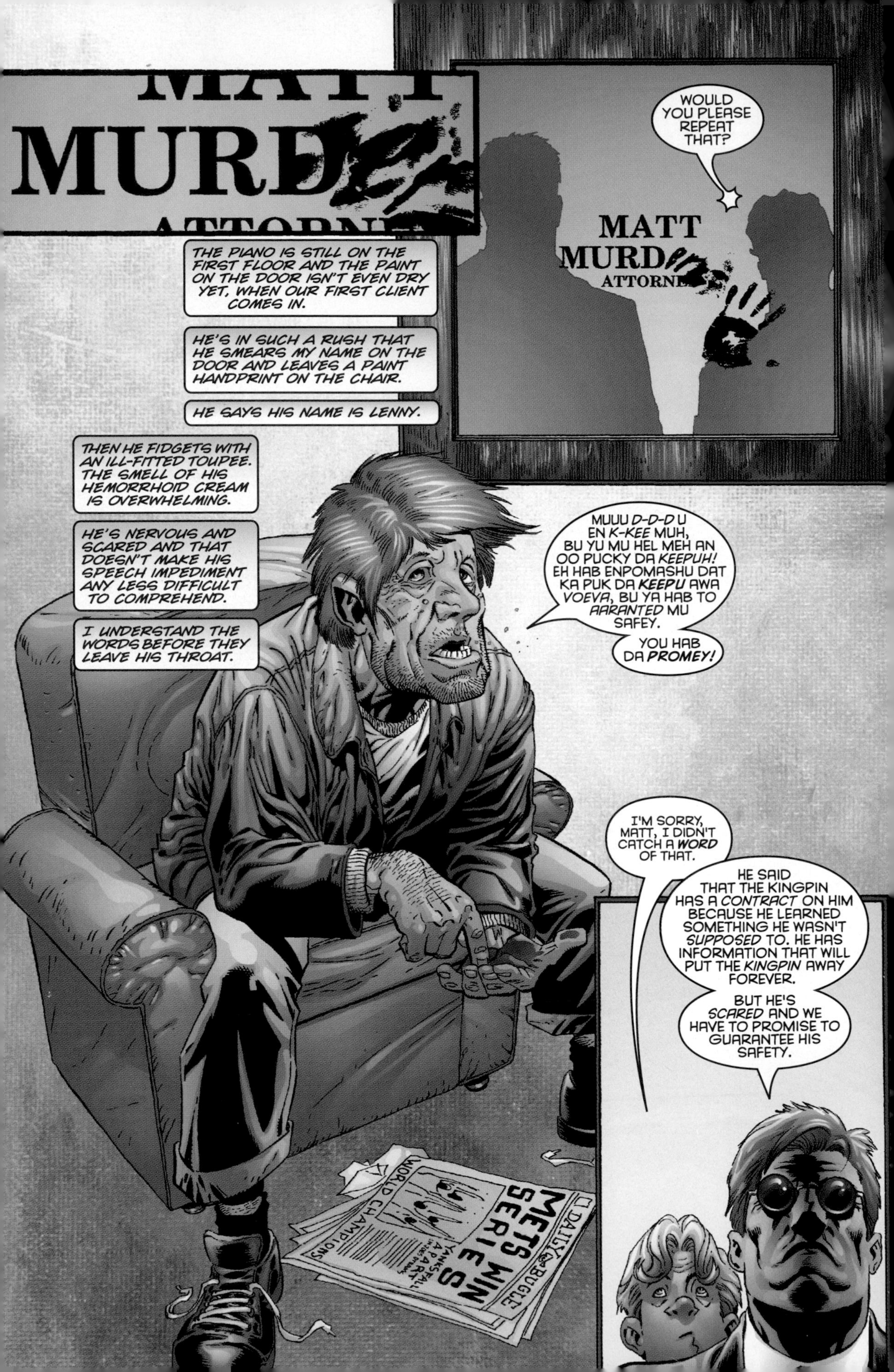
MURD
MATT MURD ATTORNE
WOULD YOU PLEASE REPEAT THAT?
THE PIANO IS STILL ON THE FIRST FLOOR AND THE PAINT ON THE DOOR ISN'T EVEN DRY YET, WHEN OUR FIRST CLIENT COMES IN.
HE'S IN SUCH A RUSH THAT HE SMEARS MY NAME ON THE DOOR AND LEAVES A PAINT HANDPRINT ON THE CHAIR.
HE SAYS HIS NAME IS LENNY.
THEN HE FIDGETS WITH AN ILL-FITTED TOUPEE. THE SMELL OF HIS HEMORRHOID CREAM IS OVERWHELMING.
HE'S NERVOUS AND SCARED AND THAT DOESN'T MAKE HIS SPEECH IMPEDIMENT ANY LESS DIFFICULT TO COMPREHEND.
I UNDERSTAND THE WORDS BEFORE THEY LEAVE HIS THROAT.
MUUU D-D-D U EN K-KEE MUH, BU YU MU HEL MEH AN OO PUCKY DA KEEPUH! EH HAB ENPOMASHU DAT KA PUK DA KEEPU AWA VOEVA, BU YA HAB TO AARANTED MU SAFEY.
YOU HAB DA PROMEY!
I'M SORRY, MATT, I DIDN'T CATCH A WORD OF THAT.
HE SAID THAT THE KINGPIN HAS A CONTRACT ON HIM BECAUSE HE LEARNED SOMETHING HE WASN'T SUPPOSED TO. HE HAS INFORMATION THAT WILL PUT THE KINGPIN AWAY FOREVER.
BUT HE'S SCARED AND WE HAVE TO PROMISE TO GUARANTEE HIS SAFETY.
DAILY BUGLE
METS WIN SERIES
WORLD CHAMPIONS

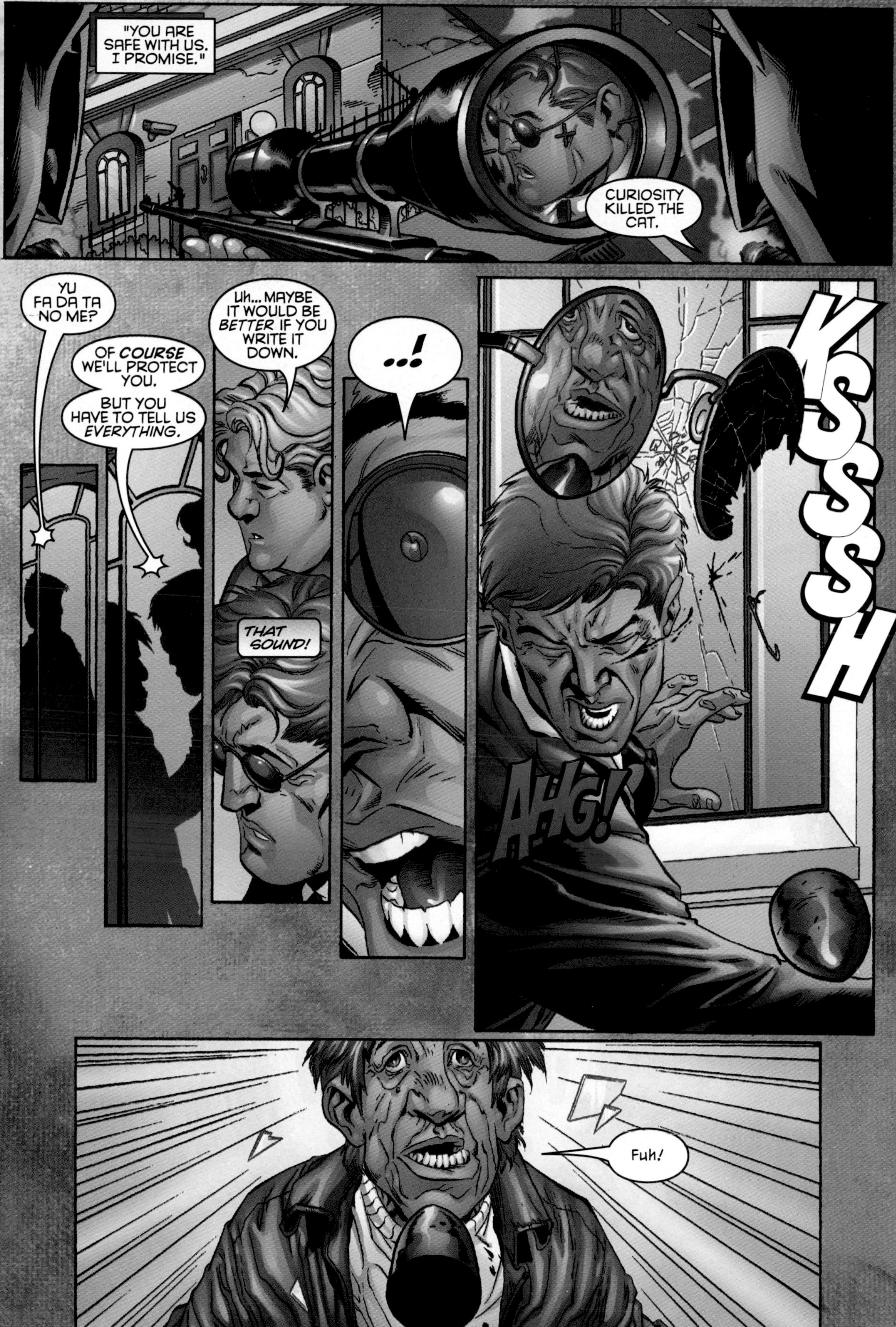
"YOU ARE SAFE WITH US. I PROMISE."
CURIOSITY KILLED THE CAT.
YU FA DA TA NO ME?
OF COURSE WE'LL PROTECT YOU.
BUT YOU HAVE TO TELL US EVERYTHING.
Uh... MAYBE IT WOULD BE BETTER IF YOU WRITE IT DOWN.
THAT SOUND!
..!
KSSSH
AHG!
Fuh!

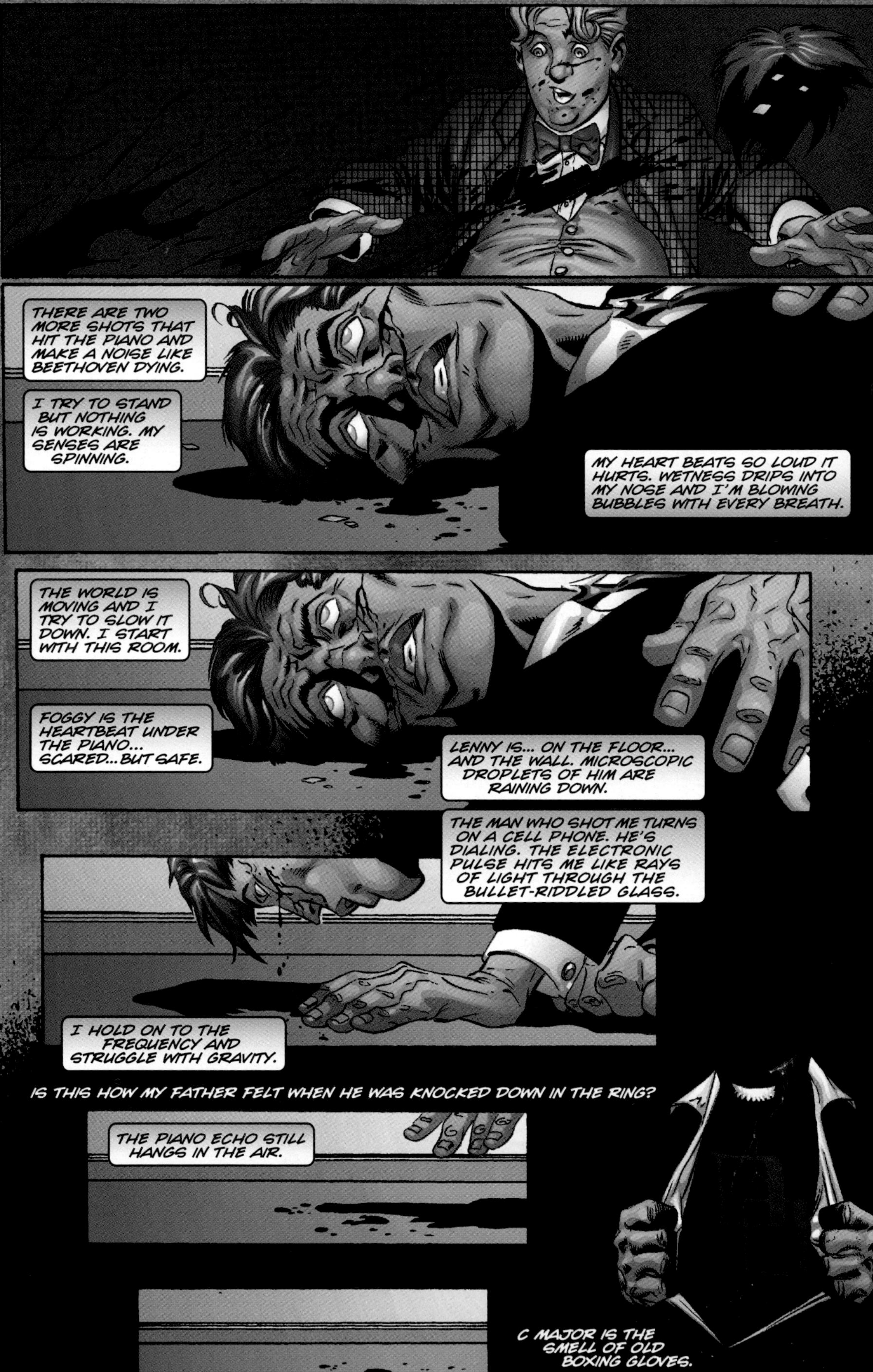
THERE ARE TWO MORE SHOTS THAT HIT THE PIANO AND MAKE A NOISE LIKE BEETHOVEN DYING.
I TRY TO STAND BUT NOTHING IS WORKING. MY SENSES ARE SPINNING.
MY HEART BEATS SO LOUD IT HURTS. WETNESS DRIPS INTO MY NOSE AND I'M BLOWING BUBBLES WITH EVERY BREATH.
THE WORLD IS MOVING AND I TRY TO SLOW IT DOWN. I START WITH THIS ROOM.
FOGGY IS THE HEARTBEAT UNDER THE PIANO... SCARED...BUT SAFE.
LENNY IS... ON THE FLOOR... AND THE WALL. MICROSCOPIC DROPLETS OF HIM ARE RAINING DOWN.
THE MAN WHO SHOT ME TURNS ON A CELL PHONE. HE'S DIALING. THE ELECTRONIC PULSE HITS ME LIKE RAYS OF LIGHT THROUGH THE BULLET-RIDDLED GLASS.
I HOLD ON TO THE FREQUENCY AND STRUGGLE WITH GRAVITY.
IS THIS HOW MY FATHER FELT WHEN HE WAS KNOCKED DOWN IN THE RING?
THE PIANO ECHO STILL HANGS IN THE AIR.
C MAJOR IS THE SMELL OF OLD BOXING GLOVES.

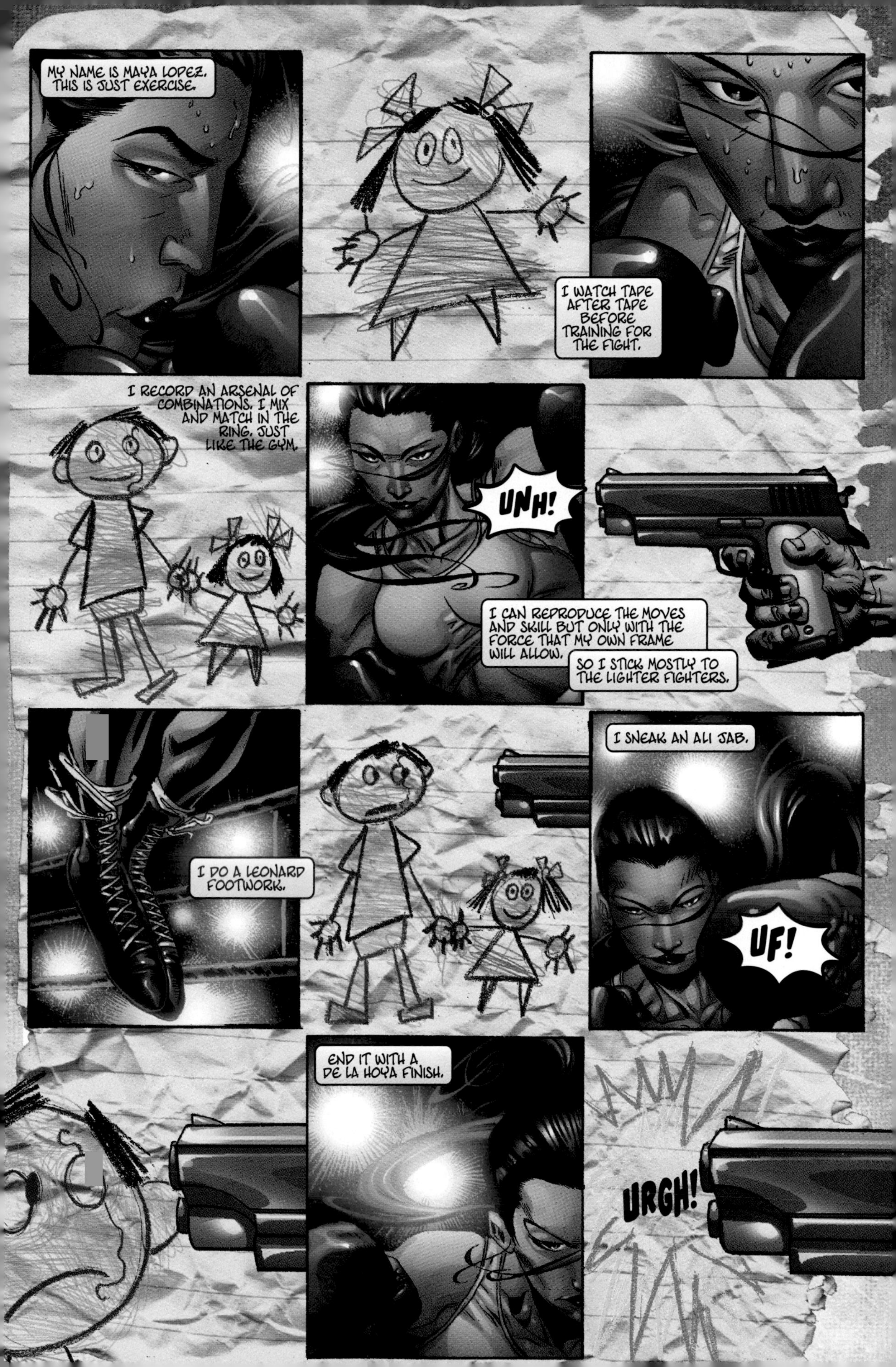
MY NAME IS MAYA LOPEZ. THIS IS JUST EXERCISE.
I WATCH TAPE AFTER TAPE BEFORE TRAINING FOR THE FIGHT.
I RECORD AN ARSENAL OF COMBINATIONS. I MIX AND MATCH IN THE RING, JUST LIKE THE GYM.
UNH!
I CAN REPRODUCE THE MOVES AND SKILL BUT ONLY WITH THE FORCE THAT MY OWN FRAME WILL ALLOW.
SO I STICK MOSTLY TO THE LIGHTER FIGHTERS.
I DO A LEONARD FOOTWORK.
I SNEAK AN ALI JAB.
UF!
END IT WITH A DE LA HOYA FINISH.
URGH!

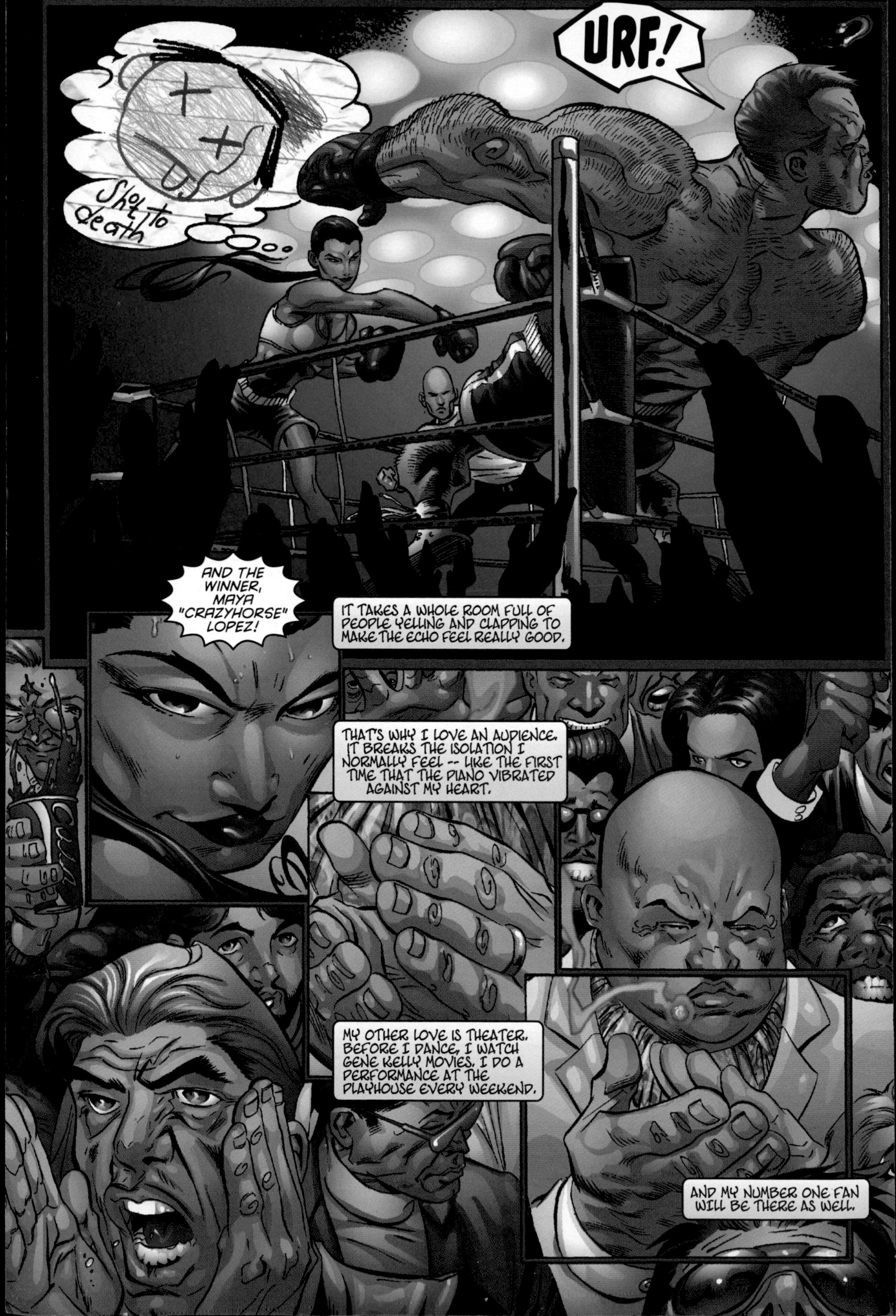
Shot to death
URF!
AND THE WINNER, MAYA "CRAZYHORSE" LOPEZ!
IT TAKES A WHOLE ROOM FULL OF PEOPLE YELLING AND CLAPPING TO MAKE THE ECHO FEEL REALLY GOOD.
THAT'S WHY I LOVE AN AUDIENCE. IT BREAKS THE ISOLATION I NORMALLY FEEL -- LIKE THE FIRST TIME THAT THE PIANO VIBRATED AGAINST MY HEART.
MY OTHER LOVE IS THEATER. BEFORE I DANCE, I WATCH GENE KELLY MOVIES. I DO A PERFORMANCE AT THE PLAYHOUSE EVERY WEEKEND.
AND MY NUMBER ONE FAN WILL BE THERE AS WELL.

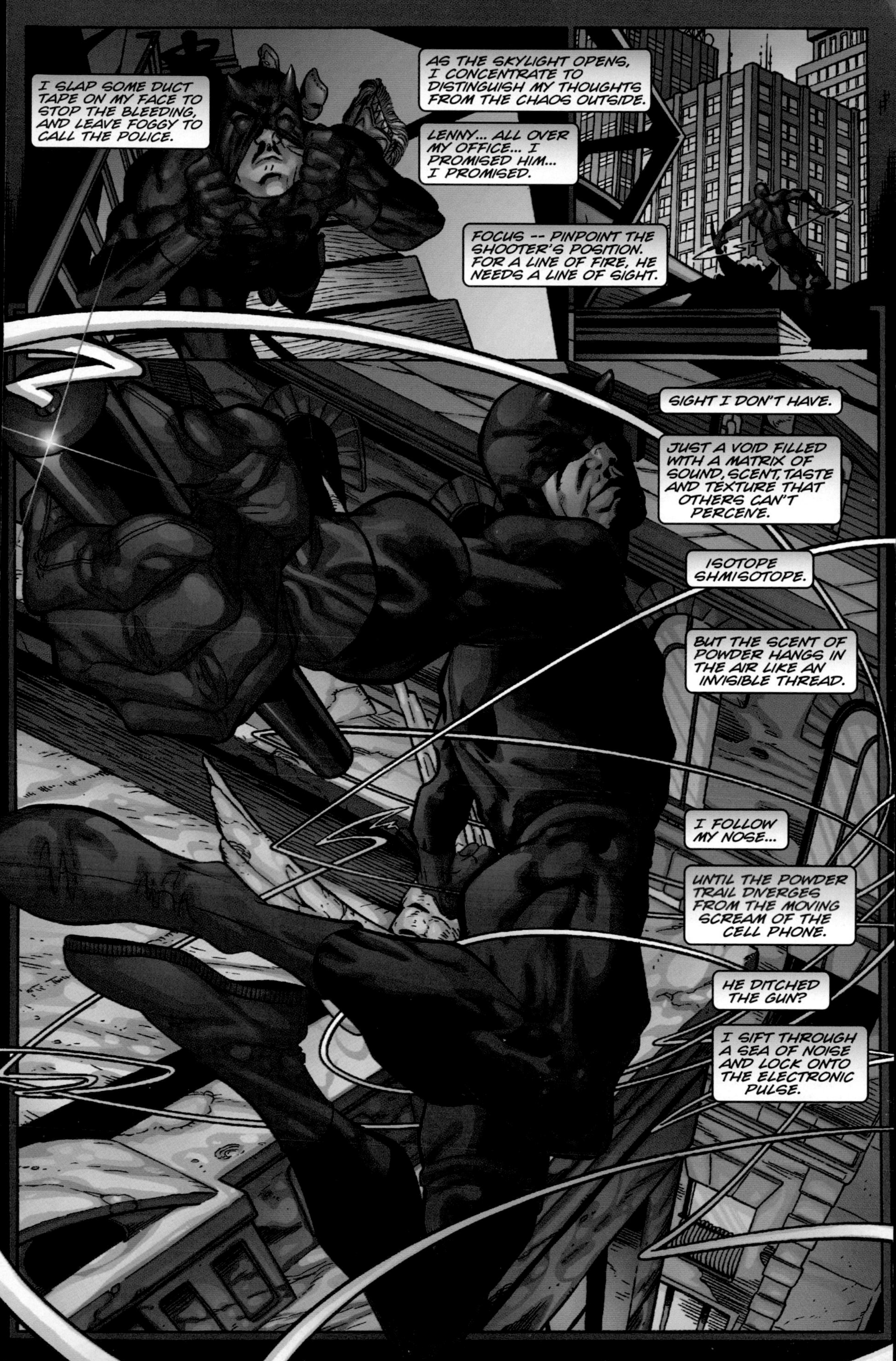
I SLAP SOME DUCT TAPE ON MY FACE TO STOP THE BLEEDING, AND LEAVE FOGGY TO CALL THE POLICE.
AS THE SKYLIGHT OPENS, I CONCENTRATE TO DISTINGUISH MY THOUGHTS FROM THE CHAOS OUTSIDE.
LENNY... ALL OVER MY OFFICE... I PROMISED HIM... I PROMISED.
FOCUS -- PINPOINT THE SHOOTER'S POSITION. FOR A LINE OF FIRE, HE NEEDS A LINE OF SIGHT.
SIGHT I DON'T HAVE.
JUST A VOID FILLED WITH A MATRIX OF SOUND, SCENT, TASTE AND TEXTURE THAT OTHERS CAN'T PERCEIVE.
ISOTOPE SHMISOTOPE.
BUT THE SCENT OF POWDER HANGS IN THE AIR LIKE AN INVISIBLE THREAD.
I FOLLOW MY NOSE...
UNTIL THE POWDER TRAIL DIVERGES FROM THE MOVING SCREAM OF THE CELL PHONE.
HE DITCHED THE GUN?
I SIFT THROUGH A SEA OF NOISE AND LOCK ONTO THE ELECTRONIC PULSE.

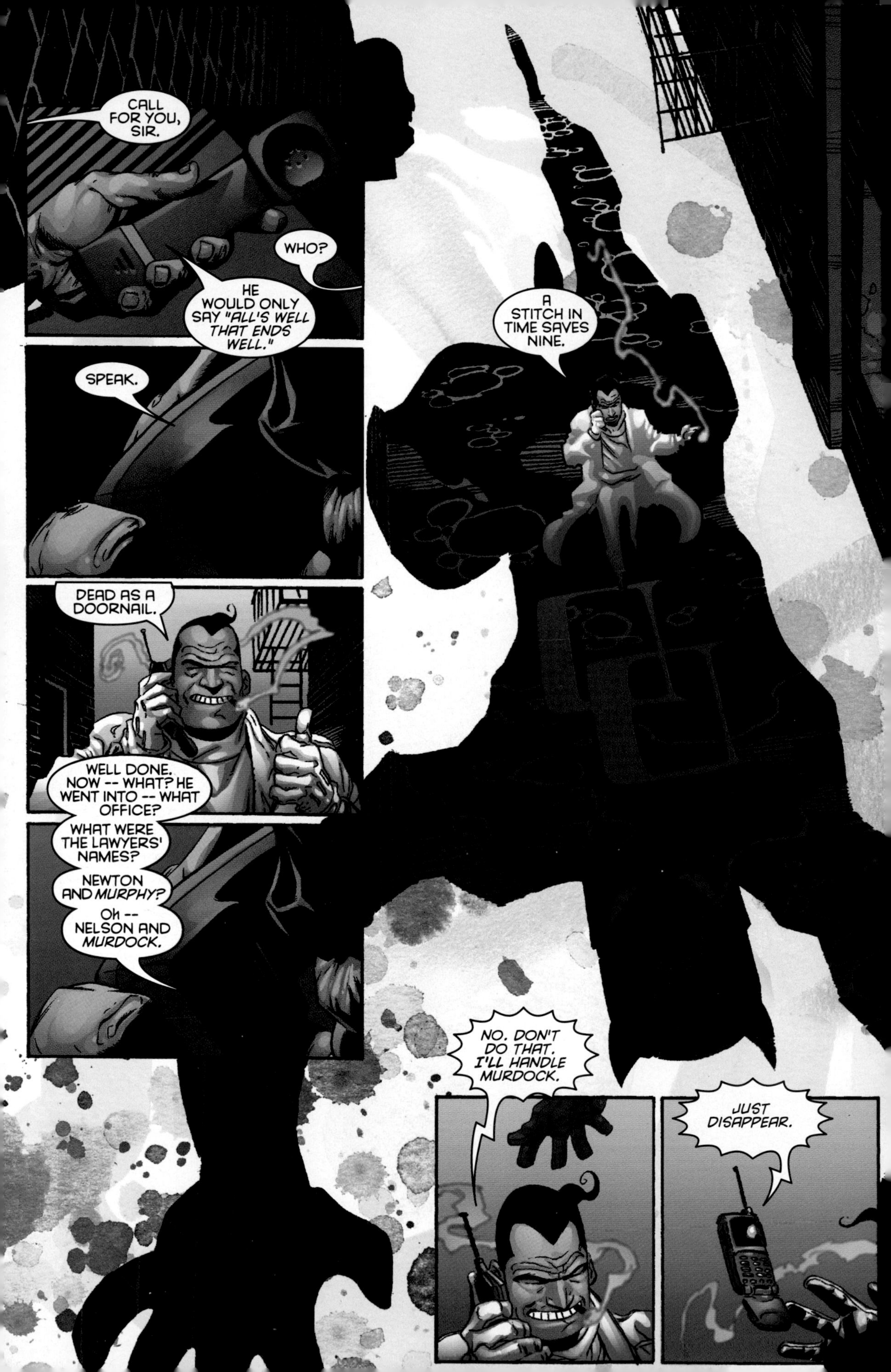
CALL FOR YOU, SIR.
WHO?
HE WOULD ONLY SAY "ALL'S WELL THAT ENDS WELL."
SPEAK.
A STITCH IN TIME SAVES NINE.
DEAD AS A DOORNAIL.
WELL DONE. NOW -- WHAT? HE WENT INTO -- WHAT OFFICE?
WHAT WERE THE LAWYERS' NAMES?
NEWTON AND MURPHY?
Oh -- NELSON AND MURDOCK.
NO. DON'T DO THAT. I'LL HANDLE MURDOCK.
JUST DISAPPEAR.

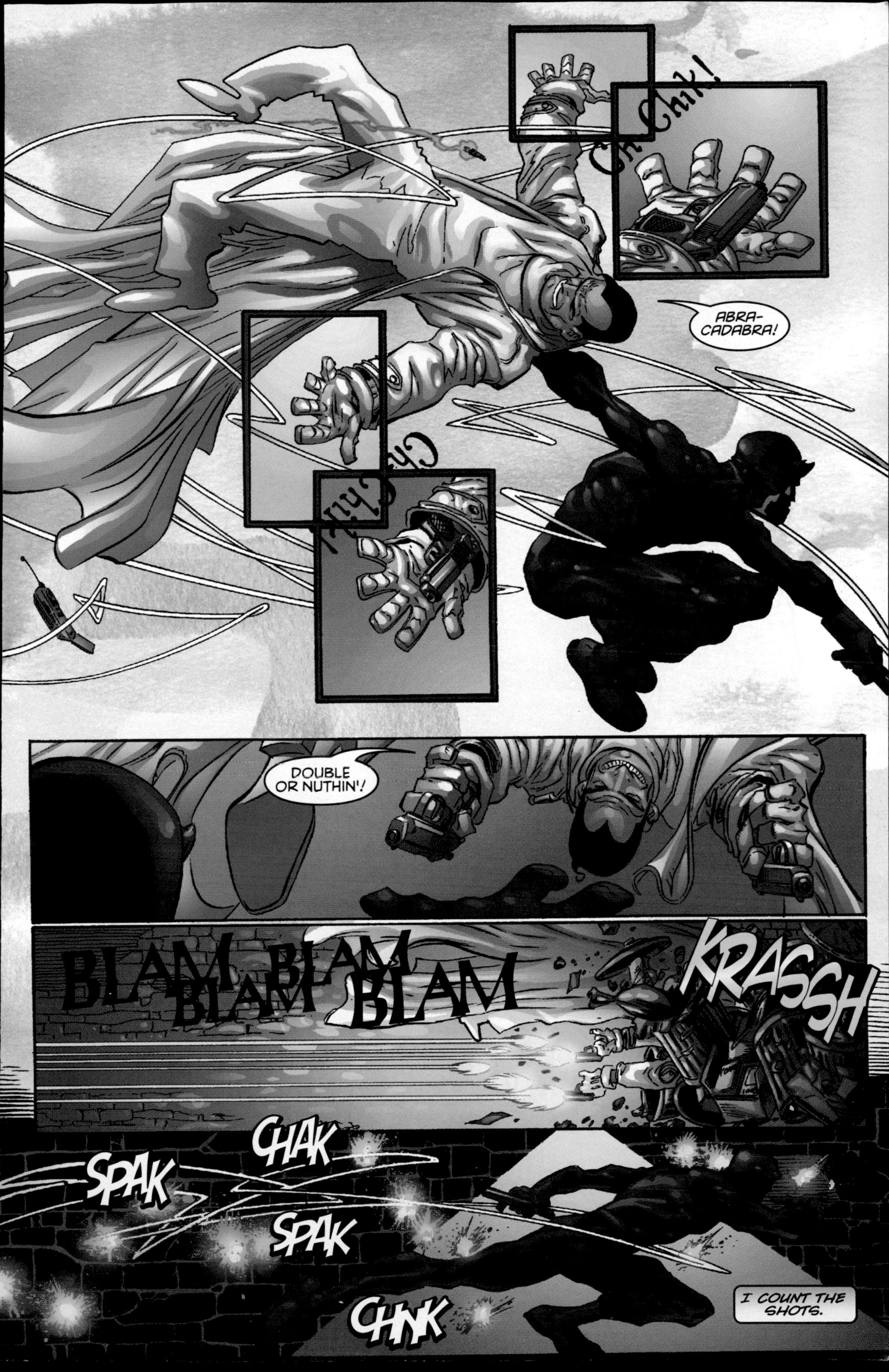
Ch Chik!
ABRA-CADABRA!
Ch Chik!
DOUBLE OR NUTHIN'!
BLAM BLAM BLAM BLAM BLAM
KRASSH
CHAK
SPAK
SPAK
CHNK
I COUNT THE SHOTS.

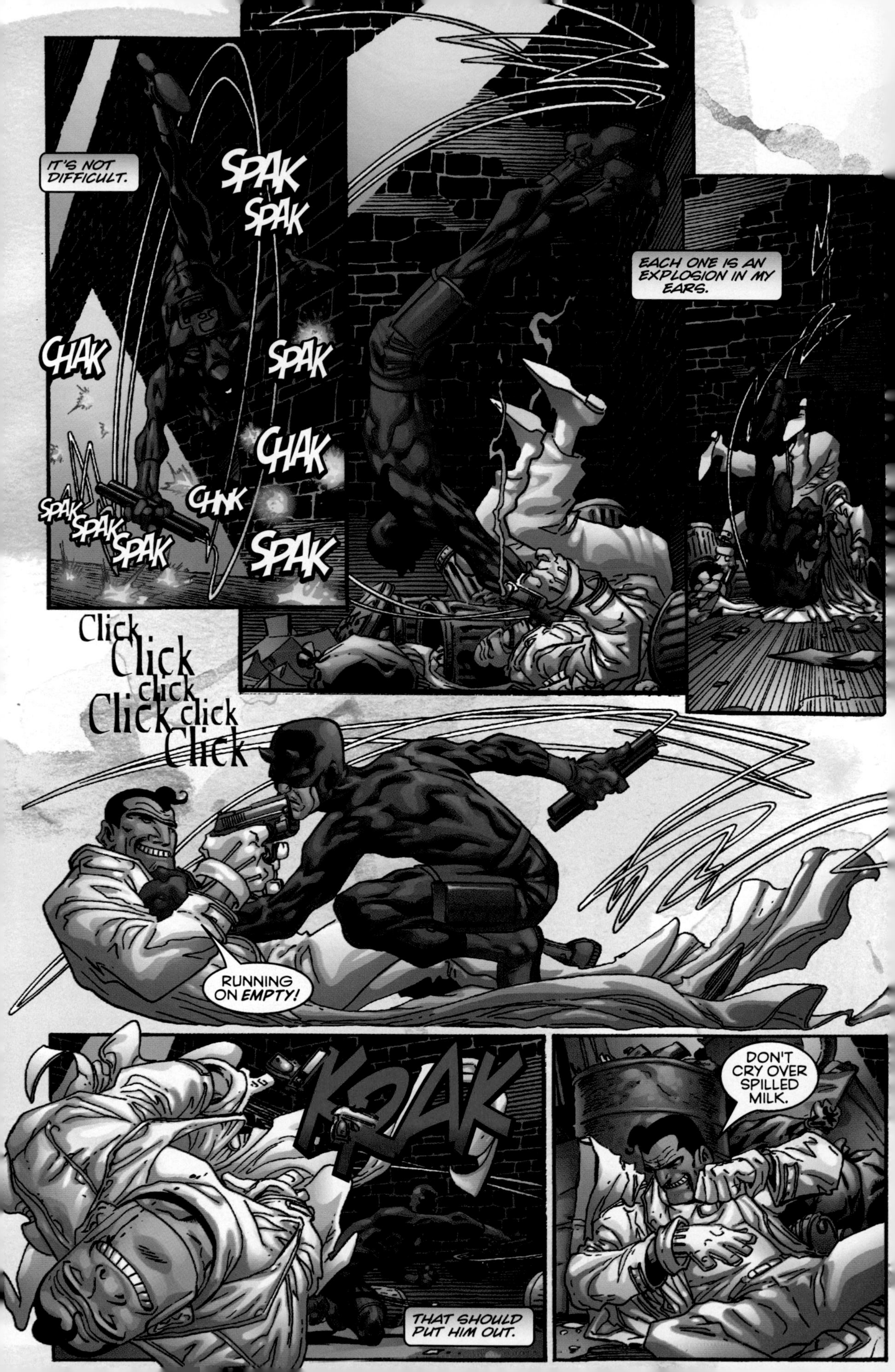
IT'S NOT DIFFICULT.
SPAK
SPAK
CHAK
SPAK
CHAK
CHNK
SPAK
SPAK
SPAK
SPAK
EACH ONE IS AN EXPLOSION IN MY EARS.
Click
Click
click
Click click
Click
RUNNING ON EMPTY!
KRAK
THAT SHOULD PUT HIM OUT.
DON'T CRY OVER SPILLED MILK.

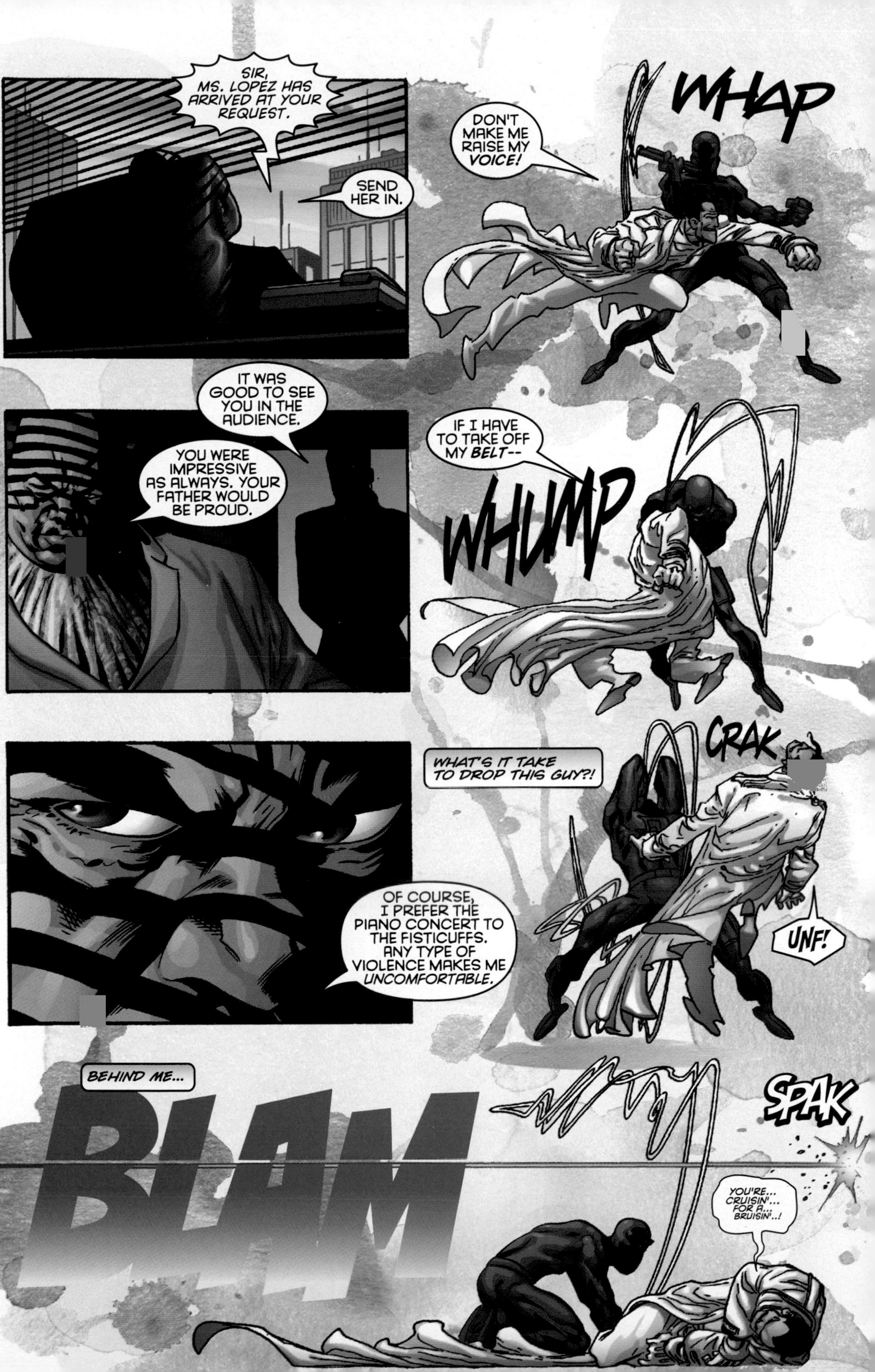
SIR, MS. LOPEZ HAS ARRIVED AT YOUR REQUEST.
SEND HER IN.
WHAP
DON'T MAKE ME RAISE MY VOICE!
IT WAS GOOD TO SEE YOU IN THE AUDIENCE.
YOU WERE IMPRESSIVE AS ALWAYS. YOUR FATHER WOULD BE PROUD.
IF I HAVE TO TAKE OFF MY BELT--
WHUMP
OF COURSE, I PREFER THE PIANO CONCERT TO THE FISTICUFFS. ANY TYPE OF VIOLENCE MAKES ME UNCOMFORTABLE.
CRAK
WHAT'S IT TAKE TO DROP THIS GUY?!
UNF!
BEHIND ME...
BLAM
SPAK
YOU'RE... CRUISIN'... FOR A... BRUISIN'...!

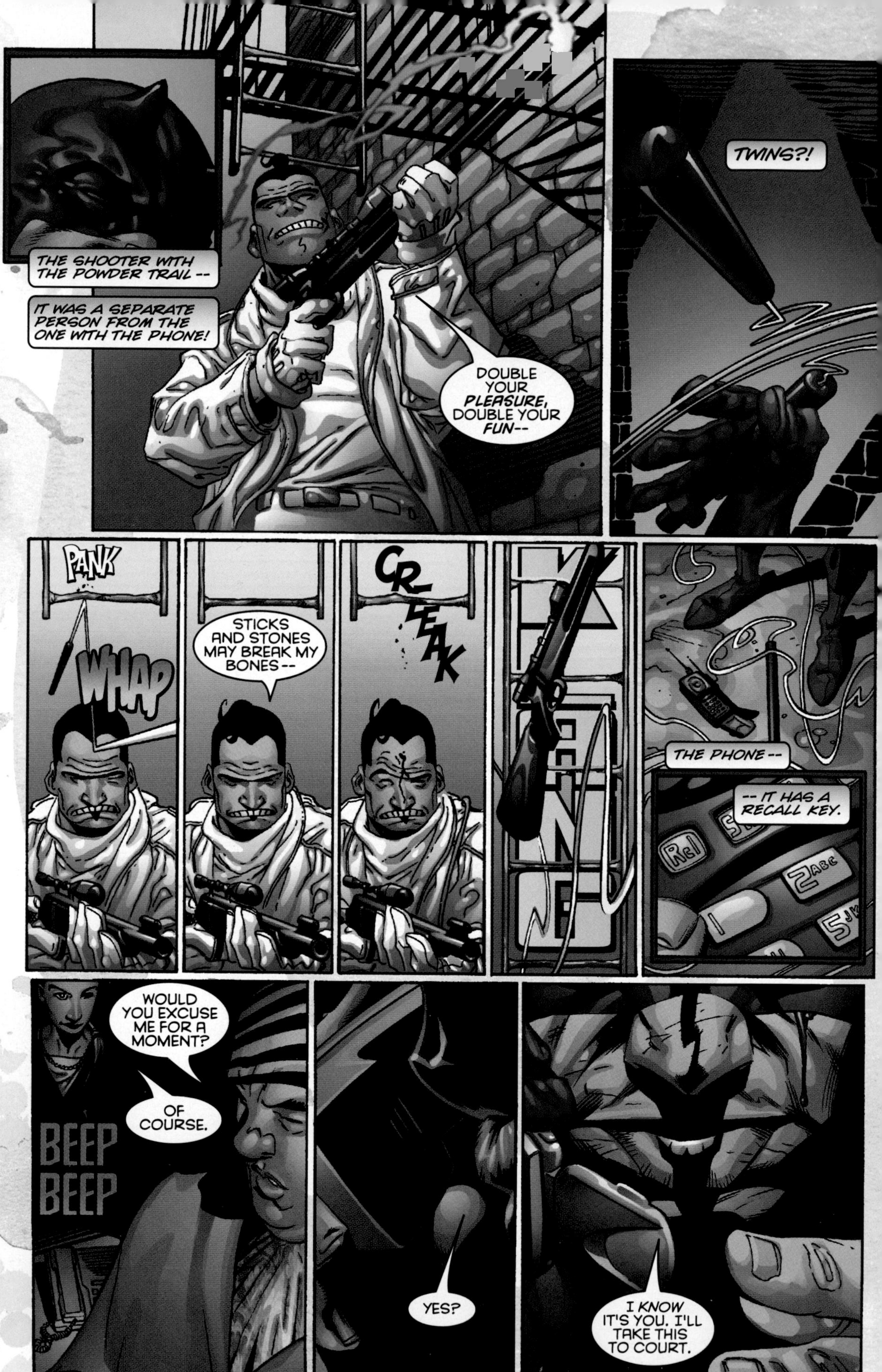
THE SHOOTER WITH THE POWDER TRAIL --
IT WAS A SEPARATE PERSON FROM THE ONE WITH THE PHONE!
DOUBLE YOUR PLEASURE, DOUBLE YOUR FUN--
TWINS?!
PANK
WHAP
STICKS AND STONES MAY BREAK MY BONES--
CREAK
THE PHONE --
-- IT HAS A RECALL KEY.
WOULD YOU EXCUSE ME FOR A MOMENT?
OF COURSE.
BEEP BEEP
YES?
I KNOW IT'S YOU. I'LL TAKE THIS TO COURT.

K-LIK

ON PAPER HE IS A SHADOW-- A BUSINESSMAN.

HIS NAME IS A HUSHED WHISPER ON NERVOUS LIPS.

BUT HIS LEGEND STILL CARRIES WEIGHT. HE IS THE KINGPIN OF CRIME.

MURDOCK. DAREDEVIL.

ALL OF OUR ADULT LIVES WE ARE BUSY TRYING TO FILL AN *EMPTINESS* THAT WE EXPERIENCED IN CHILDHOOD.

IT'S THE *CORE* OF THE CRIME FIGHTER PHENOMENON. IT'S THE MOTIVATION OF *ANY* FIGHTER, MYSELF INCLUDED.

THE REALIZATION OF THIS LEADS TO EXTRAORDINARY PERCEPTION OR METAPHORICAL *BLINDNESS.*

A MAN LIKE MURDOCK CANNOT BE DESTROYED BY TAKING EVERYTHING AWAY FROM HIM. MEN LIKE US HAVE BUILT THEMSELVES FROM NOTHING. THAT EMPTINESS IS OUR MOTIVATION.

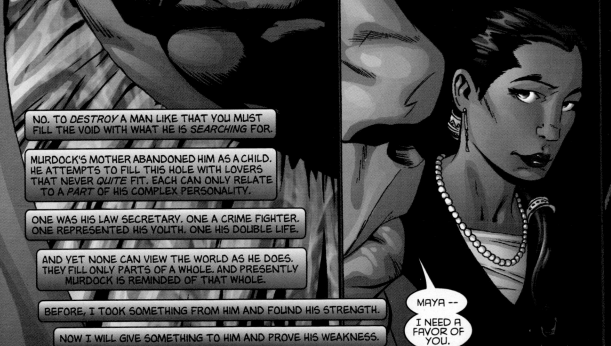

NO. TO *DESTROY* A MAN LIKE THAT YOU MUST FILL THE VOID WITH WHAT HE IS *SEARCHING* FOR.

MURDOCK'S MOTHER ABANDONED HIM AS A CHILD. HE ATTEMPTS TO FILL THIS HOLE WITH LOVERS THAT NEVER *QUITE* FIT. EACH CAN ONLY RELATE TO A *PART* OF HIS COMPLEX PERSONALITY.

ONE WAS HIS LAW SECRETARY. ONE A CRIME FIGHTER. ONE REPRESENTED HIS YOUTH. ONE HIS DOUBLE LIFE.

AND YET NONE CAN VIEW THE WORLD AS HE DOES. THEY FILL ONLY PARTS OF A WHOLE. AND PRESENTLY MURDOCK IS REMINDED OF THAT WHOLE.

BEFORE, I TOOK SOMETHING FROM HIM AND FOUND HIS STRENGTH.

NOW I WILL GIVE SOMETHING TO HIM AND PROVE HIS WEAKNESS.

MAYA -- I NEED A FAVOR OF YOU.

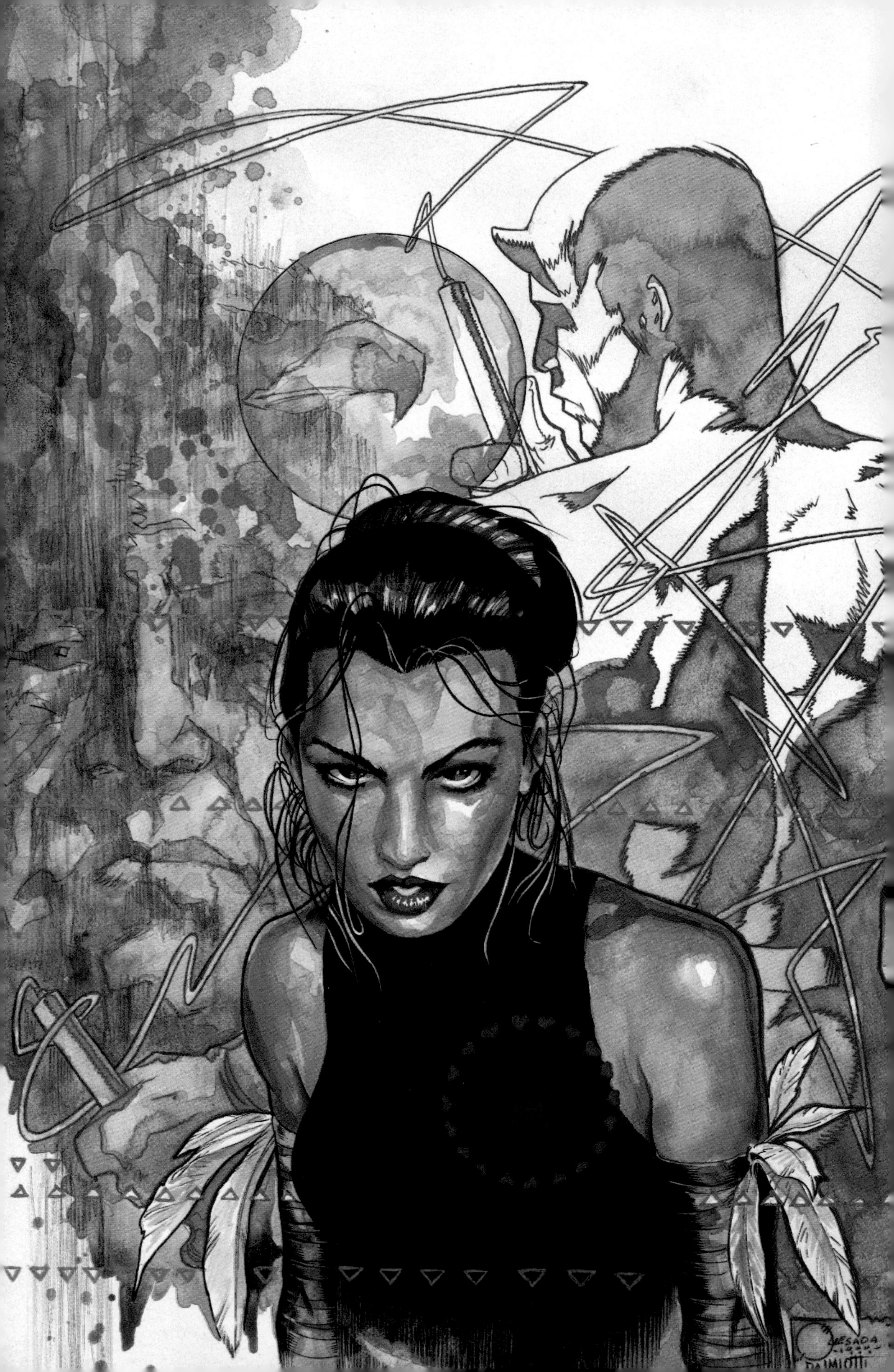

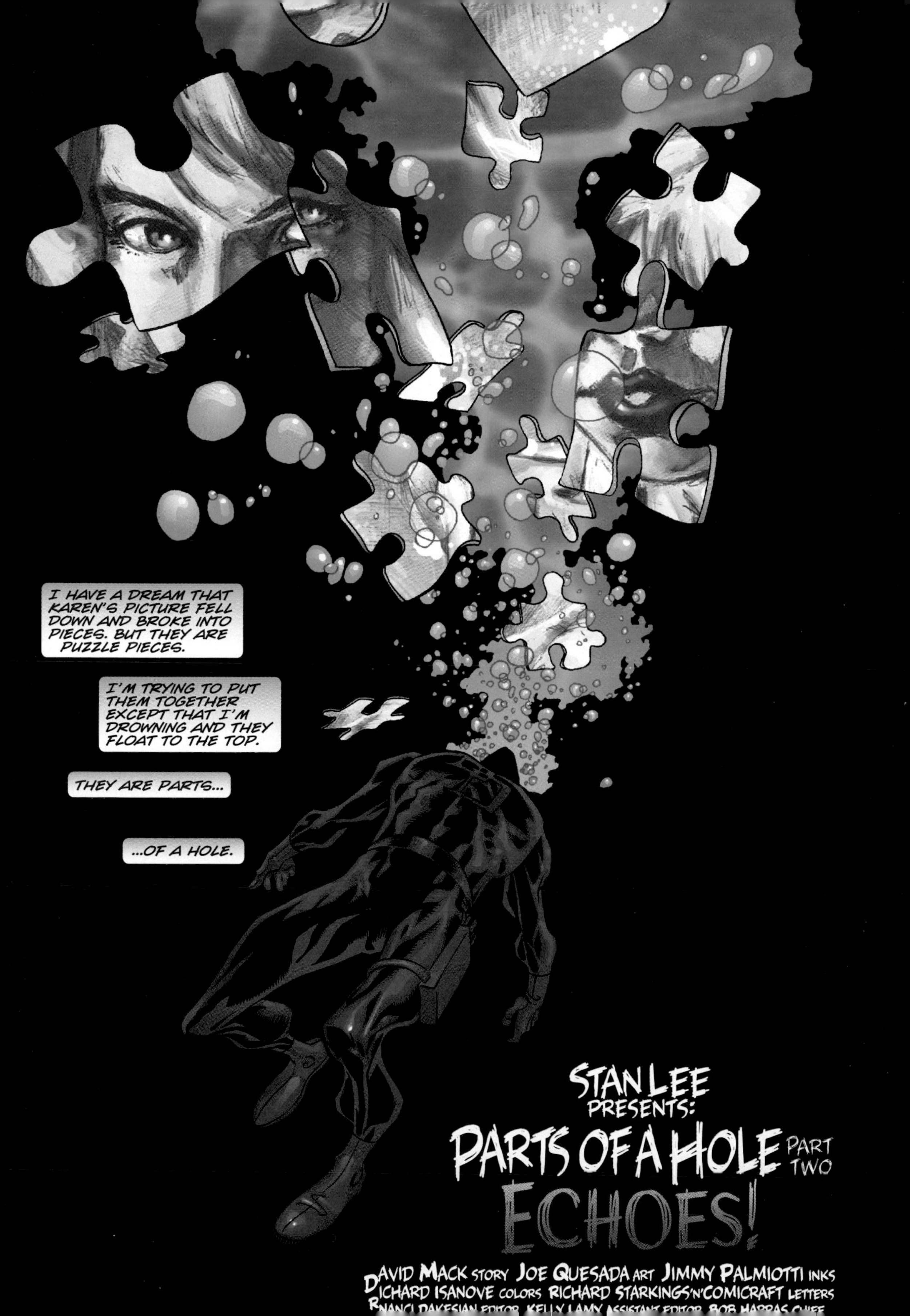
I HAVE A DREAM THAT KAREN'S PICTURE FELL DOWN AND BROKE INTO PIECES. BUT THEY ARE PUZZLE PIECES.
I'M TRYING TO PUT THEM TOGETHER EXCEPT THAT I'M DROWNING AND THEY FLOAT TO THE TOP.
THEY ARE PARTS...
...OF A HOLE.
STAN LEE PRESENTS:
PARTS OF A HOLE PART TWO
ECHOES!
DAVID MACK STORY JOE QUESADA ART JIMMY PALMIOTTI INKS
RICHARD ISANOVE COLORS RICHARD STARKINGS'N'COMICRAFT LETTERS
NANCI DAKESIAN EDITOR KELLY LAMY ASSISTANT EDITOR BOB HARRAS CHIEF

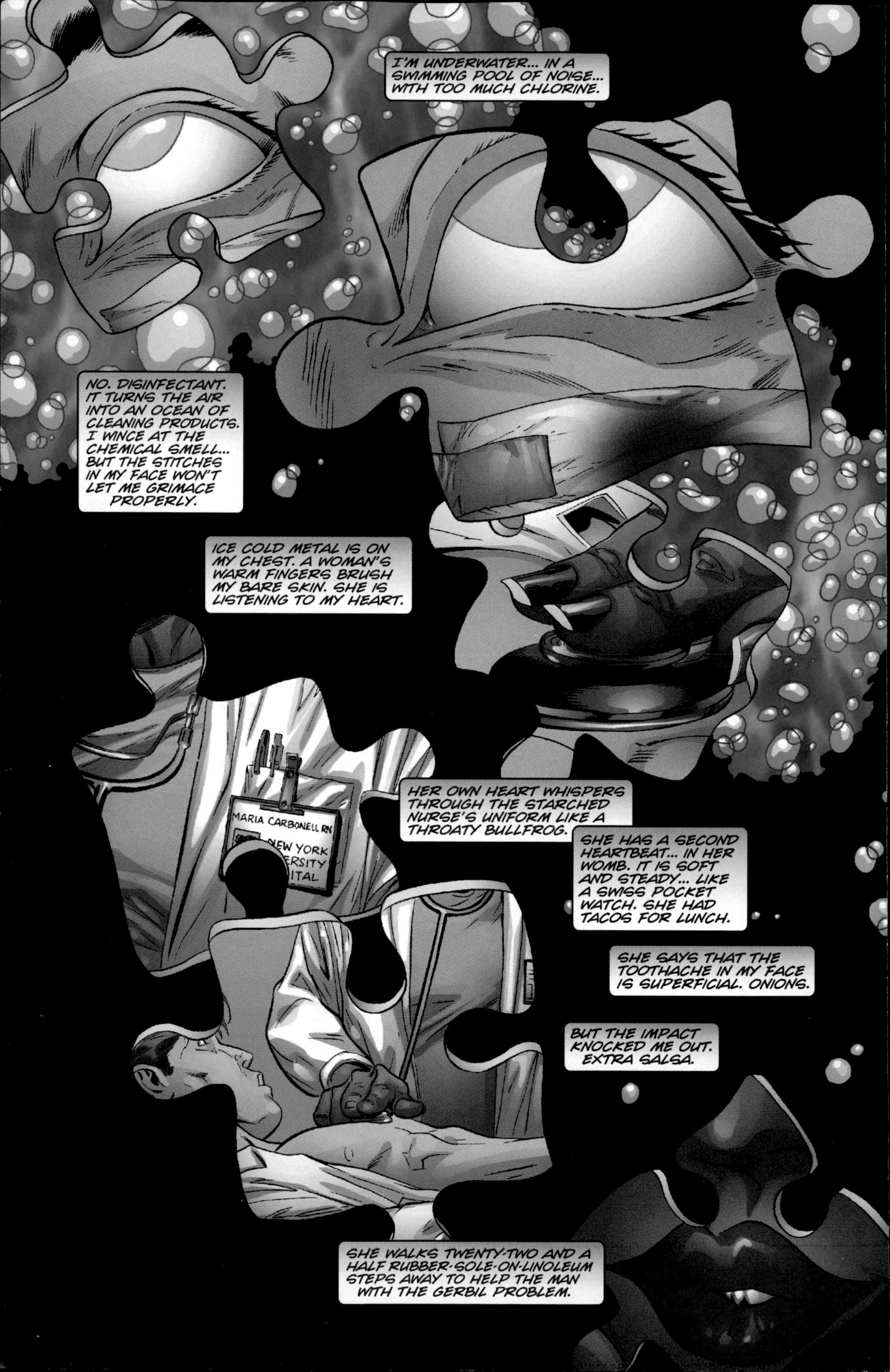

I'M UNDERWATER... IN A SWIMMING POOL OF NOISE... WITH TOO MUCH CHLORINE.
NO. DISINFECTANT. IT TURNS THE AIR INTO AN OCEAN OF CLEANING PRODUCTS. I WINCE AT THE CHEMICAL SMELL... BUT THE STITCHES IN MY FACE WON'T LET ME GRIMACE PROPERLY.
ICE COLD METAL IS ON MY CHEST. A WOMAN'S WARM FINGERS BRUSH MY BARE SKIN. SHE IS LISTENING TO MY HEART.
MARIA CARBONELL RN
NEW YORK
HER OWN HEART WHISPERS THROUGH THE STARCHED NURSE'S UNIFORM LIKE A THROATY BULLFROG.
SHE HAS A SECOND HEARTBEAT... IN HER WOMB. IT IS SOFT AND STEADY... LIKE A SWISS POCKET WATCH. SHE HAD TACOS FOR LUNCH.
SHE SAYS THAT THE TOOTHACHE IN MY FACE IS SUPERFICIAL. ONIONS.
BUT THE IMPACT KNOCKED ME OUT. EXTRA SALSA.
SHE WALKS TWENTY-TWO AND A HALF RUBBER-SOLE-ON-LINOLEUM STEPS AWAY TO HELP THE MAN WITH THE GERBIL PROBLEM.

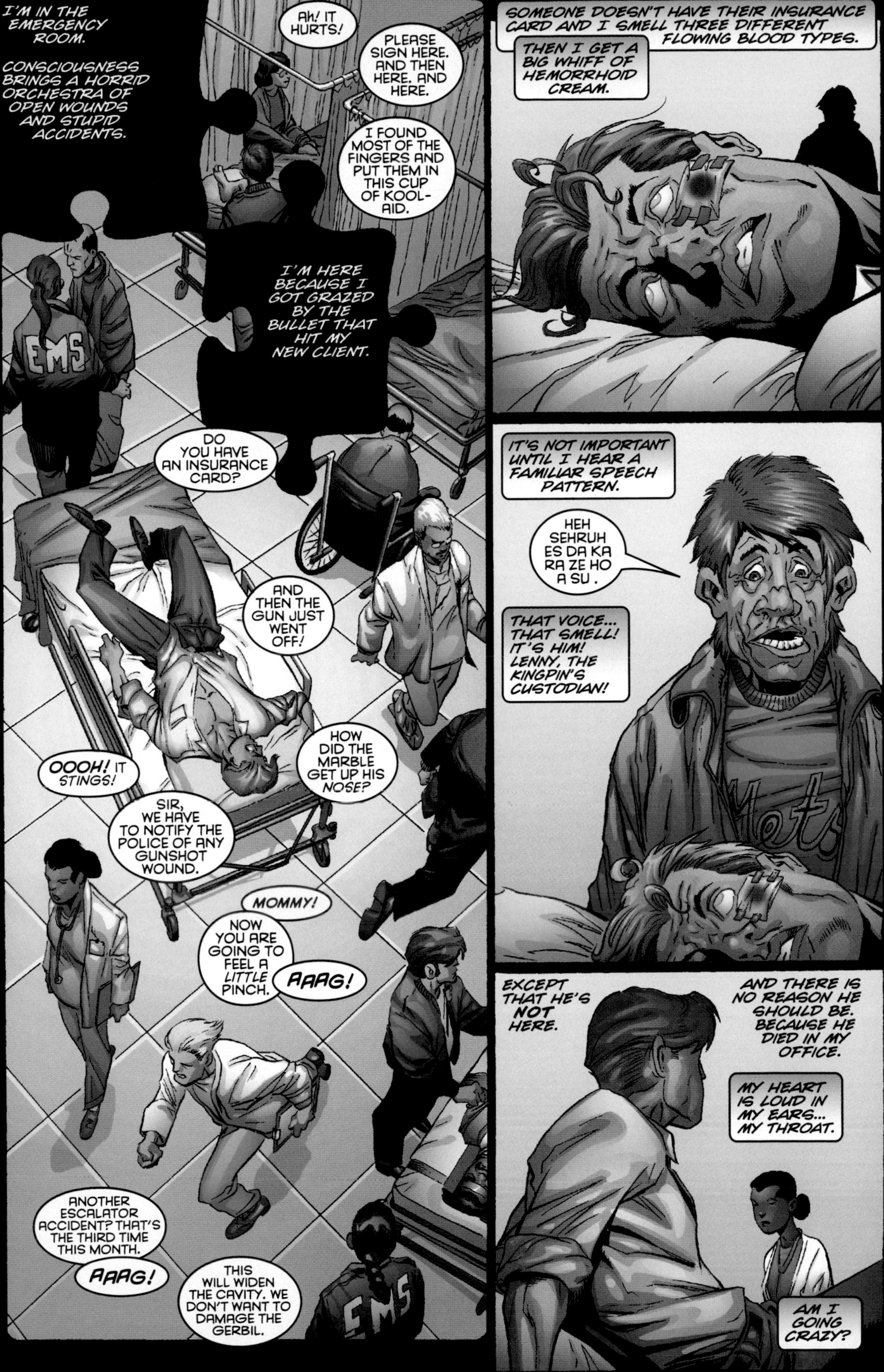
I'M IN THE EMERGENCY ROOM.
CONSCIOUSNESS BRINGS A HORRID ORCHESTRA OF OPEN WOUNDS AND STUPID ACCIDENTS.
AH! IT HURTS!
PLEASE SIGN HERE. AND THEN HERE. AND HERE.
I FOUND MOST OF THE FINGERS AND PUT THEM IN THIS CUP OF KOOL-AID.
I'M HERE BECAUSE I GOT GRAZED BY THE BULLET THAT HIT MY NEW CLIENT.
DO YOU HAVE AN INSURANCE CARD?
AND THEN THE GUN JUST WENT OFF!
HOW DID THE MARBLE GET UP HIS NOSE?
OOOH! IT STINGS!
SIR, WE HAVE TO NOTIFY THE POLICE OF ANY GUNSHOT WOUND.
MOMMY!
NOW YOU ARE GOING TO FEEL A LITTLE PINCH.
AAAG!
ANOTHER ESCALATOR ACCIDENT? THAT'S THE THIRD TIME THIS MONTH.
AAAG!
THIS WILL WIDEN THE CAVITY. WE DON'T WANT TO DAMAGE THE GERBIL.
SOMEONE DOESN'T HAVE THEIR INSURANCE CARD AND I SMELL THREE DIFFERENT FLOWING BLOOD TYPES.
THEN I GET A BIG WHIFF OF HEMORRHOID CREAM.
IT'S NOT IMPORTANT UNTIL I HEAR A FAMILIAR SPEECH PATTERN.
HEH SEHRUH ES DA KA RA ZE HO A SU.
THAT VOICE... THAT SMELL! IT'S HIM! LENNY, THE KINGPIN'S CUSTODIAN!
EXCEPT THAT HE'S NOT HERE.
AND THERE IS NO REASON HE SHOULD BE. BECAUSE HE DIED IN MY OFFICE.
MY HEART IS LOUD IN MY EARS... MY THROAT.
AM I GOING CRAZY?

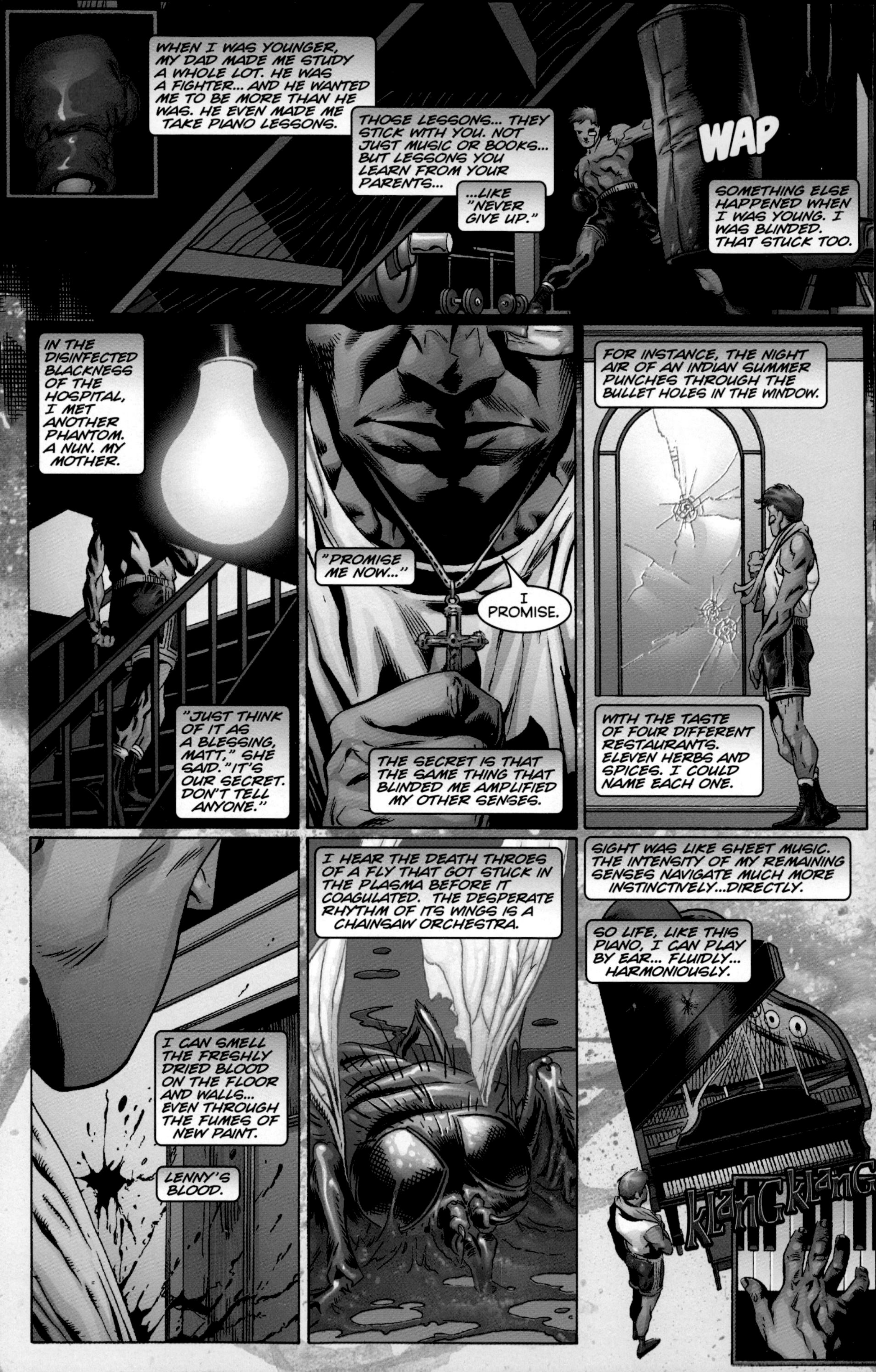

WHEN I WAS YOUNGER, MY DAD MADE ME STUDY A WHOLE LOT. HE WAS A FIGHTER... AND HE WANTED ME TO BE MORE THAN HE WAS. HE EVEN MADE ME TAKE PIANO LESSONS.
THOSE LESSONS... THEY STICK WITH YOU. NOT JUST MUSIC OR BOOKS... BUT LESSONS YOU LEARN FROM YOUR PARENTS...
...LIKE "NEVER GIVE UP."
WAP
SOMETHING ELSE HAPPENED WHEN I WAS YOUNG. I WAS BLINDED. THAT STUCK TOO.
IN THE DISINFECTED BLACKNESS OF THE HOSPITAL, I MET ANOTHER PHANTOM. A NUN. MY MOTHER.
"JUST THINK OF IT AS A BLESSING, MATT," SHE SAID. "IT'S OUR SECRET. DON'T TELL ANYONE."
"PROMISE ME NOW..."
I PROMISE.
THE SECRET IS THAT THE SAME THING THAT BLINDED ME AMPLIFIED MY OTHER SENSES.
FOR INSTANCE, THE NIGHT AIR OF AN INDIAN SUMMER PUNCHES THROUGH THE BULLET HOLES IN THE WINDOW.
WITH THE TASTE OF FOUR DIFFERENT RESTAURANTS. ELEVEN HERBS AND SPICES. I COULD NAME EACH ONE.
I CAN SMELL THE FRESHLY DRIED BLOOD ON THE FLOOR AND WALLS... EVEN THROUGH THE FUMES OF NEW PAINT.
LENNY'S BLOOD.
I HEAR THE DEATH THROES OF A FLY THAT GOT STUCK IN THE PLASMA BEFORE IT COAGULATED. THE DESPERATE RHYTHM OF ITS WINGS IS A CHAINSAW ORCHESTRA.
SIGHT WAS LIKE SHEET MUSIC. THE INTENSITY OF MY REMAINING SENSES NAVIGATE MUCH MORE INSTINCTIVELY...DIRECTLY.
SO LIFE, LIKE THIS PIANO, I CAN PLAY BY EAR... FLUIDLY... HARMONIOUSLY.
KLANG KLANG

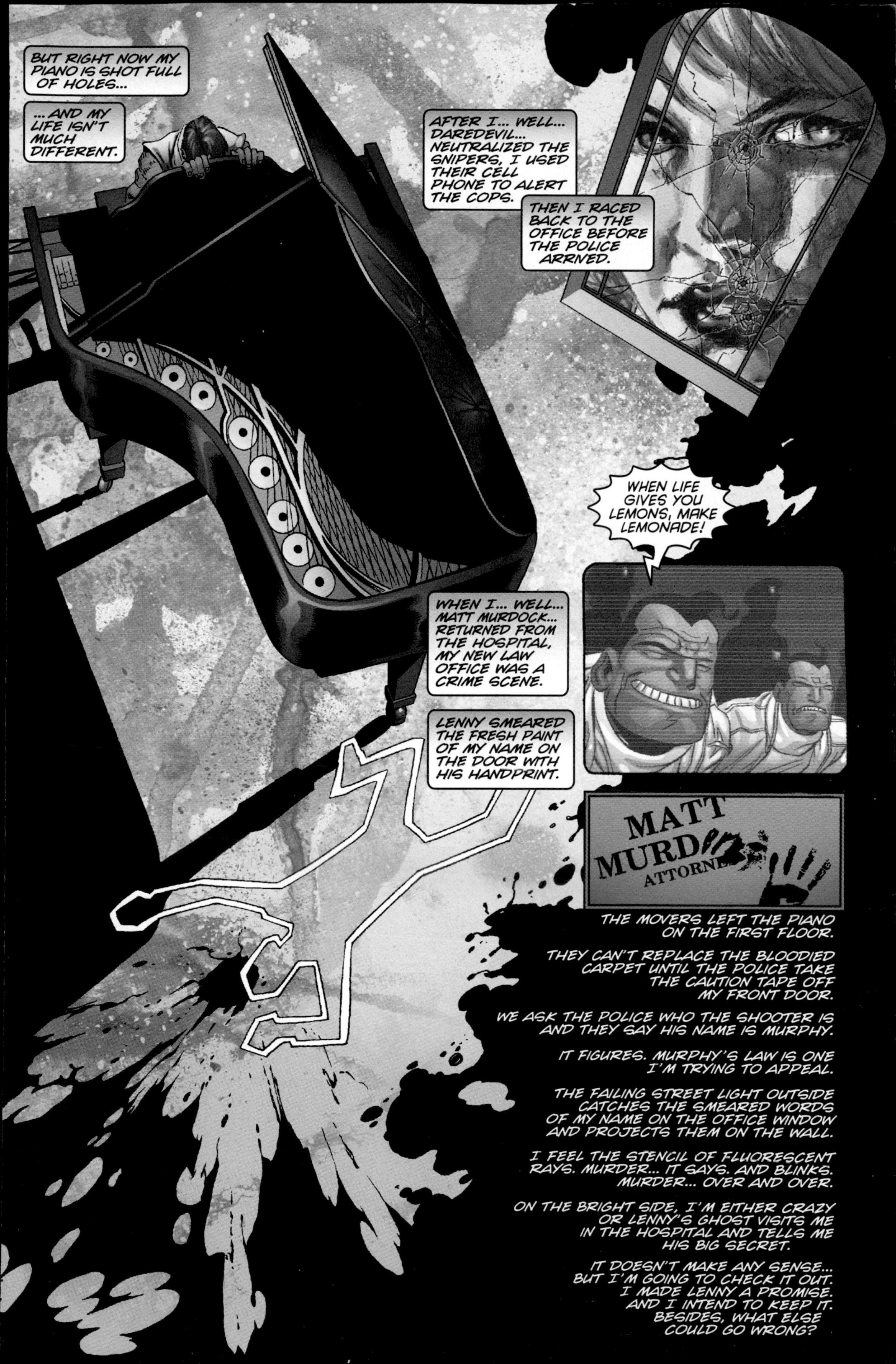
BUT RIGHT NOW MY PIANO IS SHOT FULL OF HOLES...
...AND MY LIFE ISN'T MUCH DIFFERENT.
AFTER I... WELL... DAREDEVIL... NEUTRALIZED THE SNIPERS, I USED THEIR CELL PHONE TO ALERT THE COPS.
THEN I RACED BACK TO THE OFFICE BEFORE THE POLICE ARRIVED.
WHEN LIFE GIVES YOU LEMONS, MAKE LEMONADE!
WHEN I... WELL... MATT MURDOCK... RETURNED FROM THE HOSPITAL, MY NEW LAW OFFICE WAS A CRIME SCENE.
LENNY SMEARED THE FRESH PAINT OF MY NAME ON THE DOOR WITH HIS HANDPRINT.
MATT
MURD
ATTORNE
THE MOVERS LEFT THE PIANO ON THE FIRST FLOOR.
THEY CAN'T REPLACE THE BLOODIED CARPET UNTIL THE POLICE TAKE THE CAUTION TAPE OFF MY FRONT DOOR.
WE ASK THE POLICE WHO THE SHOOTER IS AND THEY SAY HIS NAME IS MURPHY.
IT FIGURES. MURPHY'S LAW IS ONE I'M TRYING TO APPEAL.
THE FAILING STREET LIGHT OUTSIDE CATCHES THE SMEARED WORDS OF MY NAME ON THE OFFICE WINDOW AND PROJECTS THEM ON THE WALL.
I FEEL THE STENCIL OF FLUORESCENT RAYS. MURDER... IT SAYS. AND BLINKS. MURDER... OVER AND OVER.
ON THE BRIGHT SIDE, I'M EITHER CRAZY OR LENNY'S GHOST VISITS ME IN THE HOSPITAL AND TELLS ME HIS BIG SECRET.
IT DOESN'T MAKE ANY SENSE... BUT I'M GOING TO CHECK IT OUT. I MADE LENNY A PROMISE. AND I INTEND TO KEEP IT. BESIDES, WHAT ELSE COULD GO WRONG?

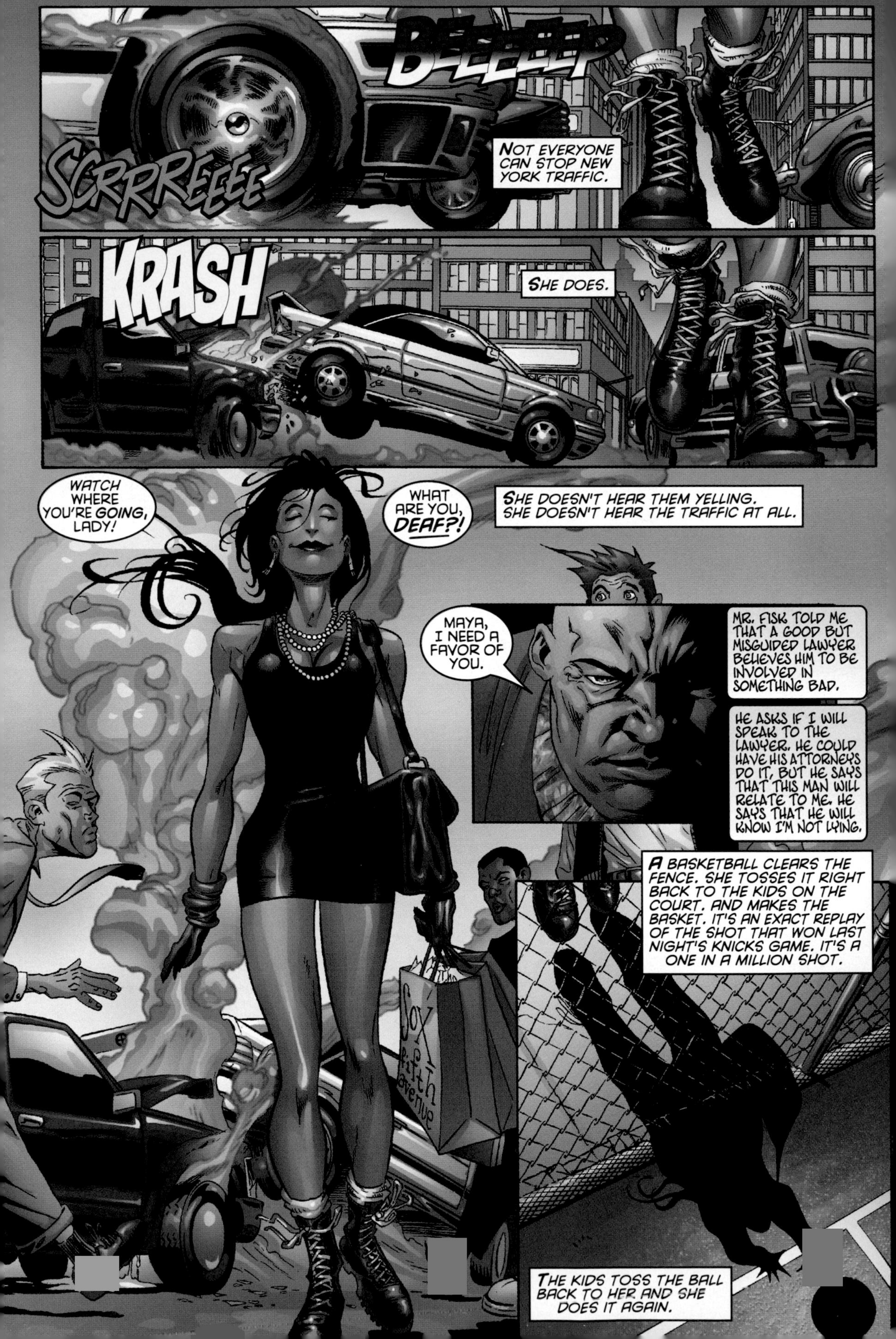

BEEEEP
SCRRREEEE
NOT EVERYONE CAN STOP NEW YORK TRAFFIC.
KRASH
SHE DOES.
WATCH WHERE YOU'RE GOING, LADY!
WHAT ARE YOU, DEAF?!
SHE DOESN'T HEAR THEM YELLING. SHE DOESN'T HEAR THE TRAFFIC AT ALL.
MAYA, I NEED A FAVOR OF YOU.
MR. FISK TOLD ME THAT A GOOD BUT MISGUIDED LAWYER BELIEVES HIM TO BE INVOLVED IN SOMETHING BAD.
HE ASKS IF I WILL SPEAK TO THE LAWYER. HE COULD HAVE HIS ATTORNEYS DO IT, BUT HE SAYS THAT THIS MAN WILL RELATE TO ME. HE SAYS THAT HE WILL KNOW I'M NOT LYING.
A BASKETBALL CLEARS THE FENCE. SHE TOSSES IT RIGHT BACK TO THE KIDS ON THE COURT. AND MAKES THE BASKET. IT'S AN EXACT REPLAY OF THE SHOT THAT WON LAST NIGHT'S KNICKS GAME. IT'S A ONE IN A MILLION SHOT.
THE KIDS TOSS THE BALL BACK TO HER AND SHE DOES IT AGAIN.

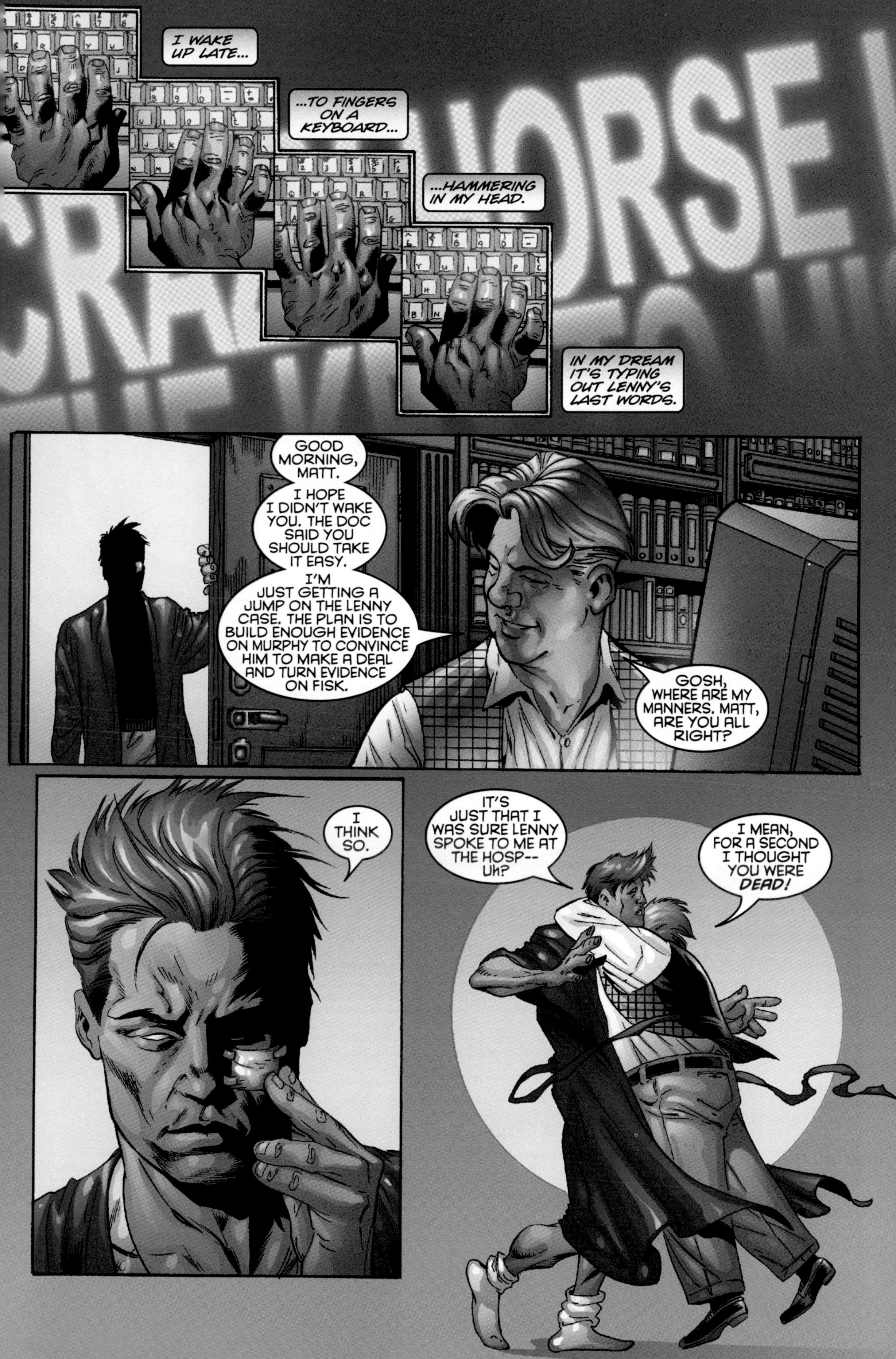
I WAKE UP LATE...
...TO FINGERS ON A KEYBOARD...
...HAMMERING IN MY HEAD.
IN MY DREAM IT'S TYPING OUT LENNY'S LAST WORDS.
GOOD MORNING, MATT.
I HOPE I DIDN'T WAKE YOU. THE DOC SAID YOU SHOULD TAKE IT EASY.
I'M JUST GETTING A JUMP ON THE LENNY CASE. THE PLAN IS TO BUILD ENOUGH EVIDENCE ON MURPHY TO CONVINCE HIM TO MAKE A DEAL AND TURN EVIDENCE ON FISK.
GOSH, WHERE ARE MY MANNERS. MATT, ARE YOU ALL RIGHT?
I THINK SO.
IT'S JUST THAT I WAS SURE LENNY SPOKE TO ME AT THE HOSP-- Uh?
I MEAN, FOR A SECOND I THOUGHT YOU WERE DEAD!

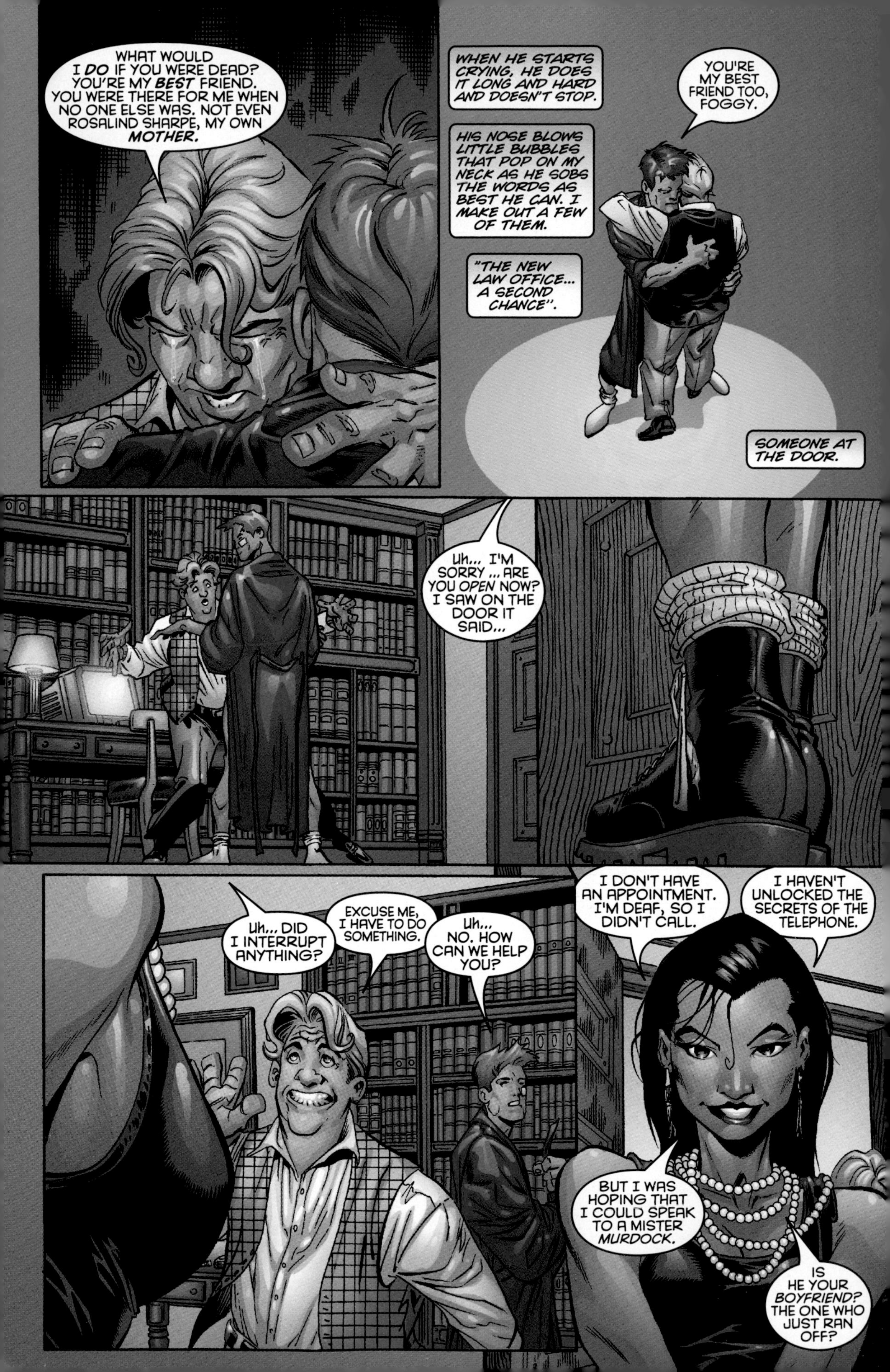
WHAT WOULD I DO IF YOU WERE DEAD? YOU'RE MY BEST FRIEND. YOU WERE THERE FOR ME WHEN NO ONE ELSE WAS. NOT EVEN ROSALIND SHARPE, MY OWN MOTHER.
WHEN HE STARTS CRYING, HE DOES IT LONG AND HARD AND DOESN'T STOP.
HIS NOSE BLOWS LITTLE BUBBLES THAT POP ON MY NECK AS HE SOBS THE WORDS AS BEST HE CAN. I MAKE OUT A FEW OF THEM.
"THE NEW LAW OFFICE... A SECOND CHANCE".
YOU'RE MY BEST FRIEND TOO, FOGGY.
SOMEONE AT THE DOOR.
UH... I'M SORRY ... ARE YOU OPEN NOW? I SAW ON THE DOOR IT SAID...
UH... DID I INTERRUPT ANYTHING?
EXCUSE ME, I HAVE TO DO SOMETHING.
UH... NO. HOW CAN WE HELP YOU?
I DON'T HAVE AN APPOINTMENT. I'M DEAF, SO I DIDN'T CALL.
I HAVEN'T UNLOCKED THE SECRETS OF THE TELEPHONE.
BUT I WAS HOPING THAT I COULD SPEAK TO A MISTER MURDOCK.
IS HE YOUR BOYFRIEND? THE ONE WHO JUST RAN OFF?

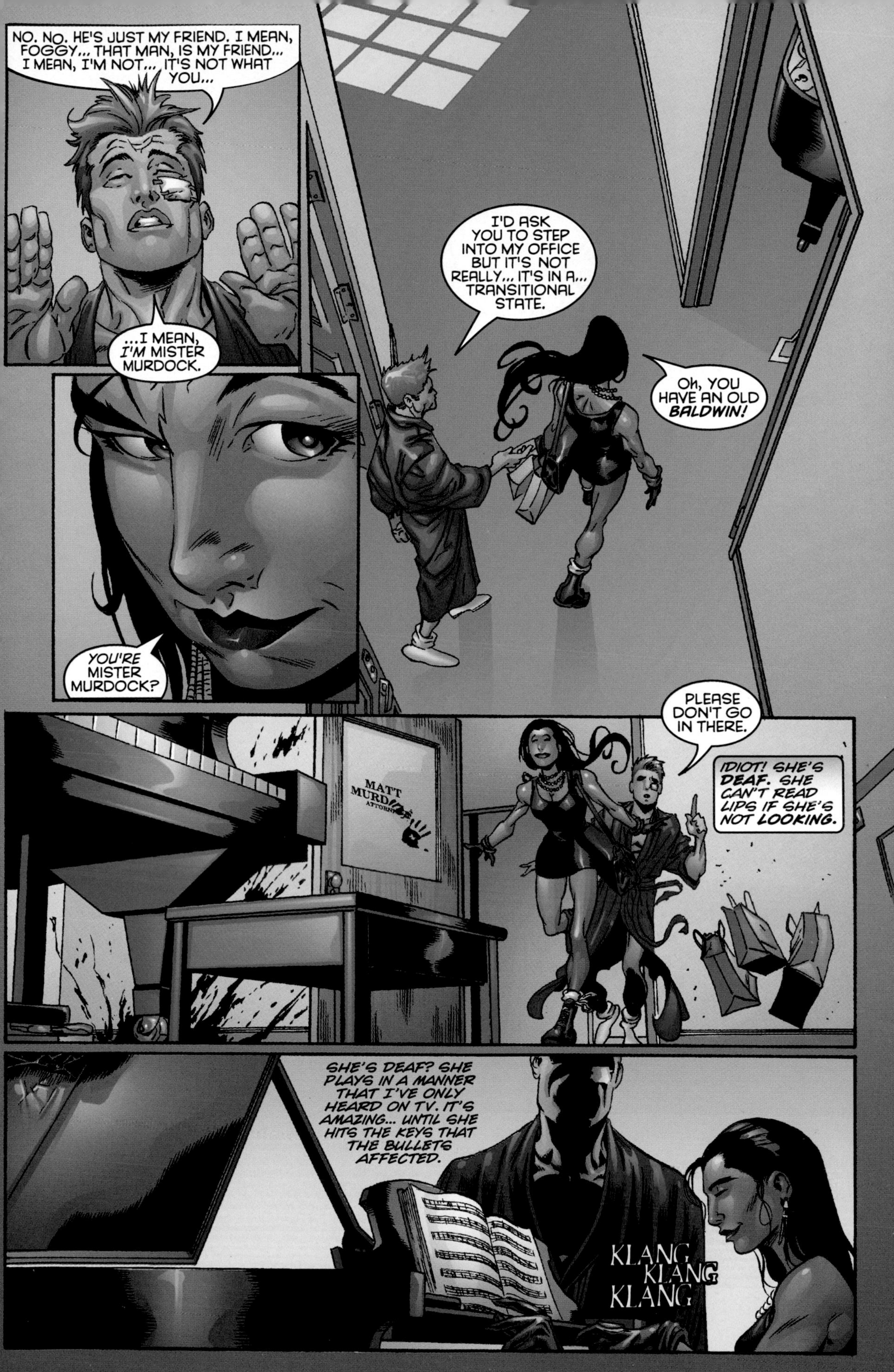
NO. NO. HE'S JUST MY FRIEND. I MEAN, FOGGY... THAT MAN, IS MY FRIEND... I MEAN, I'M NOT... IT'S NOT WHAT YOU...
...I MEAN, I'M MISTER MURDOCK.
I'D ASK YOU TO STEP INTO MY OFFICE BUT IT'S NOT REALLY... IT'S IN A... TRANSITIONAL STATE.
Oh, YOU HAVE AN OLD BALDWIN!
YOU'RE MISTER MURDOCK?
PLEASE DON'T GO IN THERE.
IDIOT! SHE'S DEAF. SHE CAN'T READ LIPS IF SHE'S NOT LOOKING.
SHE'S DEAF? SHE PLAYS IN A MANNER THAT I'VE ONLY HEARD ON TV. IT'S AMAZING... UNTIL SHE HITS THE KEYS THAT THE BULLETS AFFECTED.
KLANG KLANG KLANG

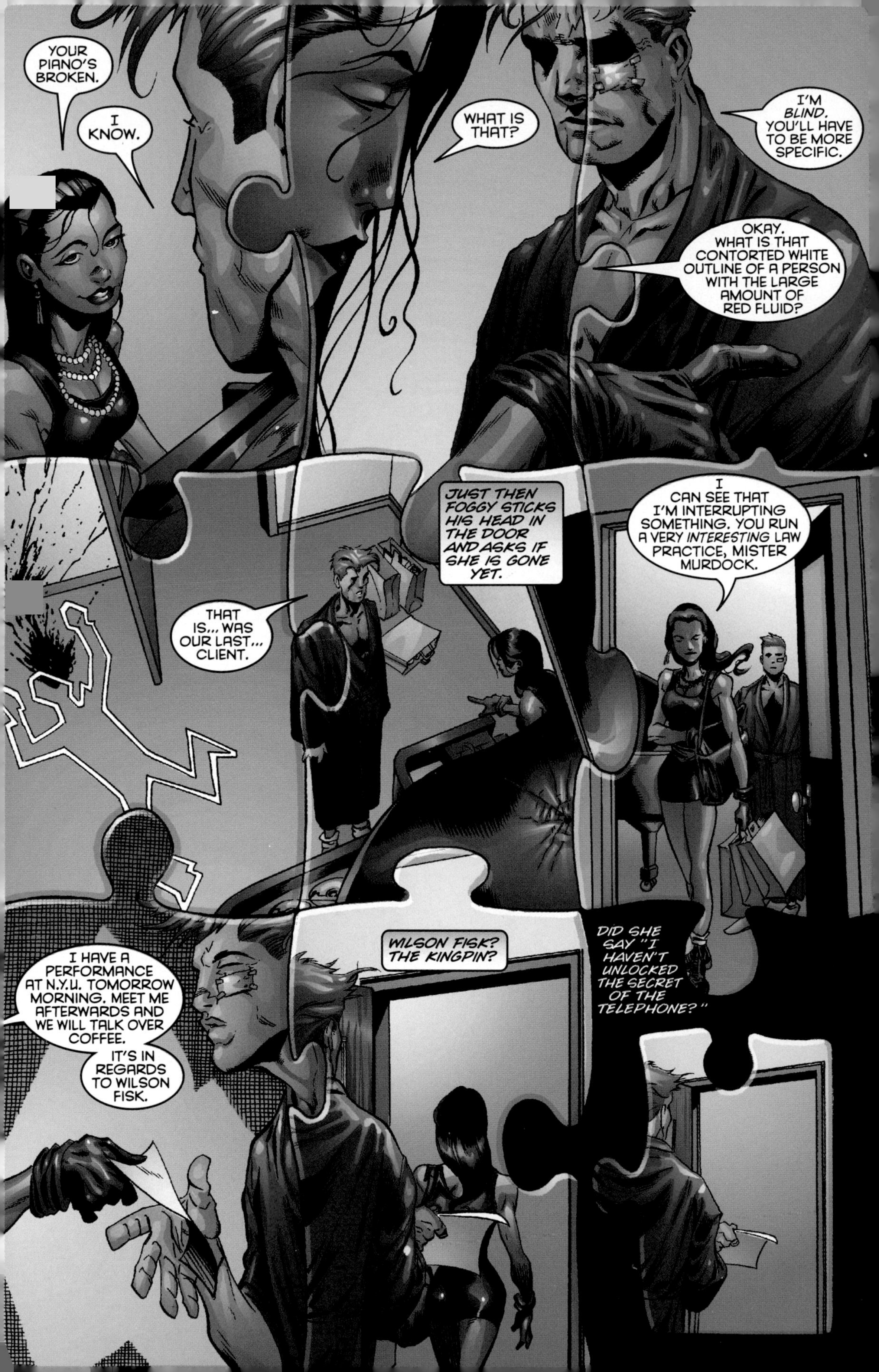

YOUR PIANO'S BROKEN.
I KNOW.
WHAT IS THAT?
I'M *BLIND*. YOU'LL HAVE TO BE MORE SPECIFIC.
OKAY. WHAT IS THAT CONTORTED WHITE OUTLINE OF A PERSON WITH THE LARGE AMOUNT OF RED FLUID?
THAT IS... WAS OUR LAST... CLIENT.
JUST THEN FOGGY STICKS HIS HEAD IN THE DOOR AND ASKS IF SHE IS GONE YET.
I CAN SEE THAT I'M INTERRUPTING SOMETHING. YOU RUN A VERY *INTERESTING* LAW PRACTICE, MISTER MURDOCK.
I HAVE A PERFORMANCE AT N.Y.U. TOMORROW MORNING. MEET ME AFTERWARDS AND WE WILL TALK OVER COFFEE.
IT'S IN REGARDS TO WILSON FISK.
WILSON FISK? THE KINGPIN?
DID SHE SAY "I HAVEN'T UNLOCKED THE SECRET OF THE TELEPHONE?"

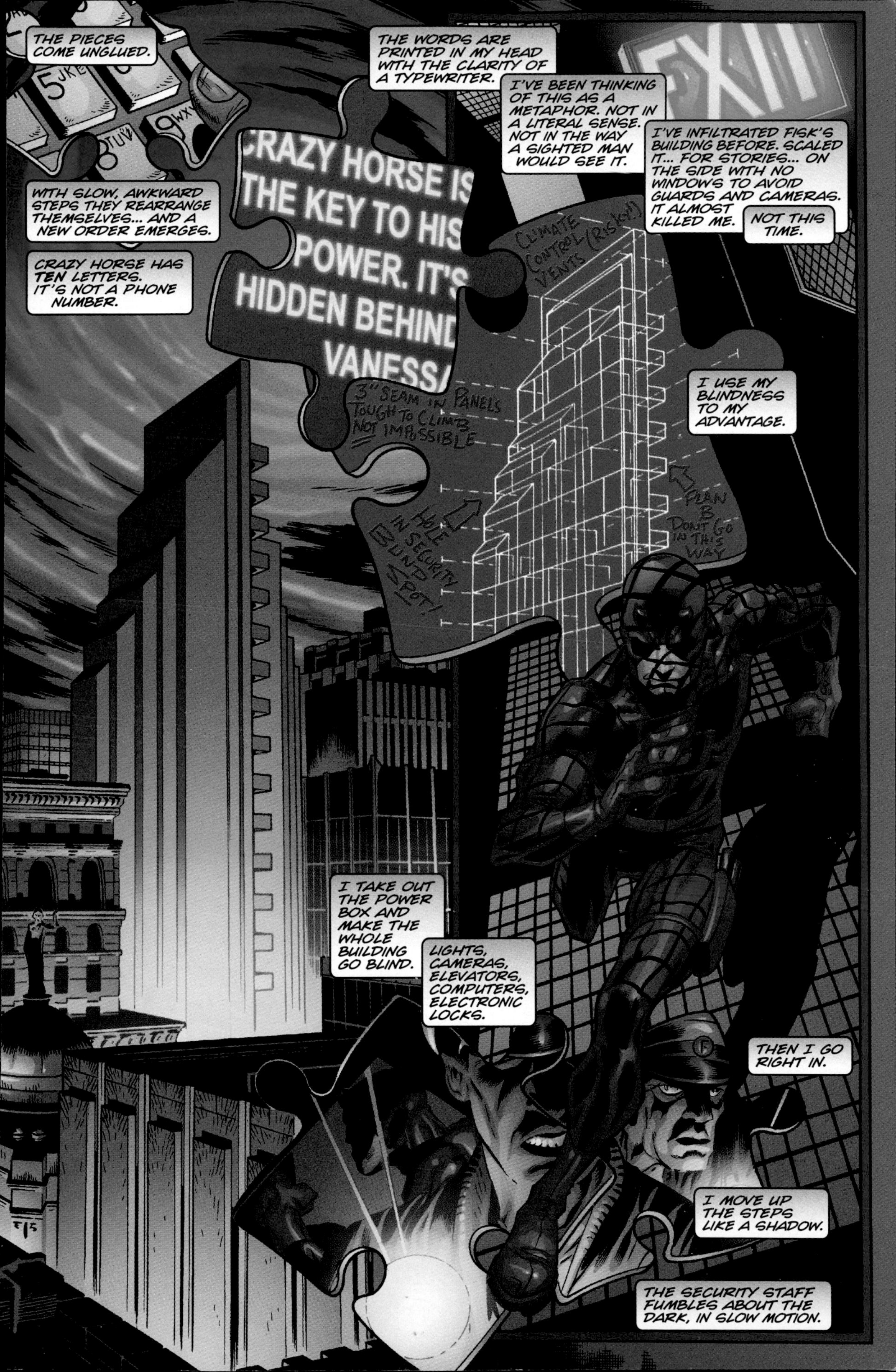
THE PIECES COME UNGLUED.
WITH SLOW, AWKWARD STEPS THEY REARRANGE THEMSELVES... AND A NEW ORDER EMERGES.
CRAZY HORSE HAS TEN LETTERS. IT'S NOT A PHONE NUMBER.
THE WORDS ARE PRINTED IN MY HEAD WITH THE CLARITY OF A TYPEWRITER.
CRAZY HORSE IS THE KEY TO HIS POWER. IT'S HIDDEN BEHIND VANESSA
I'VE BEEN THINKING OF THIS AS A METAPHOR. NOT IN A LITERAL SENSE. NOT IN THE WAY A SIGHTED MAN WOULD SEE IT.
EXIT
I'VE INFILTRATED FISK'S BUILDING BEFORE. SCALED IT... FOR STORIES... ON THE SIDE WITH NO WINDOWS TO AVOID GUARDS AND CAMERAS. IT ALMOST KILLED ME.
NOT THIS TIME.
CLIMATE CONTROL VENTS (Risky!)
3" SEAM IN PANELS TOUGH TO CLIMB NOT IMPOSSIBLE
HOLE IN SECURITY BLIND SPOT!
PLAN B DON'T GO IN THIS WAY
I USE MY BLINDNESS TO MY ADVANTAGE.
I TAKE OUT THE POWER BOX AND MAKE THE WHOLE BUILDING GO BLIND.
LIGHTS, CAMERAS, ELEVATORS, COMPUTERS, ELECTRONIC LOCKS.
THEN I GO RIGHT IN.
I MOVE UP THE STEPS LIKE A SHADOW.
THE SECURITY STAFF FUMBLES ABOUT THE DARK, IN SLOW MOTION.

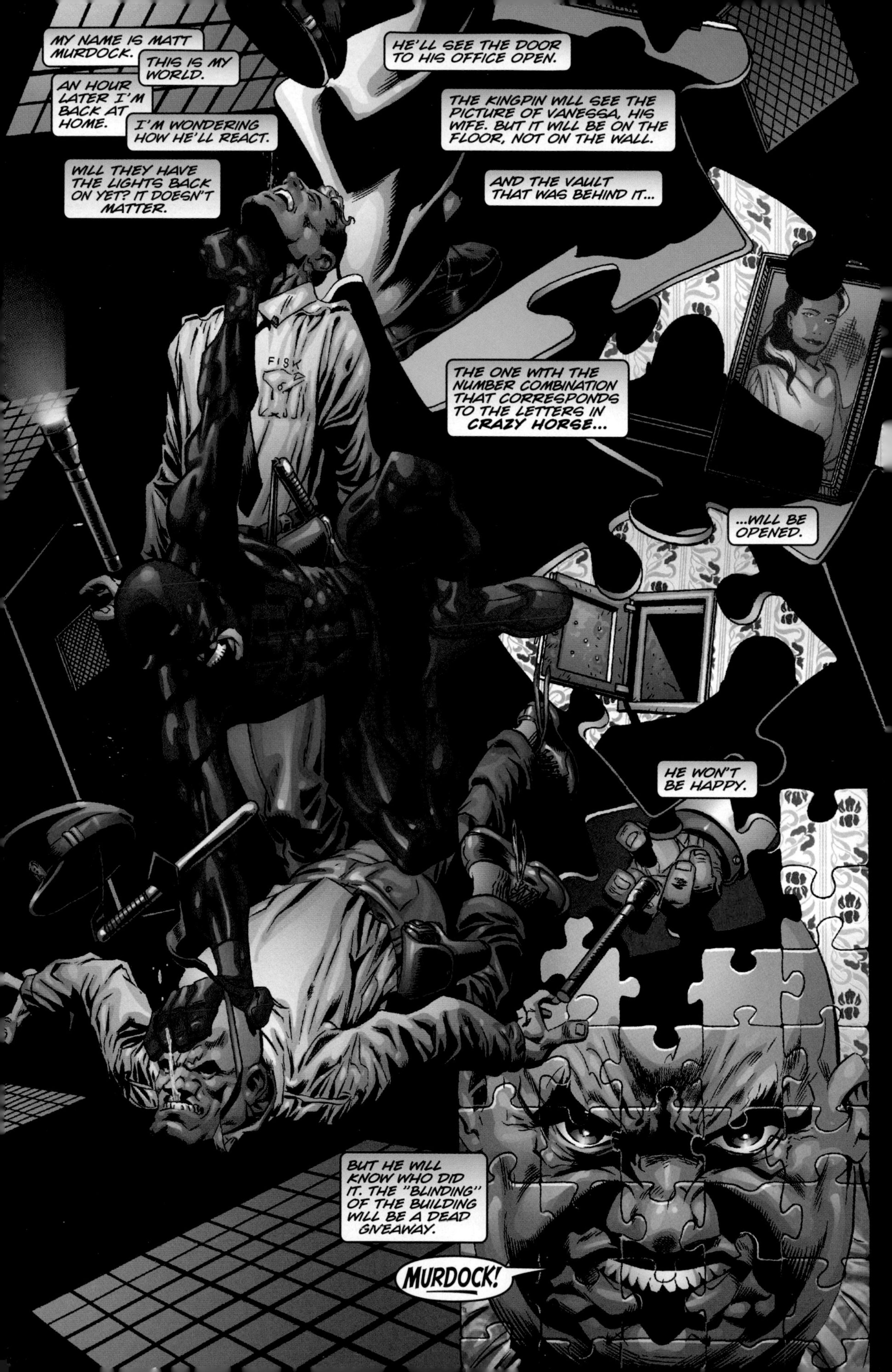
MY NAME IS MATT MURDOCK.
THIS IS MY WORLD.
AN HOUR LATER I'M BACK AT HOME.
I'M WONDERING HOW HE'LL REACT.
WILL THEY HAVE THE LIGHTS BACK ON YET? IT DOESN'T MATTER.
HE'LL SEE THE DOOR TO HIS OFFICE OPEN.
THE KINGPIN WILL SEE THE PICTURE OF VANESSA, HIS WIFE. BUT IT WILL BE ON THE FLOOR, NOT ON THE WALL.
AND THE VAULT THAT WAS BEHIND IT...
FISK
THE ONE WITH THE NUMBER COMBINATION THAT CORRESPONDS TO THE LETTERS IN CRAZY HORSE...
...WILL BE OPENED.
HE WON'T BE HAPPY.
BUT HE WILL KNOW WHO DID IT. THE "BLINDING" OF THE BUILDING WILL BE A DEAD GIVEAWAY.
MURDOCK!

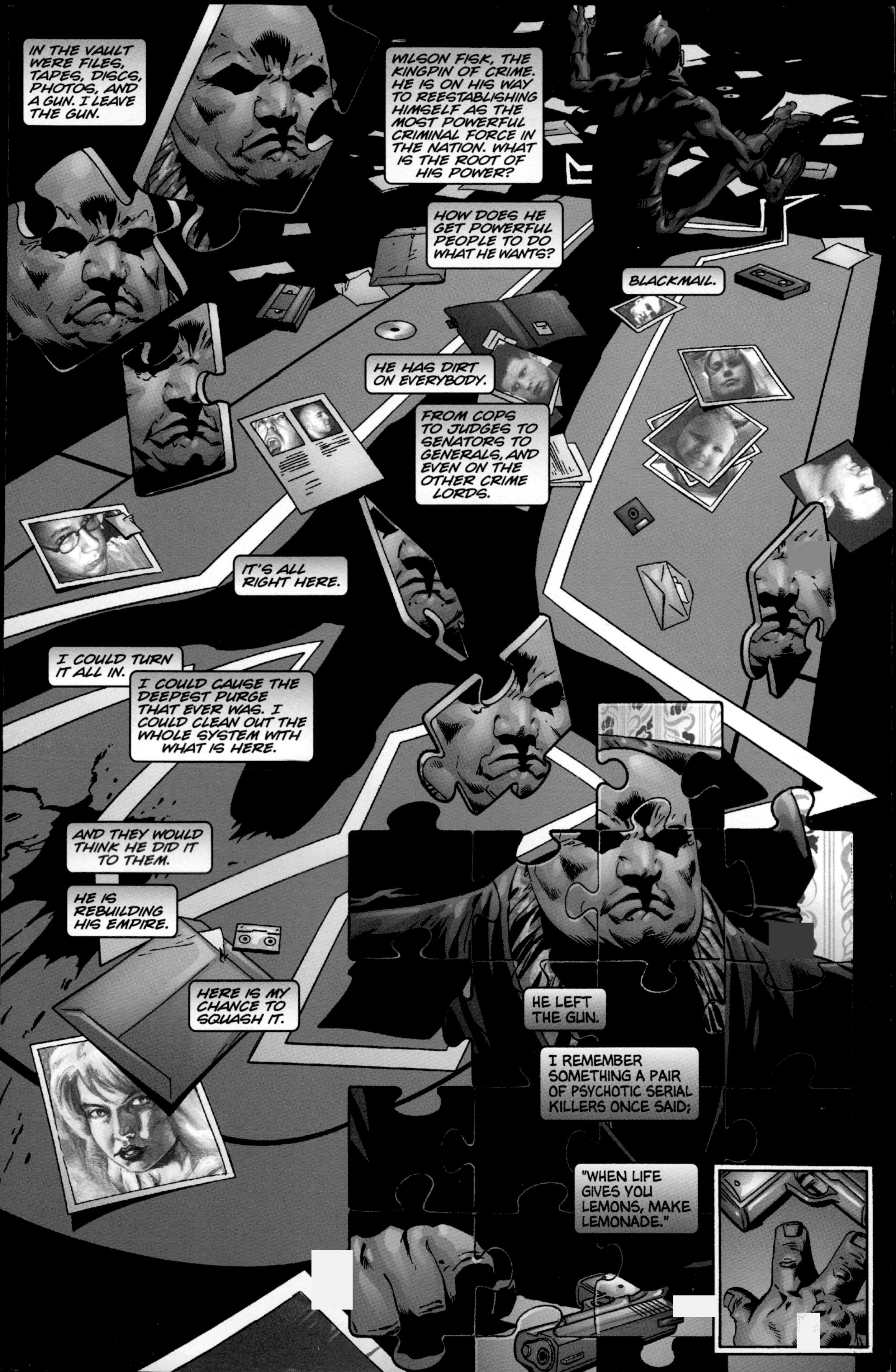
IN THE VAULT WERE FILES, TAPES, DISCS, PHOTOS, AND A GUN. I LEAVE THE GUN.
WILSON FISK, THE KINGPIN OF CRIME. HE IS ON HIS WAY TO REESTABLISHING HIMSELF AS THE MOST POWERFUL CRIMINAL FORCE IN THE NATION. WHAT IS THE ROOT OF HIS POWER?
HOW DOES HE GET POWERFUL PEOPLE TO DO WHAT HE WANTS?
BLACKMAIL.
HE HAS DIRT ON EVERYBODY.
FROM COPS TO JUDGES TO SENATORS TO GENERALS, AND EVEN ON THE OTHER CRIME LORDS.
IT'S ALL RIGHT HERE.
I COULD TURN IT ALL IN.
I COULD CAUSE THE DEEPEST PURGE THAT EVER WAS. I COULD CLEAN OUT THE WHOLE SYSTEM WITH WHAT IS HERE.
AND THEY WOULD THINK HE DID IT TO THEM.
HE IS REBUILDING HIS EMPIRE.
HERE IS MY CHANCE TO SQUASH IT.
HE LEFT THE GUN.
I REMEMBER SOMETHING A PAIR OF PSYCHOTIC SERIAL KILLERS ONCE SAID;
"WHEN LIFE GIVES YOU LEMONS, MAKE LEMONADE."

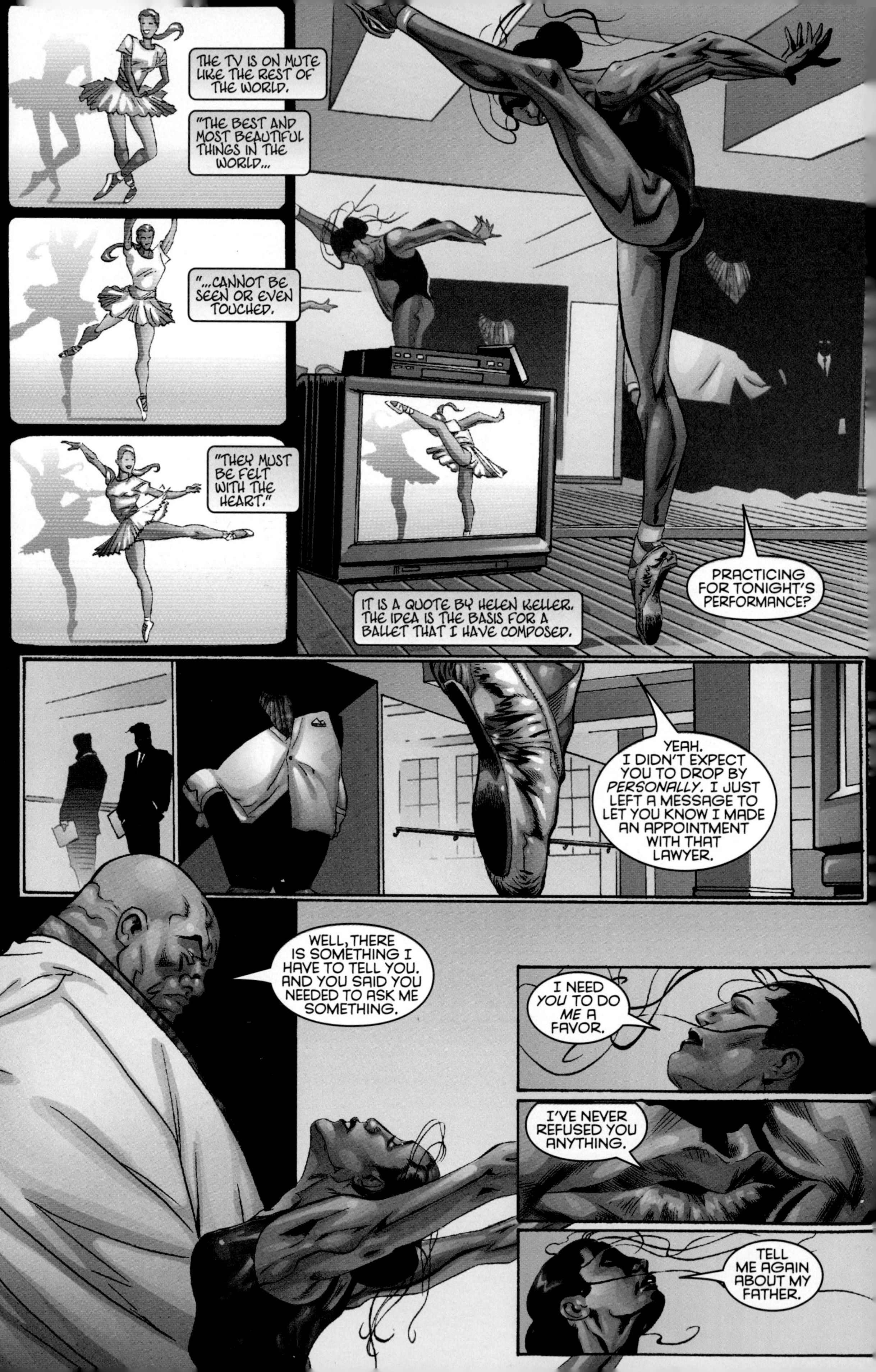
THE TV IS ON MUTE LIKE THE REST OF THE WORLD.
"THE BEST AND MOST BEAUTIFUL THINGS IN THE WORLD...
"...CANNOT BE SEEN OR EVEN TOUCHED.
"THEY MUST BE FELT WITH THE HEART."
IT IS A QUOTE BY HELEN KELLER. THE IDEA IS THE BASIS FOR A BALLET THAT I HAVE COMPOSED.
PRACTICING FOR TONIGHT'S PERFORMANCE?
YEAH. I DIDN'T EXPECT YOU TO DROP BY PERSONALLY. I JUST LEFT A MESSAGE TO LET YOU KNOW I MADE AN APPOINTMENT WITH THAT LAWYER.
WELL, THERE IS SOMETHING I HAVE TO TELL YOU. AND YOU SAID YOU NEEDED TO ASK ME SOMETHING.
I NEED YOU TO DO ME A FAVOR.
I'VE NEVER REFUSED YOU ANYTHING.
TELL ME AGAIN ABOUT MY FATHER.

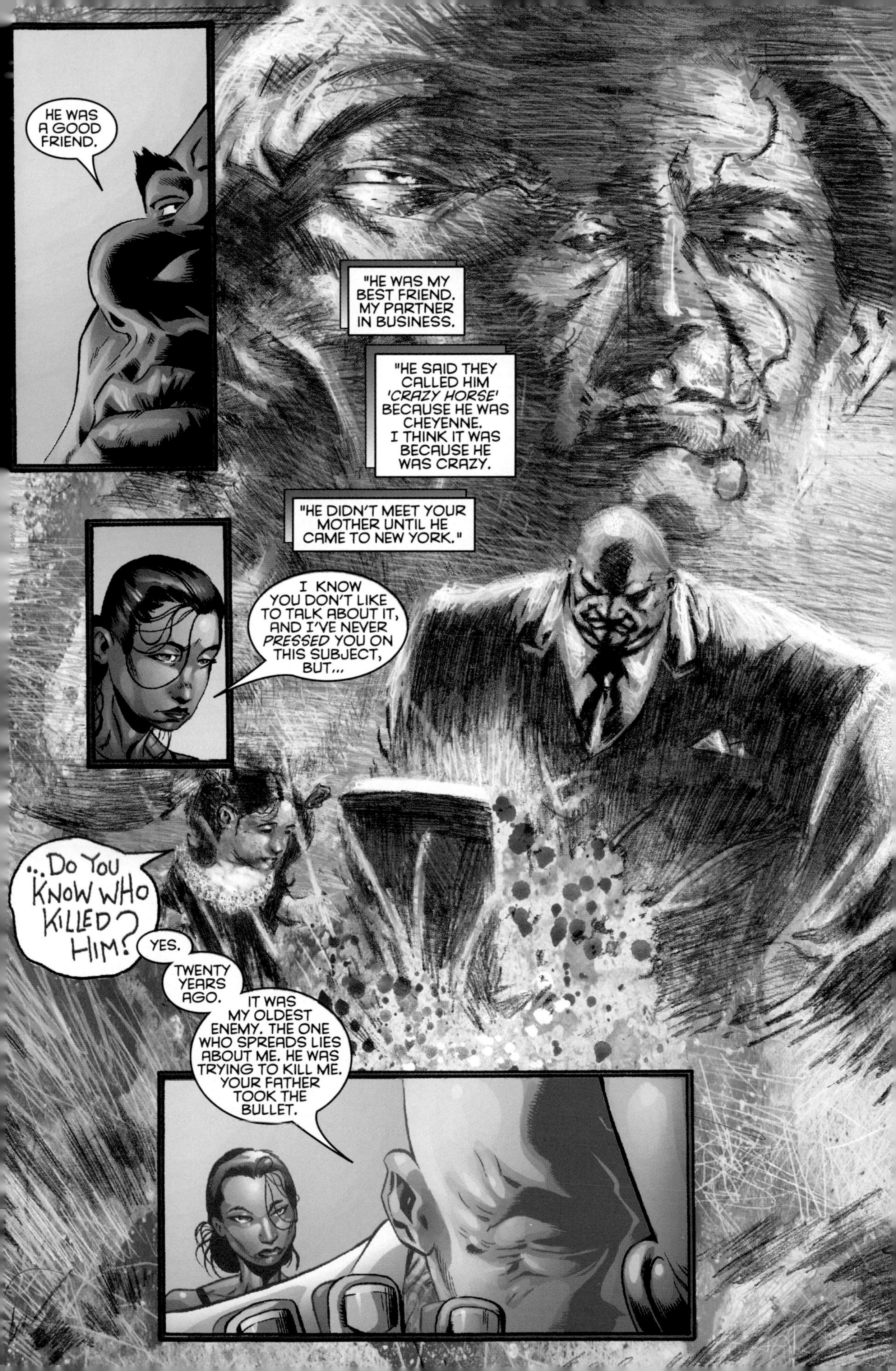
HE WAS A GOOD FRIEND.
"HE WAS MY BEST FRIEND. MY PARTNER IN BUSINESS.
"HE SAID THEY CALLED HIM 'CRAZY HORSE' BECAUSE HE WAS CHEYENNE. I THINK IT WAS BECAUSE HE WAS CRAZY.
"HE DIDN'T MEET YOUR MOTHER UNTIL HE CAME TO NEW YORK."
I KNOW YOU DON'T LIKE TO TALK ABOUT IT, AND I'VE NEVER PRESSED YOU ON THIS SUBJECT, BUT...
...DO YOU KNOW WHO KILLED HIM?
YES.
TWENTY YEARS AGO.
IT WAS MY OLDEST ENEMY. THE ONE WHO SPREADS LIES ABOUT ME. HE WAS TRYING TO KILL ME. YOUR FATHER TOOK THE BULLET.

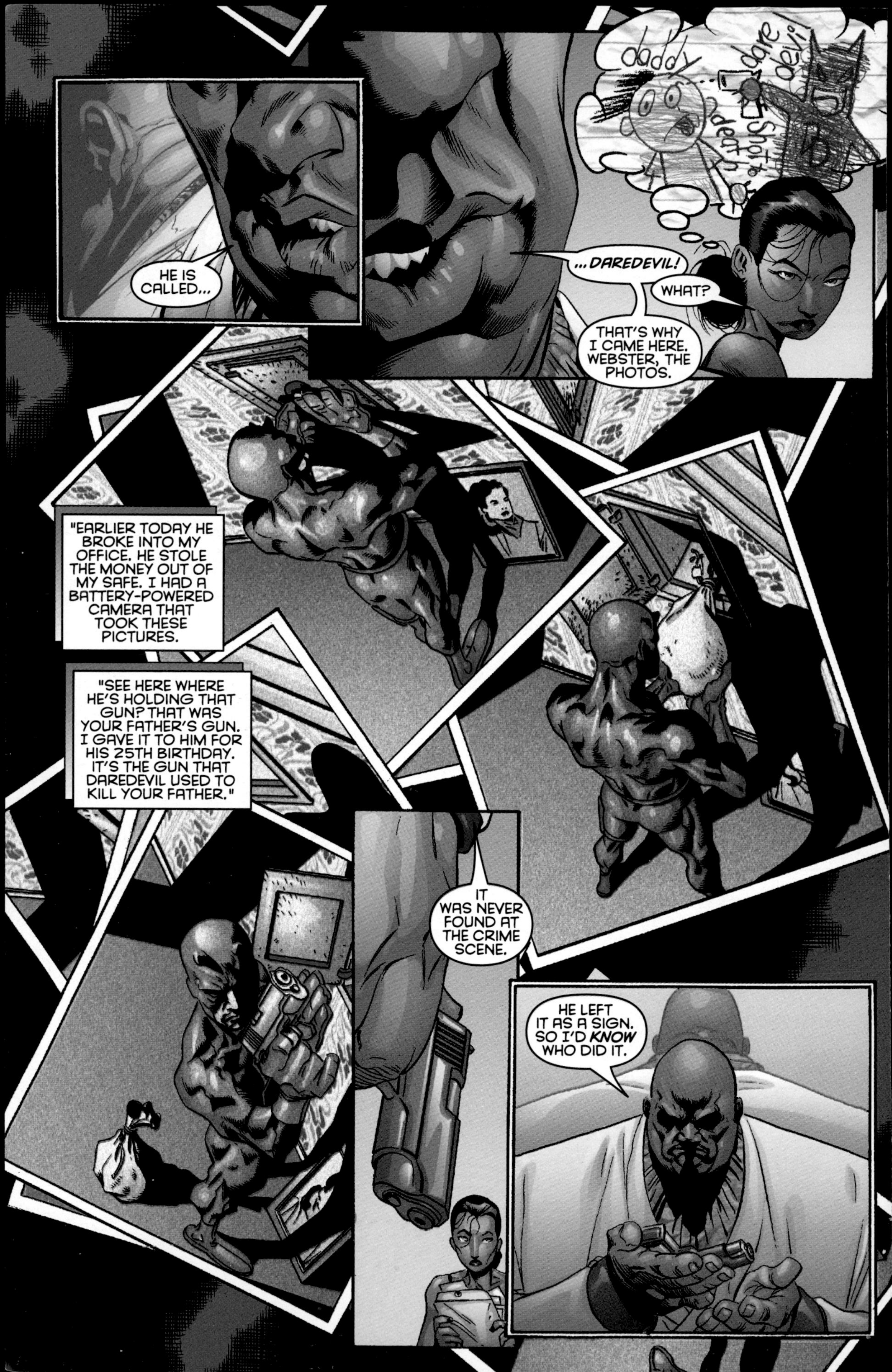

HE IS CALLED...
daddy
dare devil
Shot to death
...DAREDEVIL!
WHAT?
THAT'S WHY I CAME HERE. WEBSTER, THE PHOTOS.
"EARLIER TODAY HE BROKE INTO MY OFFICE. HE STOLE THE MONEY OUT OF MY SAFE. I HAD A BATTERY-POWERED CAMERA THAT TOOK THESE PICTURES.
"SEE HERE WHERE HE'S HOLDING THAT GUN? THAT WAS YOUR FATHER'S GUN. I GAVE IT TO HIM FOR HIS 25TH BIRTHDAY. IT'S THE GUN THAT DAREDEVIL USED TO KILL YOUR FATHER."
IT WAS NEVER FOUND AT THE CRIME SCENE.
HE LEFT IT AS A SIGN. SO I'D KNOW WHO DID IT.

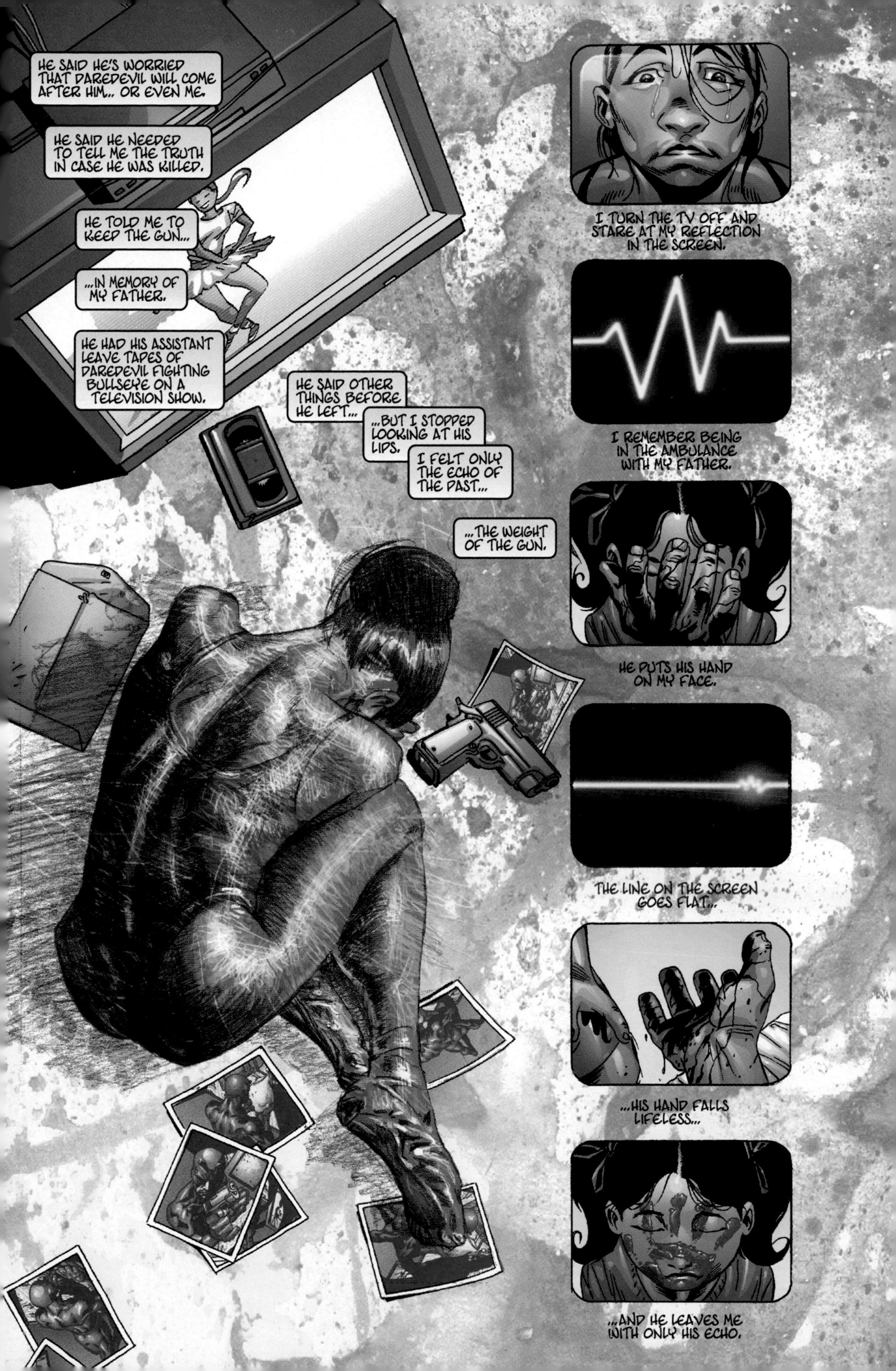

HE SAID HE'S WORRIED THAT DAREDEVIL WILL COME AFTER HIM... OR EVEN ME.
HE SAID HE NEEDED TO TELL ME THE TRUTH IN CASE HE WAS KILLED.
HE TOLD ME TO KEEP THE GUN...
...IN MEMORY OF MY FATHER.
HE HAD HIS ASSISTANT LEAVE TAPES OF DAREDEVIL FIGHTING BULLSEYE ON A TELEVISION SHOW.
HE SAID OTHER THINGS BEFORE HE LEFT...
...BUT I STOPPED LOOKING AT HIS LIPS.
I FELT ONLY THE ECHO OF THE PAST...
...THE WEIGHT OF THE GUN.
I TURN THE TV OFF AND STARE AT MY REFLECTION IN THE SCREEN.
I REMEMBER BEING IN THE AMBULANCE WITH MY FATHER.
HE PUTS HIS HAND ON MY FACE.
THE LINE ON THE SCREEN GOES FLAT...
...HIS HAND FALLS LIFELESS...
...AND HE LEAVES ME WITH ONLY HIS ECHO.

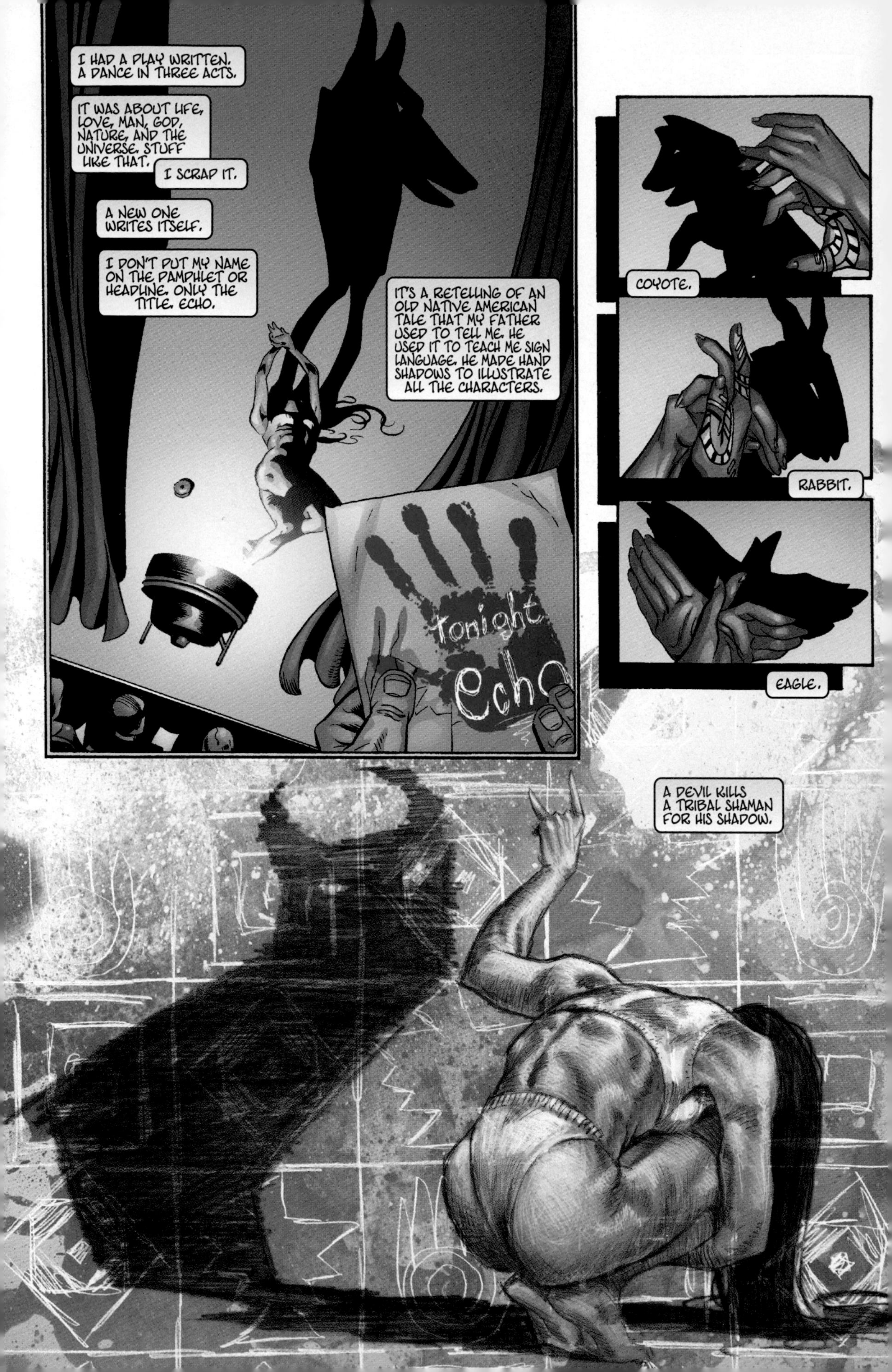
I HAD A PLAY WRITTEN. A DANCE IN THREE ACTS.
IT WAS ABOUT LIFE, LOVE, MAN, GOD, NATURE, AND THE UNIVERSE. STUFF LIKE THAT.
I SCRAP IT.
A NEW ONE WRITES ITSELF.
I DON'T PUT MY NAME ON THE PAMPHLET OR HEADLINE. ONLY THE TITLE. ECHO.
IT'S A RETELLING OF AN OLD NATIVE AMERICAN TALE THAT MY FATHER USED TO TELL ME. HE USED IT TO TEACH ME SIGN LANGUAGE. HE MADE HAND SHADOWS TO ILLUSTRATE ALL THE CHARACTERS.
Tonight
Echo
COYOTE.
RABBIT.
EAGLE.
A DEVIL KILLS A TRIBAL SHAMAN FOR HIS SHADOW.

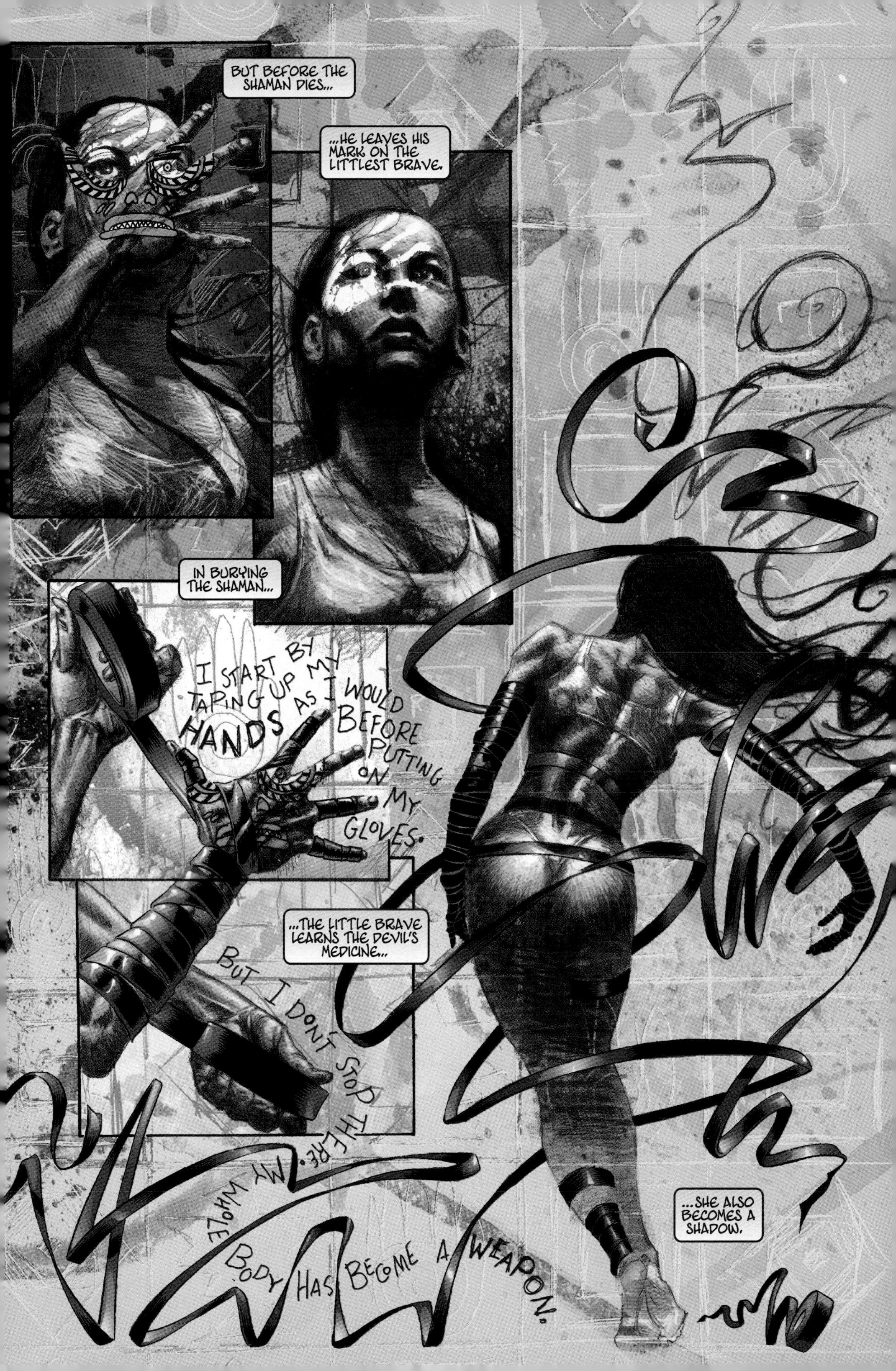
BUT BEFORE THE SHAMAN DIES...
...HE LEAVES HIS MARK ON THE LITTLEST BRAVE.
IN BURYING THE SHAMAN...
I START BY TAPING UP MY HANDS AS I WOULD BEFORE PUTTING ON MY GLOVES.
...THE LITTLE BRAVE LEARNS THE DEVIL'S MEDICINE...
BUT I DON'T STOP THERE. MY WHOLE BODY HAS BECOME A WEAPON.
...SHE ALSO BECOMES A SHADOW.

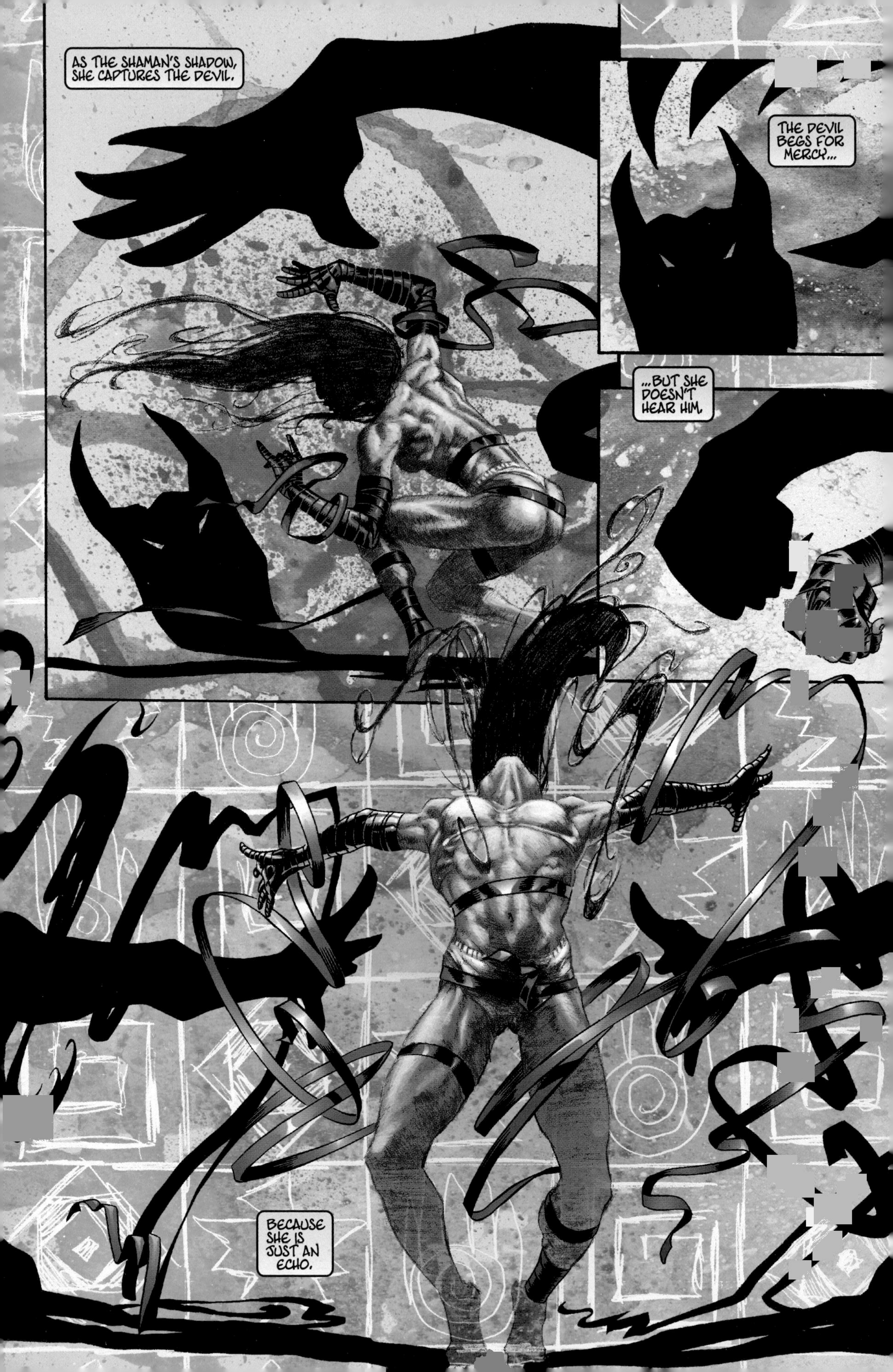
AS THE SHAMAN'S SHADOW, SHE CAPTURES THE DEVIL.
THE DEVIL BEGS FOR MERCY...
...BUT SHE DOESN'T HEAR HIM.
BECAUSE SHE IS JUST AN ECHO.

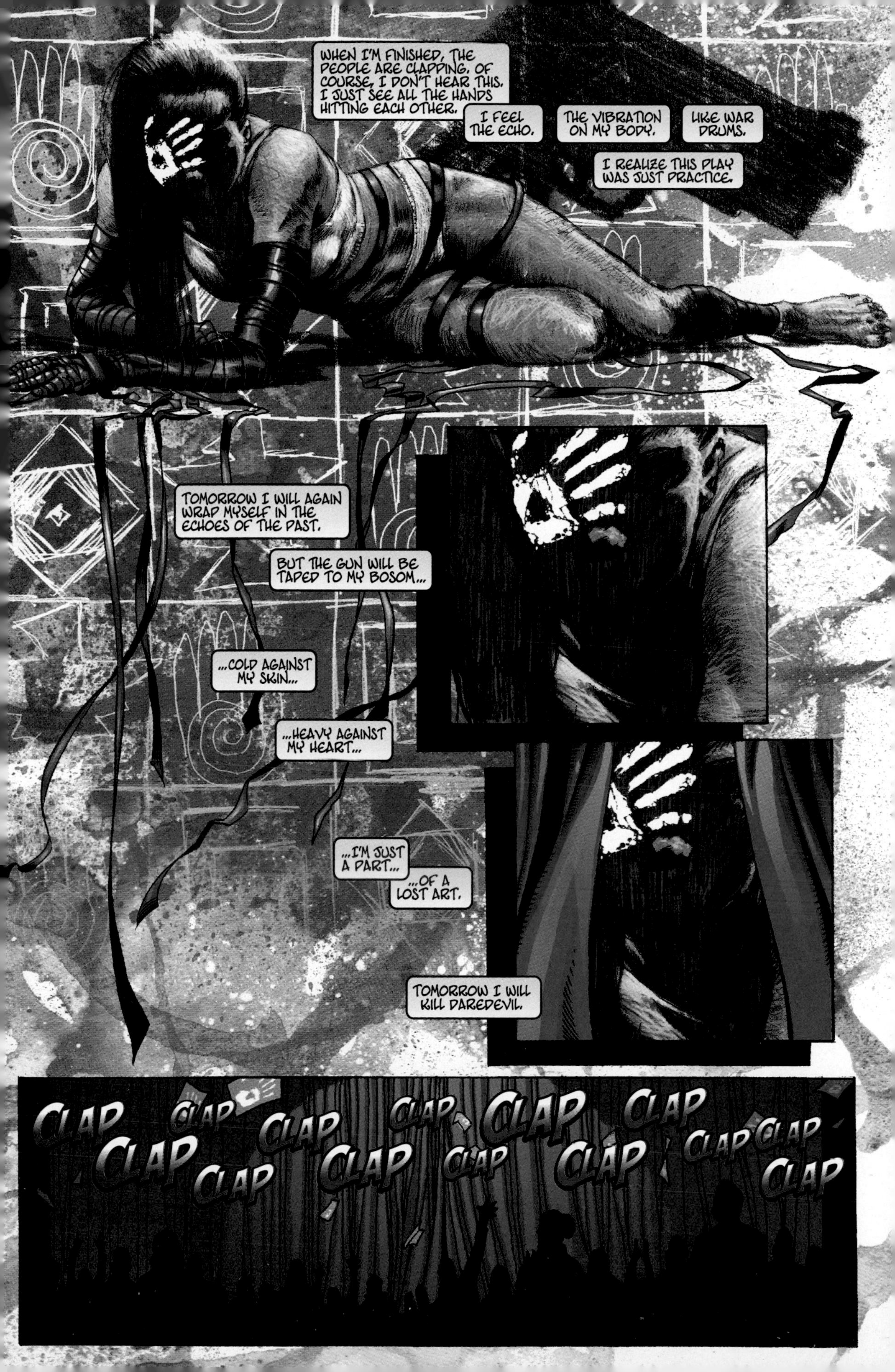
WHEN I'M FINISHED, THE PEOPLE ARE CLAPPING. OF COURSE, I DON'T HEAR THIS. I JUST SEE ALL THE HANDS HITTING EACH OTHER.
I FEEL THE ECHO.
THE VIBRATION ON MY BODY.
LIKE WAR DRUMS.
I REALIZE THIS PLAY WAS JUST PRACTICE.
TOMORROW I WILL AGAIN WRAP MYSELF IN THE ECHOES OF THE PAST.
BUT THE GUN WILL BE TAPED TO MY BOSOM...
...COLD AGAINST MY SKIN...
...HEAVY AGAINST MY HEART...
...I'M JUST A PART...
...OF A LOST ART.
TOMORROW I WILL KILL DAREDEVIL.
CLAP CLAP CLAP CLAP CLAP CLAP CLAP CLAP CLAP CLAP CLAP CLAP CLAP CLAP CLAP

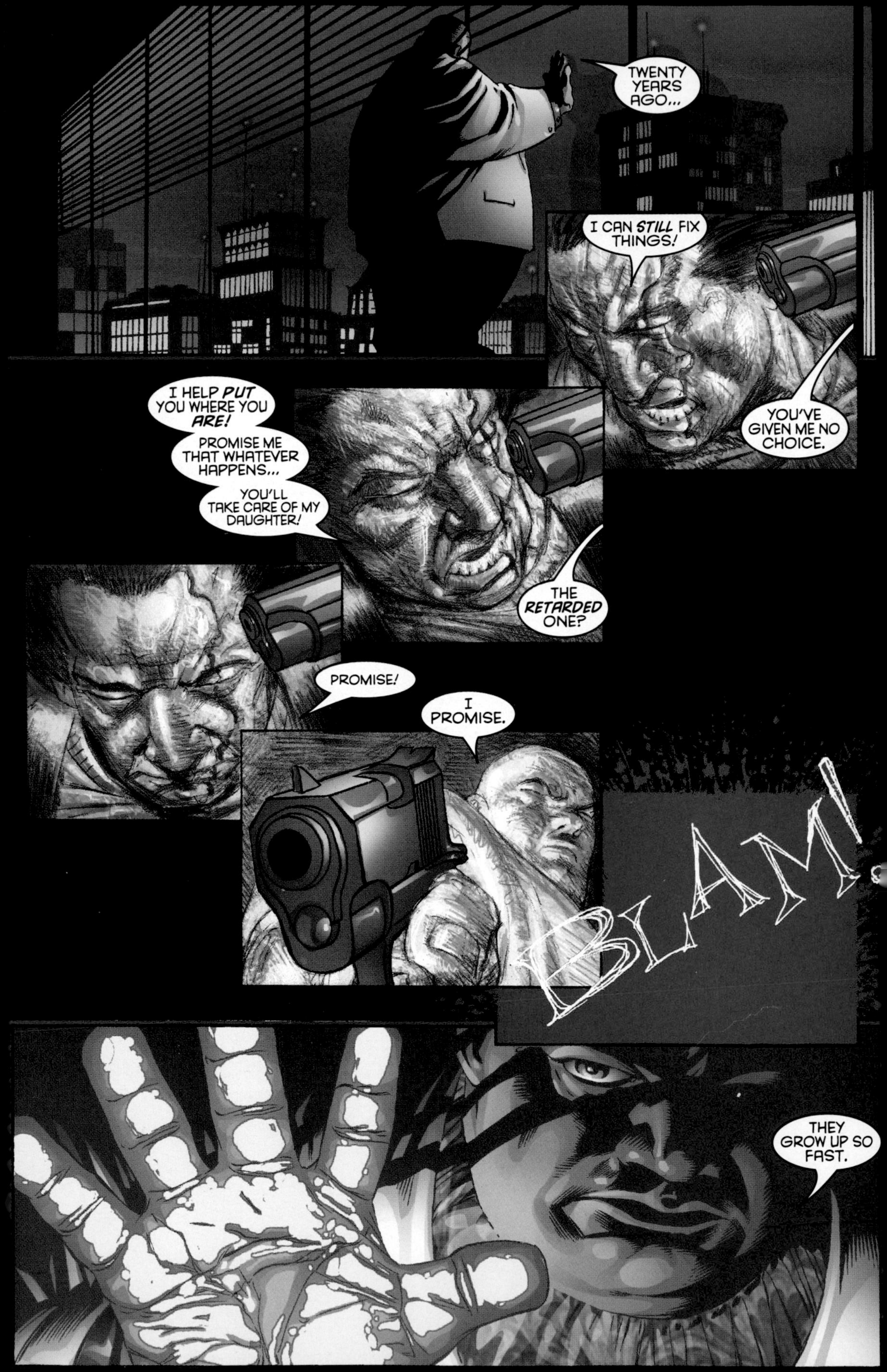
TWENTY YEARS AGO...
I CAN STILL FIX THINGS!
YOU'VE GIVEN ME NO CHOICE.
I HELP PUT YOU WHERE YOU ARE!
PROMISE ME THAT WHATEVER HAPPENS...
YOU'LL TAKE CARE OF MY DAUGHTER!
THE RETARDED ONE?
PROMISE!
I PROMISE.
BLAM!
THEY GROW UP SO FAST.

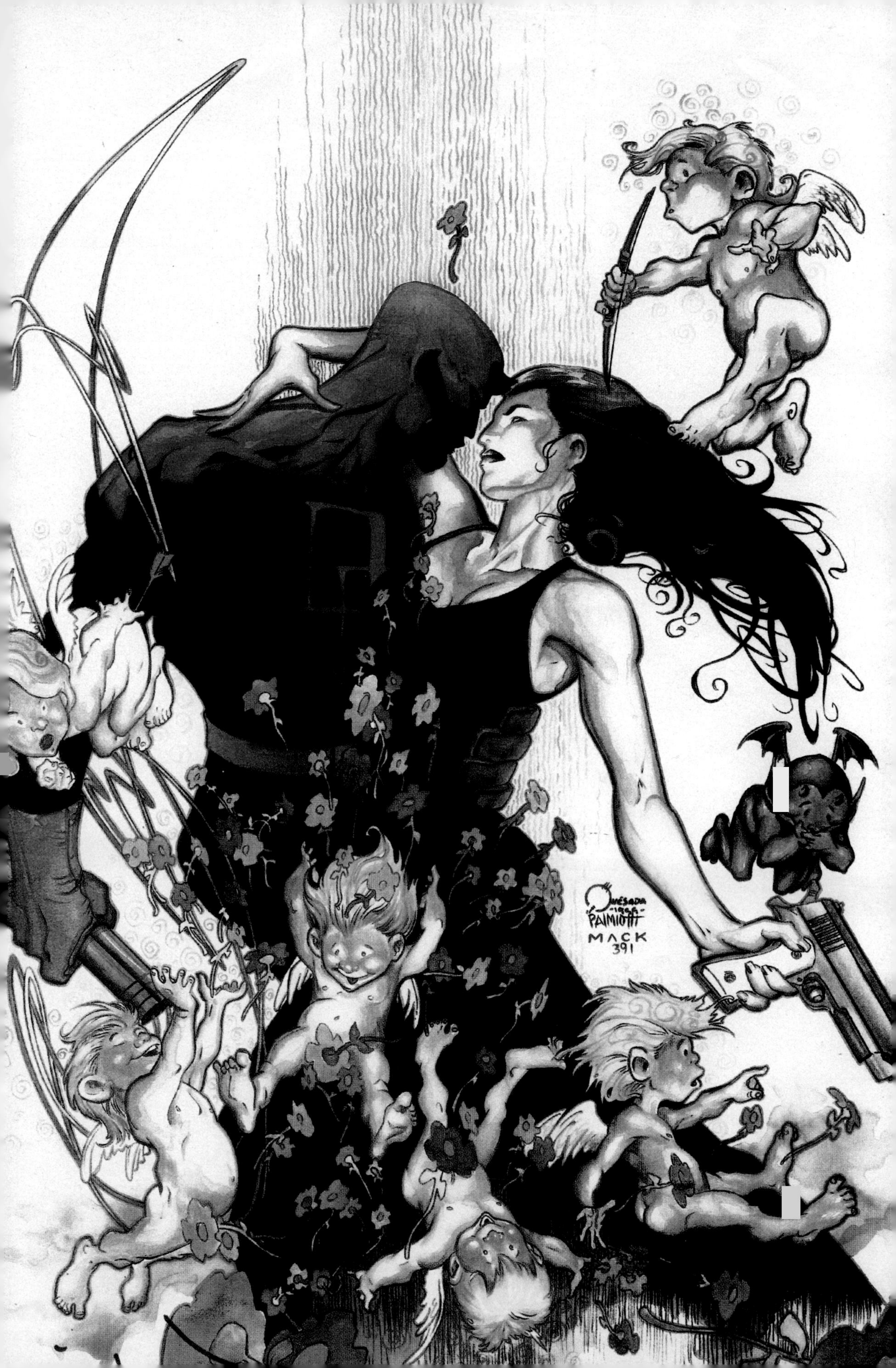
MACK
391

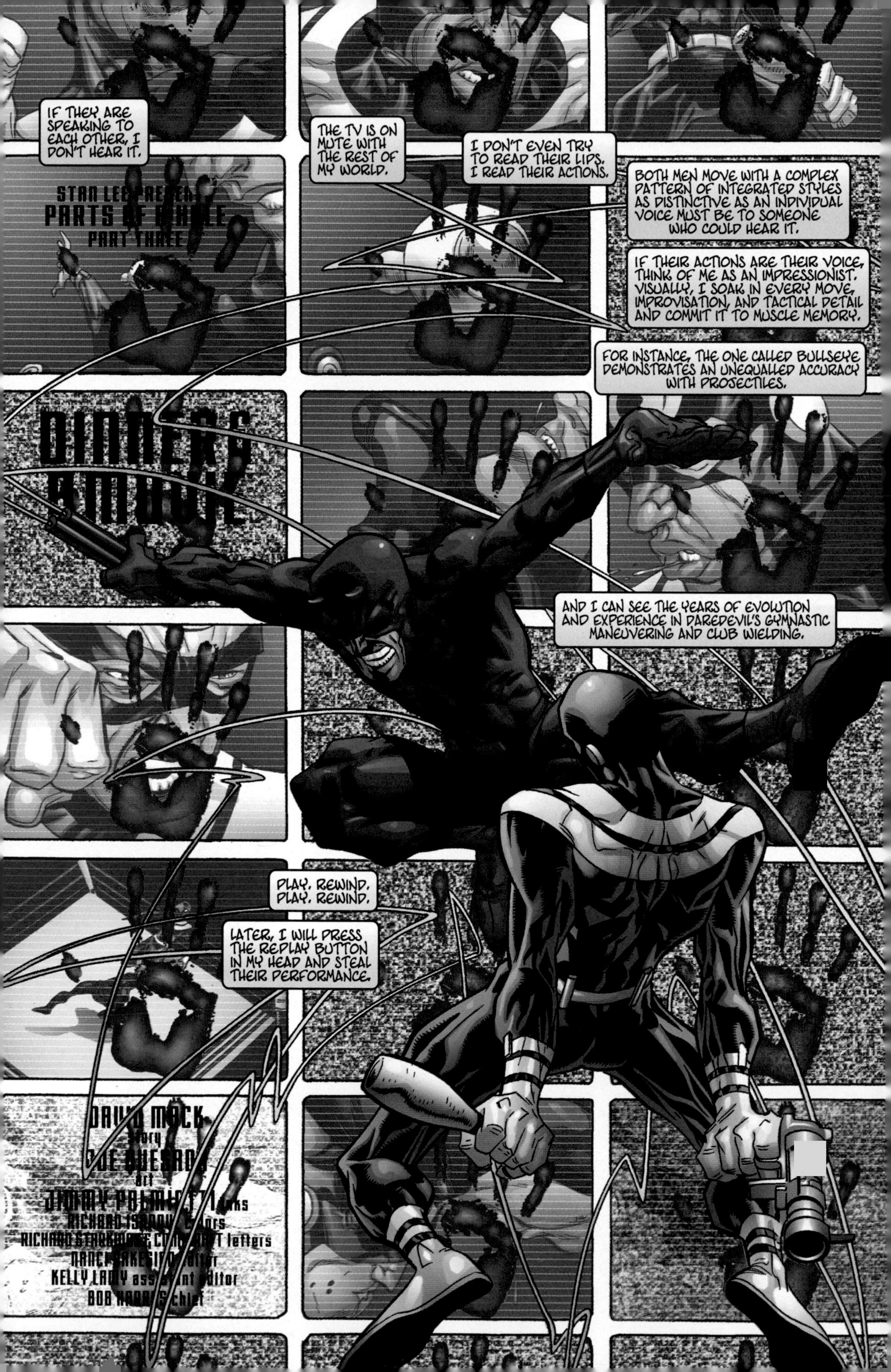
IF THEY ARE SPEAKING TO EACH OTHER, I DON'T HEAR IT.
PART THREE
THE TV IS ON MUTE WITH THE REST OF MY WORLD.
I DON'T EVEN TRY TO READ THEIR LIPS. I READ THEIR ACTIONS.
BOTH MEN MOVE WITH A COMPLEX PATTERN OF INTEGRATED STYLES AS DISTINCTIVE AS AN INDIVIDUAL VOICE MUST BE TO SOMEONE WHO COULD HEAR IT.
IF THEIR ACTIONS ARE THEIR VOICE, THINK OF ME AS AN IMPRESSIONIST. VISUALLY, I SOAK IN EVERY MOVE, IMPROVISATION, AND TACTICAL DETAIL AND COMMIT IT TO MUSCLE MEMORY.
FOR INSTANCE, THE ONE CALLED BULLSEYE DEMONSTRATES AN UNEQUALLED ACCURACY WITH PROJECTILES.
AND I CAN SEE THE YEARS OF EVOLUTION AND EXPERIENCE IN DAREDEVIL'S GYMNASTIC MANEUVERING AND CLUB WIELDING.
PLAY. REWIND. PLAY. REWIND.
LATER, I WILL PRESS THE REPLAY BUTTON IN MY HEAD AND STEAL THEIR PERFORMANCE.
story
art
letters

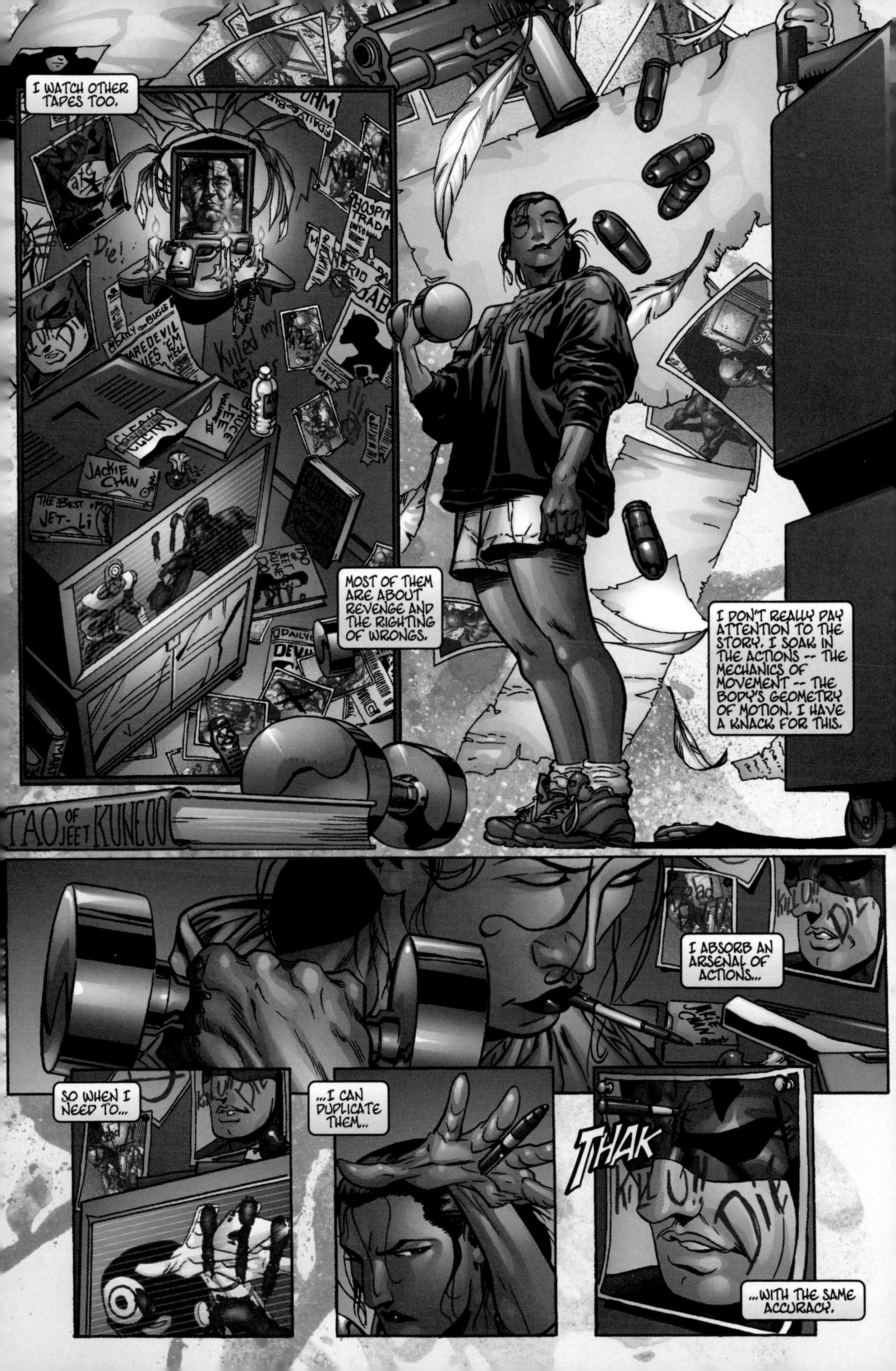
I WATCH OTHER TAPES TOO.
MOST OF THEM ARE ABOUT REVENGE AND THE RIGHTING OF WRONGS.
I DON'T REALLY PAY ATTENTION TO THE STORY. I SOAK IN THE ACTIONS -- THE MECHANICS OF MOVEMENT -- THE BODY'S GEOMETRY OF MOTION. I HAVE A KNACK FOR THIS.
TAO OF JEET KUNE DO
I ABSORB AN ARSENAL OF ACTIONS...
SO WHEN I NEED TO...
...I CAN DUPLICATE THEM...
THAK
...WITH THE SAME ACCURACY.

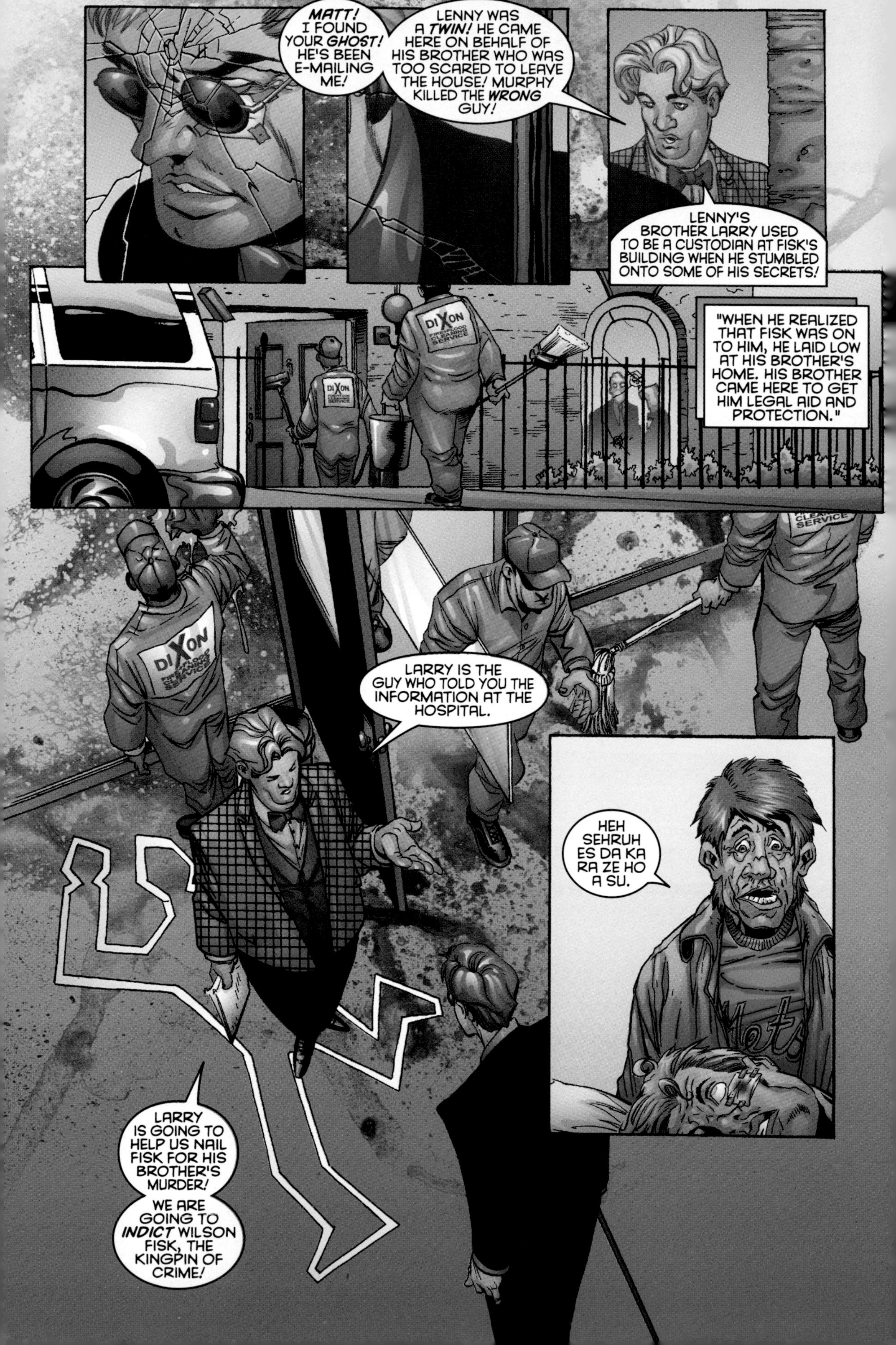
MATT! I FOUND YOUR GHOST! HE'S BEEN E-MAILING ME!
LENNY WAS A TWIN! HE CAME HERE ON BEHALF OF HIS BROTHER WHO WAS TOO SCARED TO LEAVE THE HOUSE! MURPHY KILLED THE WRONG GUY!
LENNY'S BROTHER LARRY USED TO BE A CUSTODIAN AT FISK'S BUILDING WHEN HE STUMBLED ONTO SOME OF HIS SECRETS!
DIXON FIRE/FLOOD CLEANING SERVICE
"WHEN HE REALIZED THAT FISK WAS ON TO HIM, HE LAID LOW AT HIS BROTHER'S HOME. HIS BROTHER CAME HERE TO GET HIM LEGAL AID AND PROTECTION."
LARRY IS THE GUY WHO TOLD YOU THE INFORMATION AT THE HOSPITAL.
HEH SEHRUH ES DA KA RA ZE HO A SU.
LARRY IS GOING TO HELP US NAIL FISK FOR HIS BROTHER'S MURDER!
WE ARE GOING TO INDICT WILSON FISK, THE KINGPIN OF CRIME!

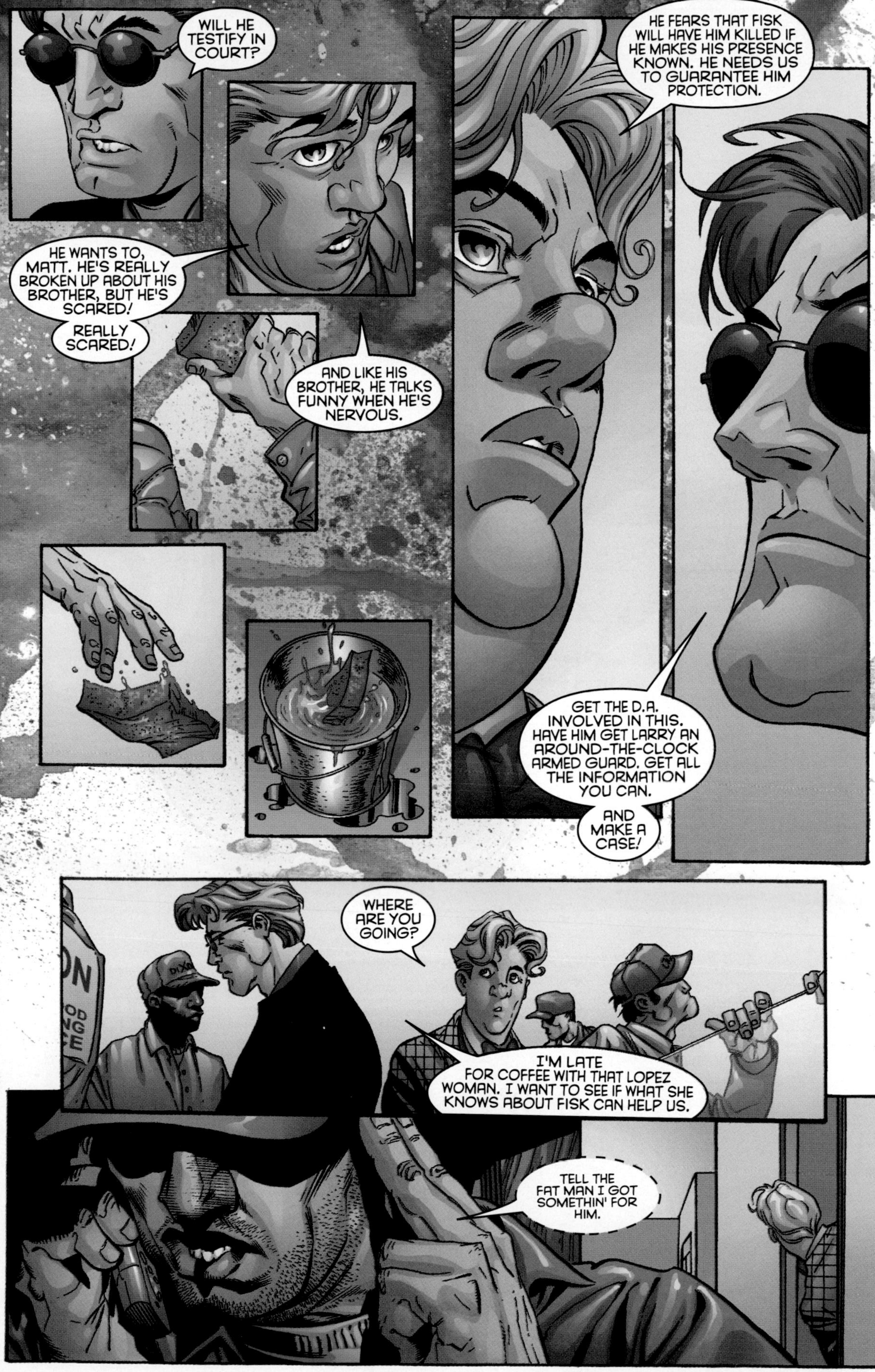
WILL HE TESTIFY IN COURT?
HE WANTS TO, MATT. HE'S REALLY BROKEN UP ABOUT HIS BROTHER, BUT HE'S SCARED!
REALLY SCARED!
AND LIKE HIS BROTHER, HE TALKS FUNNY WHEN HE'S NERVOUS.
HE FEARS THAT FISK WILL HAVE HIM KILLED IF HE MAKES HIS PRESENCE KNOWN. HE NEEDS US TO GUARANTEE HIM PROTECTION.
GET THE D.A. INVOLVED IN THIS. HAVE HIM GET LARRY AN AROUND-THE-CLOCK ARMED GUARD. GET ALL THE INFORMATION YOU CAN.
AND MAKE A CASE!
WHERE ARE YOU GOING?
I'M LATE FOR COFFEE WITH THAT LOPEZ WOMAN. I WANT TO SEE IF WHAT SHE KNOWS ABOUT FISK CAN HELP US.
TELL THE FAT MAN I GOT SOMETHIN' FOR HIM.

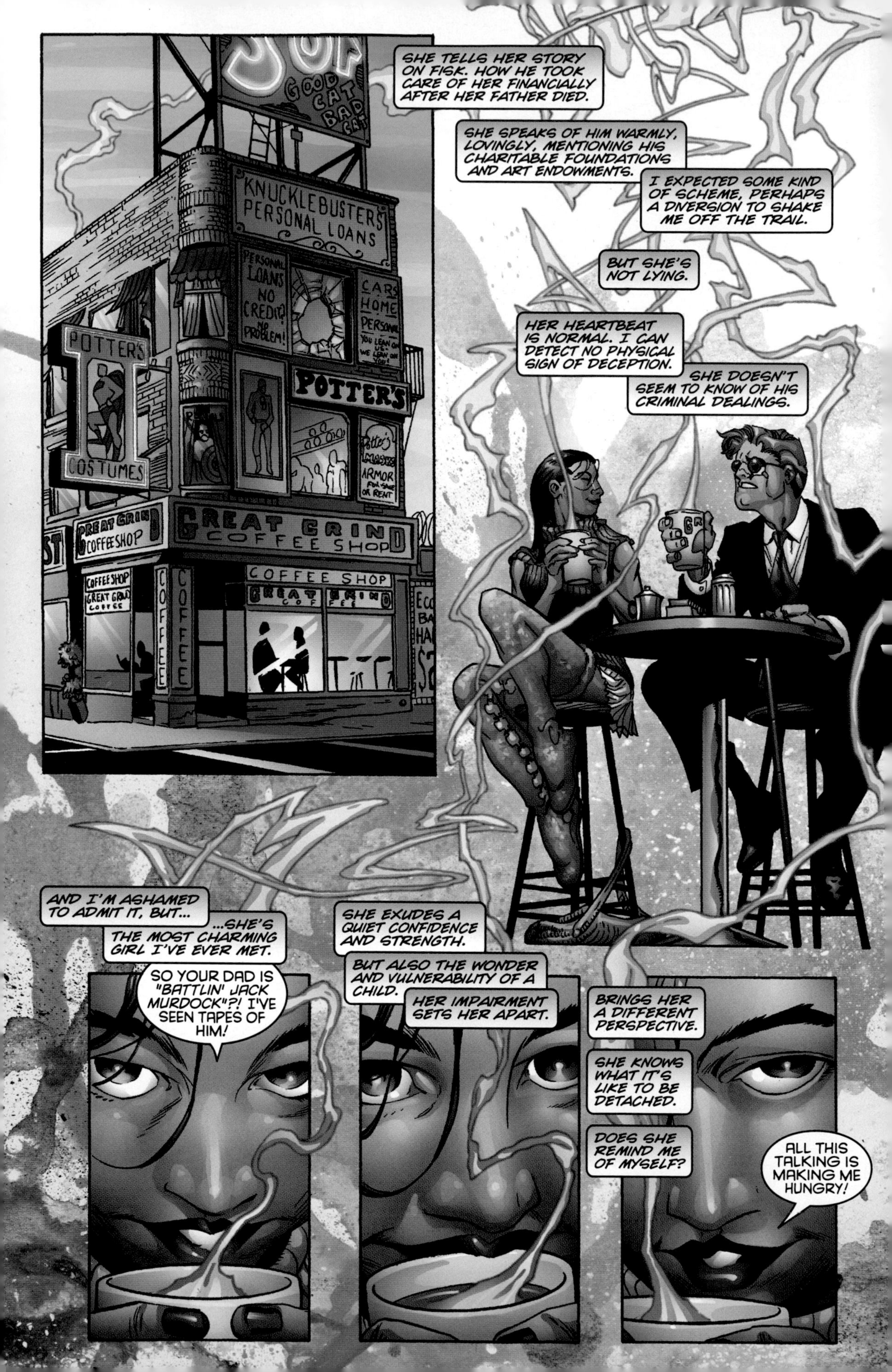
GOOD CAT BAD CAT
KNUCKLEBUSTERS PERSONAL LOANS
PERSONAL LOANS NO CREDIT? NO PROBLEM!
CARS HOME PERSONAL
POTTER'S COSTUMES
POTTER'S
ARMOR
GREAT GRIND COFFEE SHOP
COFFEE SHOP GREAT GRIND COFFEE
COFFEE
SHE TELLS HER STORY ON FISK. HOW HE TOOK CARE OF HER FINANCIALLY AFTER HER FATHER DIED.
SHE SPEAKS OF HIM WARMLY, LOVINGLY, MENTIONING HIS CHARITABLE FOUNDATIONS AND ART ENDOWMENTS.
I EXPECTED SOME KIND OF SCHEME, PERHAPS A DIVERSION TO SHAKE ME OFF THE TRAIL.
BUT SHE'S NOT LYING.
HER HEARTBEAT IS NORMAL. I CAN DETECT NO PHYSICAL SIGN OF DECEPTION.
SHE DOESN'T SEEM TO KNOW OF HIS CRIMINAL DEALINGS.
AND I'M ASHAMED TO ADMIT IT, BUT...
...SHE'S THE MOST CHARMING GIRL I'VE EVER MET.
SO YOUR DAD IS "BATTLIN' JACK MURDOCK"?! I'VE SEEN TAPES OF HIM!
SHE EXUDES A QUIET CONFIDENCE AND STRENGTH.
BUT ALSO THE WONDER AND VULNERABILITY OF A CHILD.
HER IMPAIRMENT SETS HER APART.
BRINGS HER A DIFFERENT PERSPECTIVE.
SHE KNOWS WHAT IT'S LIKE TO BE DETACHED.
DOES SHE REMIND ME OF MYSELF?
ALL THIS TALKING IS MAKING ME HUNGRY!

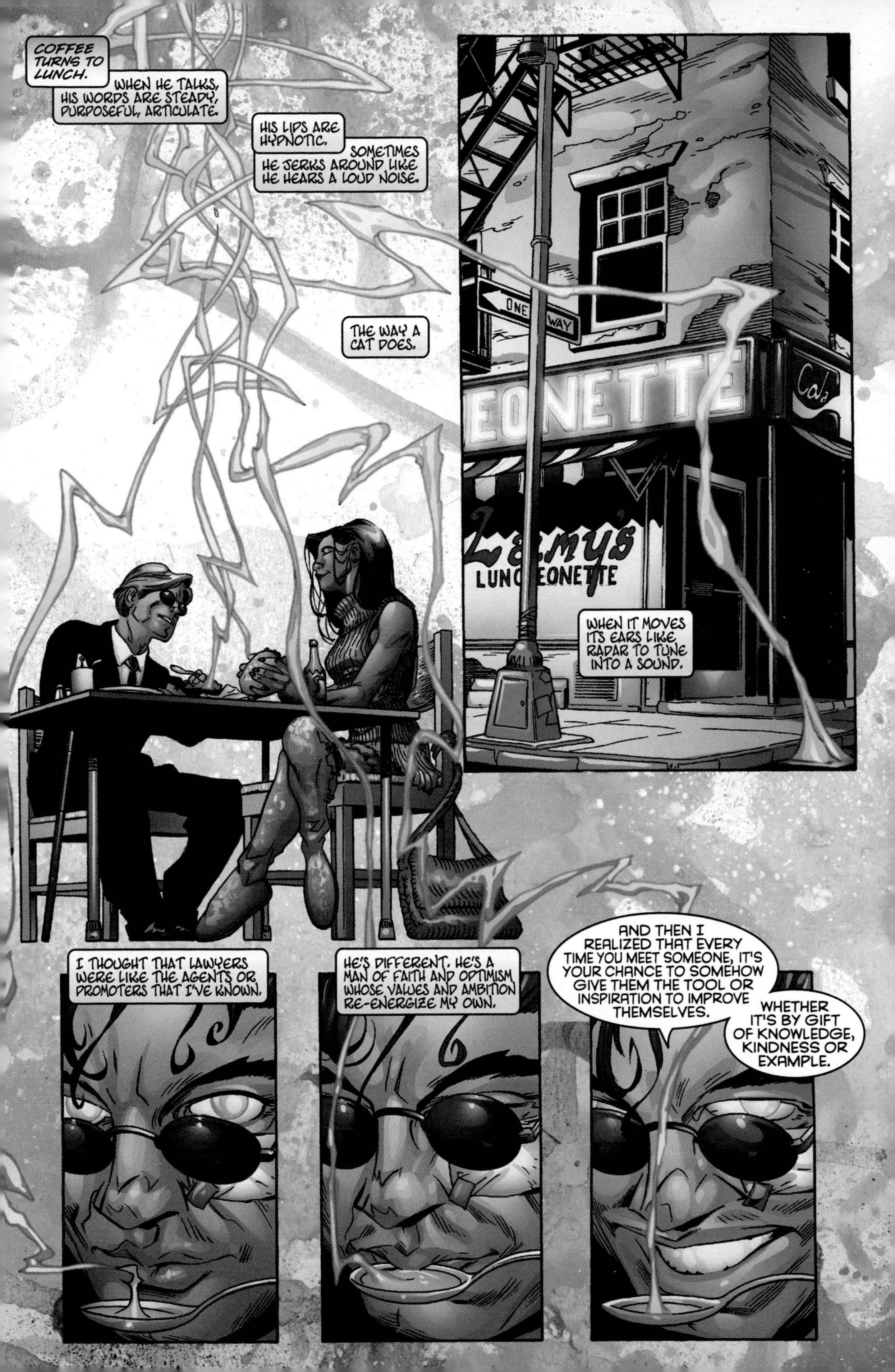
COFFEE TURNS TO LUNCH.
WHEN HE TALKS, HIS WORDS ARE STEADY, PURPOSEFUL, ARTICULATE.
HIS LIPS ARE HYPNOTIC.
SOMETIMES HE JERKS AROUND LIKE HE HEARS A LOUD NOISE.
THE WAY A CAT DOES.
ONE WAY
EONETTE
Lamy's
LUNCHEONETTE
WHEN IT MOVES ITS EARS LIKE RADAR TO TUNE INTO A SOUND.
I THOUGHT THAT LAWYERS WERE LIKE THE AGENTS OR PROMOTERS THAT I'VE KNOWN.
HE'S DIFFERENT. HE'S A MAN OF FAITH AND OPTIMISM WHOSE VALUES AND AMBITION RE-ENERGIZE MY OWN.
AND THEN I REALIZED THAT EVERY TIME YOU MEET SOMEONE, IT'S YOUR CHANCE TO SOMEHOW GIVE THEM THE TOOL OR INSPIRATION TO IMPROVE THEMSELVES.
WHETHER IT'S BY GIFT OF KNOWLEDGE, KINDNESS OR EXAMPLE.

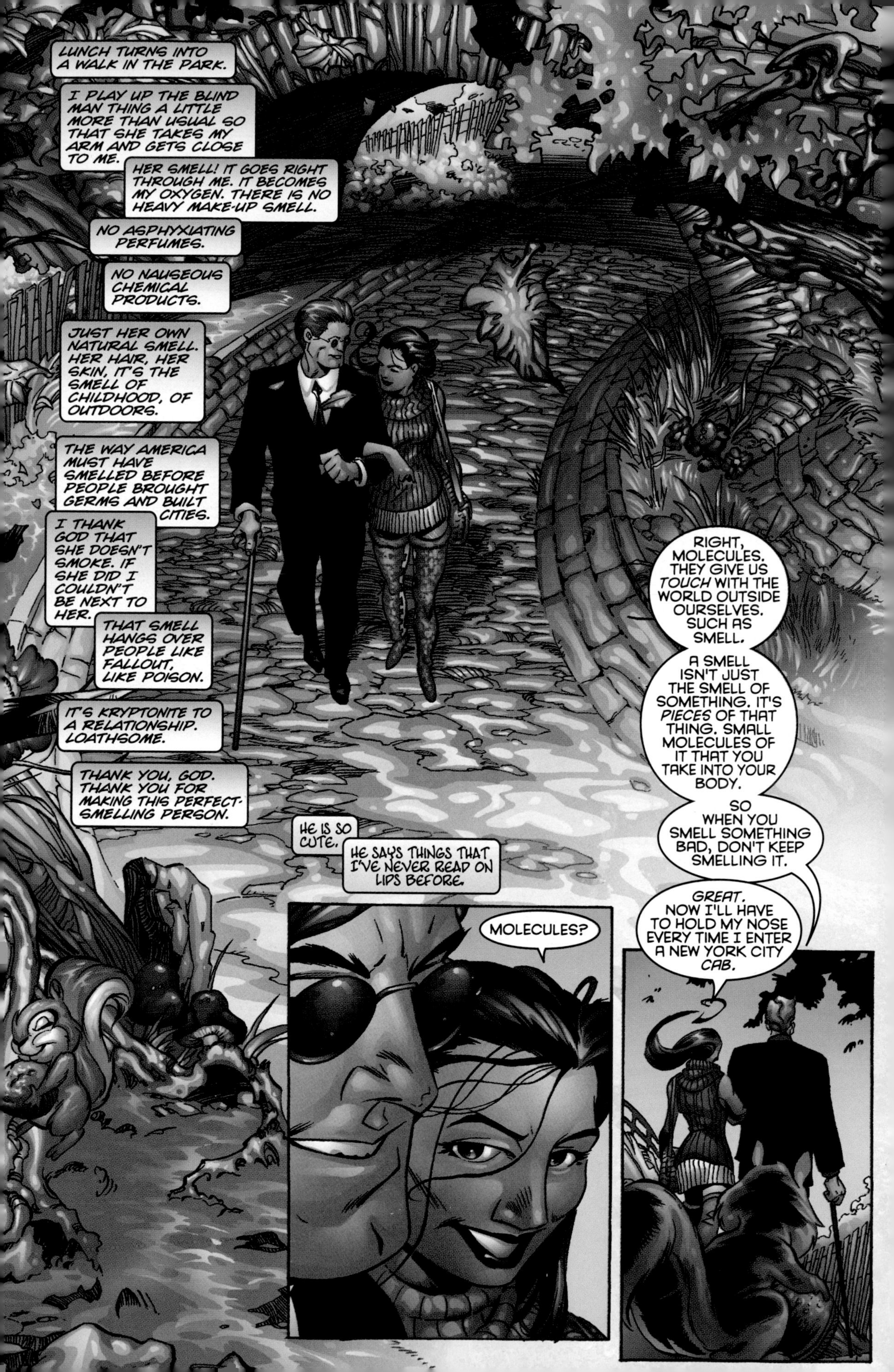
LUNCH TURNS INTO A WALK IN THE PARK.
I PLAY UP THE BLIND MAN THING A LITTLE MORE THAN USUAL SO THAT SHE TAKES MY ARM AND GETS CLOSE TO ME.
HER SMELL! IT GOES RIGHT THROUGH ME. IT BECOMES MY OXYGEN. THERE IS NO HEAVY MAKE-UP SMELL.
NO ASPHYXIATING PERFUMES.
NO NAUSEOUS CHEMICAL PRODUCTS.
JUST HER OWN NATURAL SMELL. HER HAIR, HER SKIN, IT'S THE SMELL OF CHILDHOOD, OF OUTDOORS.
THE WAY AMERICA MUST HAVE SMELLED BEFORE PEOPLE BROUGHT GERMS AND BUILT CITIES.
I THANK GOD THAT SHE DOESN'T SMOKE. IF SHE DID I COULDN'T BE NEXT TO HER.
THAT SMELL HANGS OVER PEOPLE LIKE FALLOUT, LIKE POISON.
IT'S KRYPTONITE TO A RELATIONSHIP. LOATHSOME.
THANK YOU, GOD. THANK YOU FOR MAKING THIS PERFECT-SMELLING PERSON.
RIGHT, MOLECULES. THEY GIVE US *TOUCH* WITH THE WORLD OUTSIDE OURSELVES. SUCH AS SMELL.
A SMELL ISN'T JUST THE SMELL OF SOMETHING. IT'S *PIECES* OF THAT THING. SMALL MOLECULES OF IT THAT YOU TAKE INTO YOUR BODY.
SO WHEN YOU SMELL SOMETHING BAD, DON'T KEEP SMELLING IT.
HE IS SO CUTE.
HE SAYS THINGS THAT I'VE NEVER READ ON LIPS BEFORE.
MOLECULES?
GREAT. NOW I'LL HAVE TO HOLD MY NOSE EVERY TIME I ENTER A NEW YORK CITY CAB.

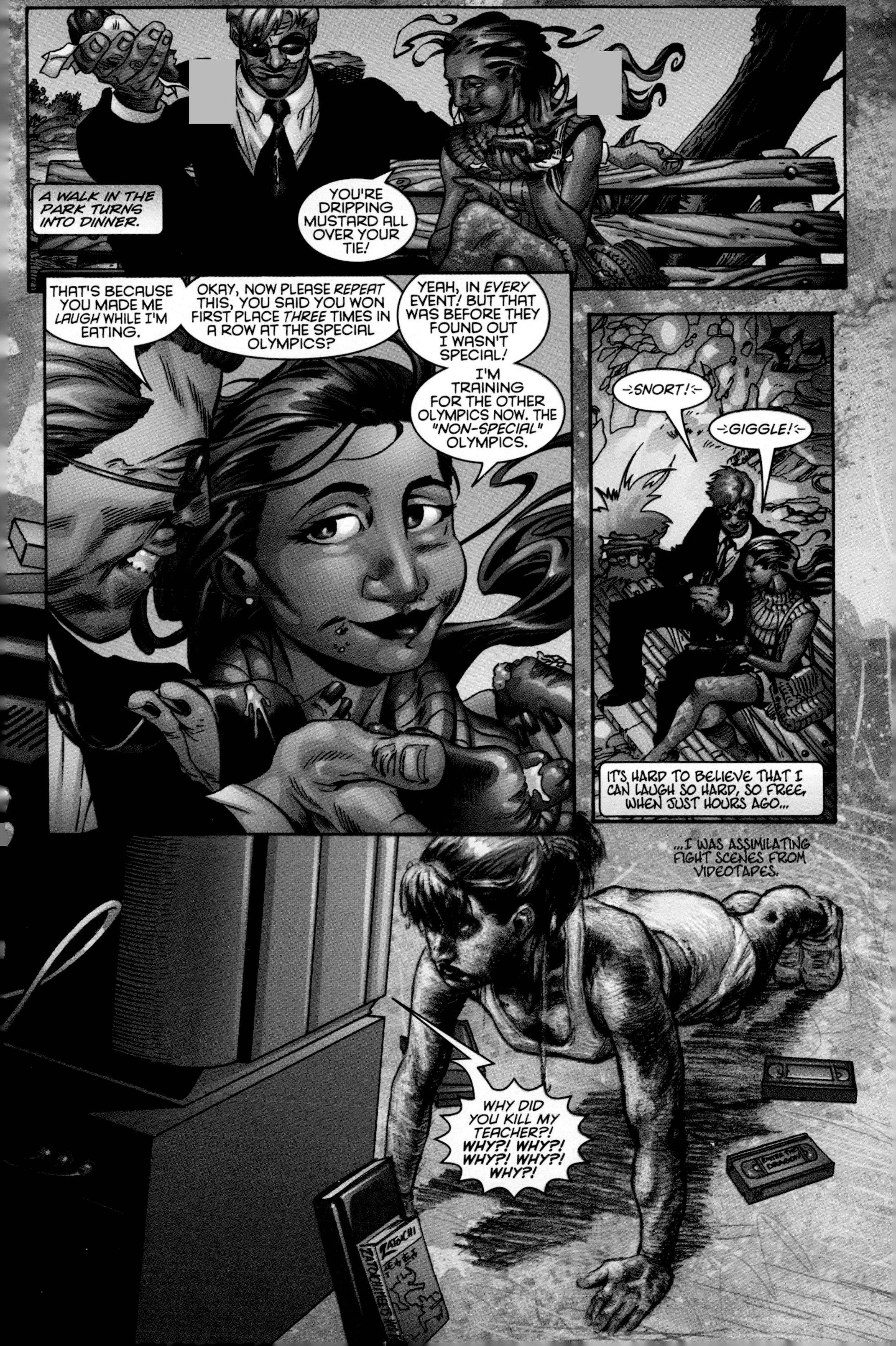

A WALK IN THE PARK TURNS INTO DINNER.
YOU'RE DRIPPING MUSTARD ALL OVER YOUR TIE!
THAT'S BECAUSE YOU MADE ME LAUGH WHILE I'M EATING.
OKAY, NOW PLEASE REPEAT THIS, YOU SAID YOU WON FIRST PLACE THREE TIMES IN A ROW AT THE SPECIAL OLYMPICS?
YEAH, IN EVERY EVENT! BUT THAT WAS BEFORE THEY FOUND OUT I WASN'T SPECIAL!
I'M TRAINING FOR THE OTHER OLYMPICS NOW. THE "NON-SPECIAL" OLYMPICS.
SNORT!
GIGGLE!
IT'S HARD TO BELIEVE THAT I CAN LAUGH SO HARD, SO FREE, WHEN JUST HOURS AGO...
...I WAS ASSIMILATING FIGHT SCENES FROM VIDEOTAPES.
WHY DID YOU KILL MY TEACHER?! WHY?! WHY?! WHY?! WHY?! WHY?!

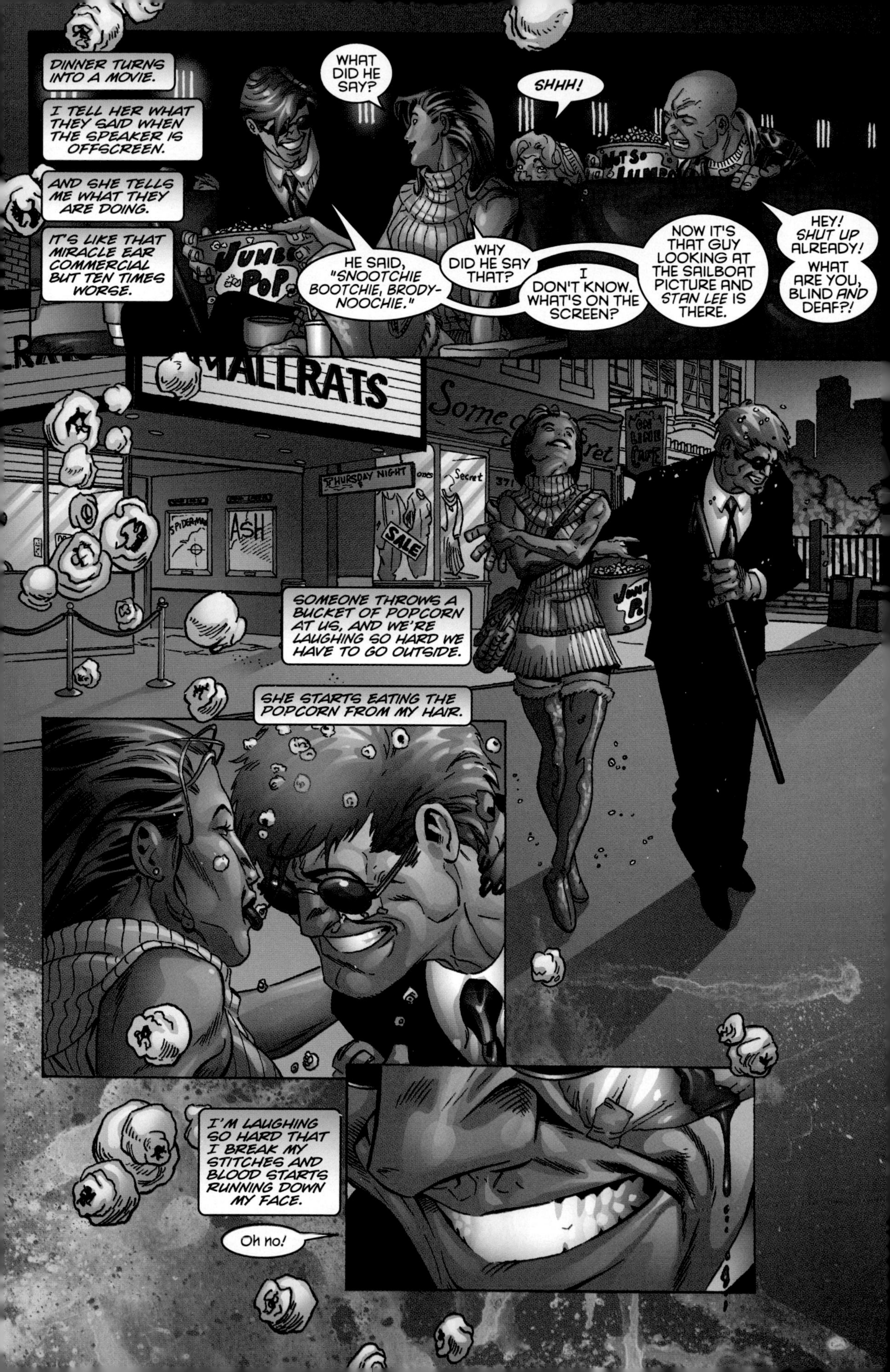

DINNER TURNS INTO A MOVIE.
I TELL HER WHAT THEY SAID WHEN THE SPEAKER IS OFFSCREEN.
AND SHE TELLS ME WHAT THEY ARE DOING.
IT'S LIKE THAT MIRACLE EAR COMMERCIAL BUT TEN TIMES WORSE.
WHAT DID HE SAY?
HE SAID, "SNOOTCHIE BOOTCHIE, BRODY-NOOCHIE."
SHHH!
WHY DID HE SAY THAT?
I DON'T KNOW. WHAT'S ON THE SCREEN?
NOW IT'S THAT GUY LOOKING AT THE SAILBOAT PICTURE AND STAN LEE IS THERE.
HEY! SHUT UP ALREADY!
WHAT ARE YOU, BLIND AND DEAF?!
MALLRATS
THURSDAY NIGHT
SALE
SOMEONE THROWS A BUCKET OF POPCORN AT US, AND WE'RE LAUGHING SO HARD WE HAVE TO GO OUTSIDE.
SHE STARTS EATING THE POPCORN FROM MY HAIR.
I'M LAUGHING SO HARD THAT I BREAK MY STITCHES AND BLOOD STARTS RUNNING DOWN MY FACE.
Oh no!

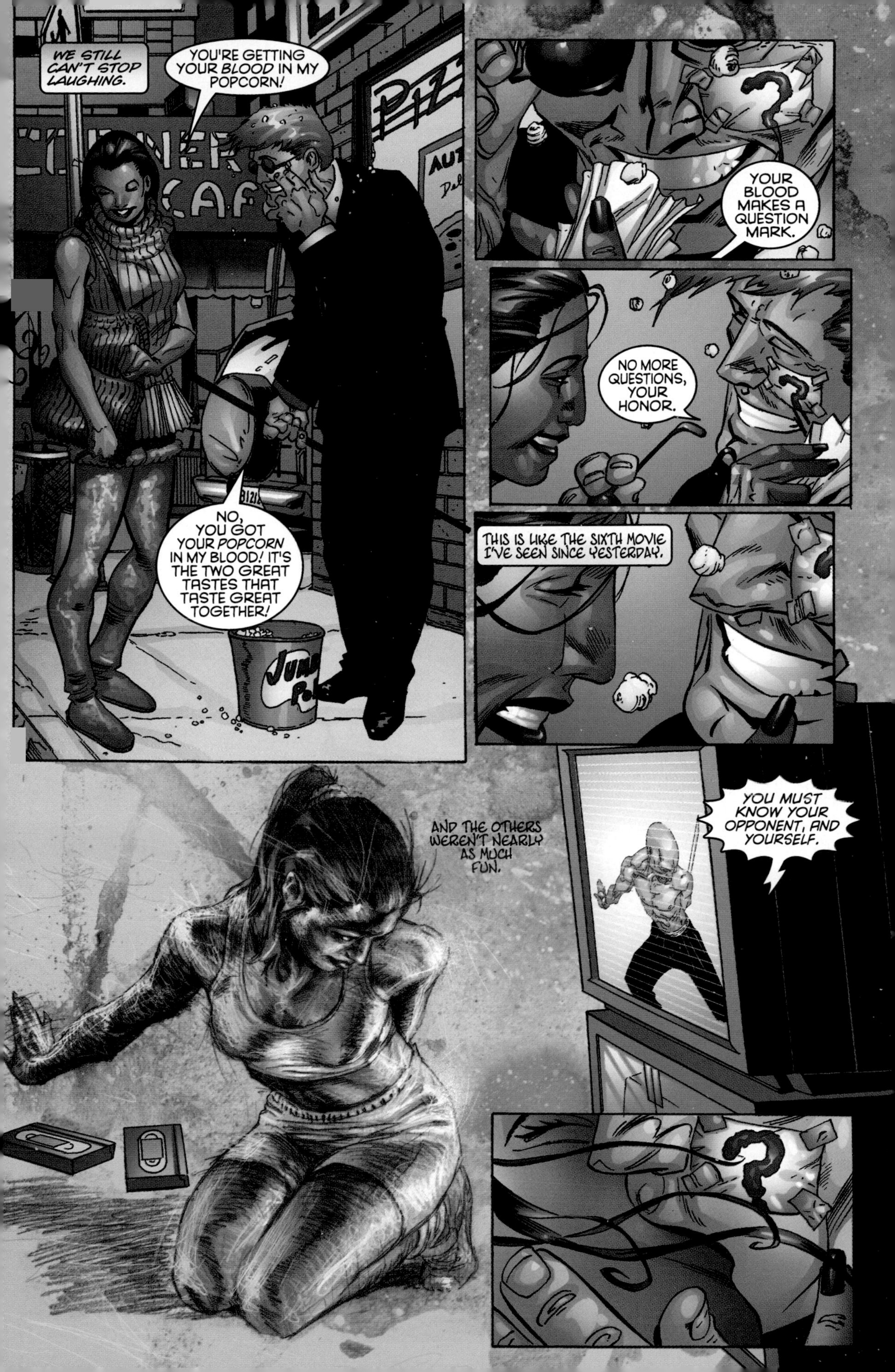
WE STILL CAN'T STOP LAUGHING.
YOU'RE GETTING YOUR BLOOD IN MY POPCORN!
NO, YOU GOT YOUR POPCORN IN MY BLOOD! IT'S THE TWO GREAT TASTES THAT TASTE GREAT TOGETHER!
YOUR BLOOD MAKES A QUESTION MARK.
NO MORE QUESTIONS, YOUR HONOR.
THIS IS LIKE THE SIXTH MOVIE I'VE SEEN SINCE YESTERDAY.
AND THE OTHERS WEREN'T NEARLY AS MUCH FUN.
YOU MUST KNOW YOUR OPPONENT, AND YOURSELF.

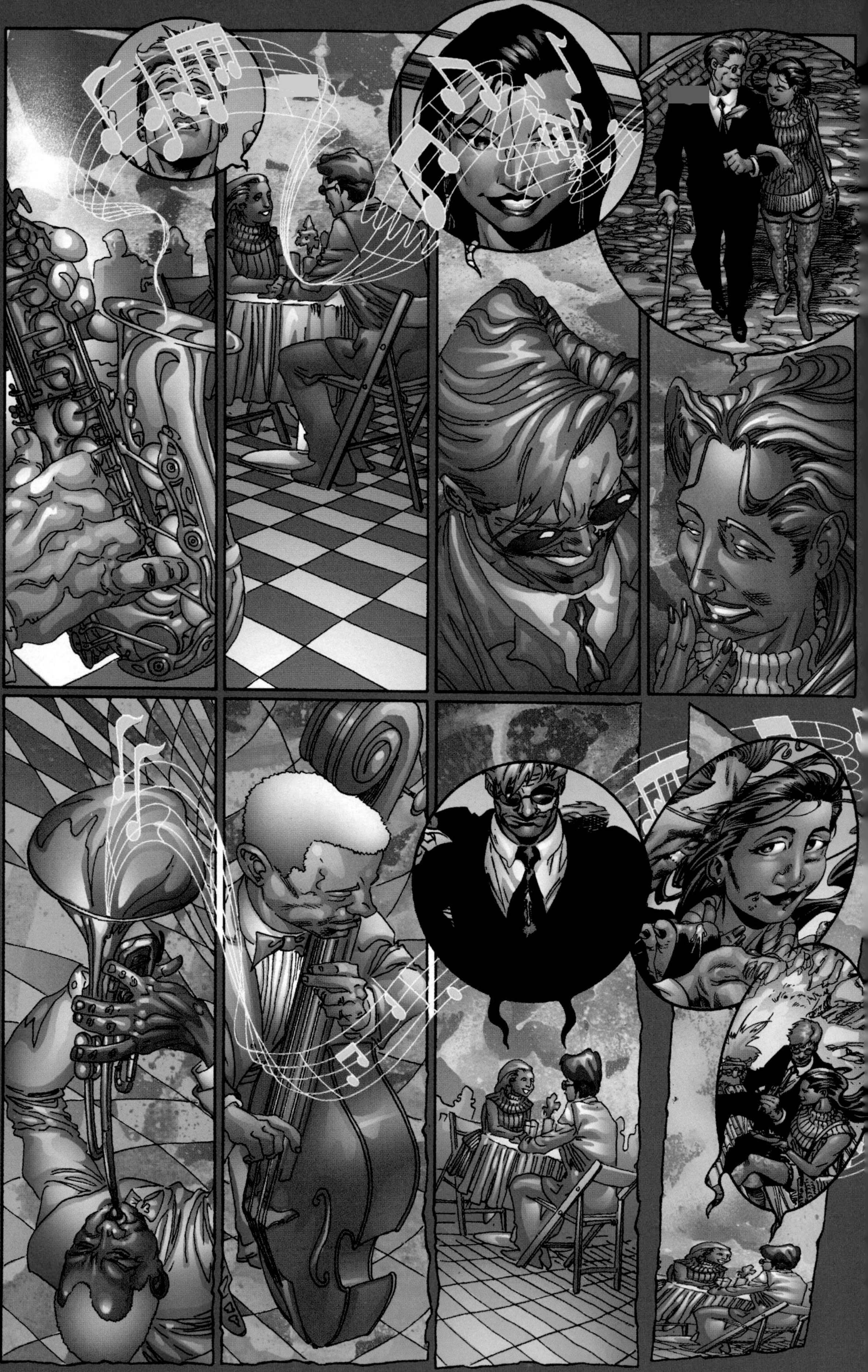

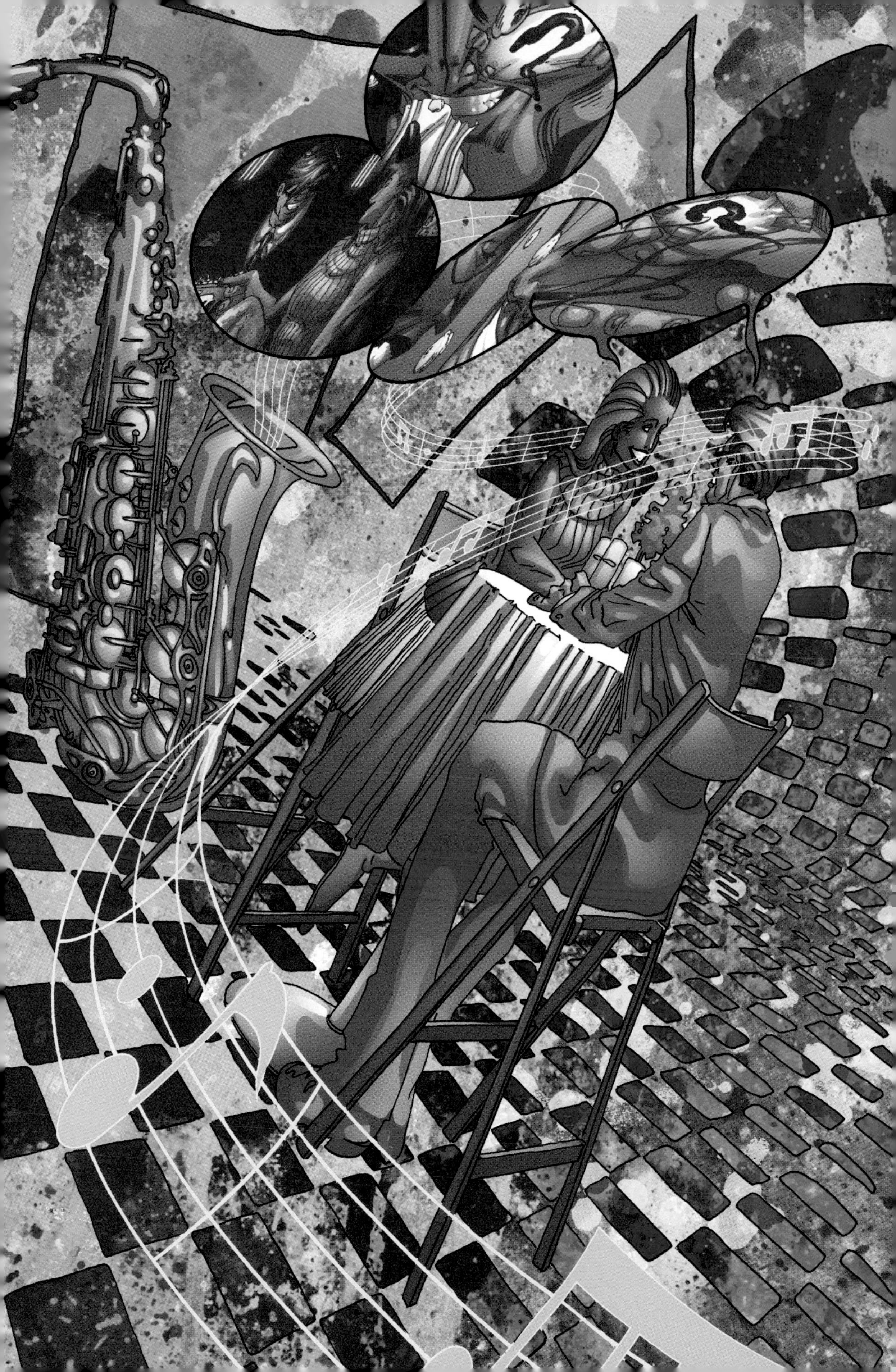

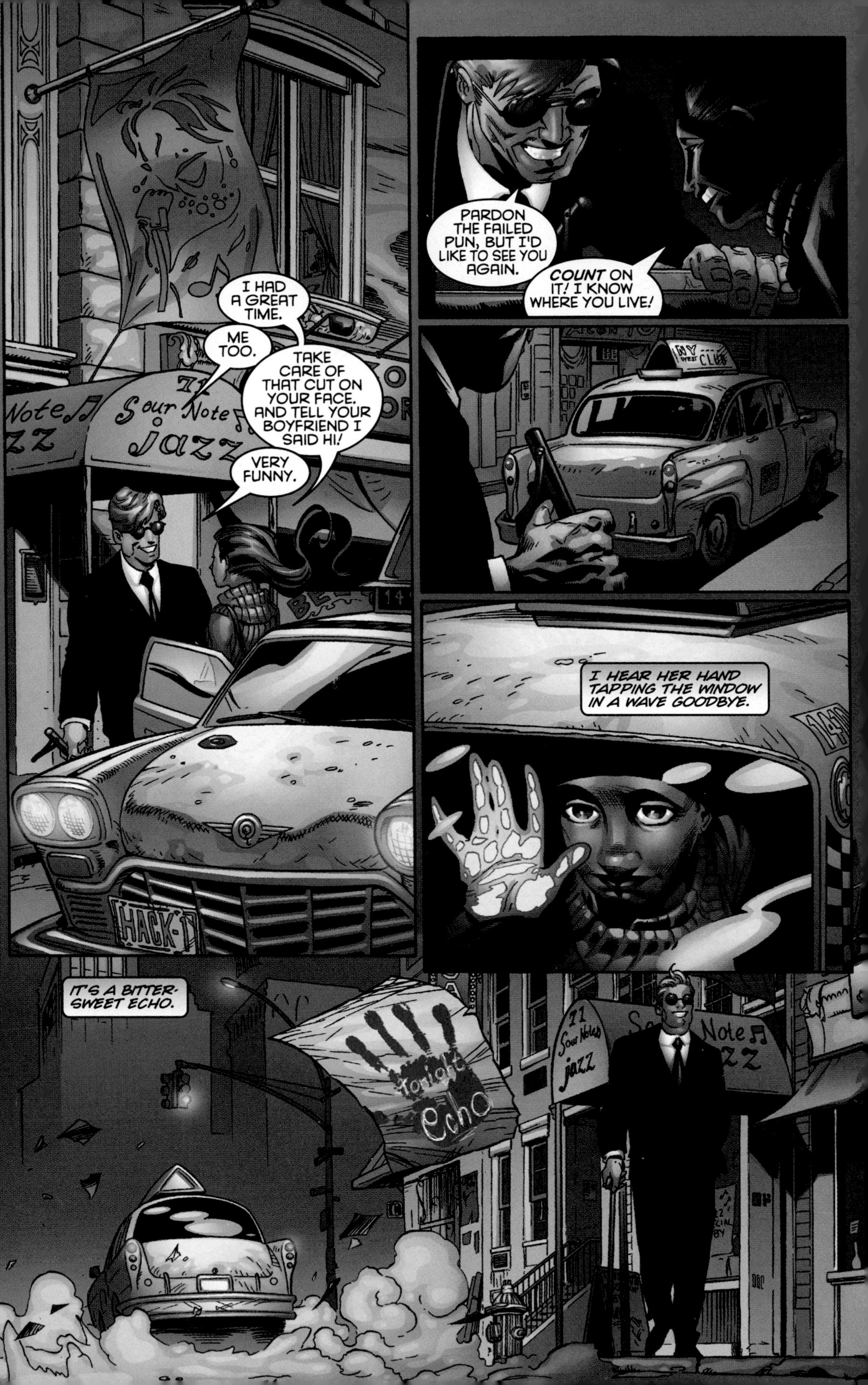
I HAD A GREAT TIME.
ME TOO.
TAKE CARE OF THAT CUT ON YOUR FACE. AND TELL YOUR BOYFRIEND I SAID HI!
VERY FUNNY.
71 Sour Note jazz
HACK-1
PARDON THE FAILED PUN, BUT I'D LIKE TO SEE YOU AGAIN.
COUNT ON IT! I KNOW WHERE YOU LIVE!
I HEAR HER HAND TAPPING THE WINDOW IN A WAVE GOODBYE.
IT'S A BITTER-SWEET ECHO.
Tonight Echo
71 Sour Note jazz

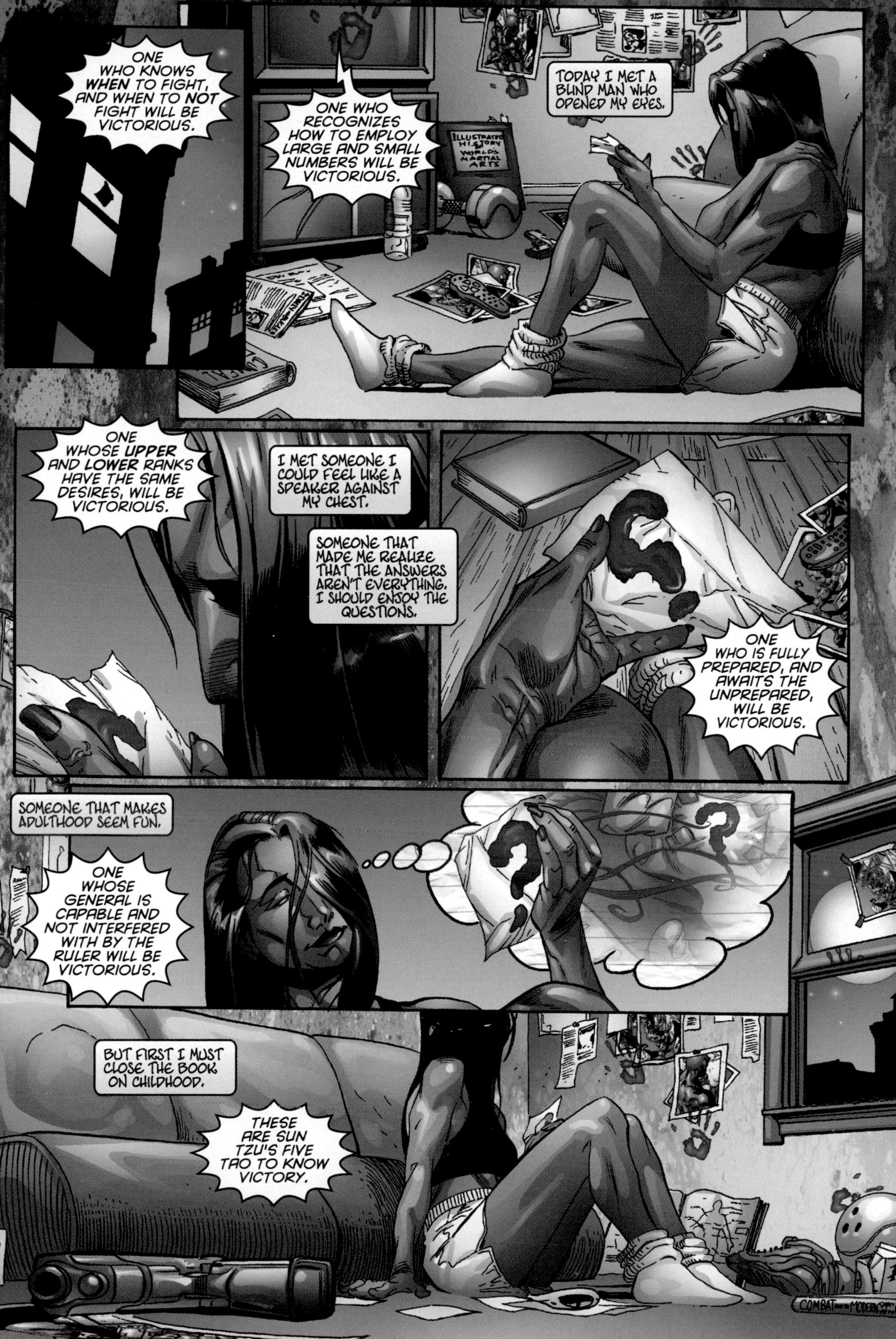

ONE WHO KNOWS **WHEN** TO FIGHT, AND WHEN TO **NOT** FIGHT WILL BE VICTORIOUS.
ONE WHO RECOGNIZES HOW TO EMPLOY LARGE AND SMALL NUMBERS WILL BE VICTORIOUS.
ILLUSTRATED HISTORY OF WORLD'S MARTIAL ARTS
TODAY I MET A BLIND MAN WHO OPENED MY EYES.
ONE WHOSE **UPPER** AND **LOWER** RANKS HAVE THE SAME DESIRES, WILL BE VICTORIOUS.
I MET SOMEONE I COULD FEEL LIKE A SPEAKER AGAINST MY CHEST.
SOMEONE THAT MADE ME REALIZE THAT THE ANSWERS AREN'T EVERYTHING. I SHOULD ENJOY THE QUESTIONS.
ONE WHO IS FULLY PREPARED, AND AWAITS THE UNPREPARED, WILL BE VICTORIOUS.
SOMEONE THAT MAKES ADULTHOOD SEEM FUN.
ONE WHOSE GENERAL IS CAPABLE AND NOT INTERFERED WITH BY THE RULER WILL BE VICTORIOUS.
BUT FIRST I MUST CLOSE THE BOOK ON CHILDHOOD.
THESE ARE SUN TZU'S FIVE TAO TO KNOW VICTORY.

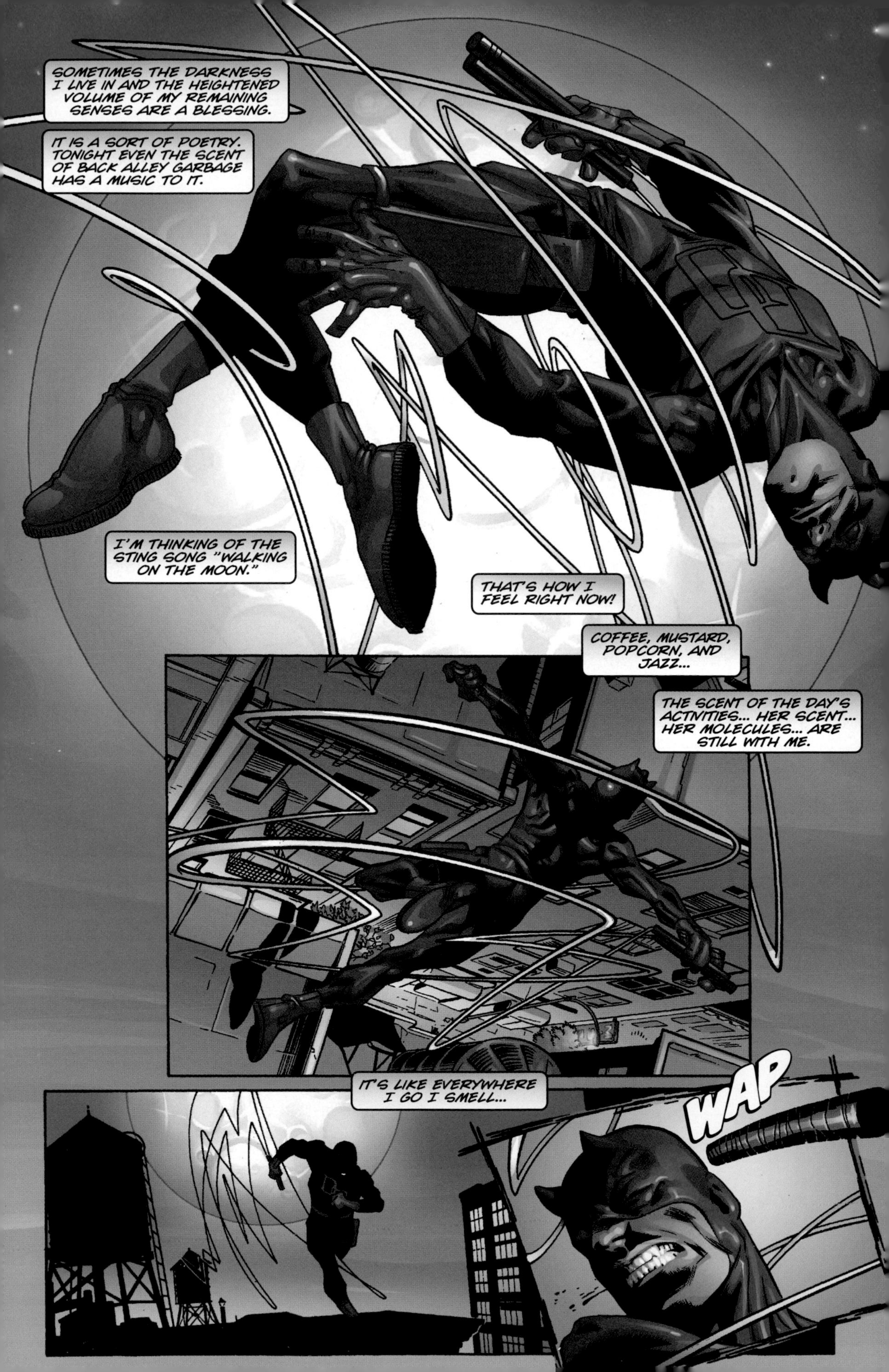
SOMETIMES THE DARKNESS I LIVE IN AND THE HEIGHTENED VOLUME OF MY REMAINING SENSES ARE A BLESSING.
IT IS A SORT OF POETRY. TONIGHT EVEN THE SCENT OF BACK ALLEY GARBAGE HAS A MUSIC TO IT.
I'M THINKING OF THE STING SONG "WALKING ON THE MOON."
THAT'S HOW I FEEL RIGHT NOW!
COFFEE, MUSTARD, POPCORN, AND JAZZ...
THE SCENT OF THE DAY'S ACTIVITIES... HER SCENT... HER MOLECULES... ARE STILL WITH ME.
IT'S LIKE EVERYWHERE I GO I SMELL...
WAP

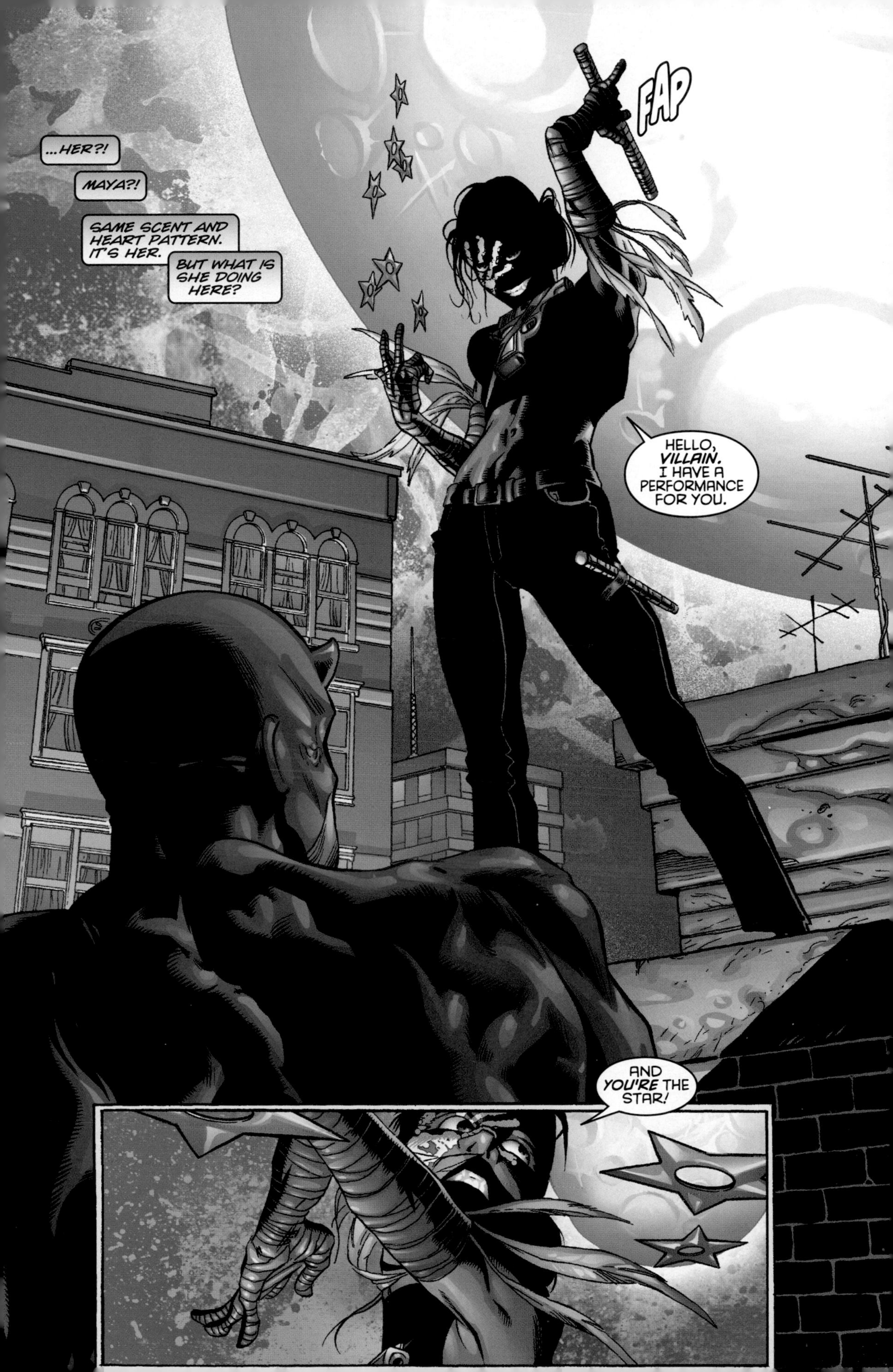

...HER?!
MAYA?!
SAME SCENT AND HEART PATTERN. IT'S HER.
BUT WHAT IS SHE DOING HERE?
FAP
HELLO, VILLAIN. I HAVE A PERFORMANCE FOR YOU.
AND YOU'RE THE STAR!

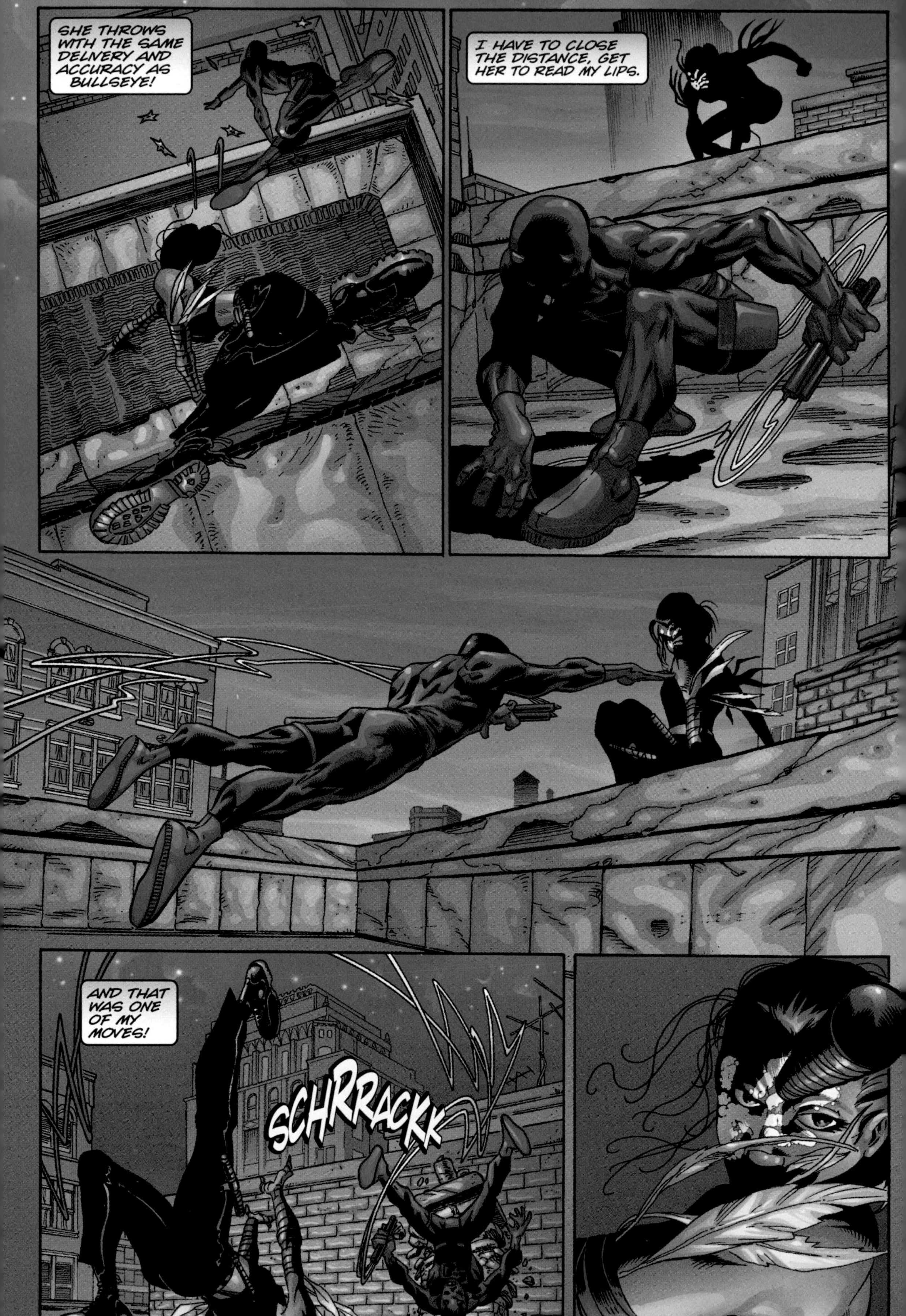
SHE THROWS WITH THE SAME DELIVERY AND ACCURACY AS BULLSEYE!
I HAVE TO CLOSE THE DISTANCE, GET HER TO READ MY LIPS.
AND THAT WAS ONE OF MY MOVES!
SCHRRACKK

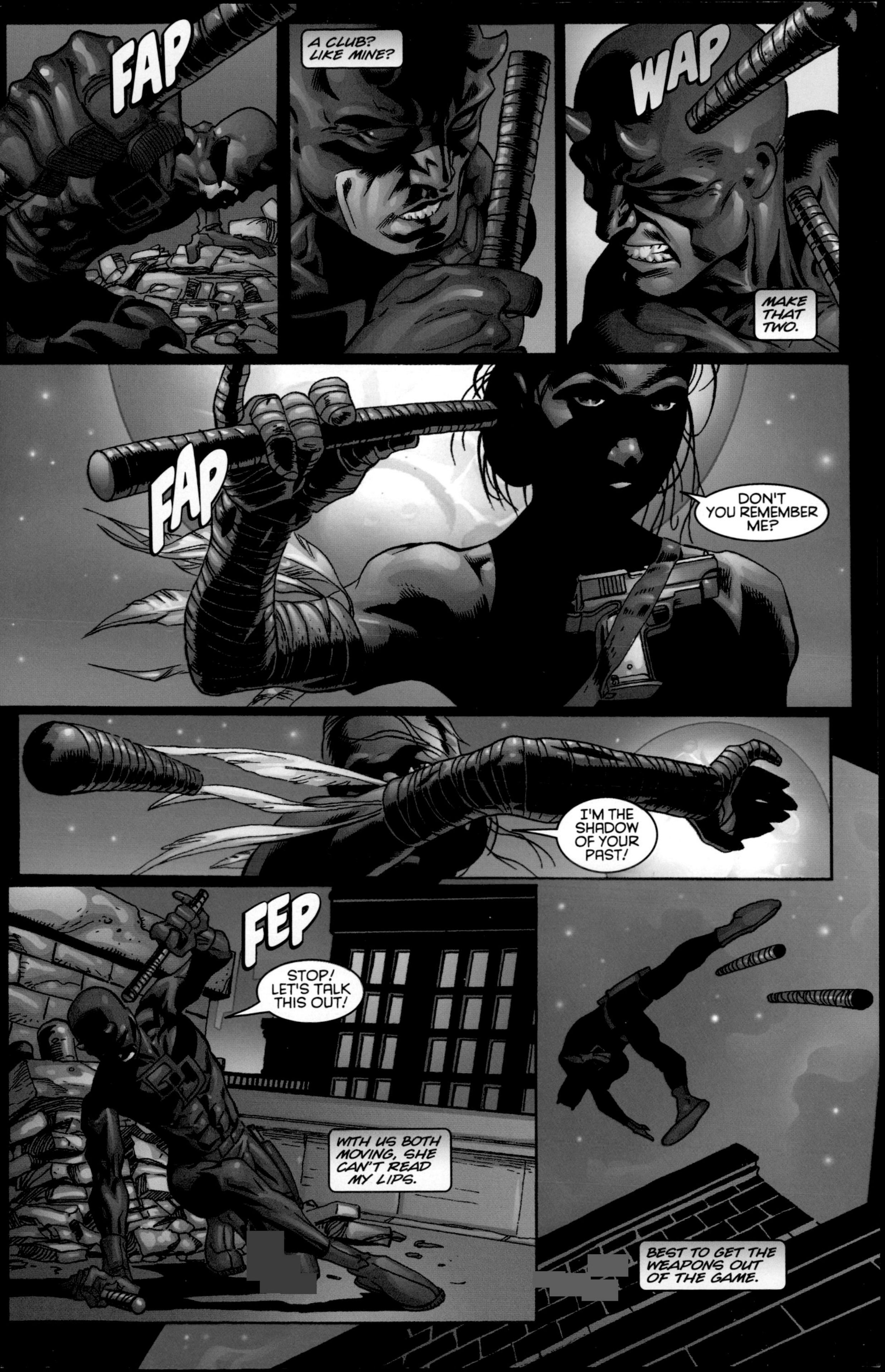
FAP
A CLUB? LIKE MINE?
WAP
MAKE THAT TWO.
FAP
DON'T YOU REMEMBER ME?
I'M THE SHADOW OF YOUR PAST!
FEP
STOP! LET'S TALK THIS OUT!
WITH US BOTH MOVING, SHE CAN'T READ MY LIPS.
BEST TO GET THE WEAPONS OUT OF THE GAME.

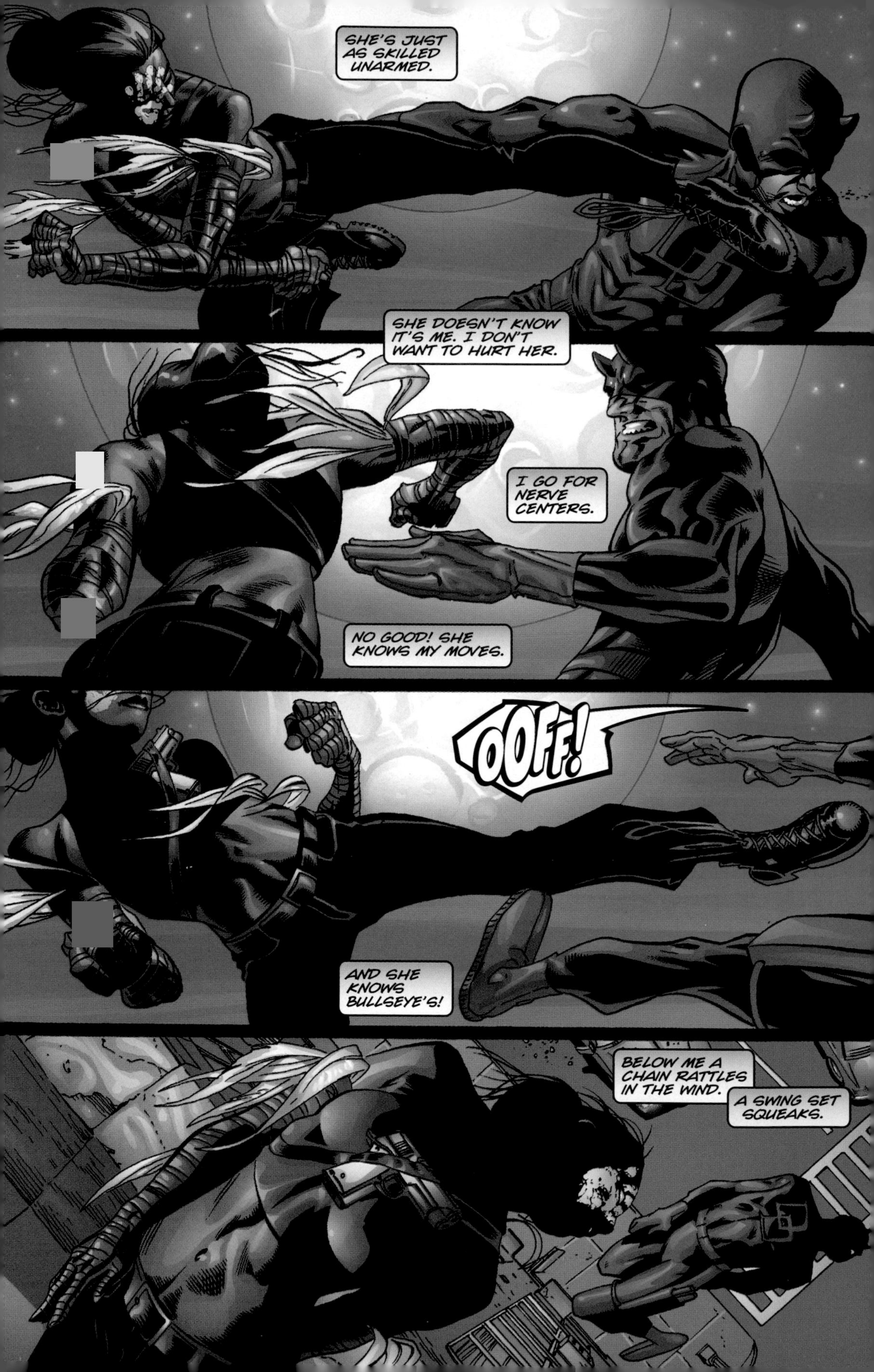

SHE'S JUST AS SKILLED UNARMED.
SHE DOESN'T KNOW IT'S ME. I DON'T WANT TO HURT HER.
I GO FOR NERVE CENTERS.
NO GOOD! SHE KNOWS MY MOVES.
OOFF!
AND SHE KNOWS BULLSEYE'S!
BELOW ME A CHAIN RATTLES IN THE WIND.
A SWING SET SQUEAKS.

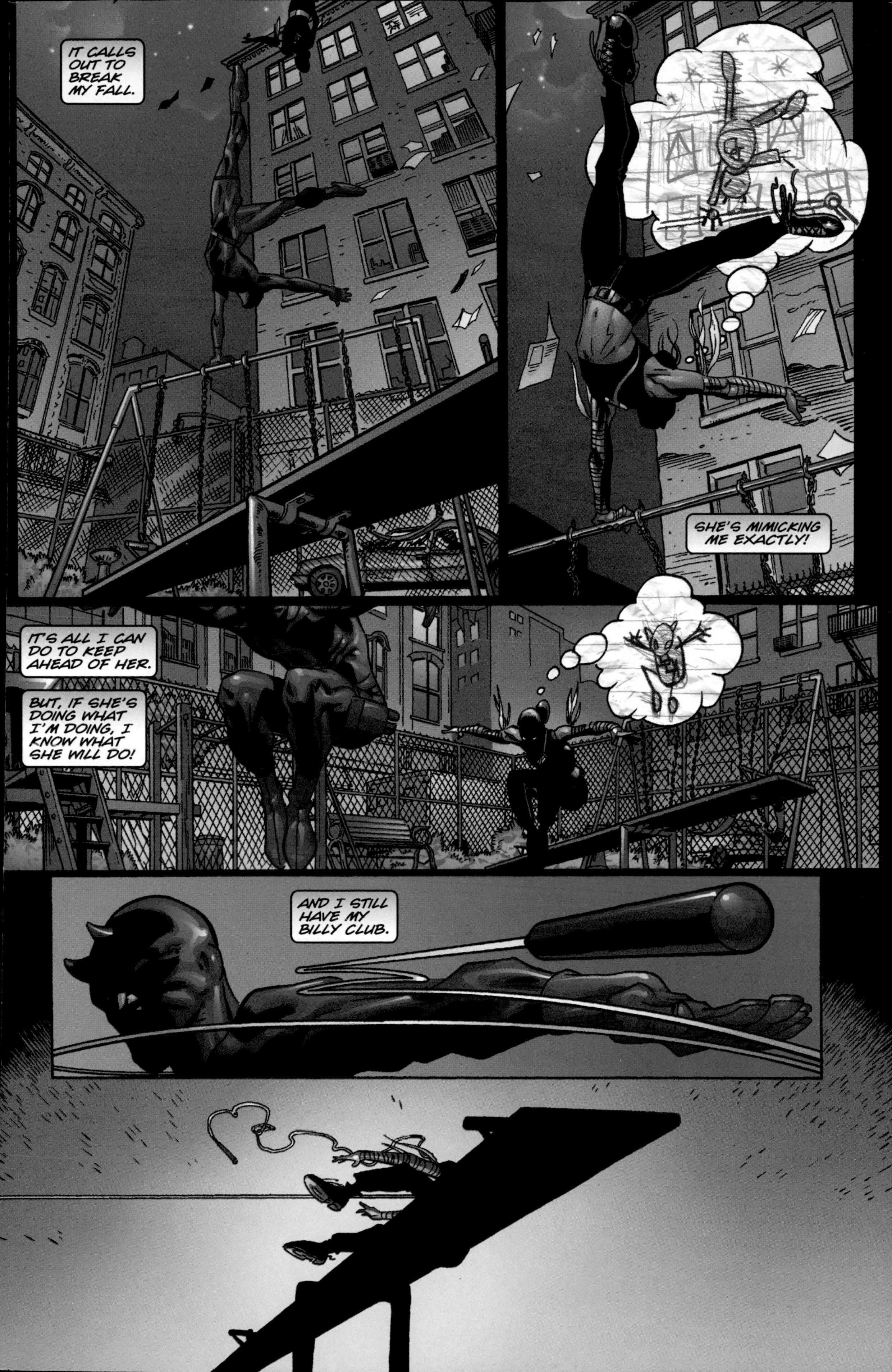
IT CALLS OUT TO BREAK MY FALL.
SHE'S MIMICKING ME EXACTLY!
IT'S ALL I CAN DO TO KEEP AHEAD OF HER.
BUT, IF SHE'S DOING WHAT I'M DOING, I KNOW WHAT SHE WILL DO!
AND I STILL HAVE MY BILLY CLUB.

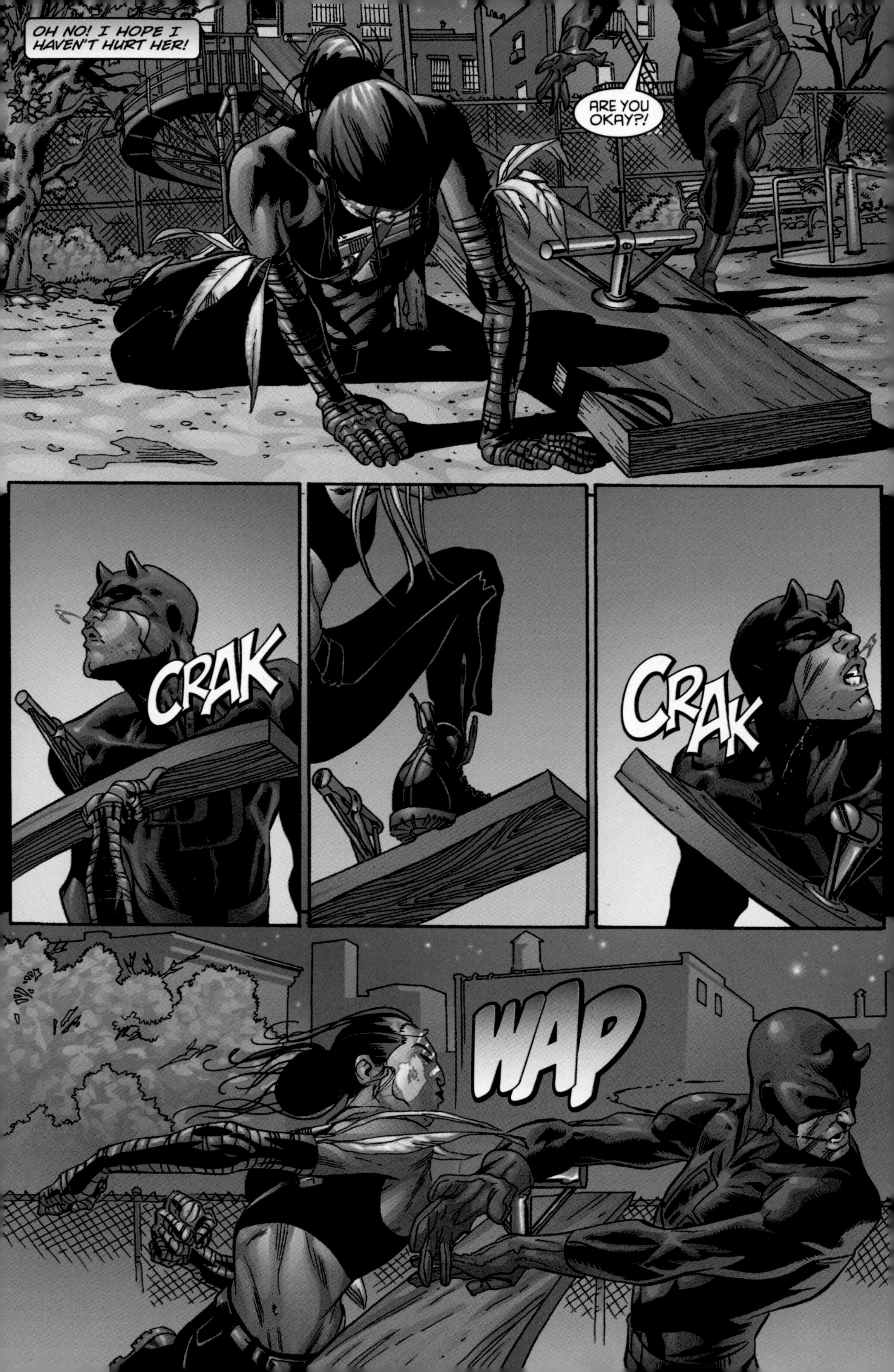
OH NO! I HOPE I HAVEN'T HURT HER!
ARE YOU OKAY?!
CRAK
CRAK
WAP

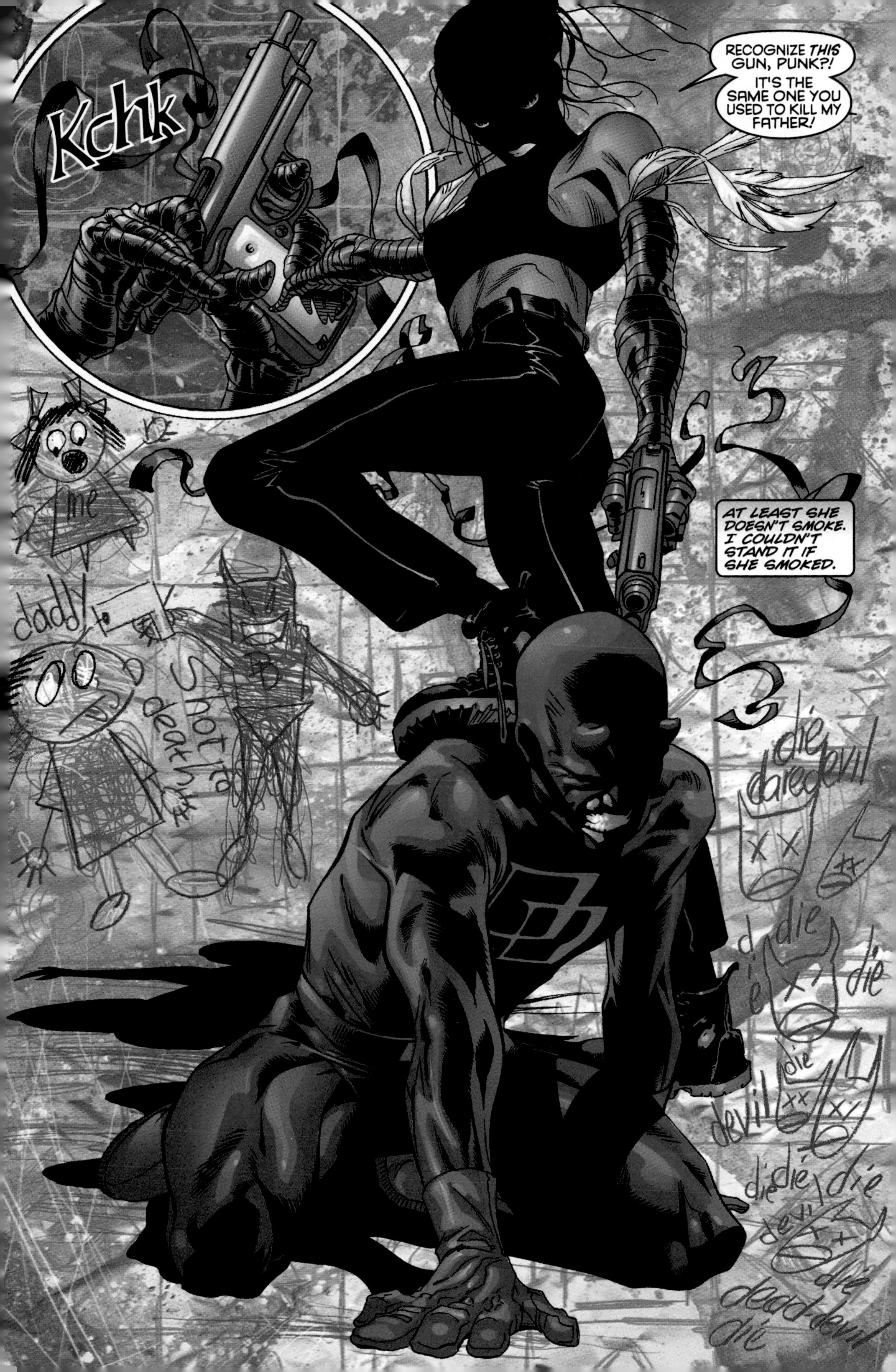

Kchk
RECOGNIZE *THIS* GUN, PUNK?!
IT'S THE SAME ONE YOU USED TO KILL MY FATHER!
AT LEAST SHE DOESN'T SMOKE. I COULDN'T STAND IT IF SHE SMOKED.
me
daddy
shot ta death
die daregevil
die
die
die
devil die
die die die
devil
die
dead-devil
die

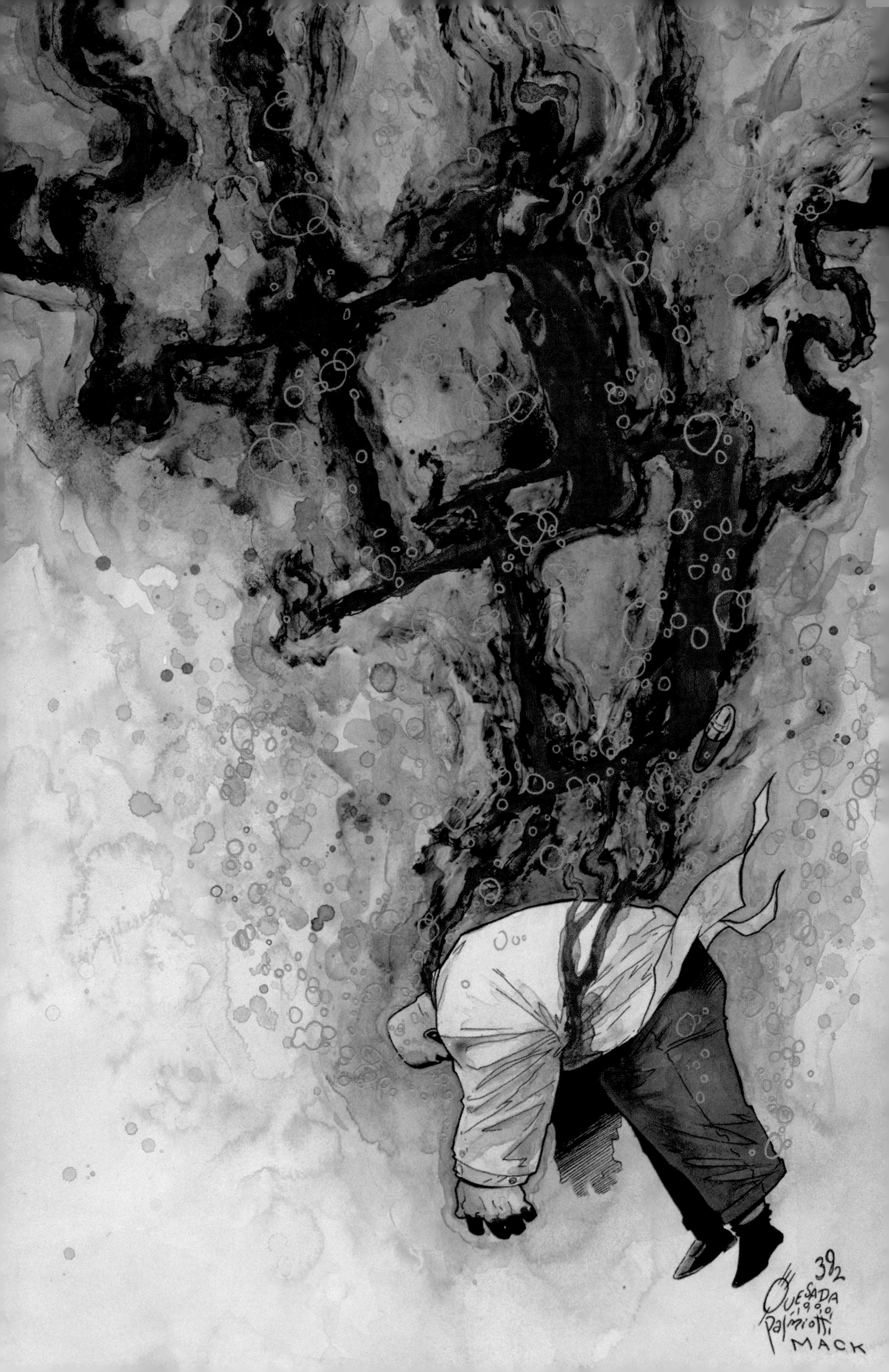
3½
QUESADA '99
Palmiotti
MACK

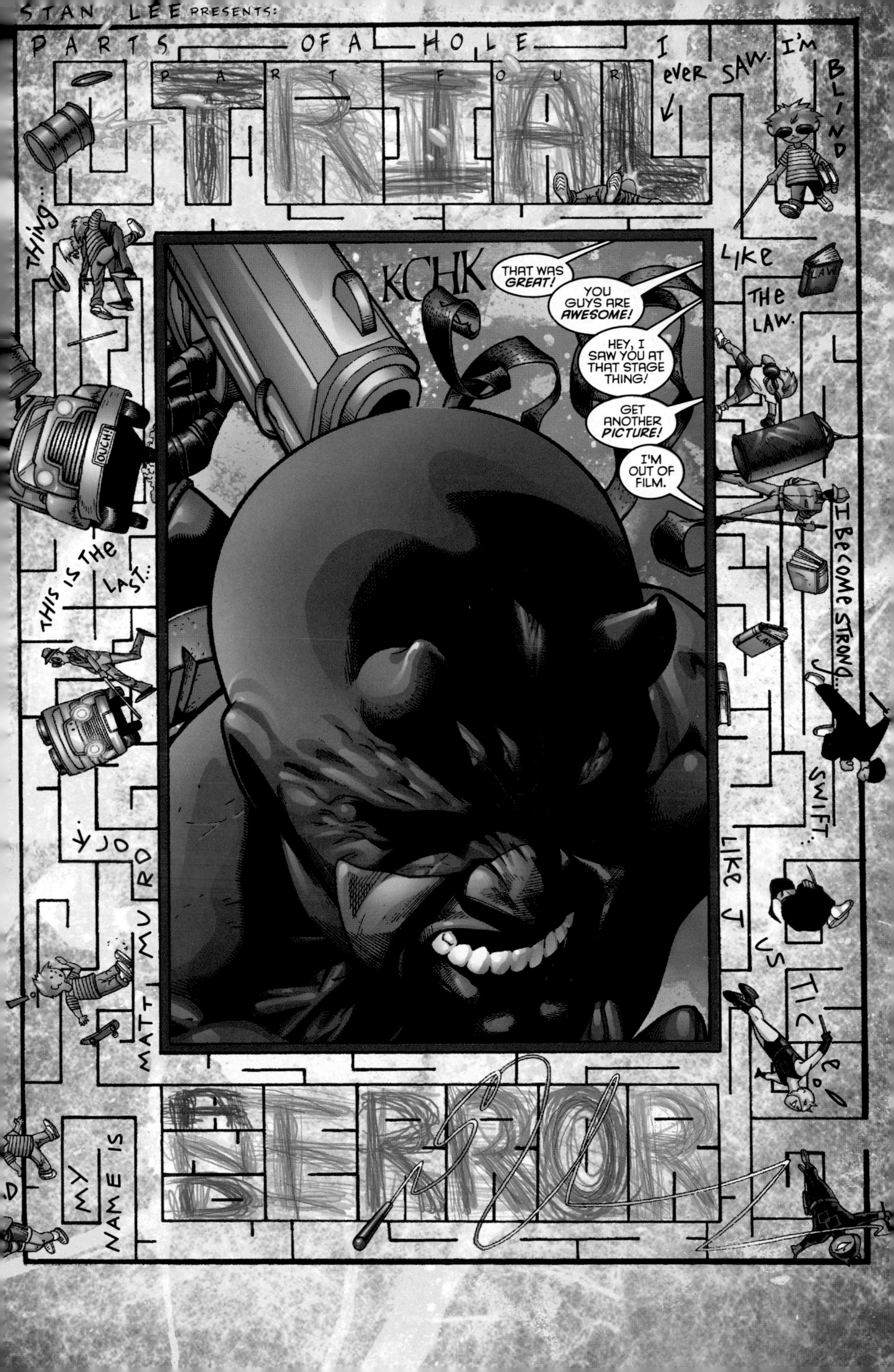
STAN LEE PRESENTS:
PARTS OF A HOLE
PART FOUR
TRIAL
I ever SAW. I'M BLIND
THING...
KCHK
THAT WAS GREAT!
YOU GUYS ARE AWESOME!
HEY, I SAW YOU AT THAT STAGE THING!
GET ANOTHER PICTURE!
I'M OUT OF FILM.
LIKE THE LAW.
LAW
OUCH!
THIS IS THE LAST...
I BECOME STRONG...
SWIFT...
LIKE JUSTICE
MATT MURDOCK
MY NAME IS
ERROR

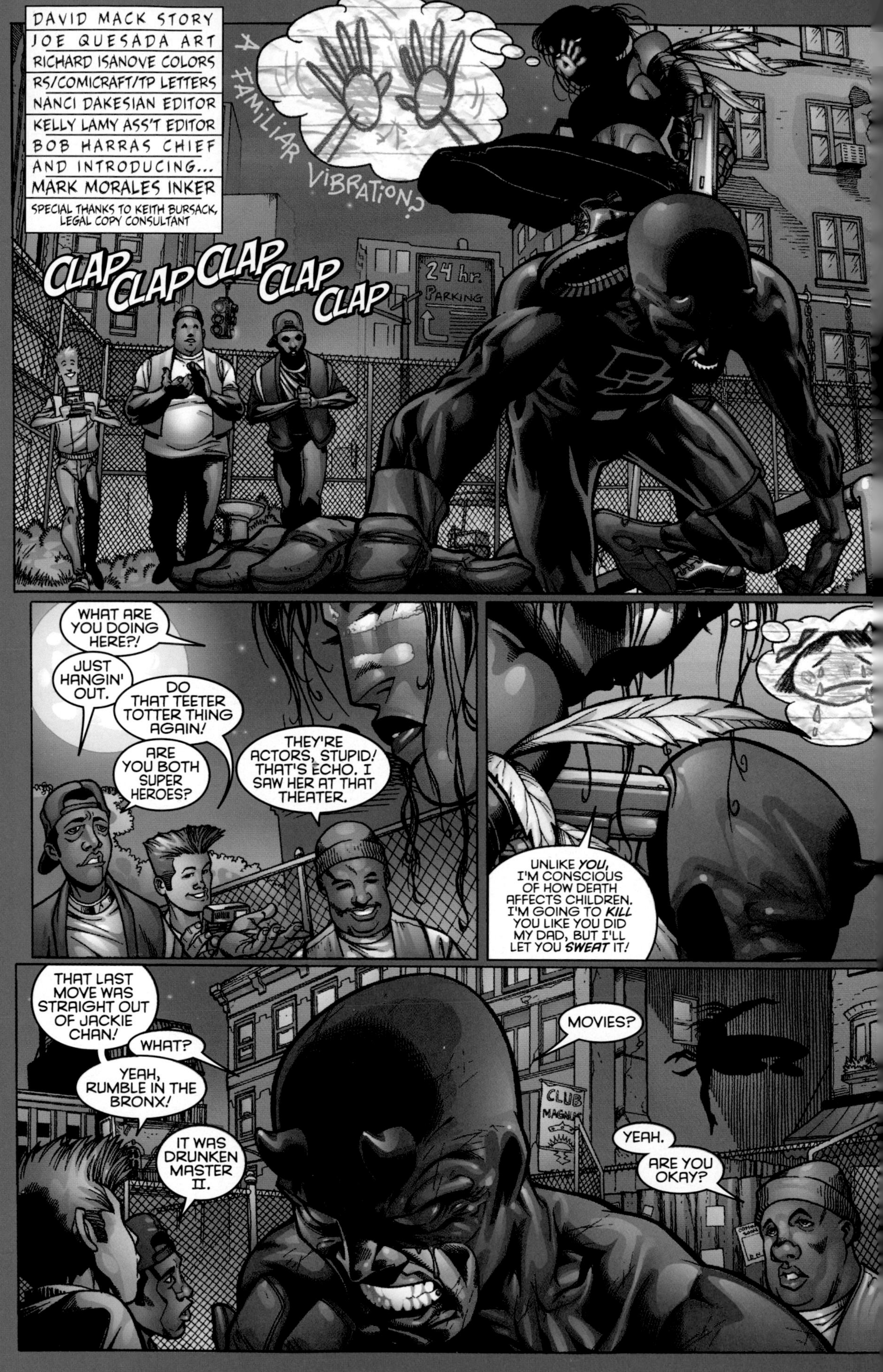

DAVID MACK STORY
JOE QUESADA ART
RICHARD ISANOVE COLORS
RS/COMICRAFT/TP LETTERS
NANCI DAKESIAN EDITOR
KELLY LAMY ASS'T EDITOR
BOB HARRAS CHIEF
AND INTRODUCING...
MARK MORALES INKER
SPECIAL THANKS TO KEITH BURSACK, LEGAL COPY CONSULTANT
A FAMILIAR VIBRATION?
CLAP CLAP CLAP CLAP CLAP
24 hr. PARKING
WHAT ARE YOU DOING HERE?!
JUST HANGIN' OUT.
DO THAT TEETER TOTTER THING AGAIN!
ARE YOU BOTH SUPER HEROES?
THEY'RE ACTORS, STUPID! THAT'S ECHO. I SAW HER AT THAT THEATER.
UNLIKE YOU, I'M CONSCIOUS OF HOW DEATH AFFECTS CHILDREN. I'M GOING TO KILL YOU LIKE YOU DID MY DAD, BUT I'LL LET YOU SWEAT IT!
THAT LAST MOVE WAS STRAIGHT OUT OF JACKIE CHAN!
WHAT?
YEAH, RUMBLE IN THE BRONX!
IT WAS DRUNKEN MASTER II.
MOVIES?
YEAH.
ARE YOU OKAY?
CLUB MAGNUS

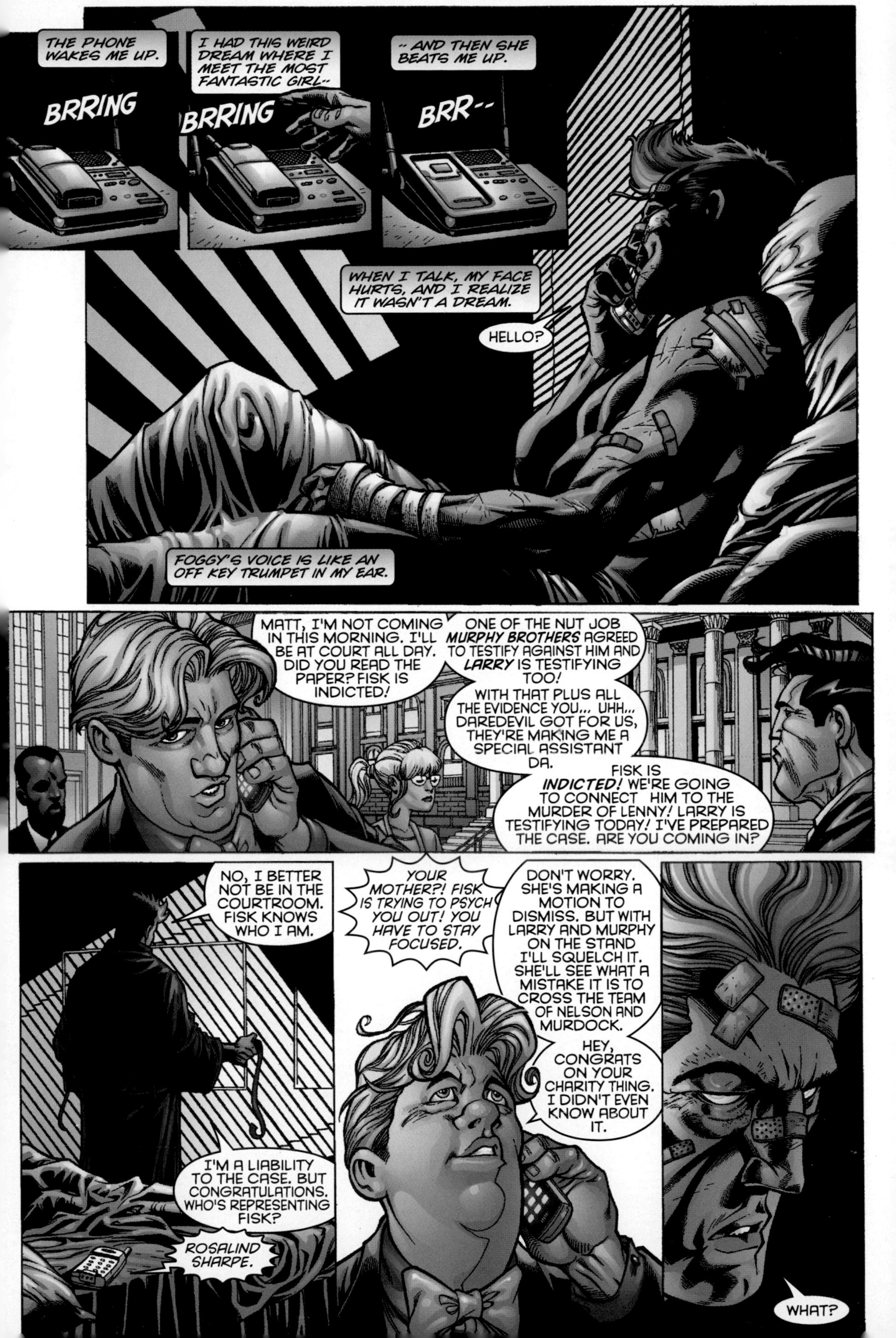

THE PHONE WAKES ME UP.
BRRING
I HAD THIS WEIRD DREAM WHERE I MEET THE MOST FANTASTIC GIRL--
BRRING
-- AND THEN SHE BEATS ME UP.
BRR--
WHEN I TALK, MY FACE HURTS, AND I REALIZE IT WASN'T A DREAM.
HELLO?
FOGGY'S VOICE IS LIKE AN OFF KEY TRUMPET IN MY EAR.
MATT, I'M NOT COMING IN THIS MORNING. I'LL BE AT COURT ALL DAY. DID YOU READ THE PAPER? FISK IS INDICTED!
ONE OF THE NUT JOB MURPHY BROTHERS AGREED TO TESTIFY AGAINST HIM AND LARRY IS TESTIFYING TOO!
WITH THAT PLUS ALL THE EVIDENCE YOU... UHH... DAREDEVIL GOT FOR US, THEY'RE MAKING ME A SPECIAL ASSISTANT DA.
FISK IS INDICTED! WE'RE GOING TO CONNECT HIM TO THE MURDER OF LENNY! LARRY IS TESTIFYING TODAY! I'VE PREPARED THE CASE. ARE YOU COMING IN?
NO, I BETTER NOT BE IN THE COURTROOM. FISK KNOWS WHO I AM.
I'M A LIABILITY TO THE CASE. BUT CONGRATULATIONS. WHO'S REPRESENTING FISK?
ROSALIND SHARPE.
YOUR MOTHER?! FISK IS TRYING TO PSYCH YOU OUT! YOU HAVE TO STAY FOCUSED.
DON'T WORRY. SHE'S MAKING A MOTION TO DISMISS. BUT WITH LARRY AND MURPHY ON THE STAND I'LL SQUELCH IT. SHE'LL SEE WHAT A MISTAKE IT IS TO CROSS THE TEAM OF NELSON AND MURDOCK.
HEY, CONGRATS ON YOUR CHARITY THING. I DIDN'T EVEN KNOW ABOUT IT.
WHAT?

DAILY BUGLE

NEW YORK'S FINEST DAILY NEWSPAPER

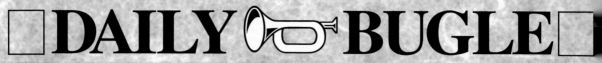

SPICE DEALER ACCUSED

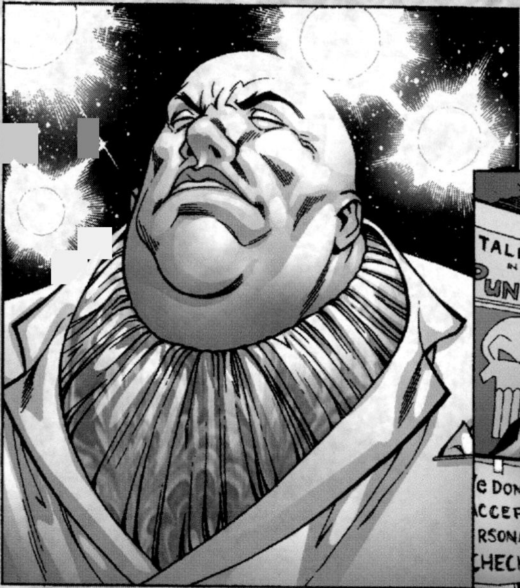

SUSPECTED KINGPIN OF CRIME INDICTED IN MURDER CASE

by Ben Urich

Wilson Fisk, international entrepreneur, will be in court to answer to charges of

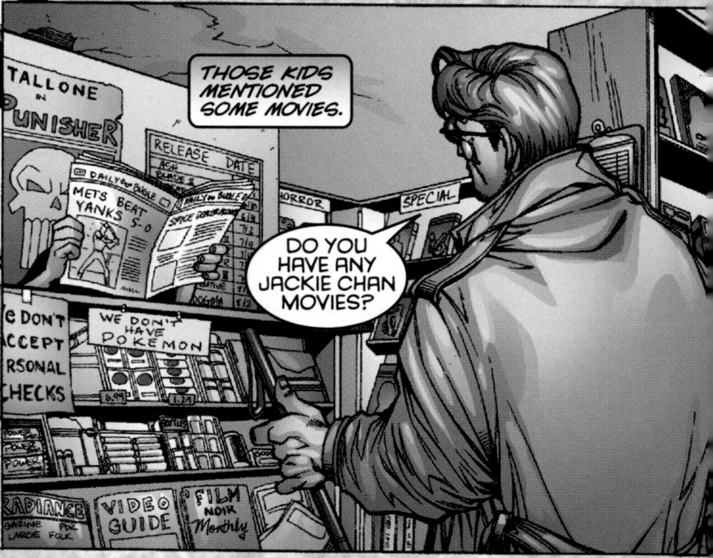

TALLONE
UNISHER
RELEASE DATE
DAILY BUGLE
METS BEAT YANKS 5-0
HORROR
SPECIAL
THOSE KIDS MENTIONED SOME MOVIES.
DO YOU HAVE ANY JACKIE CHAN MOVIES?
WE DON'T HAVE POKEMON
VIDEO GUIDE
FILM NOIR Monthly

ECHOES IN THE PLAYGROUND!

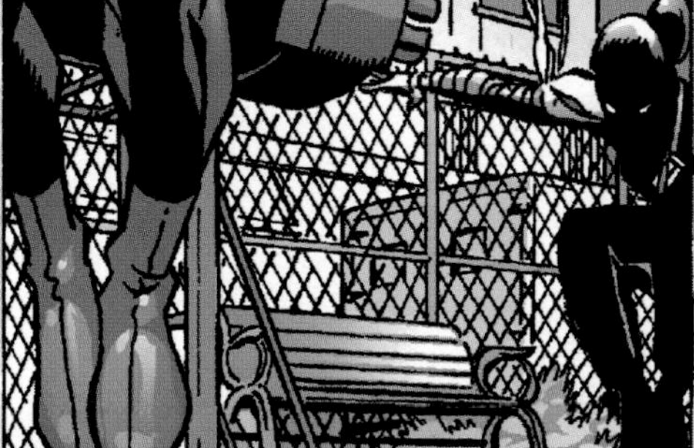

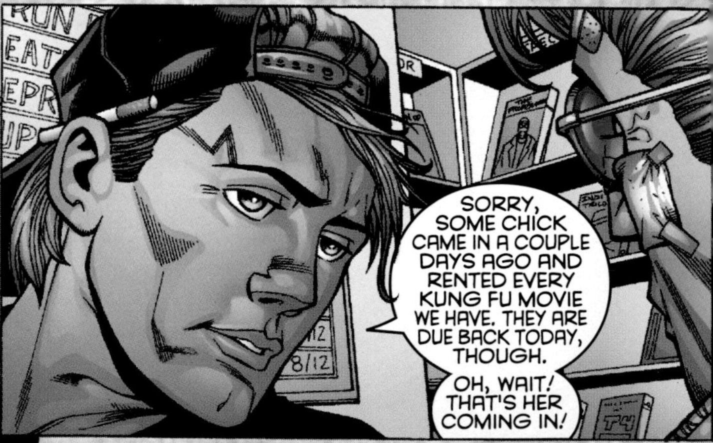

SORRY, SOME CHICK CAME IN A COUPLE DAYS AGO AND RENTED EVERY KUNG FU MOVIE WE HAVE. THEY ARE DUE BACK TODAY, THOUGH.
OH, WAIT! THAT'S HER COMING IN!

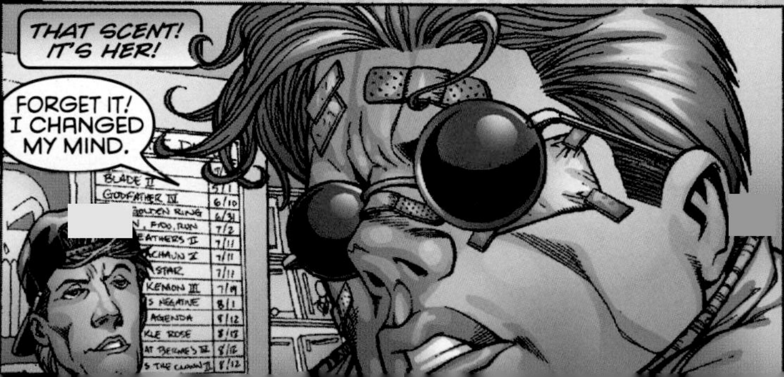

THAT SCENT! IT'S HER!
FORGET IT! I CHANGED MY MIND.

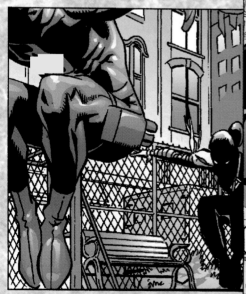

Daredevil joins Echo to reenact her play at a playground performance for children.

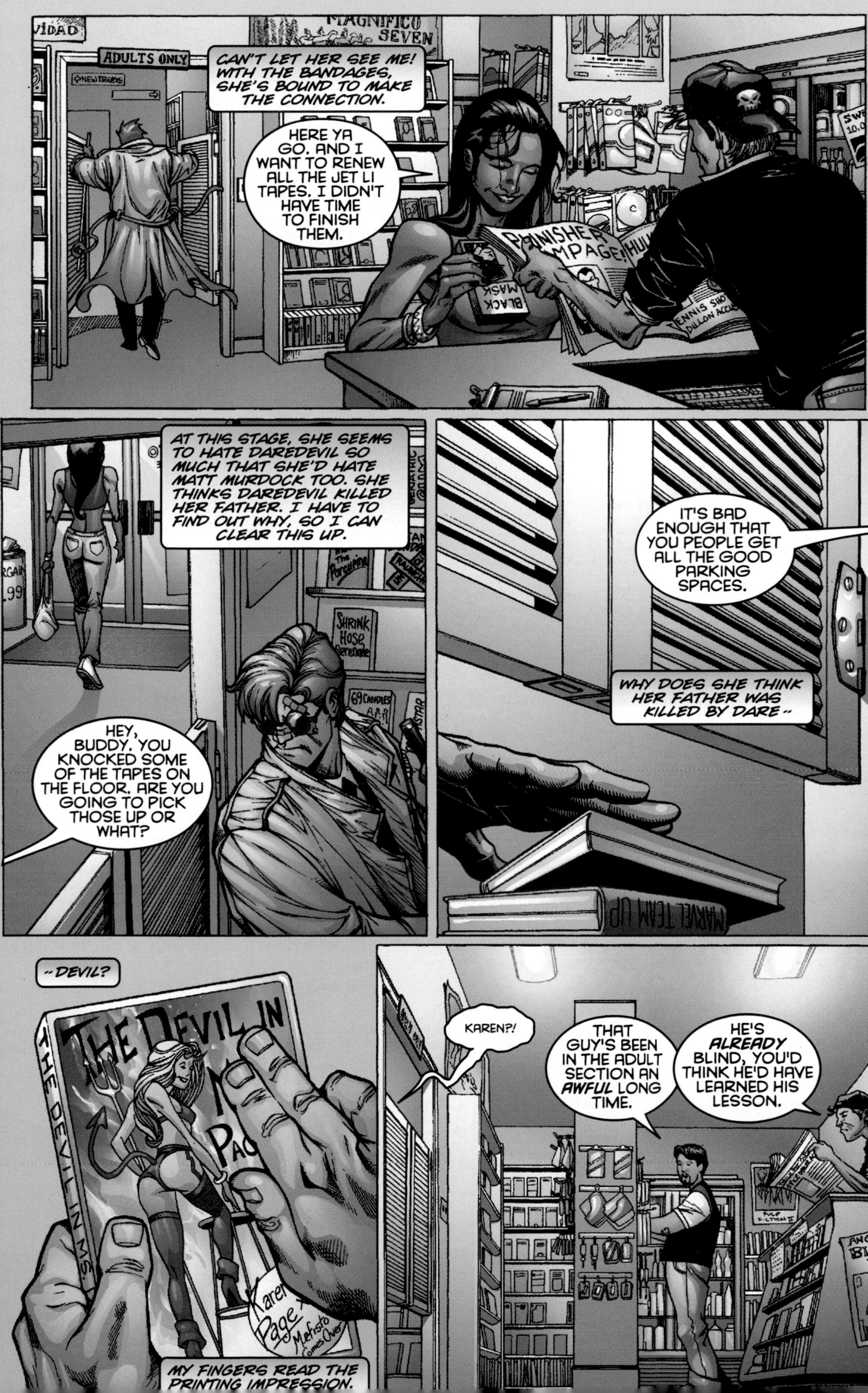
VIDAD
MAGNIFICO SEVEN
ADULTS ONLY
NEW RELEASES
CAN'T LET HER SEE ME! WITH THE BANDAGES, SHE'S BOUND TO MAKE THE CONNECTION.
HERE YA GO. AND I WANT TO RENEW ALL THE JET LI TAPES. I DIDN'T HAVE TIME TO FINISH THEM.
PUNISHER RAMPAGE! HULK
BLACK MASK
ENNIS SHOT DILLON ACCU
AT THIS STAGE, SHE SEEMS TO HATE DAREDEVIL SO MUCH THAT SHE'D HATE MATT MURDOCK TOO. SHE THINKS DAREDEVIL KILLED HER FATHER. I HAVE TO FIND OUT WHY, SO I CAN CLEAR THIS UP.
SHRINK Hose Serenade
69 CANDLES
HEY, BUDDY. YOU KNOCKED SOME OF THE TAPES ON THE FLOOR. ARE YOU GOING TO PICK THOSE UP OR WHAT?
IT'S BAD ENOUGH THAT YOU PEOPLE GET ALL THE GOOD PARKING SPACES.
WHY DOES SHE THINK HER FATHER WAS KILLED BY DARE--
MARVEL TEAM UP
--DEVIL?
THE DEVIL IN MS
THE DEVIL IN MS
Karen Page
Mefisto Comes Over
MY FINGERS READ THE PRINTING IMPRESSION.
KAREN?!
THAT GUY'S BEEN IN THE ADULT SECTION AN AWFUL LONG TIME.
HE'S ALREADY BLIND, YOU'D THINK HE'D HAVE LEARNED HIS LESSON.
PULP FICTION II

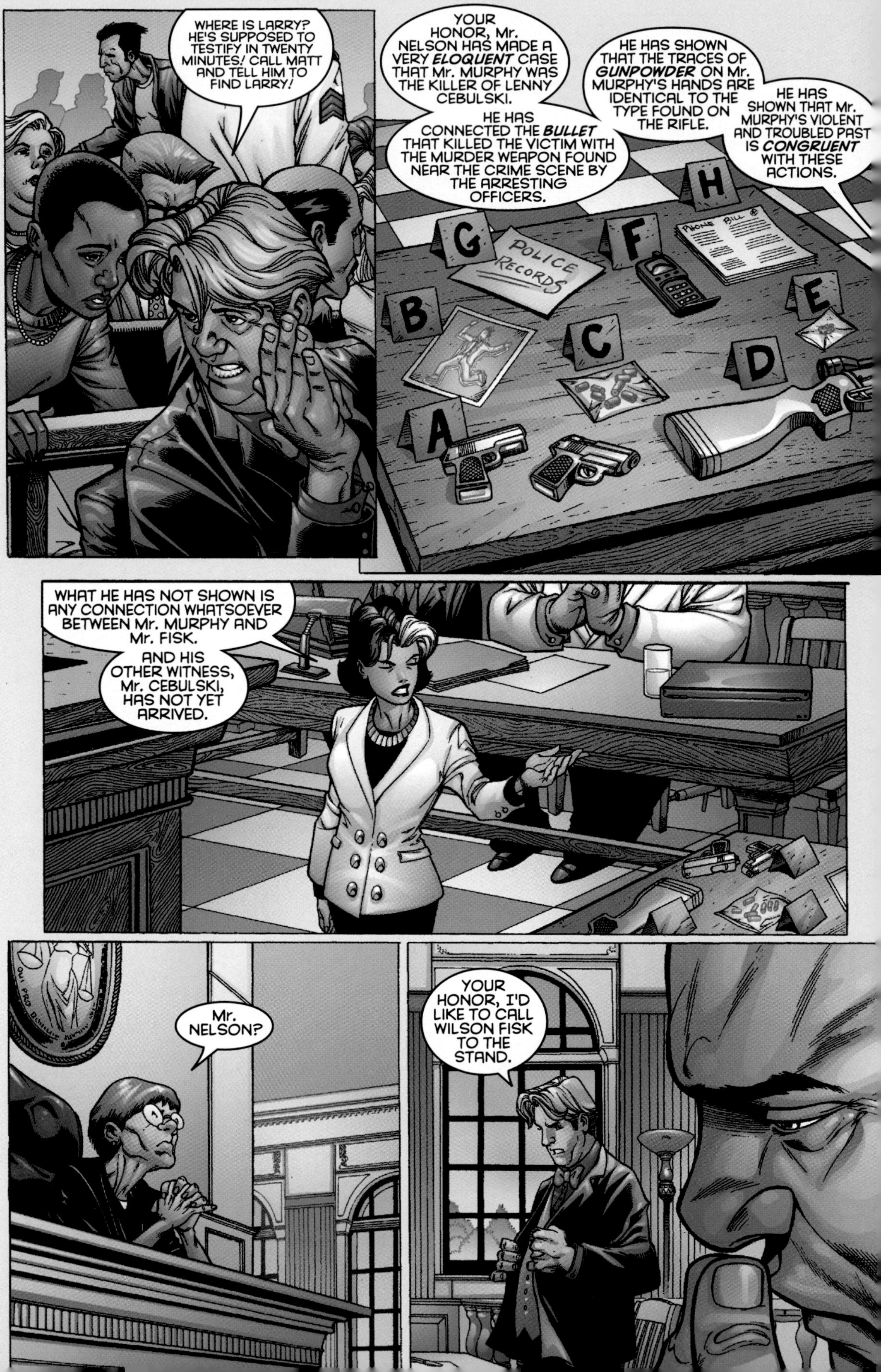

WHERE IS LARRY? HE'S SUPPOSED TO TESTIFY IN TWENTY MINUTES! CALL MATT AND TELL HIM TO FIND LARRY!
YOUR HONOR, Mr. NELSON HAS MADE A VERY ELOQUENT CASE THAT Mr. MURPHY WAS THE KILLER OF LENNY CEBULSKI.
HE HAS CONNECTED THE BULLET THAT KILLED THE VICTIM WITH THE MURDER WEAPON FOUND NEAR THE CRIME SCENE BY THE ARRESTING OFFICERS.
HE HAS SHOWN THAT THE TRACES OF GUNPOWDER ON Mr. MURPHY'S HANDS ARE IDENTICAL TO THE TYPE FOUND ON THE RIFLE.
HE HAS SHOWN THAT Mr. MURPHY'S VIOLENT AND TROUBLED PAST IS CONGRUENT WITH THESE ACTIONS.
G
POLICE RECORDS
H
F
PHONE BILL
B
C
E
D
A
WHAT HE HAS NOT SHOWN IS ANY CONNECTION WHATSOEVER BETWEEN Mr. MURPHY AND Mr. FISK.
AND HIS OTHER WITNESS, Mr. CEBULSKI, HAS NOT YET ARRIVED.
Mr. NELSON?
YOUR HONOR, I'D LIKE TO CALL WILSON FISK TO THE STAND.

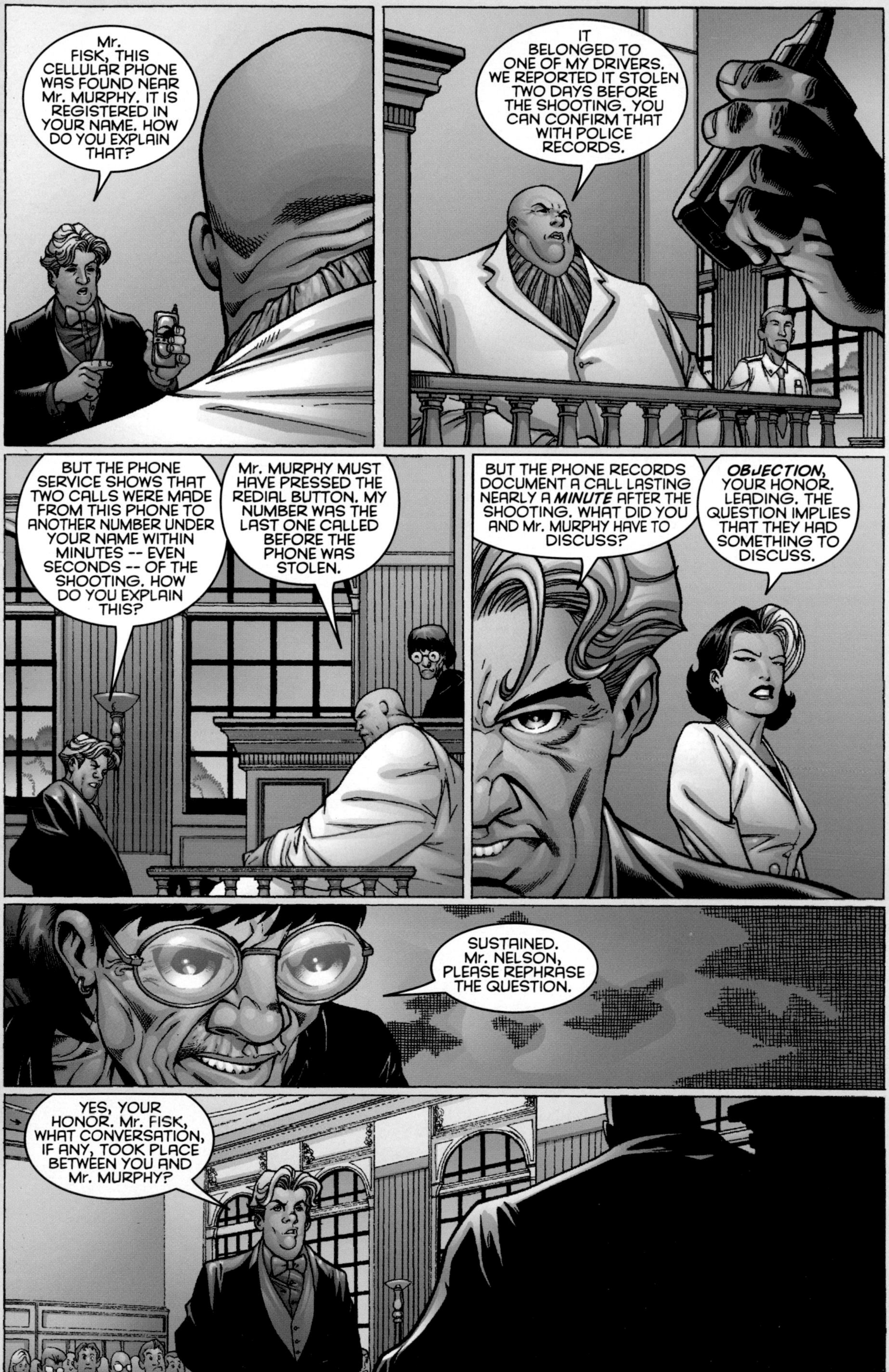
Mr. FISK, THIS CELLULAR PHONE WAS FOUND NEAR Mr. MURPHY. IT IS REGISTERED IN YOUR NAME. HOW DO YOU EXPLAIN THAT?
IT BELONGED TO ONE OF MY DRIVERS. WE REPORTED IT STOLEN TWO DAYS BEFORE THE SHOOTING. YOU CAN CONFIRM THAT WITH POLICE RECORDS.
BUT THE PHONE SERVICE SHOWS THAT TWO CALLS WERE MADE FROM THIS PHONE TO ANOTHER NUMBER UNDER YOUR NAME WITHIN MINUTES -- EVEN SECONDS -- OF THE SHOOTING. HOW DO YOU EXPLAIN THIS?
Mr. MURPHY MUST HAVE PRESSED THE REDIAL BUTTON. MY NUMBER WAS THE LAST ONE CALLED BEFORE THE PHONE WAS STOLEN.
BUT THE PHONE RECORDS DOCUMENT A CALL LASTING NEARLY A *MINUTE* AFTER THE SHOOTING. WHAT DID YOU AND Mr. MURPHY HAVE TO DISCUSS?
OBJECTION, YOUR HONOR. LEADING. THE QUESTION IMPLIES THAT THEY HAD SOMETHING TO DISCUSS.
SUSTAINED. Mr. NELSON, PLEASE REPHRASE THE QUESTION.
YES, YOUR HONOR. Mr. FISK, WHAT CONVERSATION, IF ANY, TOOK PLACE BETWEEN YOU AND Mr. MURPHY?

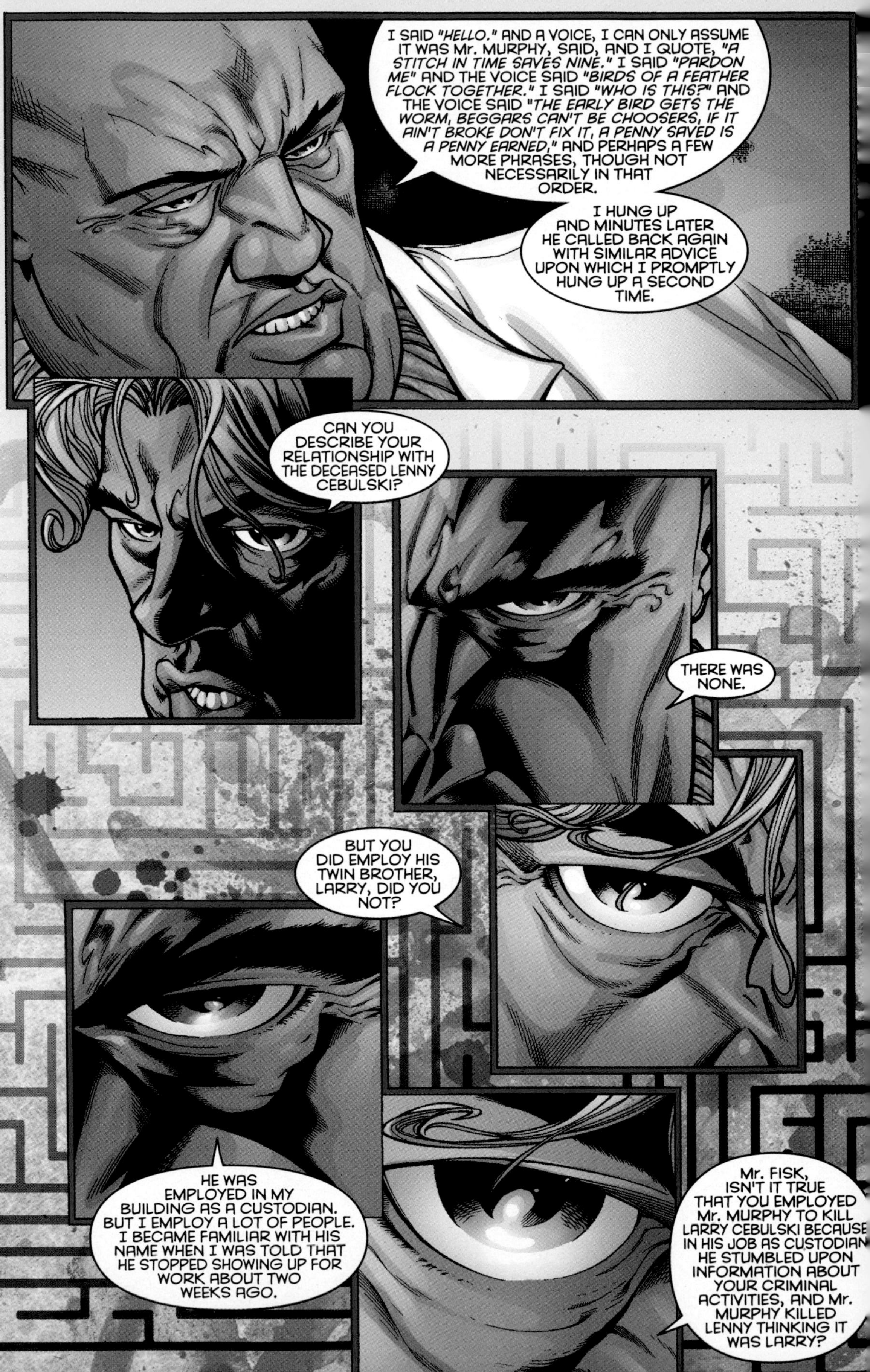

I SAID "*HELLO.*" AND A VOICE, I CAN ONLY ASSUME IT WAS Mr. MURPHY, SAID, AND I QUOTE, "*A STITCH IN TIME SAVES NINE.*" I SAID "*PARDON ME*" AND THE VOICE SAID "*BIRDS OF A FEATHER FLOCK TOGETHER.*" I SAID "*WHO IS THIS?*" AND THE VOICE SAID "*THE EARLY BIRD GETS THE WORM, BEGGARS CAN'T BE CHOOSERS, IF IT AIN'T BROKE DON'T FIX IT, A PENNY SAVED IS A PENNY EARNED,*" AND PERHAPS A FEW MORE PHRASES, THOUGH NOT NECESSARILY IN THAT ORDER.
I HUNG UP AND MINUTES LATER HE CALLED BACK AGAIN WITH SIMILAR ADVICE UPON WHICH I PROMPTLY HUNG UP A SECOND TIME.
CAN YOU DESCRIBE YOUR RELATIONSHIP WITH THE DECEASED LENNY CEBULSKI?
THERE WAS NONE.
BUT YOU DID EMPLOY HIS TWIN BROTHER, LARRY, DID YOU NOT?
HE WAS EMPLOYED IN MY BUILDING AS A CUSTODIAN. BUT I EMPLOY A LOT OF PEOPLE. I BECAME FAMILIAR WITH HIS NAME WHEN I WAS TOLD THAT HE STOPPED SHOWING UP FOR WORK ABOUT TWO WEEKS AGO.
Mr. FISK, ISN'T IT TRUE THAT YOU EMPLOYED Mr. MURPHY TO KILL LARRY CEBULSKI BECAUSE IN HIS JOB AS CUSTODIAN HE STUMBLED UPON INFORMATION ABOUT YOUR CRIMINAL ACTIVITIES, AND Mr. MURPHY KILLED LENNY THINKING IT WAS LARRY?

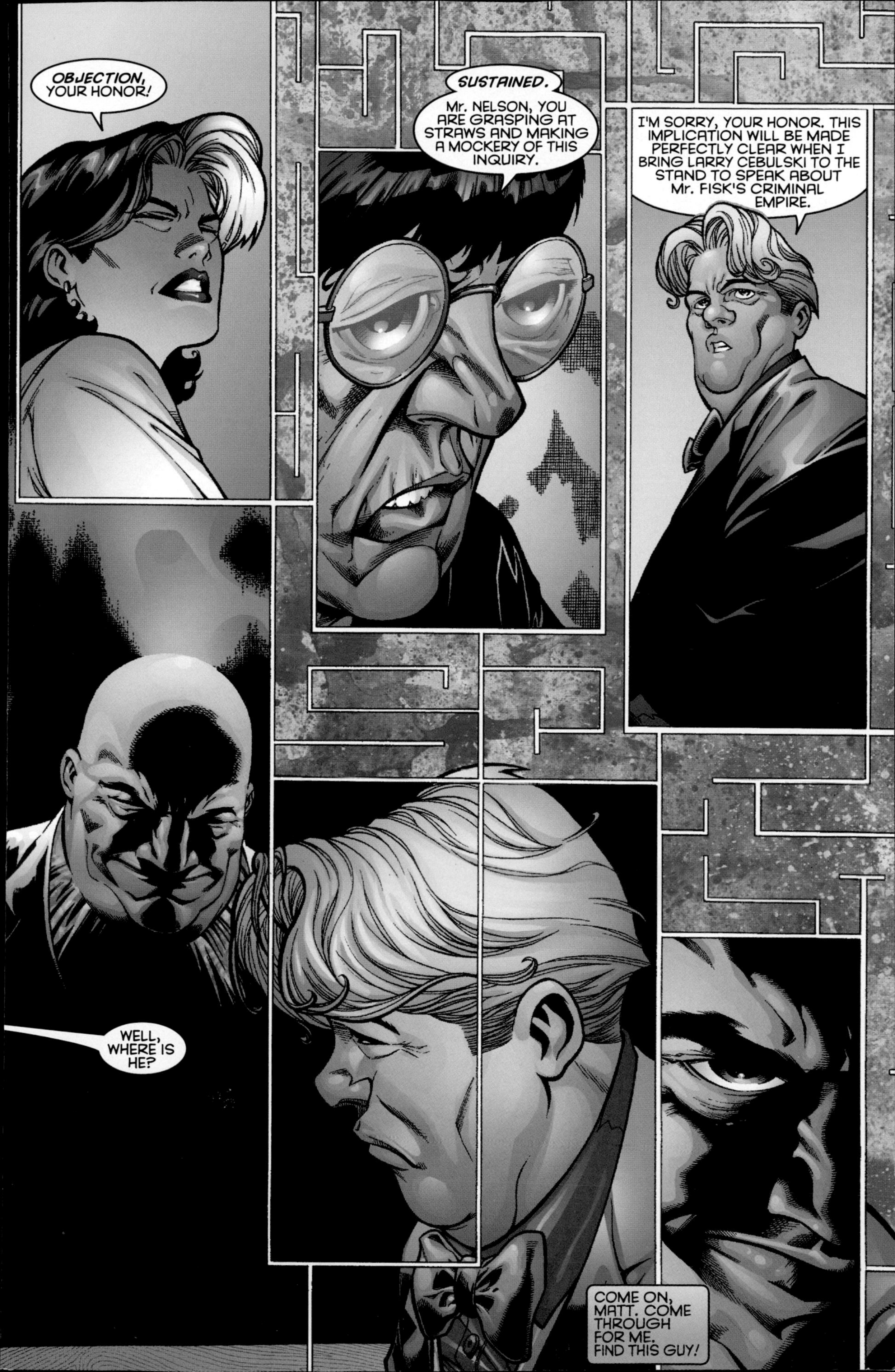
OBJECTION, YOUR HONOR!
SUSTAINED.
Mr. NELSON, YOU ARE GRASPING AT STRAWS AND MAKING A MOCKERY OF THIS INQUIRY.
I'M SORRY, YOUR HONOR. THIS IMPLICATION WILL BE MADE PERFECTLY CLEAR WHEN I BRING LARRY CEBULSKI TO THE STAND TO SPEAK ABOUT Mr. FISK'S CRIMINAL EMPIRE.
WELL, WHERE IS HE?
COME ON, MATT. COME THROUGH FOR ME. FIND THIS GUY!

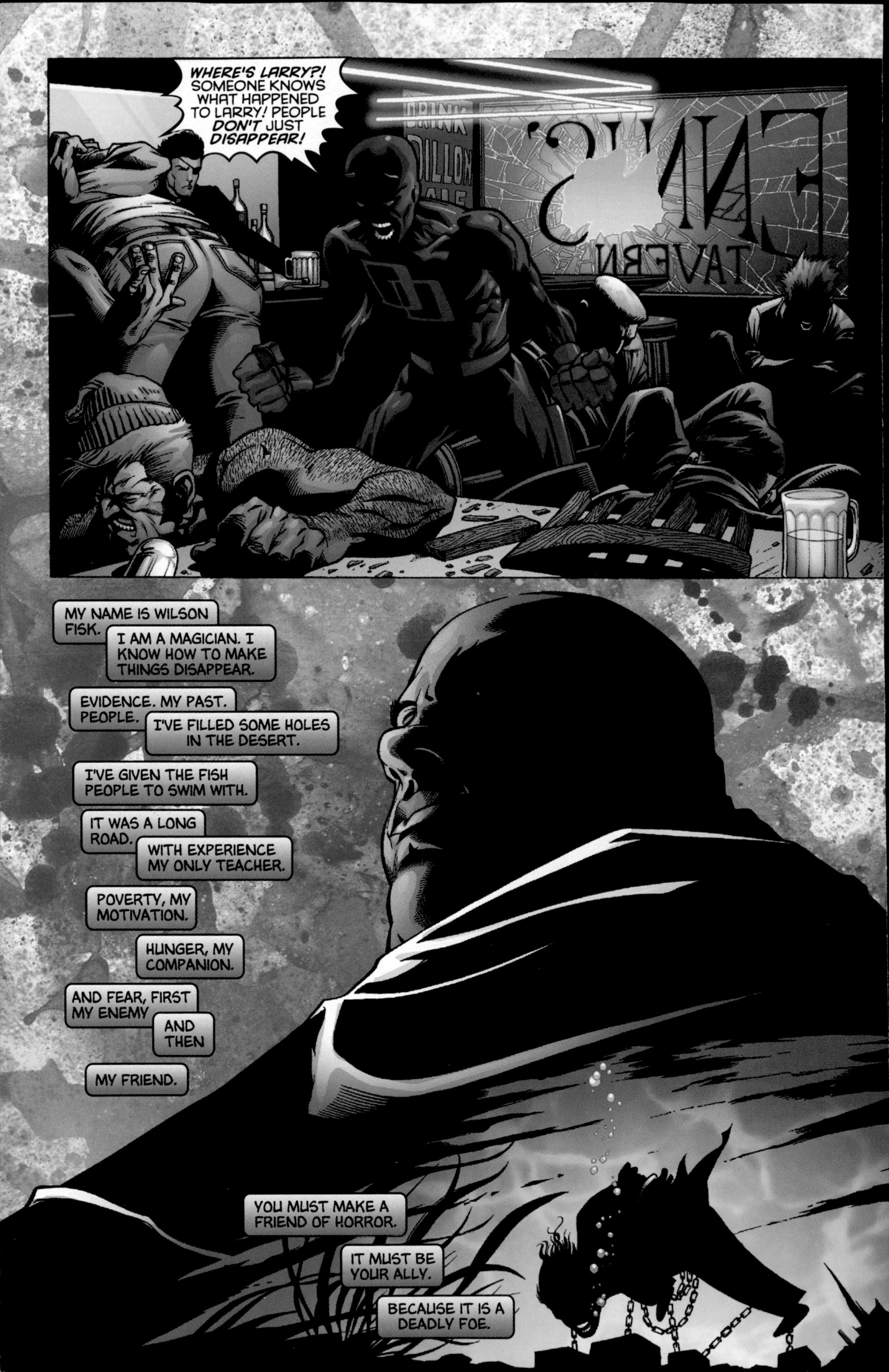

WHERE'S LARRY?! SOMEONE KNOWS WHAT HAPPENED TO LARRY! PEOPLE DON'T JUST DISAPPEAR!
DRINK DILLON ALE
ENN'S TAVERN
MY NAME IS WILSON FISK.
I AM A MAGICIAN. I KNOW HOW TO MAKE THINGS DISAPPEAR.
EVIDENCE. MY PAST. PEOPLE.
I'VE FILLED SOME HOLES IN THE DESERT.
I'VE GIVEN THE FISH PEOPLE TO SWIM WITH.
IT WAS A LONG ROAD.
WITH EXPERIENCE MY ONLY TEACHER.
POVERTY, MY MOTIVATION.
HUNGER, MY COMPANION.
AND FEAR, FIRST MY ENEMY
AND THEN
MY FRIEND.
YOU MUST MAKE A FRIEND OF HORROR.
IT MUST BE YOUR ALLY.
BECAUSE IT IS A DEADLY FOE.

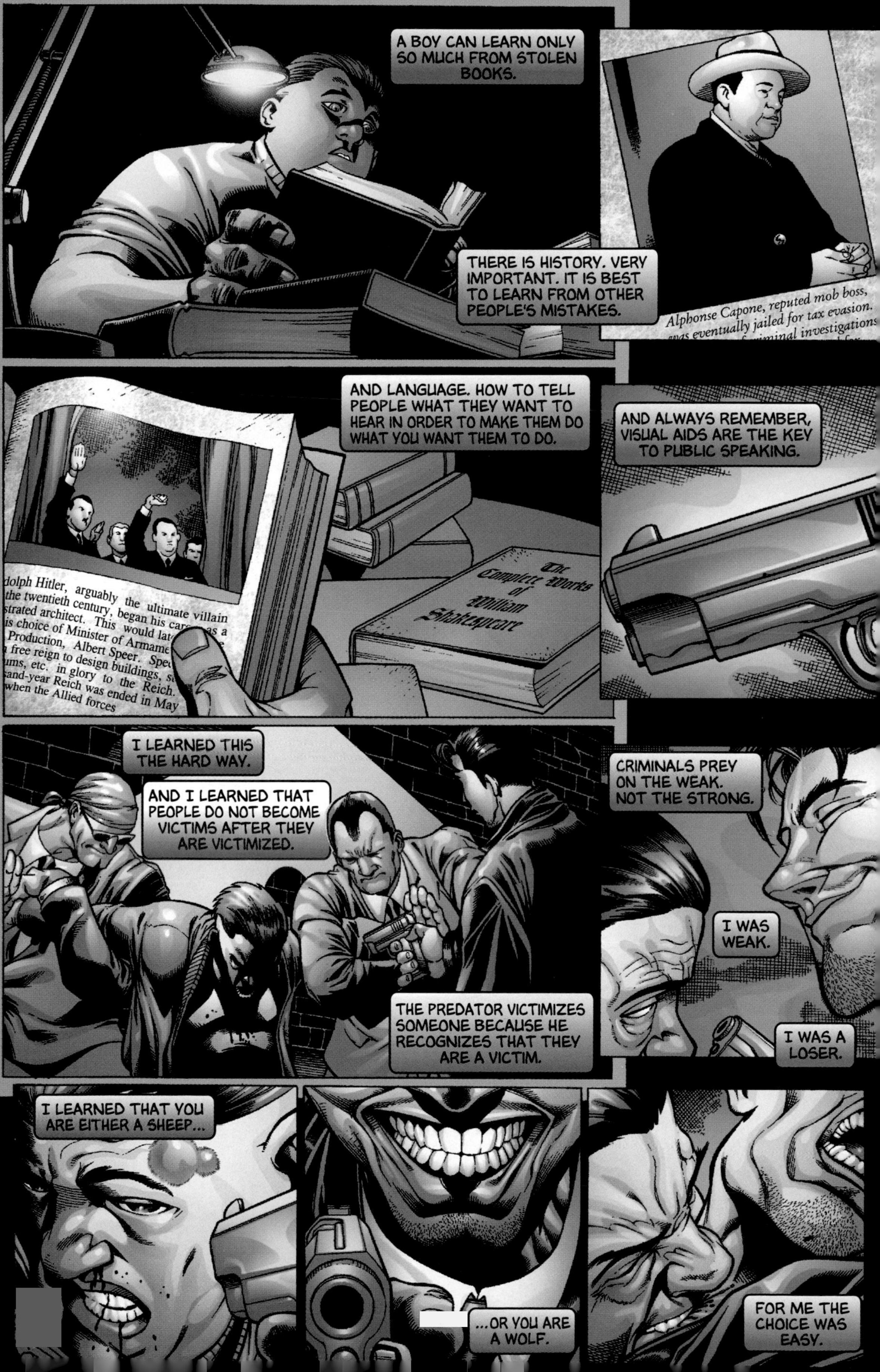
A BOY CAN LEARN ONLY SO MUCH FROM STOLEN BOOKS.
THERE IS HISTORY. VERY IMPORTANT. IT IS BEST TO LEARN FROM OTHER PEOPLE'S MISTAKES.
Alphonse Capone, reputed mob boss,
was eventually jailed for tax evasion.
AND LANGUAGE. HOW TO TELL PEOPLE WHAT THEY WANT TO HEAR IN ORDER TO MAKE THEM DO WHAT YOU WANT THEM TO DO.
dolph Hitler, arguably the ultimate villain
the twentieth century, began his car as a
strated architect. This would lat
is choice of Minister of Armame
Production, Albert Speer. Spe
free reign to design buildings,
ums, etc. in glory to the Reich.
sand-year Reich was ended in May
when the Allied forces
The Complete Works of William Shakespeare
AND ALWAYS REMEMBER, VISUAL AIDS ARE THE KEY TO PUBLIC SPEAKING.
I LEARNED THIS THE HARD WAY.
AND I LEARNED THAT PEOPLE DO NOT BECOME VICTIMS AFTER THEY ARE VICTIMIZED.
THE PREDATOR VICTIMIZES SOMEONE BECAUSE HE RECOGNIZES THAT THEY ARE A VICTIM.
CRIMINALS PREY ON THE WEAK. NOT THE STRONG.
I WAS WEAK.
I WAS A LOSER.
I LEARNED THAT YOU ARE EITHER A SHEEP...
...OR YOU ARE A WOLF.
FOR ME THE CHOICE WAS EASY.

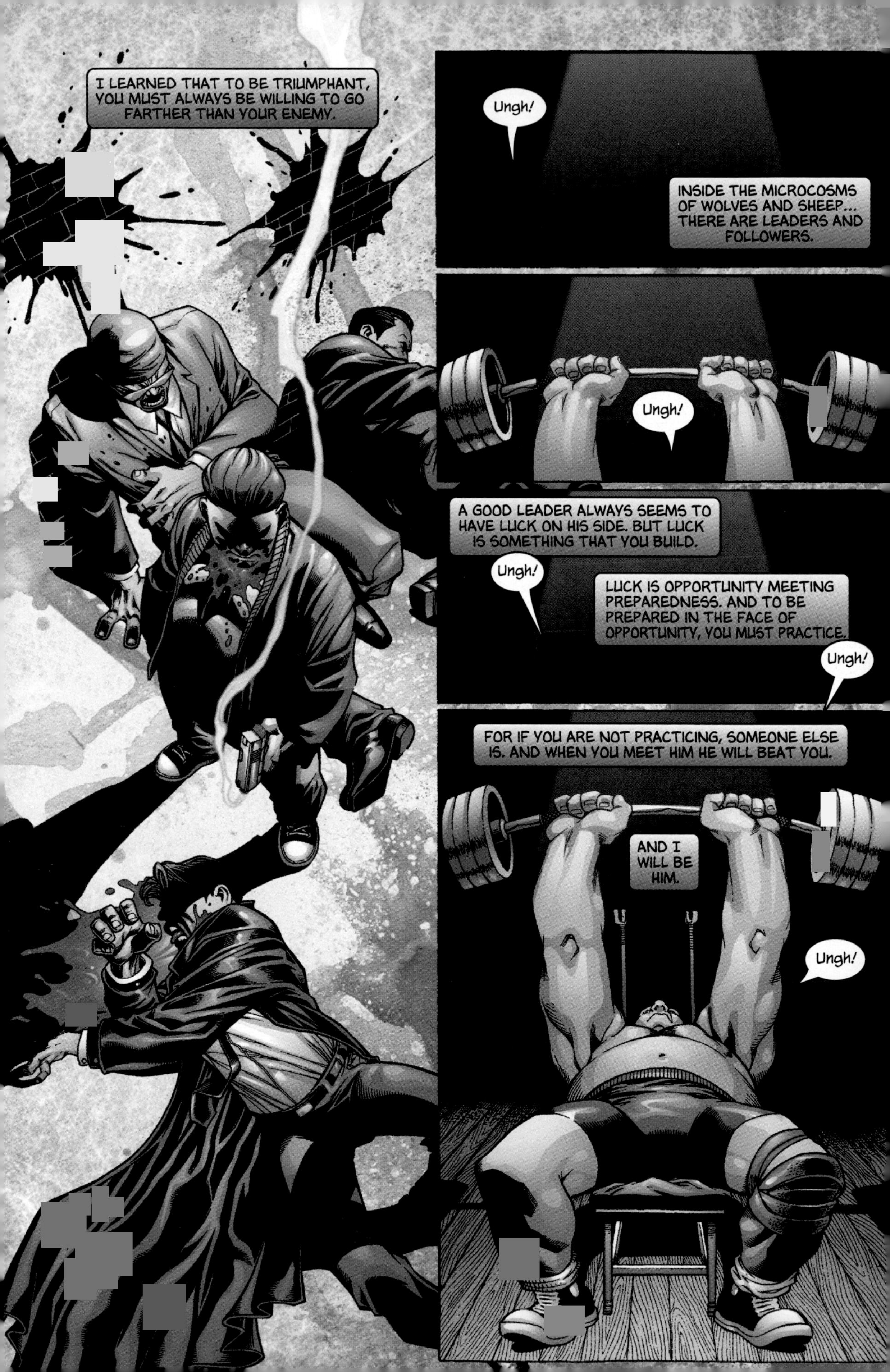
I LEARNED THAT TO BE TRIUMPHANT, YOU MUST ALWAYS BE WILLING TO GO FARTHER THAN YOUR ENEMY.
Ungh!
INSIDE THE MICROCOSMS OF WOLVES AND SHEEP... THERE ARE LEADERS AND FOLLOWERS.
Ungh!
A GOOD LEADER ALWAYS SEEMS TO HAVE LUCK ON HIS SIDE. BUT LUCK IS SOMETHING THAT YOU BUILD.
Ungh!
LUCK IS OPPORTUNITY MEETING PREPAREDNESS. AND TO BE PREPARED IN THE FACE OF OPPORTUNITY, YOU MUST PRACTICE.
Ungh!
FOR IF YOU ARE NOT PRACTICING, SOMEONE ELSE IS. AND WHEN YOU MEET HIM HE WILL BEAT YOU.
AND I WILL BE HIM.
Ungh!

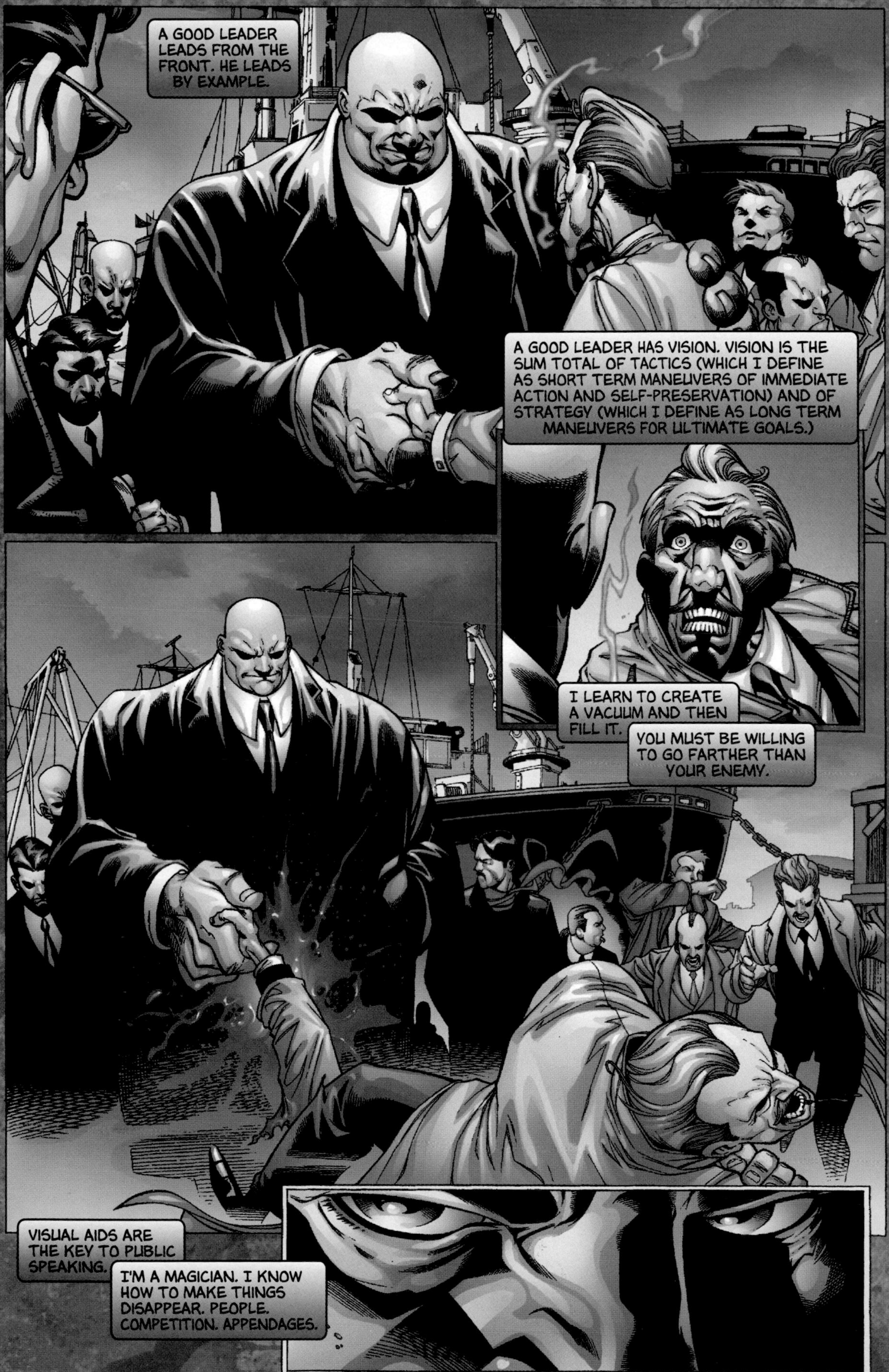
A GOOD LEADER LEADS FROM THE FRONT. HE LEADS BY EXAMPLE.
A GOOD LEADER HAS VISION. VISION IS THE SUM TOTAL OF TACTICS (WHICH I DEFINE AS SHORT TERM MANEUVERS OF IMMEDIATE ACTION AND SELF-PRESERVATION) AND OF STRATEGY (WHICH I DEFINE AS LONG TERM MANEUVERS FOR ULTIMATE GOALS.)
I LEARN TO CREATE A VACUUM AND THEN FILL IT.
YOU MUST BE WILLING TO GO FARTHER THAN YOUR ENEMY.
VISUAL AIDS ARE THE KEY TO PUBLIC SPEAKING.
I'M A MAGICIAN. I KNOW HOW TO MAKE THINGS DISAPPEAR. PEOPLE. COMPETITION. APPENDAGES.

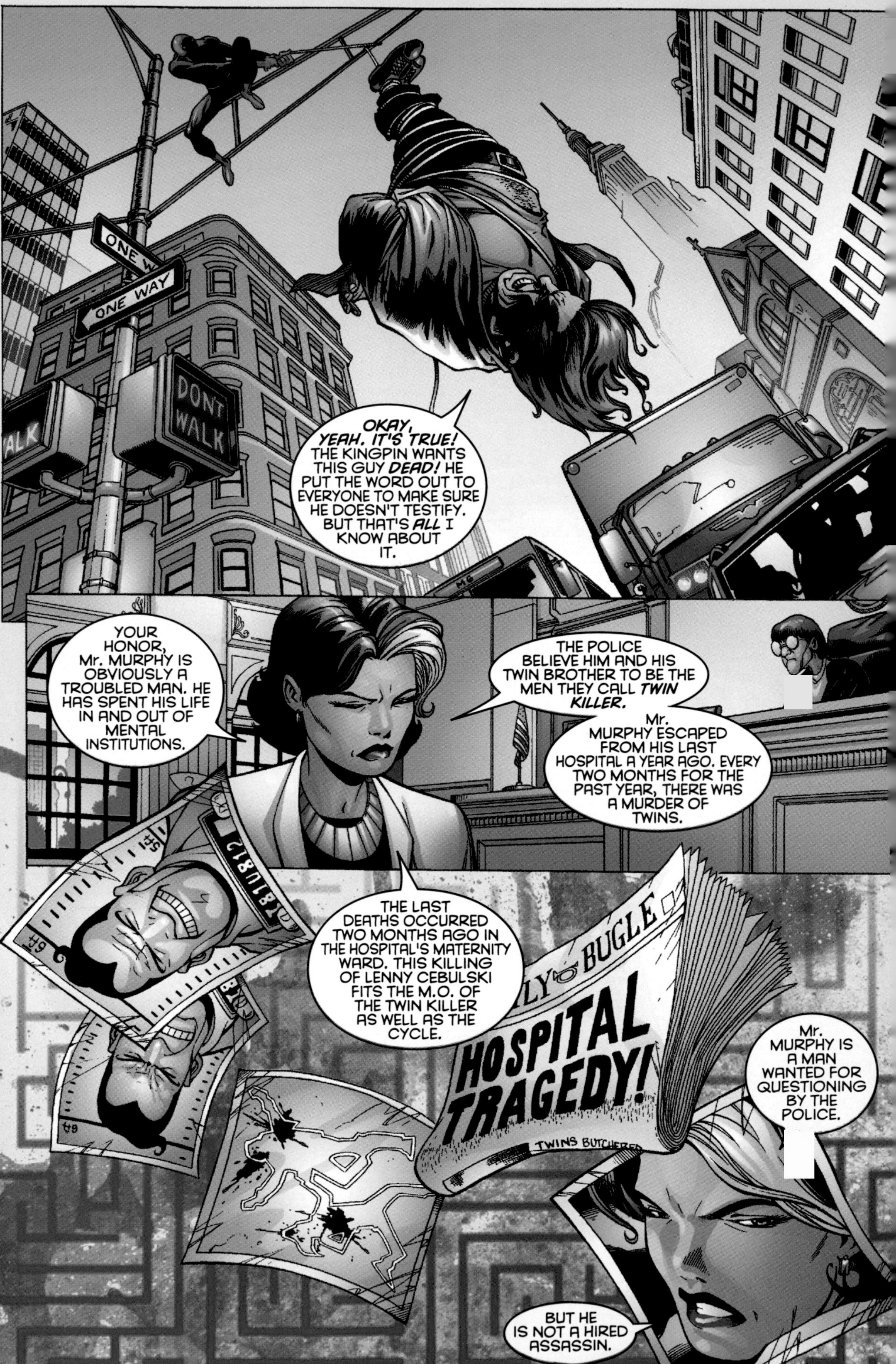
ONE WAY
ONE WAY
DON'T WALK
WALK
OKAY, YEAH. IT'S TRUE! THE KINGPIN WANTS THIS GUY DEAD! HE PUT THE WORD OUT TO EVERYONE TO MAKE SURE HE DOESN'T TESTIFY. BUT THAT'S ALL I KNOW ABOUT IT.
YOUR HONOR, Mr. MURPHY IS OBVIOUSLY A TROUBLED MAN. HE HAS SPENT HIS LIFE IN AND OUT OF MENTAL INSTITUTIONS.
THE POLICE BELIEVE HIM AND HIS TWIN BROTHER TO BE THE MEN THEY CALL TWIN KILLER.
Mr. MURPHY ESCAPED FROM HIS LAST HOSPITAL A YEAR AGO. EVERY TWO MONTHS FOR THE PAST YEAR, THERE WAS A MURDER OF TWINS.
THE LAST DEATHS OCCURRED TWO MONTHS AGO IN THE HOSPITAL'S MATERNITY WARD. THIS KILLING OF LENNY CEBULSKI FITS THE M.O. OF THE TWIN KILLER AS WELL AS THE CYCLE.
BUGLE
HOSPITAL TRAGEDY!
TWINS BUTCHERED
Mr. MURPHY IS A MAN WANTED FOR QUESTIONING BY THE POLICE.
BUT HE IS NOT A HIRED ASSASSIN.

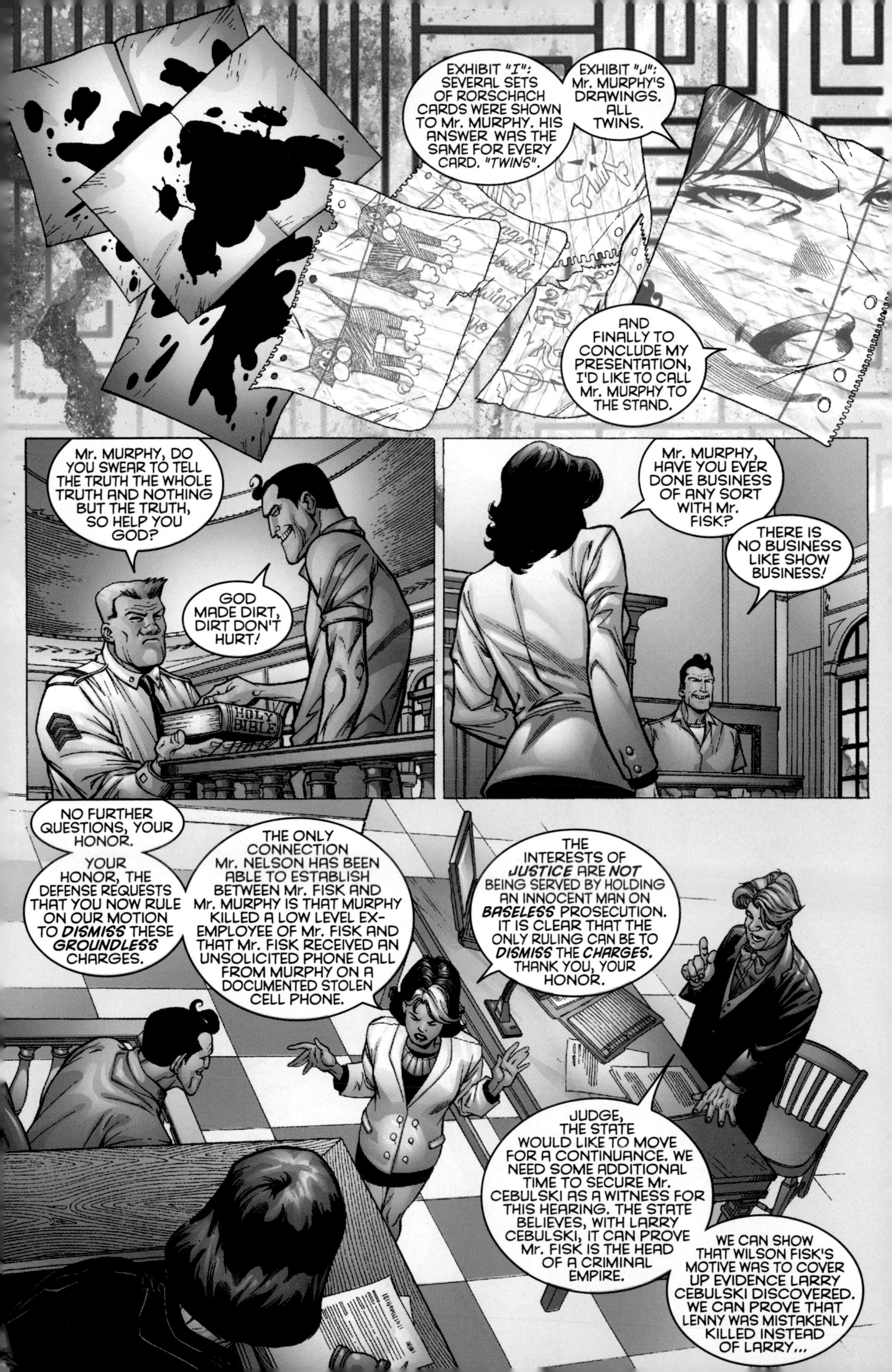

EXHIBIT "I": SEVERAL SETS OF RORSCHACH CARDS WERE SHOWN TO Mr. MURPHY. HIS ANSWER WAS THE SAME FOR EVERY CARD. "TWINS".
EXHIBIT "J": Mr. MURPHY'S DRAWINGS. ALL TWINS.
AND FINALLY TO CONCLUDE MY PRESENTATION, I'D LIKE TO CALL Mr. MURPHY TO THE STAND.
Mr. MURPHY, DO YOU SWEAR TO TELL THE TRUTH THE WHOLE TRUTH AND NOTHING BUT THE TRUTH, SO HELP YOU GOD?
GOD MADE DIRT, DIRT DON'T HURT!
HOLY BIBLE
Mr. MURPHY, HAVE YOU EVER DONE BUSINESS OF ANY SORT WITH Mr. FISK?
THERE IS NO BUSINESS LIKE SHOW BUSINESS!
NO FURTHER QUESTIONS, YOUR HONOR.
YOUR HONOR, THE DEFENSE REQUESTS THAT YOU NOW RULE ON OUR MOTION TO DISMISS THESE GROUNDLESS CHARGES.
THE ONLY CONNECTION Mr. NELSON HAS BEEN ABLE TO ESTABLISH BETWEEN Mr. FISK AND Mr. MURPHY IS THAT MURPHY KILLED A LOW LEVEL EX-EMPLOYEE OF Mr. FISK AND THAT Mr. FISK RECEIVED AN UNSOLICITED PHONE CALL FROM MURPHY ON A DOCUMENTED STOLEN CELL PHONE.
THE INTERESTS OF JUSTICE ARE NOT BEING SERVED BY HOLDING AN INNOCENT MAN ON BASELESS PROSECUTION. IT IS CLEAR THAT THE ONLY RULING CAN BE TO DISMISS THE CHARGES. THANK YOU, YOUR HONOR.
JUDGE, THE STATE WOULD LIKE TO MOVE FOR A CONTINUANCE. WE NEED SOME ADDITIONAL TIME TO SECURE Mr. CEBULSKI AS A WITNESS FOR THIS HEARING. THE STATE BELIEVES, WITH LARRY CEBULSKI, IT CAN PROVE Mr. FISK IS THE HEAD OF A CRIMINAL EMPIRE.
WE CAN SHOW THAT WILSON FISK'S MOTIVE WAS TO COVER UP EVIDENCE LARRY CEBULSKI DISCOVERED. WE CAN PROVE THAT LENNY WAS MISTAKENLY KILLED INSTEAD OF LARRY...

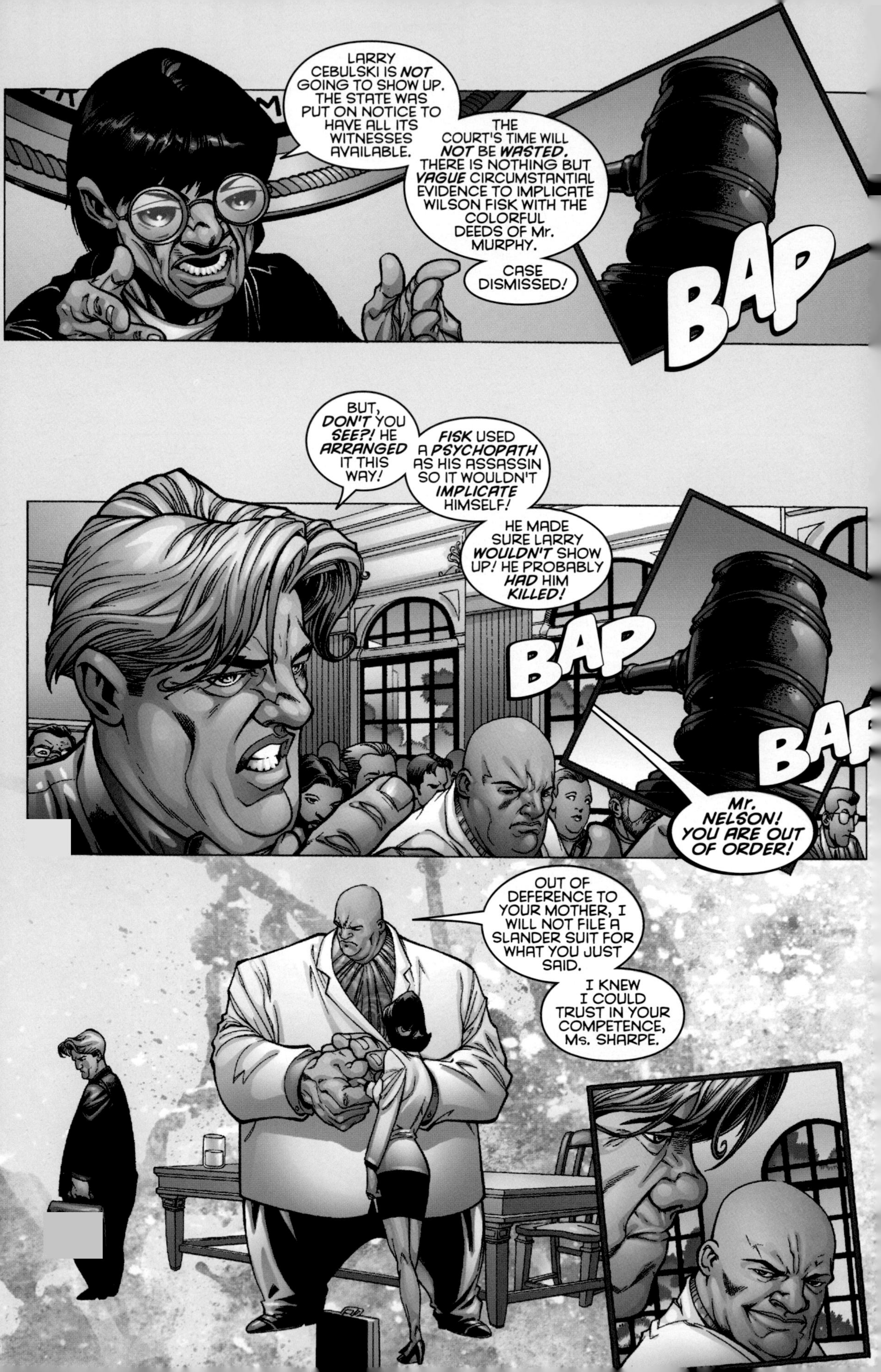
LARRY CEBULSKI IS NOT GOING TO SHOW UP. THE STATE WAS PUT ON NOTICE TO HAVE ALL ITS WITNESSES AVAILABLE.
THE COURT'S TIME WILL NOT BE WASTED. THERE IS NOTHING BUT VAGUE CIRCUMSTANTIAL EVIDENCE TO IMPLICATE WILSON FISK WITH THE COLORFUL DEEDS OF Mr. MURPHY.
CASE DISMISSED!
BAP
BUT, DON'T YOU SEE?! HE ARRANGED IT THIS WAY!
FISK USED A PSYCHOPATH AS HIS ASSASSIN SO IT WOULDN'T IMPLICATE HIMSELF!
HE MADE SURE LARRY WOULDN'T SHOW UP! HE PROBABLY HAD HIM KILLED!
BAP
Mr. NELSON! YOU ARE OUT OF ORDER!
OUT OF DEFERENCE TO YOUR MOTHER, I WILL NOT FILE A SLANDER SUIT FOR WHAT YOU JUST SAID.
I KNEW I COULD TRUST IN YOUR COMPETENCE, Ms. SHARPE.

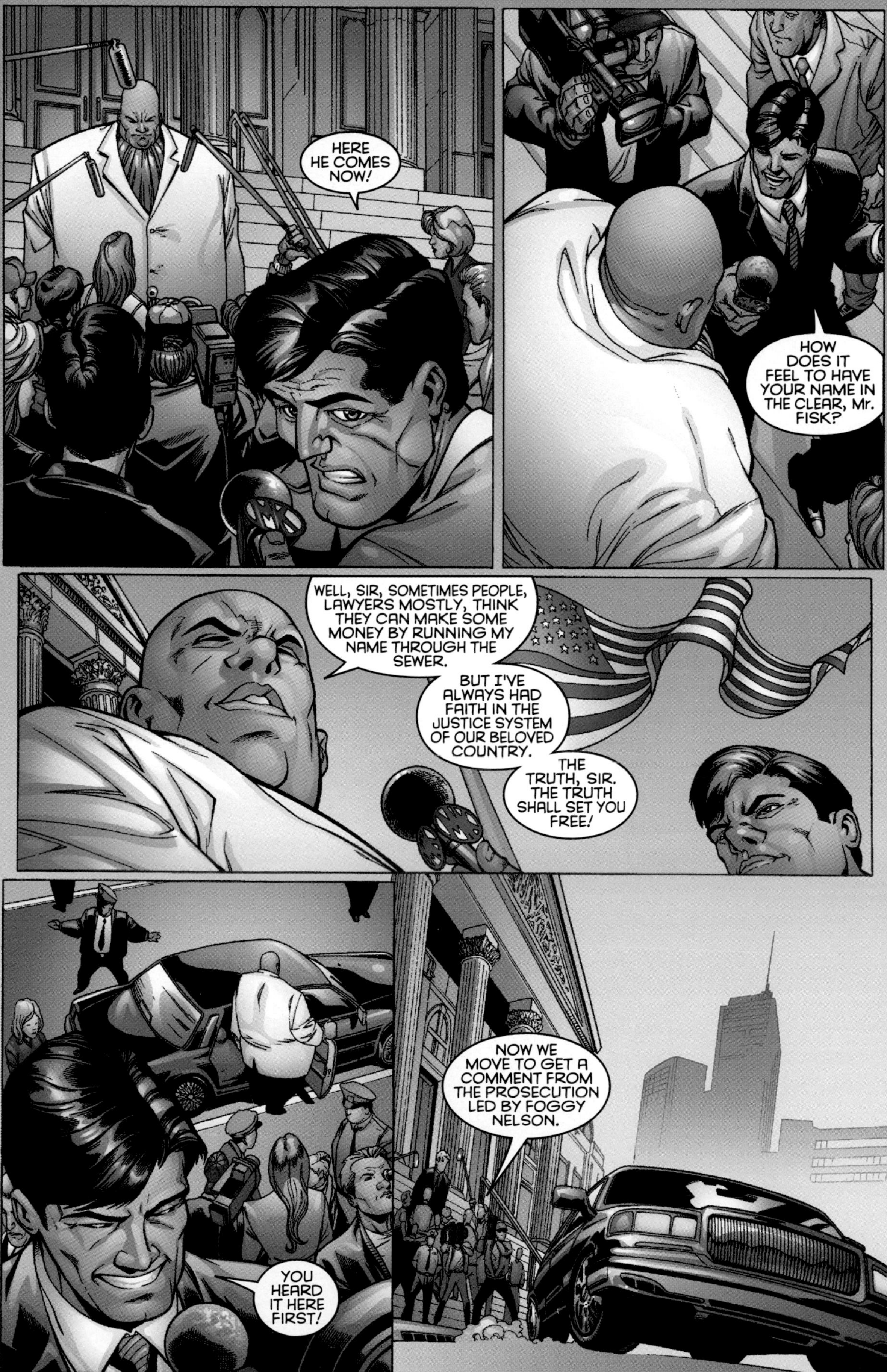
HERE HE COMES NOW!
HOW DOES IT FEEL TO HAVE YOUR NAME IN THE CLEAR, Mr. FISK?
WELL, SIR, SOMETIMES PEOPLE, LAWYERS MOSTLY, THINK THEY CAN MAKE SOME MONEY BY RUNNING MY NAME THROUGH THE SEWER.
BUT I'VE ALWAYS HAD FAITH IN THE JUSTICE SYSTEM OF OUR BELOVED COUNTRY.
THE TRUTH, SIR. THE TRUTH SHALL SET YOU FREE!
YOU HEARD IT HERE FIRST!
NOW WE MOVE TO GET A COMMENT FROM THE PROSECUTION LED BY FOGGY NELSON.

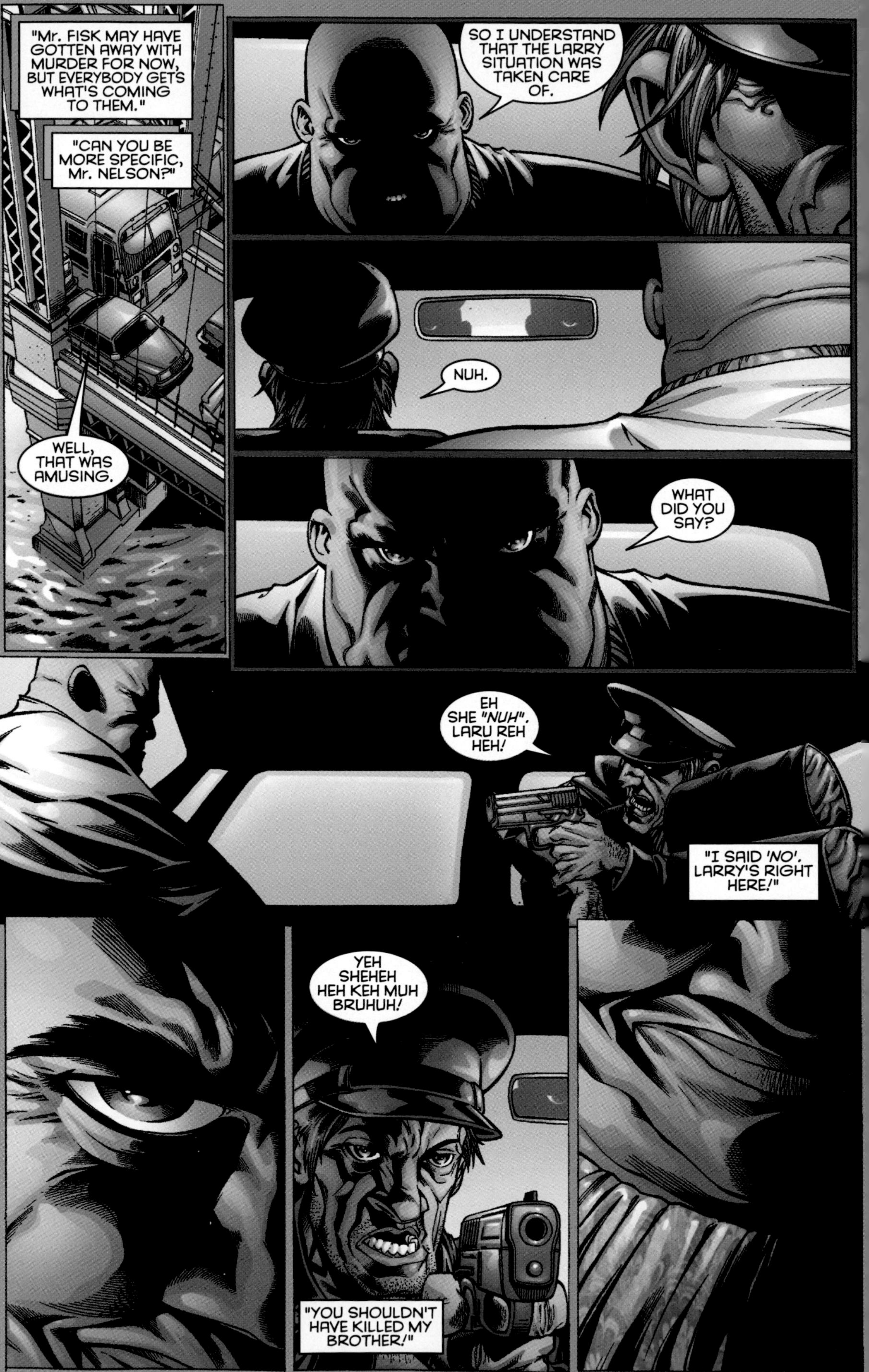
"Mr. FISK MAY HAVE GOTTEN AWAY WITH MURDER FOR NOW, BUT EVERYBODY GETS WHAT'S COMING TO THEM."
"CAN YOU BE MORE SPECIFIC, Mr. NELSON?"
WELL, THAT WAS AMUSING.
SO I UNDERSTAND THAT THE LARRY SITUATION WAS TAKEN CARE OF.
NUH.
WHAT DID YOU SAY?
EH SHE "NUH". LARU REH HEH!
"I SAID 'NO'. LARRY'S RIGHT HERE!"
YEH SHEHEH HEH KEH MUH BRUHUH!
"YOU SHOULDN'T HAVE KILLED MY BROTHER!"

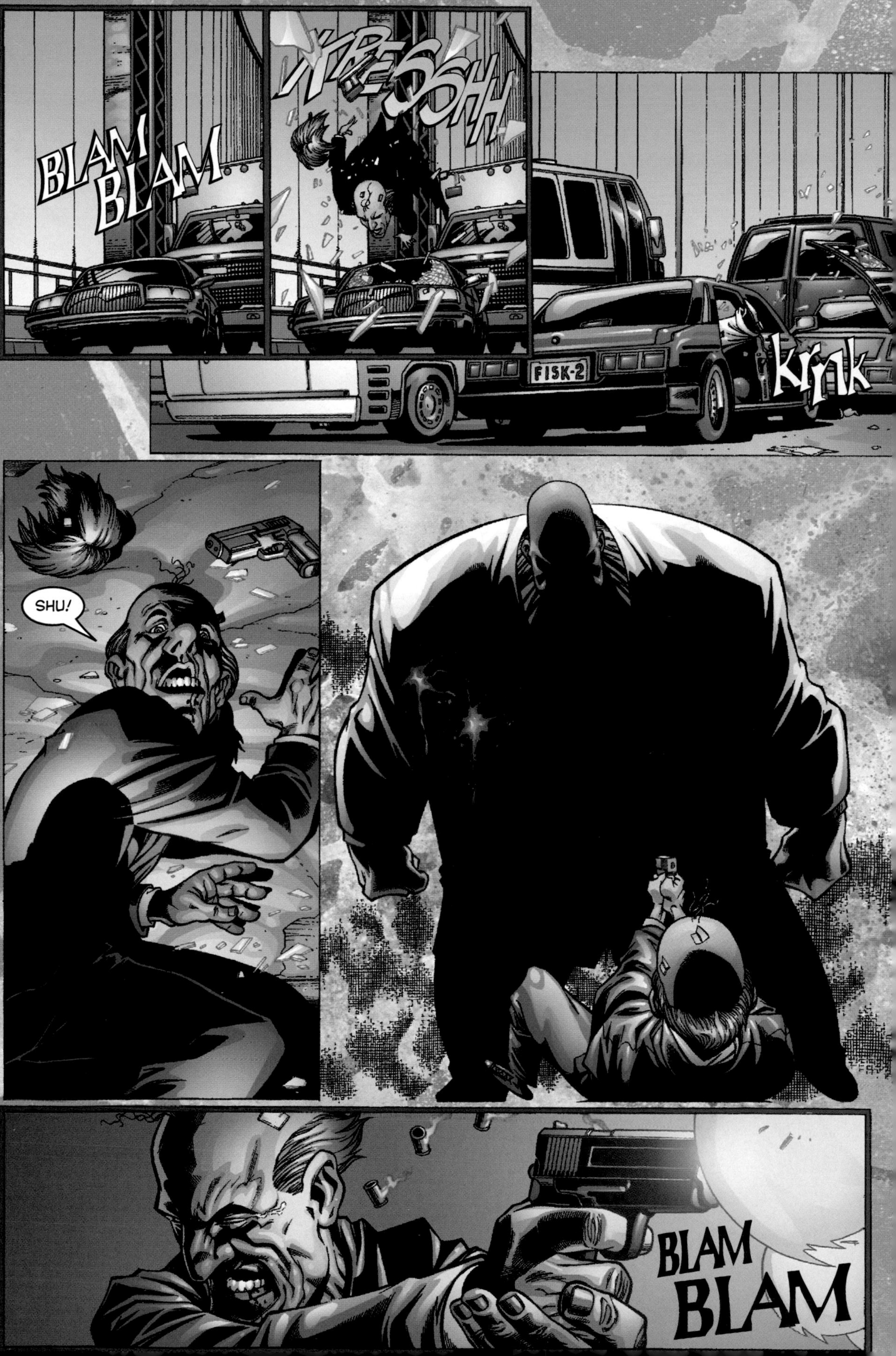
BLAM BLAM
KRESSHH
FISK-2
KRNK
SHU!
BLAM BLAM

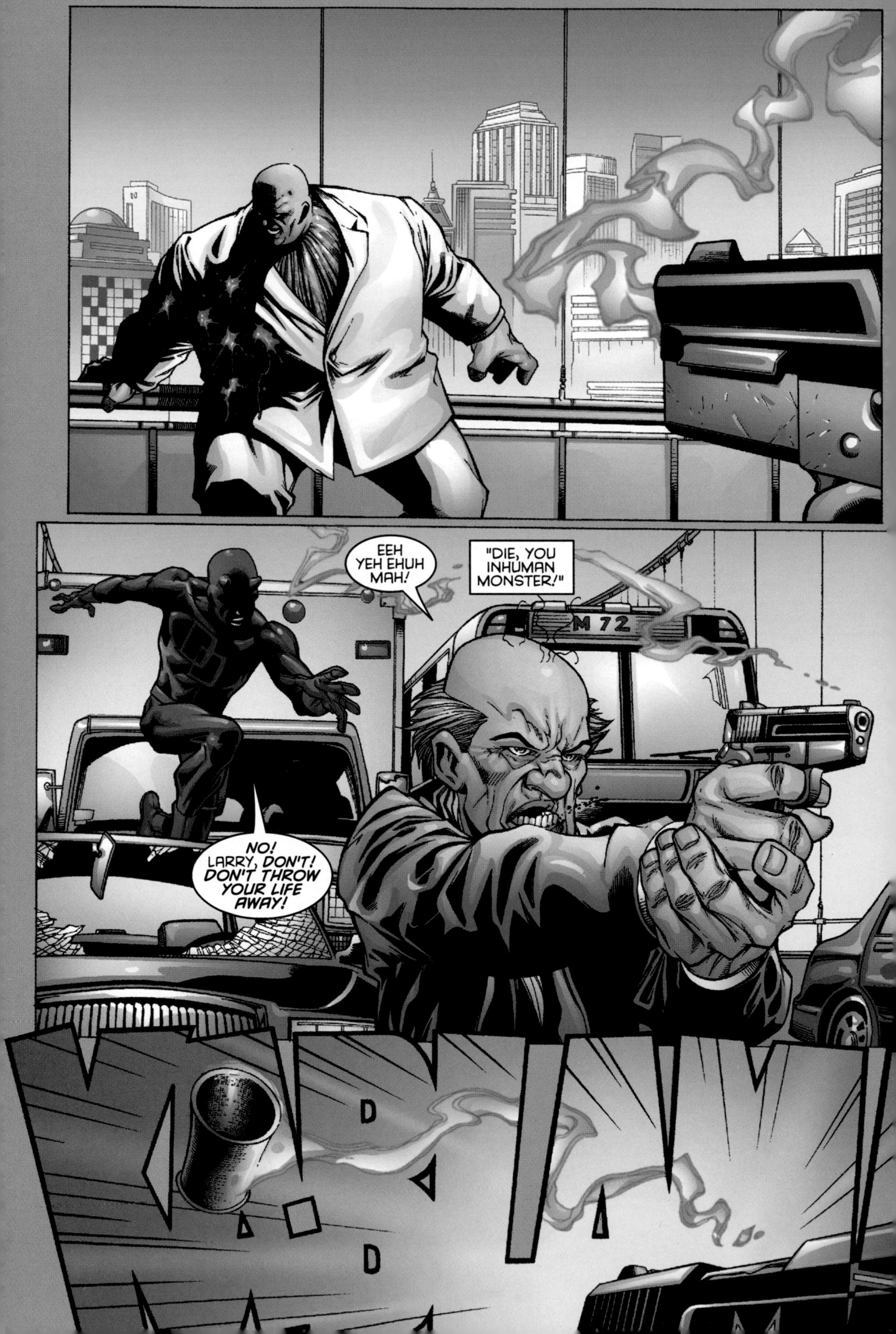
EEH YEH EHUH MAH!
"DIE, YOU INHUMAN MONSTER!"
NO! LARRY, DON'T! DON'T THROW YOUR LIFE AWAY!

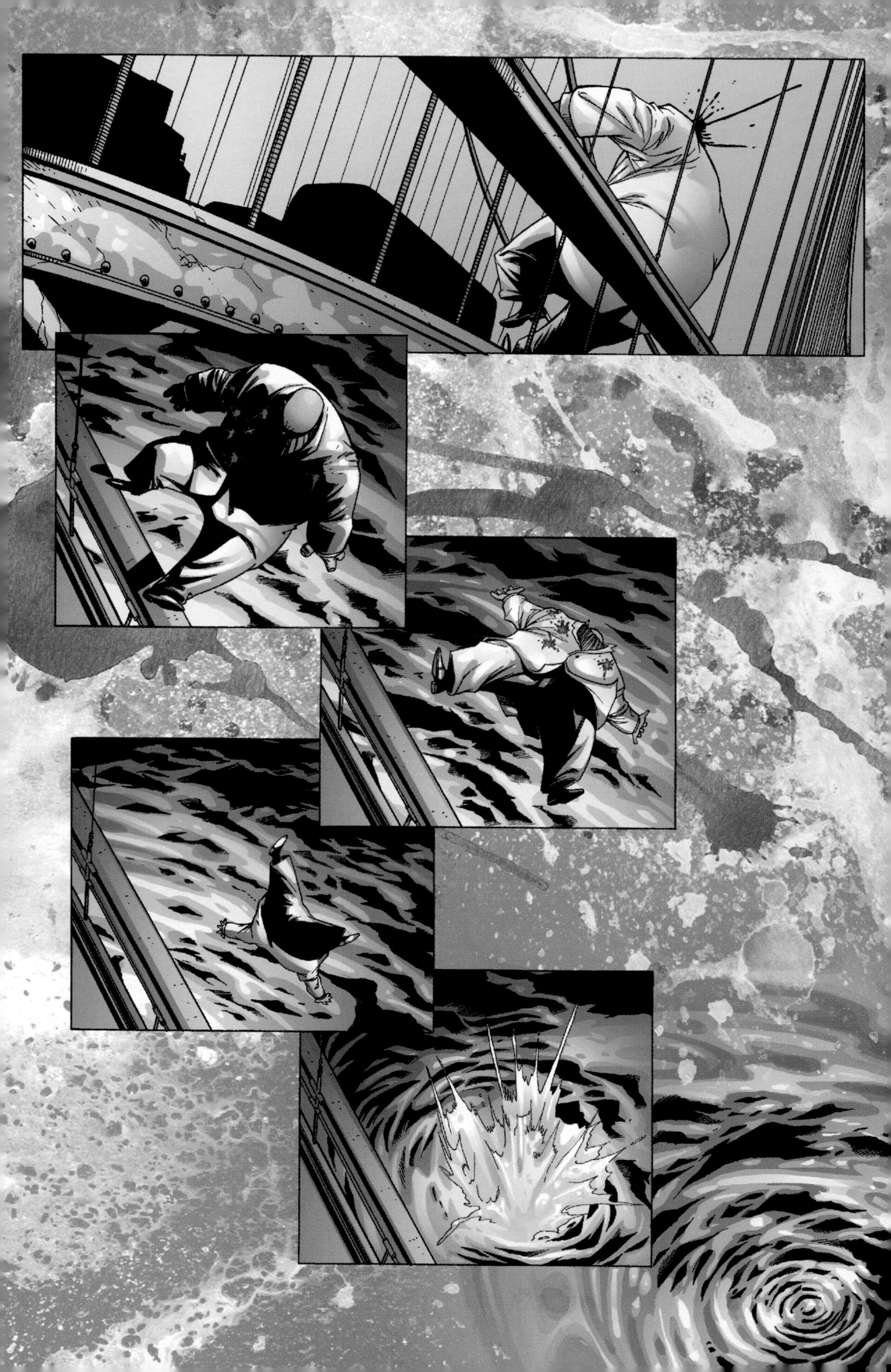

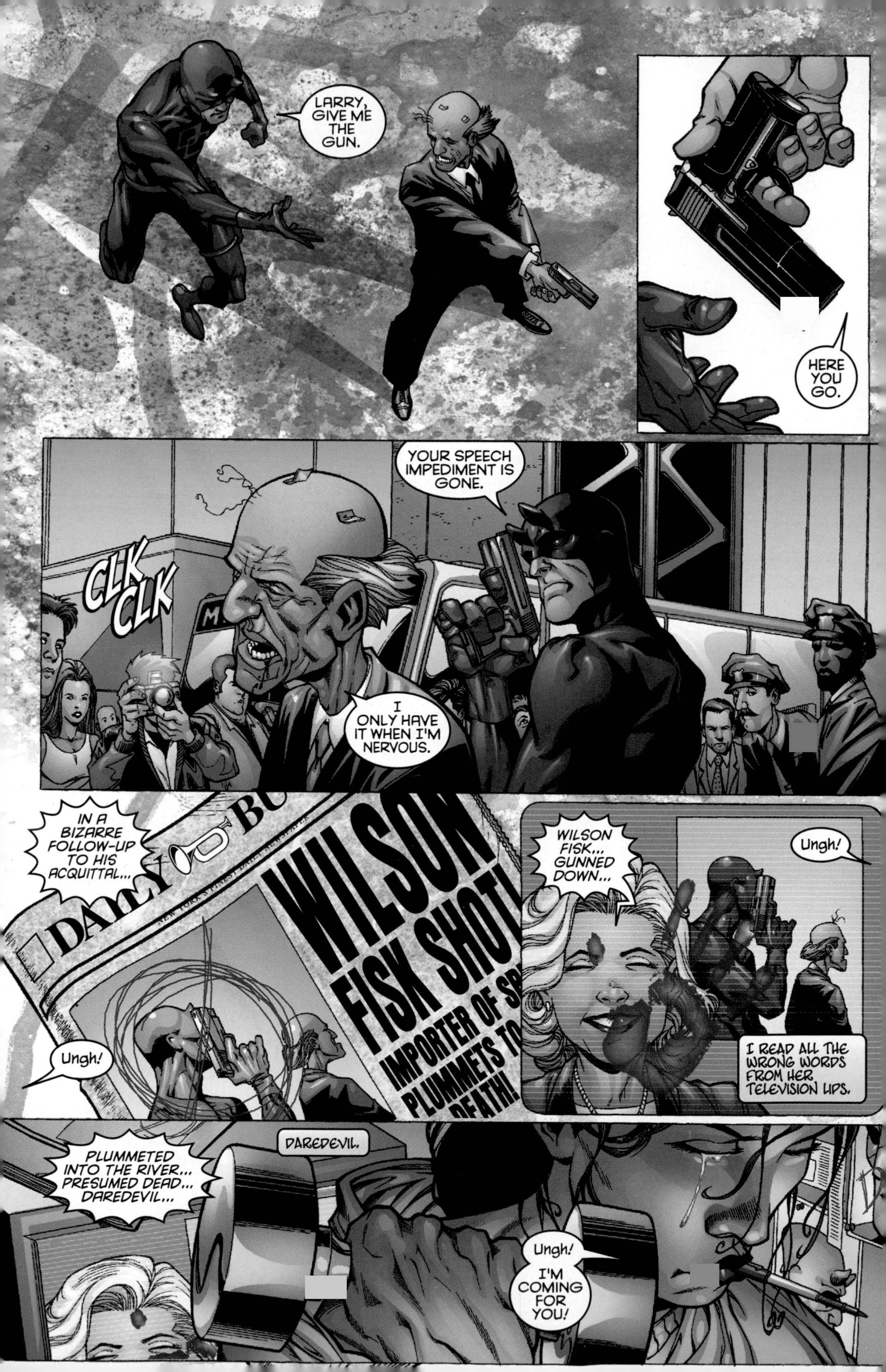
LARRY, GIVE ME THE GUN.
HERE YOU GO.
YOUR SPEECH IMPEDIMENT IS GONE.
CLK CLK
I ONLY HAVE IT WHEN I'M NERVOUS.
IN A BIZARRE FOLLOW-UP TO HIS ACQUITTAL...
DAILY
WILSON
FISK
DEATH!
Ungh!
WILSON FISK... GUNNED DOWN...
Ungh!
I READ ALL THE WRONG WORDS FROM HER TELEVISION LIPS.
PLUMMETED INTO THE RIVER... PRESUMED DEAD... DAREDEVIL...
DAREDEVIL.
Ungh!
I'M COMING FOR YOU!

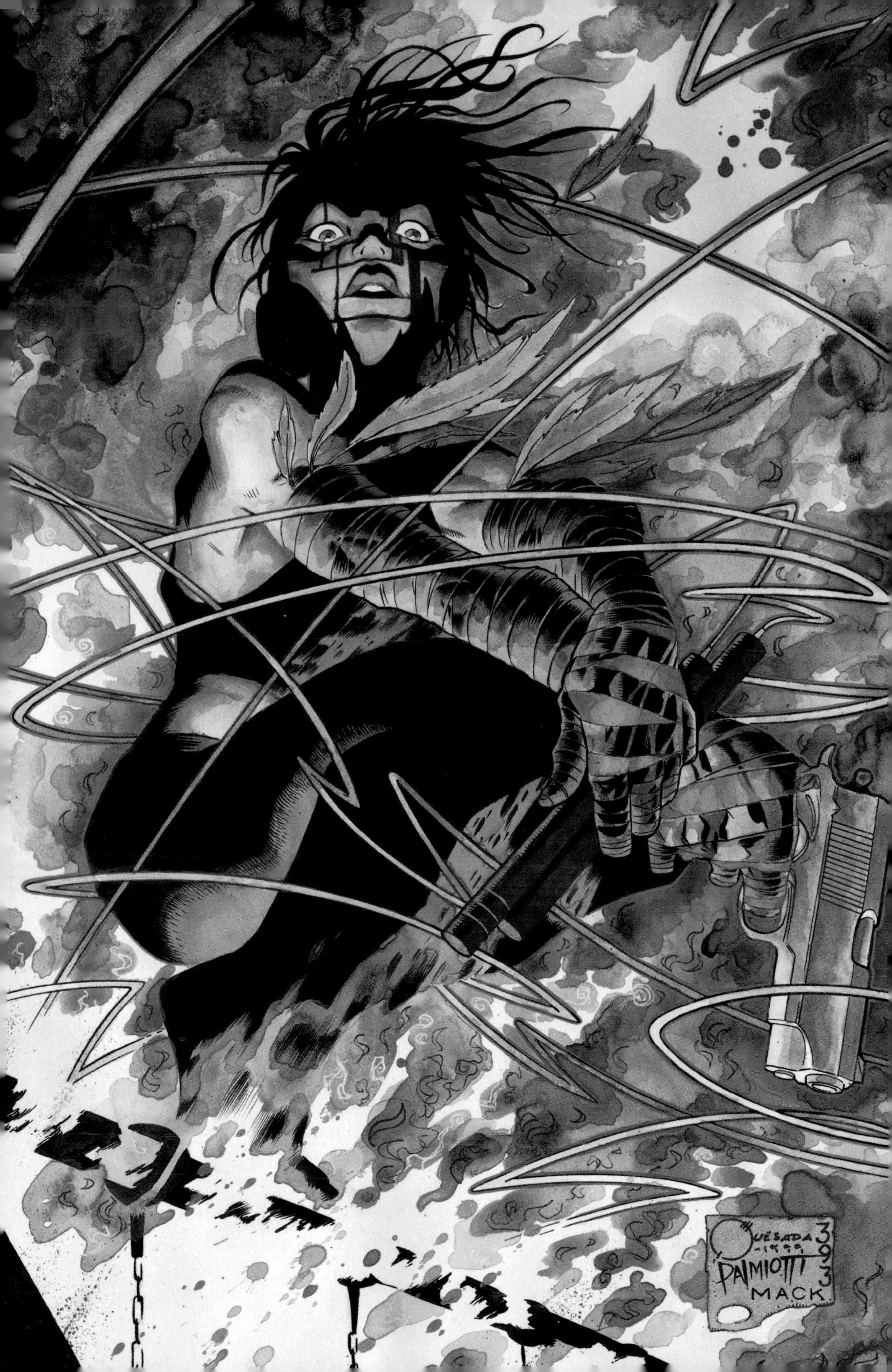
QUESADA
1999
PALMIOTTI
MACK
393

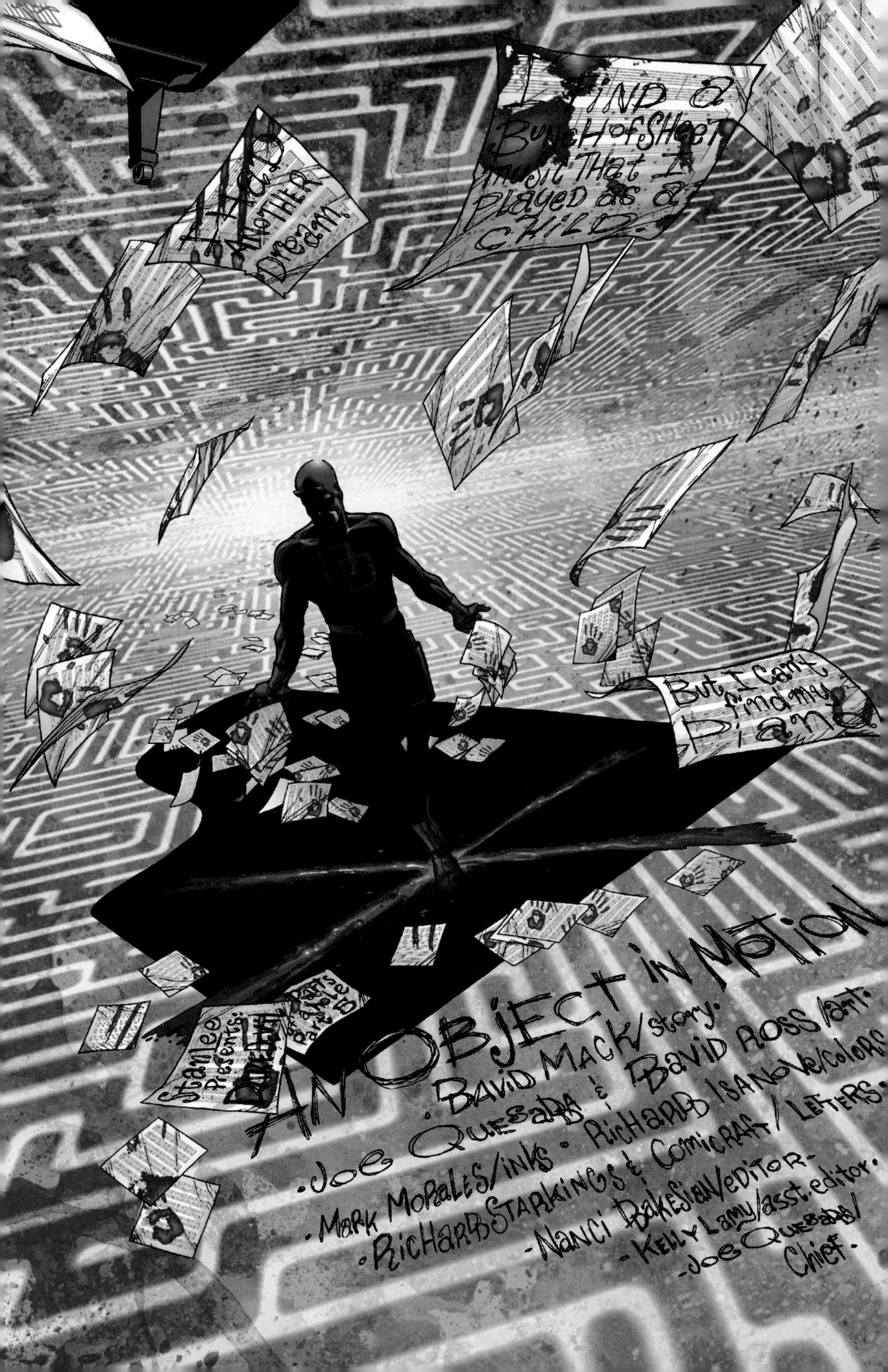
I Had Another Dream.
I find a Bunch of Sheet Music That I Played as a Child.
But I Can't find my Piano.
Stan Lee Presents:
An Object in Motion
David Mack/story.
David Ross/art.
Joe Quesada &
Richard Isanove/colors.
Mark Morales/inks.
Richard Starkings & Comicraft/Letters.
Nanci Dakesian/editor.
Kelly Lamy/asst. editor.
Joe Quesada/Chief.

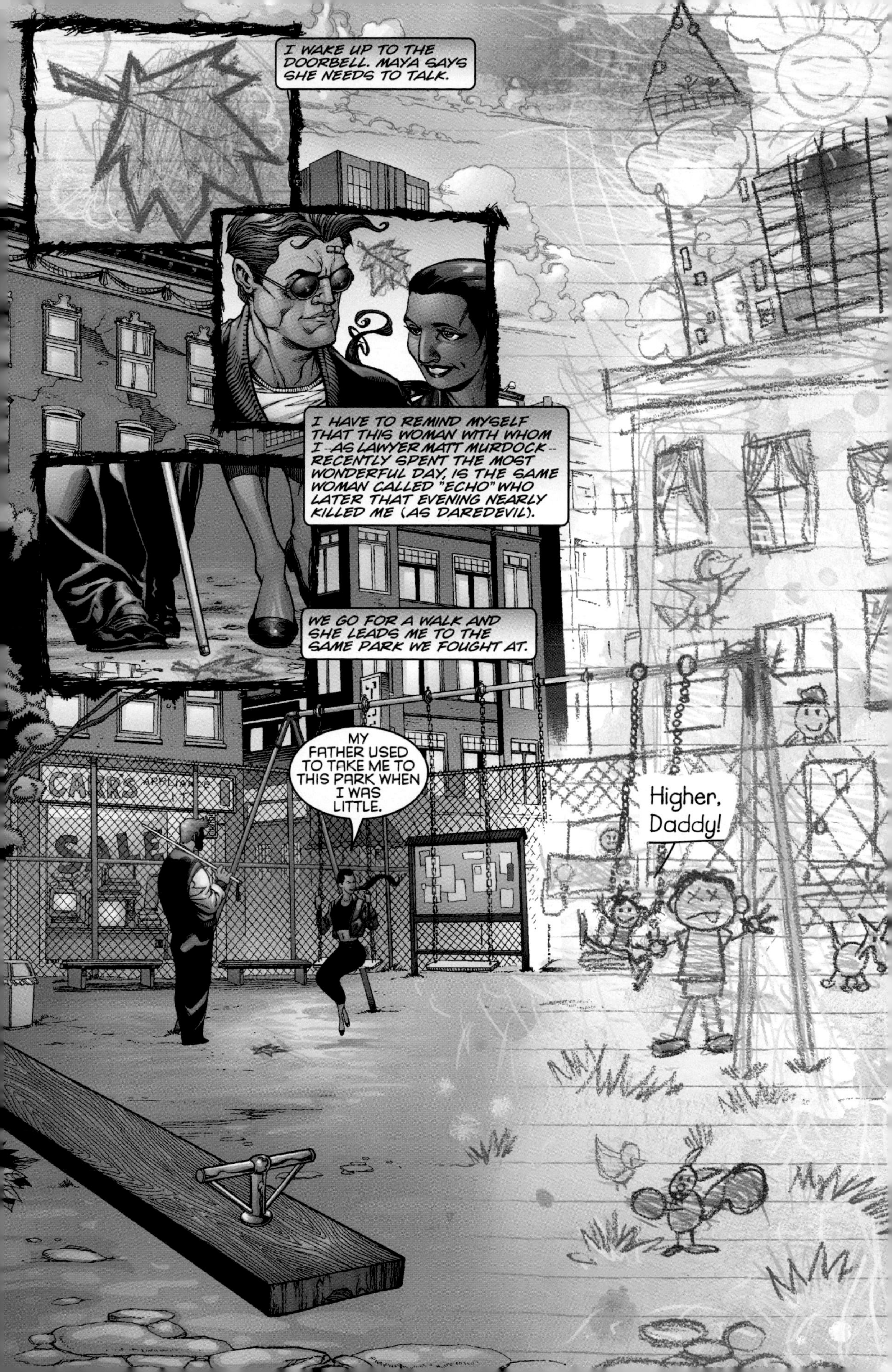
I WAKE UP TO THE DOORBELL. MAYA SAYS SHE NEEDS TO TALK.
I HAVE TO REMIND MYSELF THAT THIS WOMAN WITH WHOM I--AS LAWYER MATT MURDOCK--RECENTLY SPENT THE MOST WONDERFUL DAY, IS THE SAME WOMAN CALLED "ECHO" WHO LATER THAT EVENING NEARLY KILLED ME (AS DAREDEVIL).
WE GO FOR A WALK AND SHE LEADS ME TO THE SAME PARK WE FOUGHT AT.
MY FATHER USED TO TAKE ME TO THIS PARK WHEN I WAS LITTLE.
Higher, Daddy!
CARR'S
SALE

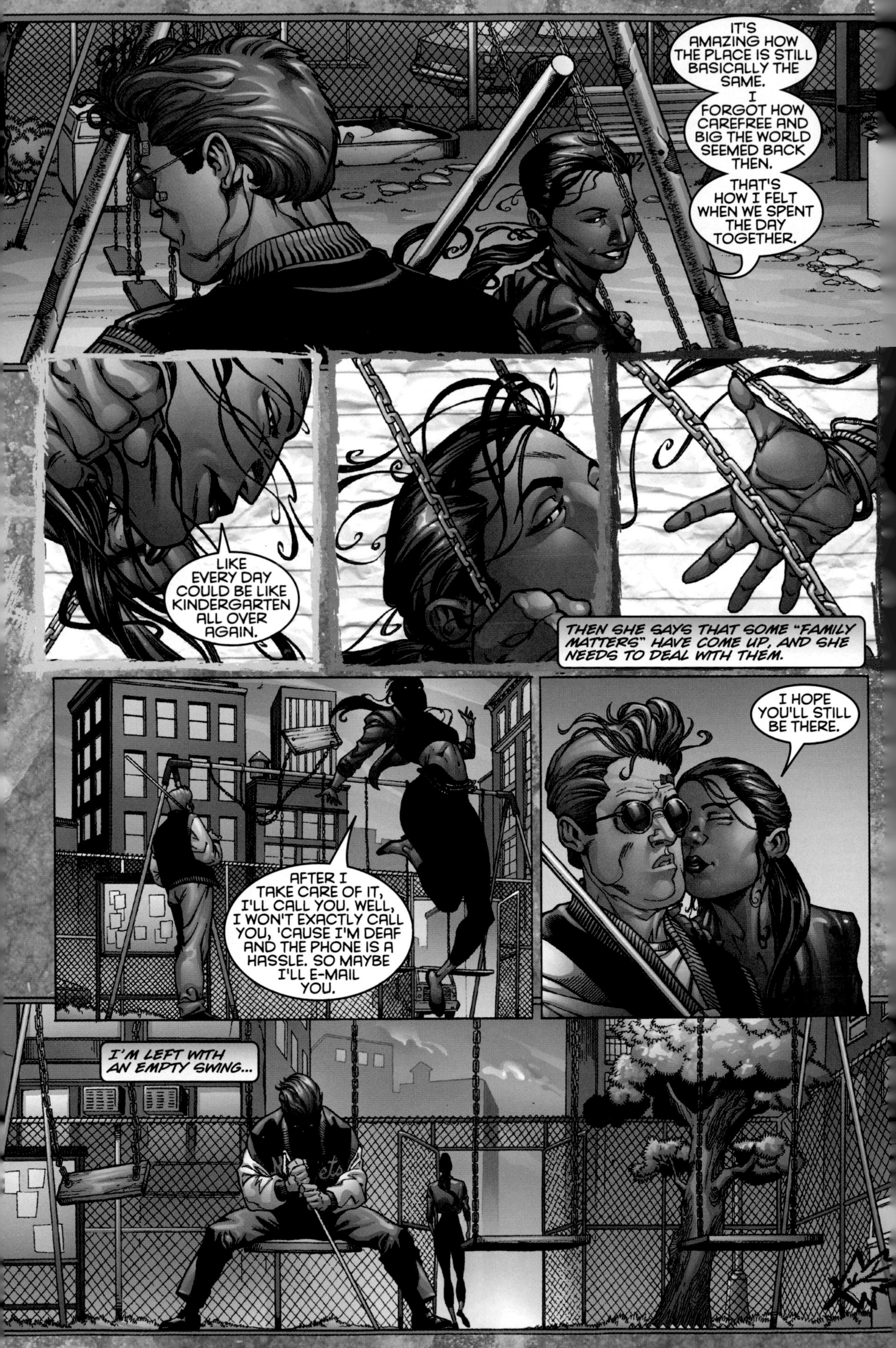

IT'S AMAZING HOW THE PLACE IS STILL BASICALLY THE SAME.
I FORGOT HOW CAREFREE AND BIG THE WORLD SEEMED BACK THEN.
THAT'S HOW I FELT WHEN WE SPENT THE DAY TOGETHER.
LIKE EVERY DAY COULD BE LIKE KINDERGARTEN ALL OVER AGAIN.
THEN SHE SAYS THAT SOME "FAMILY MATTERS" HAVE COME UP, AND SHE NEEDS TO DEAL WITH THEM.
AFTER I TAKE CARE OF IT, I'LL CALL YOU. WELL, I WON'T EXACTLY CALL YOU, 'CAUSE I'M DEAF AND THE PHONE IS A HASSLE. SO MAYBE I'LL E-MAIL YOU.
I HOPE YOU'LL STILL BE THERE.
I'M LEFT WITH AN EMPTY SWING...

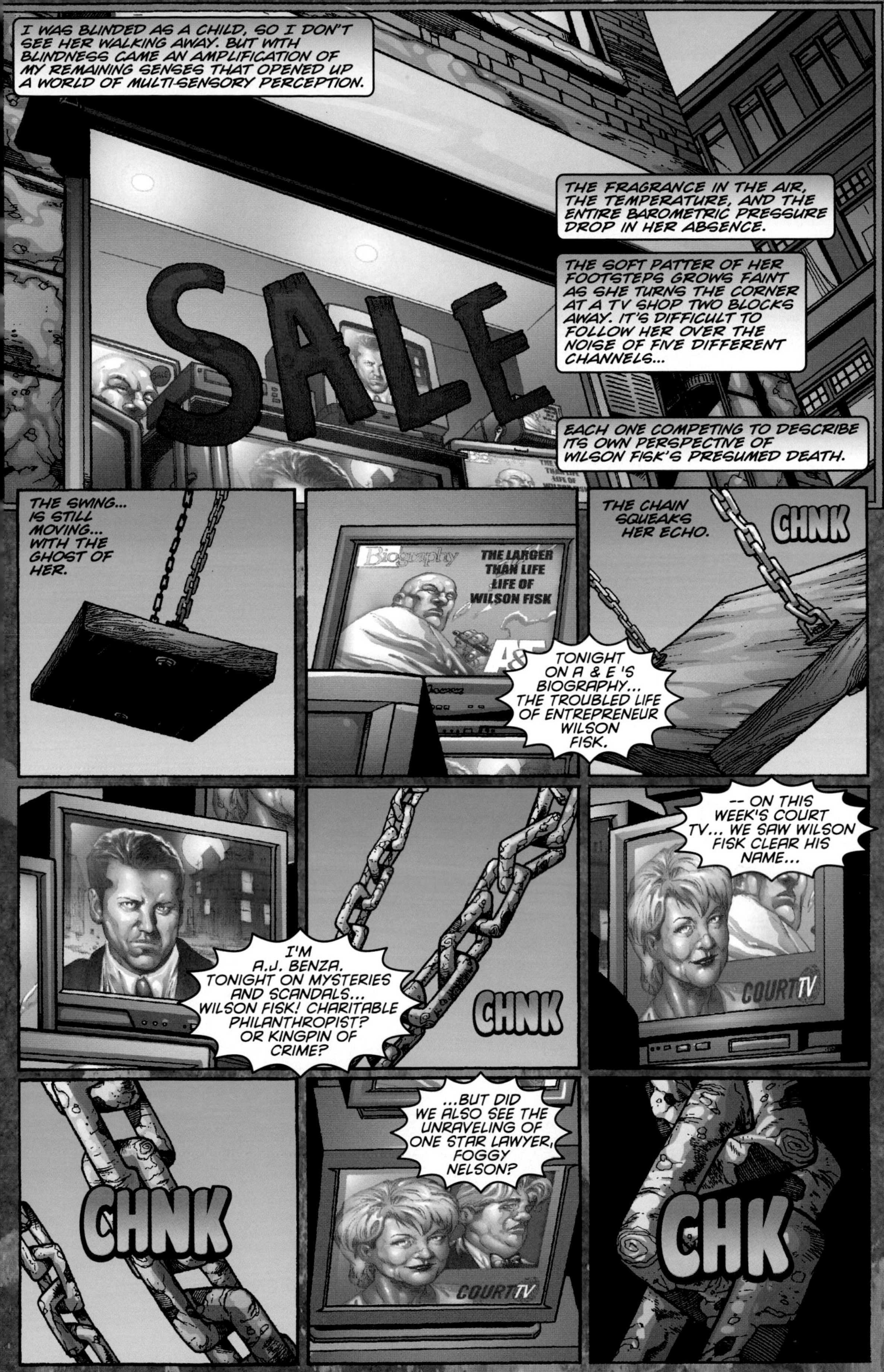
I WAS BLINDED AS A CHILD, SO I DON'T SEE HER WALKING AWAY. BUT WITH BLINDNESS CAME AN AMPLIFICATION OF MY REMAINING SENSES THAT OPENED UP A WORLD OF MULTI-SENSORY PERCEPTION.
SALE
THE FRAGRANCE IN THE AIR, THE TEMPERATURE, AND THE ENTIRE BAROMETRIC PRESSURE DROP IN HER ABSENCE.
THE SOFT PATTER OF HER FOOTSTEPS GROWS FAINT AS SHE TURNS THE CORNER AT A TV SHOP TWO BLOCKS AWAY. IT'S DIFFICULT TO FOLLOW HER OVER THE NOISE OF FIVE DIFFERENT CHANNELS...
EACH ONE COMPETING TO DESCRIBE ITS OWN PERSPECTIVE OF WILSON FISK'S PRESUMED DEATH.
THE SWING... IS STILL MOVING... WITH THE GHOST OF HER.
Biography
THE LARGER THAN LIFE LIFE OF WILSON FISK
TONIGHT ON A & E'S BIOGRAPHY... THE TROUBLED LIFE OF ENTREPRENEUR WILSON FISK.
THE CHAIN SQUEAKS HER ECHO.
CHNK
I'M A.J. BENZA. TONIGHT ON MYSTERIES AND SCANDALS... WILSON FISK! CHARITABLE PHILANTHROPIST? OR KINGPIN OF CRIME?
CHNK
-- ON THIS WEEK'S COURT TV... WE SAW WILSON FISK CLEAR HIS NAME...
COURT TV
CHNK
...BUT DID WE ALSO SEE THE UNRAVELING OF ONE STAR LAWYER, FOGGY NELSON?
COURT TV
CHK

CHNK

FAP

CHNK

FAP

WITH THE KINGPIN GONE, THE OTHER CRIME FAMILIES WILL WANT TO FILL THE VACUUM.

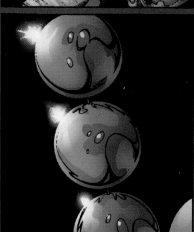

I TURN OVER THE REST OF THE KINGPIN'S FILES TO FOGGY.

ALL THE DIRT... FROM COPS TO CARDINALS, TO THE OTHER FAMILIES, TO PRIVATE INDUSTRY, TO SENATORS.

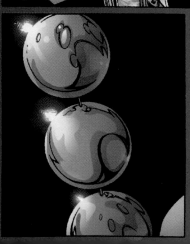

SPECIAL ASSISTANT DISTRICT ATTORNEY FOGGY NELSON TAKES IT TO COURT.

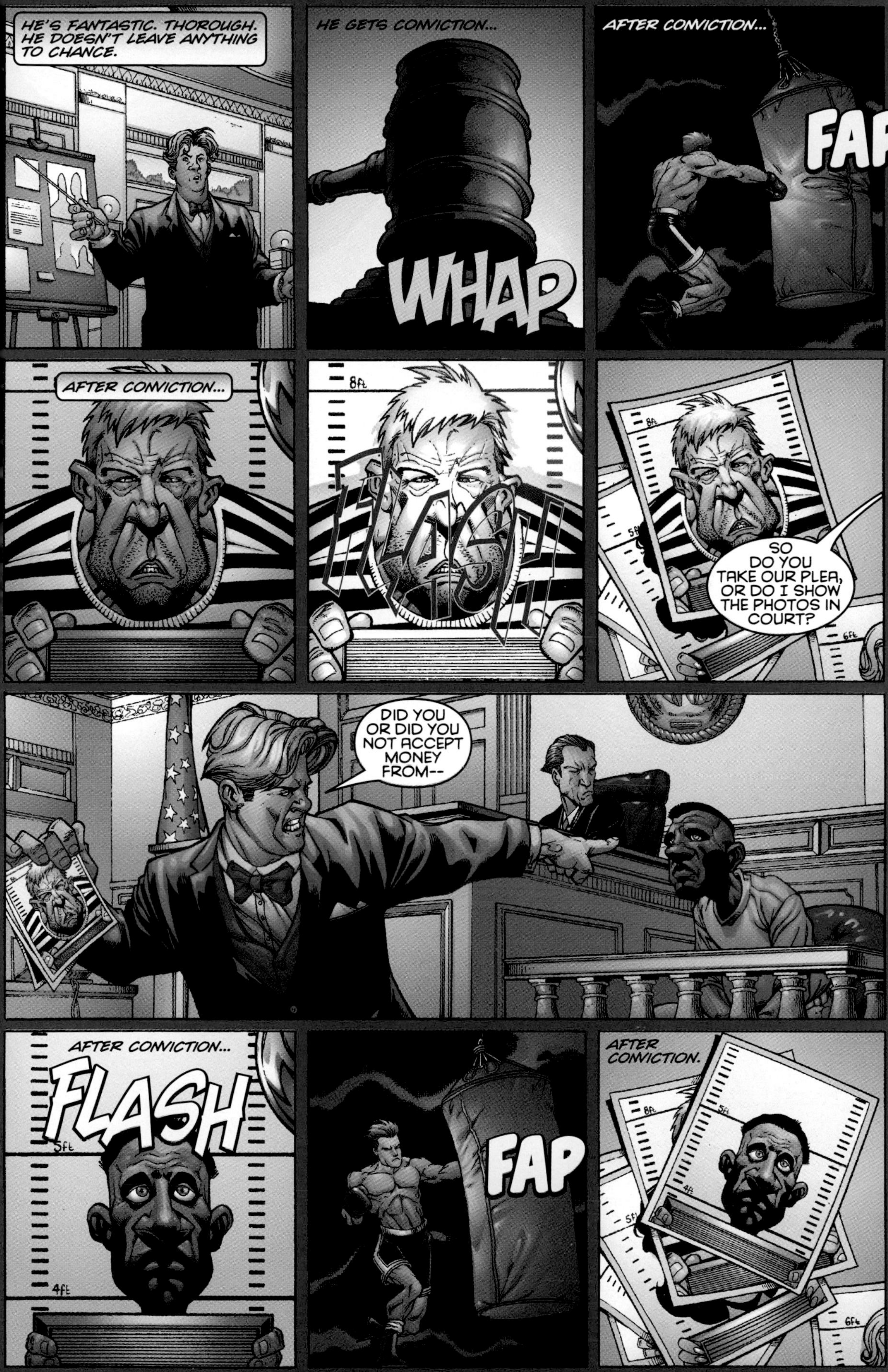
HE'S FANTASTIC. THOROUGH. HE DOESN'T LEAVE ANYTHING TO CHANCE.
HE GETS CONVICTION...
WHAP
AFTER CONVICTION...
FAP
AFTER CONVICTION...
8ft
FLASH
8ft
5ft
6ft
SO DO YOU TAKE OUR PLEA, OR DO I SHOW THE PHOTOS IN COURT?
DID YOU OR DID YOU NOT ACCEPT MONEY FROM--
AFTER CONVICTION...
FLASH
5ft
4ft
FAP
AFTER CONVICTION.
8ft
5ft
4ft
5ft
6ft

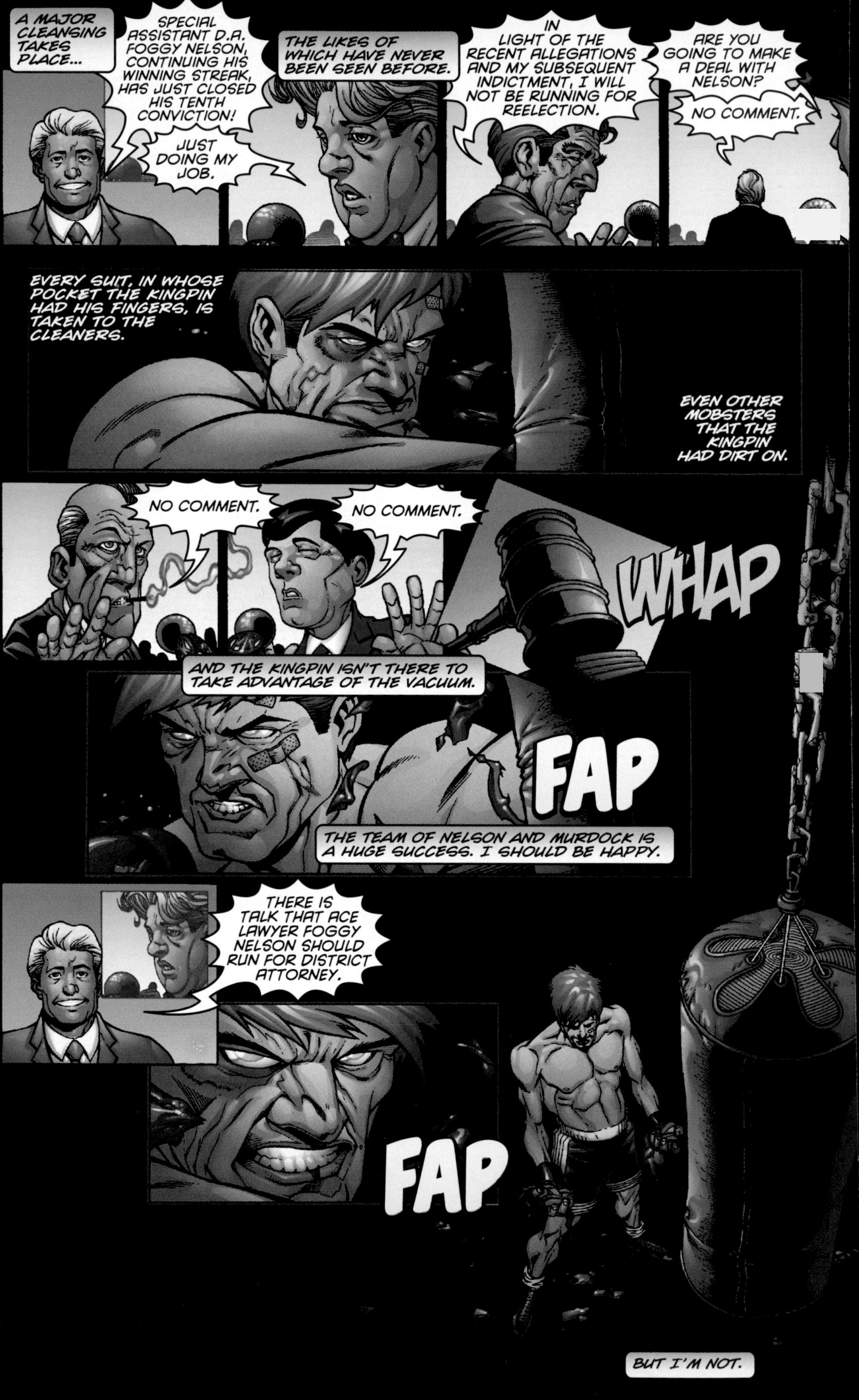
A MAJOR CLEANSING TAKES PLACE...
SPECIAL ASSISTANT D.A. FOGGY NELSON, CONTINUING HIS WINNING STREAK, HAS JUST CLOSED HIS TENTH CONVICTION!
JUST DOING MY JOB.
THE LIKES OF WHICH HAVE NEVER BEEN SEEN BEFORE.
IN LIGHT OF THE RECENT ALLEGATIONS AND MY SUBSEQUENT INDICTMENT, I WILL NOT BE RUNNING FOR REELECTION.
ARE YOU GOING TO MAKE A DEAL WITH NELSON?
NO COMMENT.
EVERY SUIT, IN WHOSE POCKET THE KINGPIN HAD HIS FINGERS, IS TAKEN TO THE CLEANERS.
EVEN OTHER MOBSTERS THAT THE KINGPIN HAD DIRT ON.
NO COMMENT.
NO COMMENT.
WHAP
AND THE KINGPIN ISN'T THERE TO TAKE ADVANTAGE OF THE VACUUM.
FAP
THE TEAM OF NELSON AND MURDOCK IS A HUGE SUCCESS. I SHOULD BE HAPPY.
THERE IS TALK THAT ACE LAWYER FOGGY NELSON SHOULD RUN FOR DISTRICT ATTORNEY.
FAP
BUT I'M NOT.

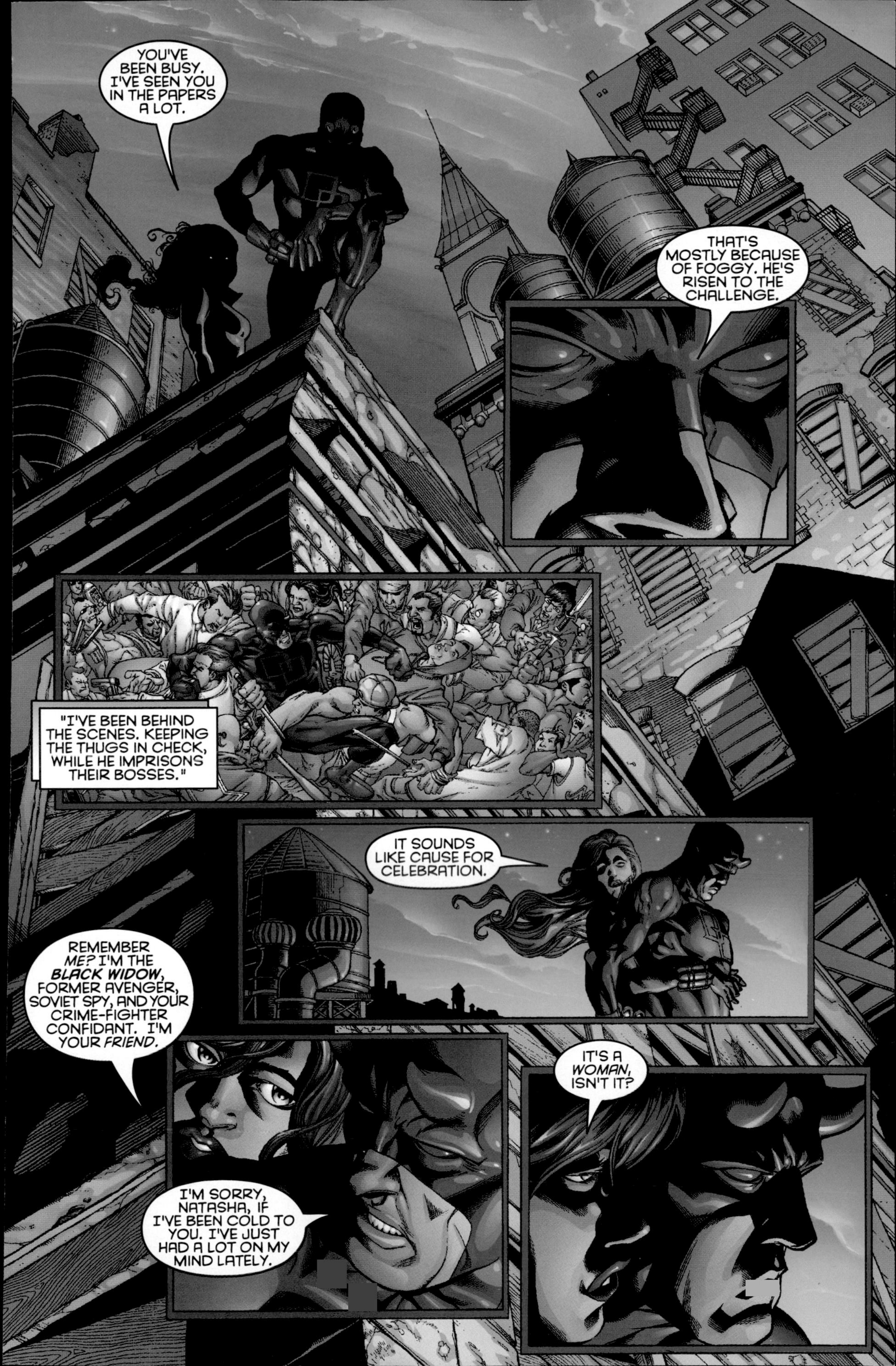
YOU'VE BEEN BUSY. I'VE SEEN YOU IN THE PAPERS A LOT.
THAT'S MOSTLY BECAUSE OF FOGGY. HE'S RISEN TO THE CHALLENGE.
"I'VE BEEN BEHIND THE SCENES. KEEPING THE THUGS IN CHECK, WHILE HE IMPRISONS THEIR BOSSES."
IT SOUNDS LIKE CAUSE FOR CELEBRATION.
REMEMBER *ME?* I'M THE ***BLACK WIDOW***, FORMER AVENGER, SOVIET SPY, AND YOUR CRIME-FIGHTER CONFIDANT. I'M YOUR *FRIEND*.
I'M SORRY, NATASHA, IF I'VE BEEN COLD TO YOU. I'VE JUST HAD A LOT ON MY MIND LATELY.
IT'S A *WOMAN*, ISN'T IT?

"IT'S SORT OF COMPLICATED."

I'LL BET. WITH YOU IT ALWAYS IS.

"I'M NOT EXACTLY SURE HOW ALL THE PIECES FIT TOGETHER."

OR WHY HER ANGER...

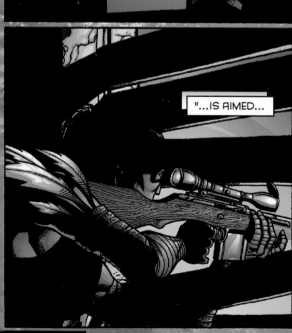

"...IS AIMED...

"...AT DAREDEVIL."

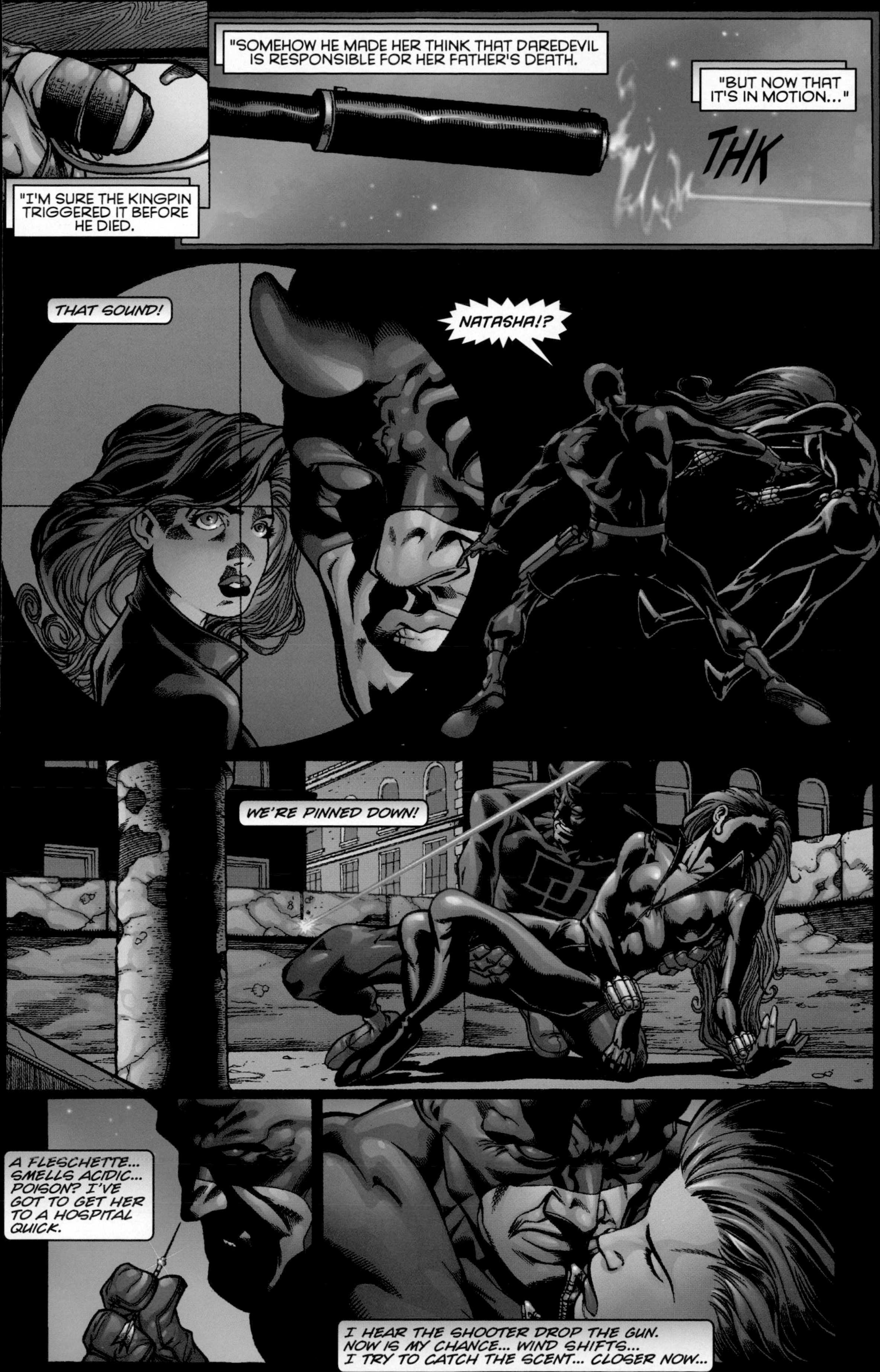
"SOMEHOW HE MADE HER THINK THAT DAREDEVIL IS RESPONSIBLE FOR HER FATHER'S DEATH.
"I'M SURE THE KINGPIN TRIGGERED IT BEFORE HE DIED.
"BUT NOW THAT IT'S IN MOTION..."
THK
THAT SOUND!
NATASHA!?
WE'RE PINNED DOWN!
A FLESCHETTE... SMELLS ACIDIC... POISON? I'VE GOT TO GET HER TO A HOSPITAL QUICK.
I HEAR THE SHOOTER DROP THE GUN. NOW IS MY CHANCE... WIND SHIFTS... I TRY TO CATCH THE SCENT... CLOSER NOW...

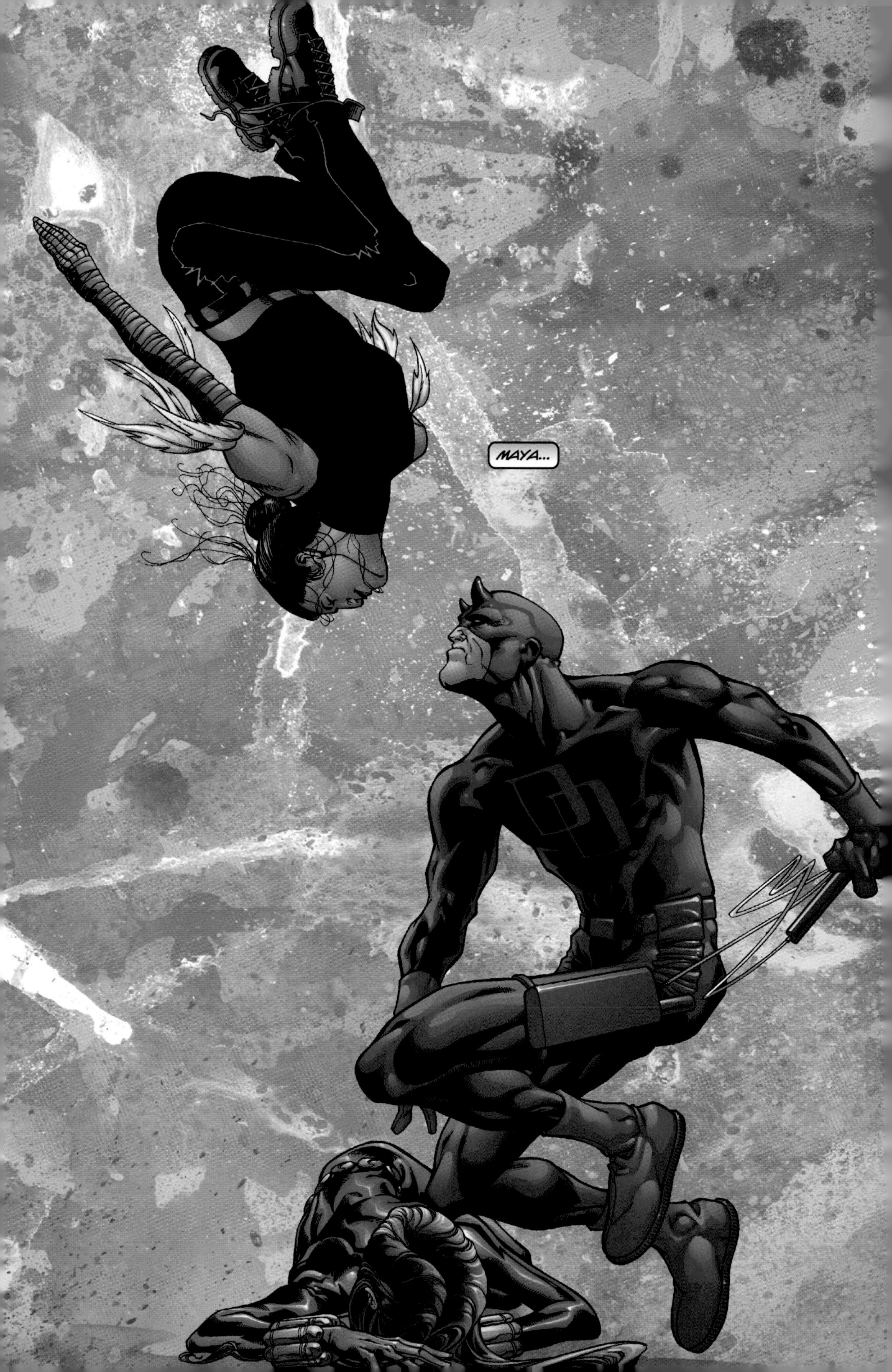
MAYA...

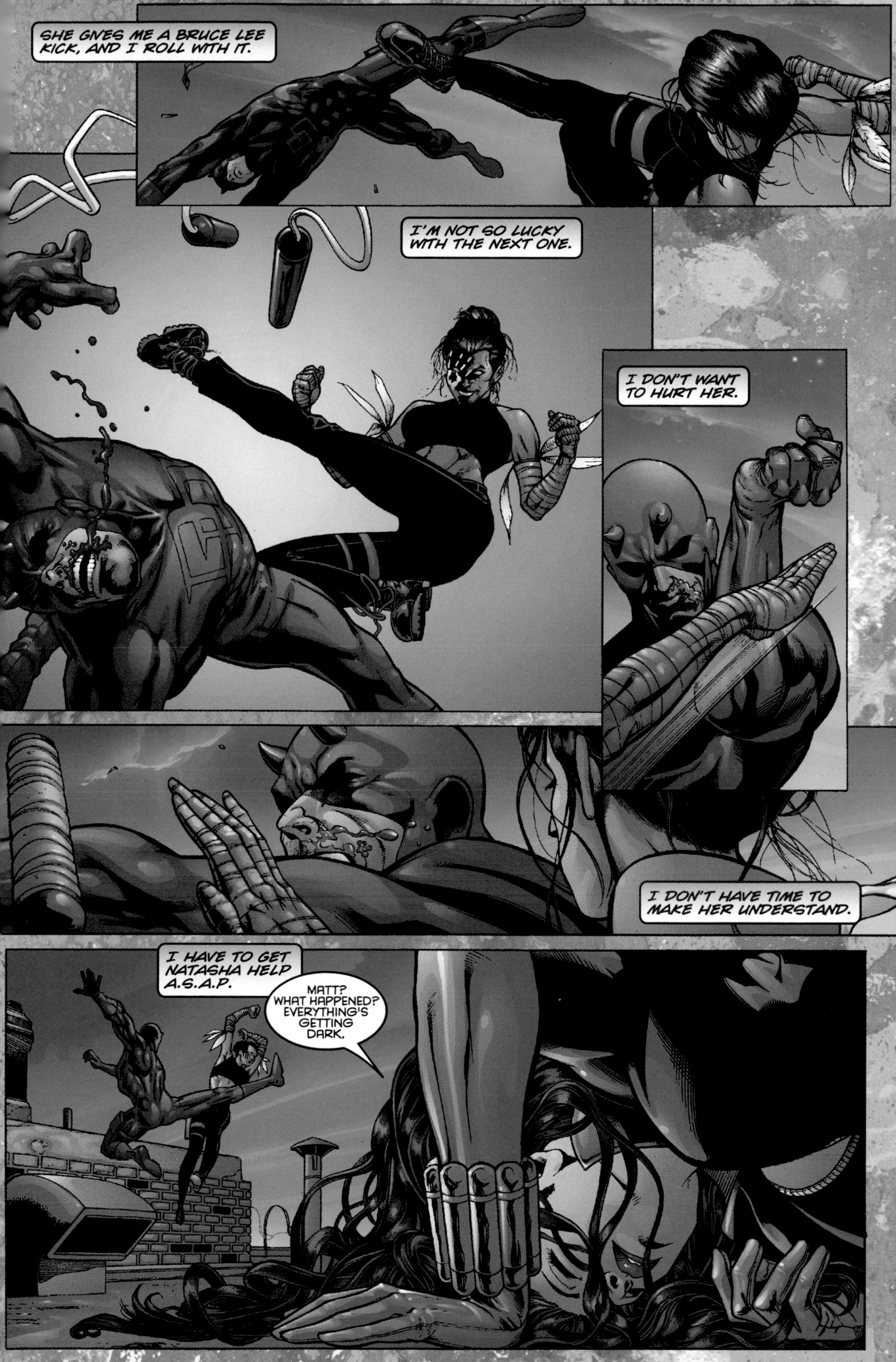
SHE GIVES ME A BRUCE LEE KICK, AND I ROLL WITH IT.
I'M NOT SO LUCKY WITH THE NEXT ONE.
I DON'T WANT TO HURT HER.
I DON'T HAVE TIME TO MAKE HER UNDERSTAND.
I HAVE TO GET NATASHA HELP A.S.A.P.
MATT? WHAT HAPPENED? EVERYTHING'S GETTING DARK.

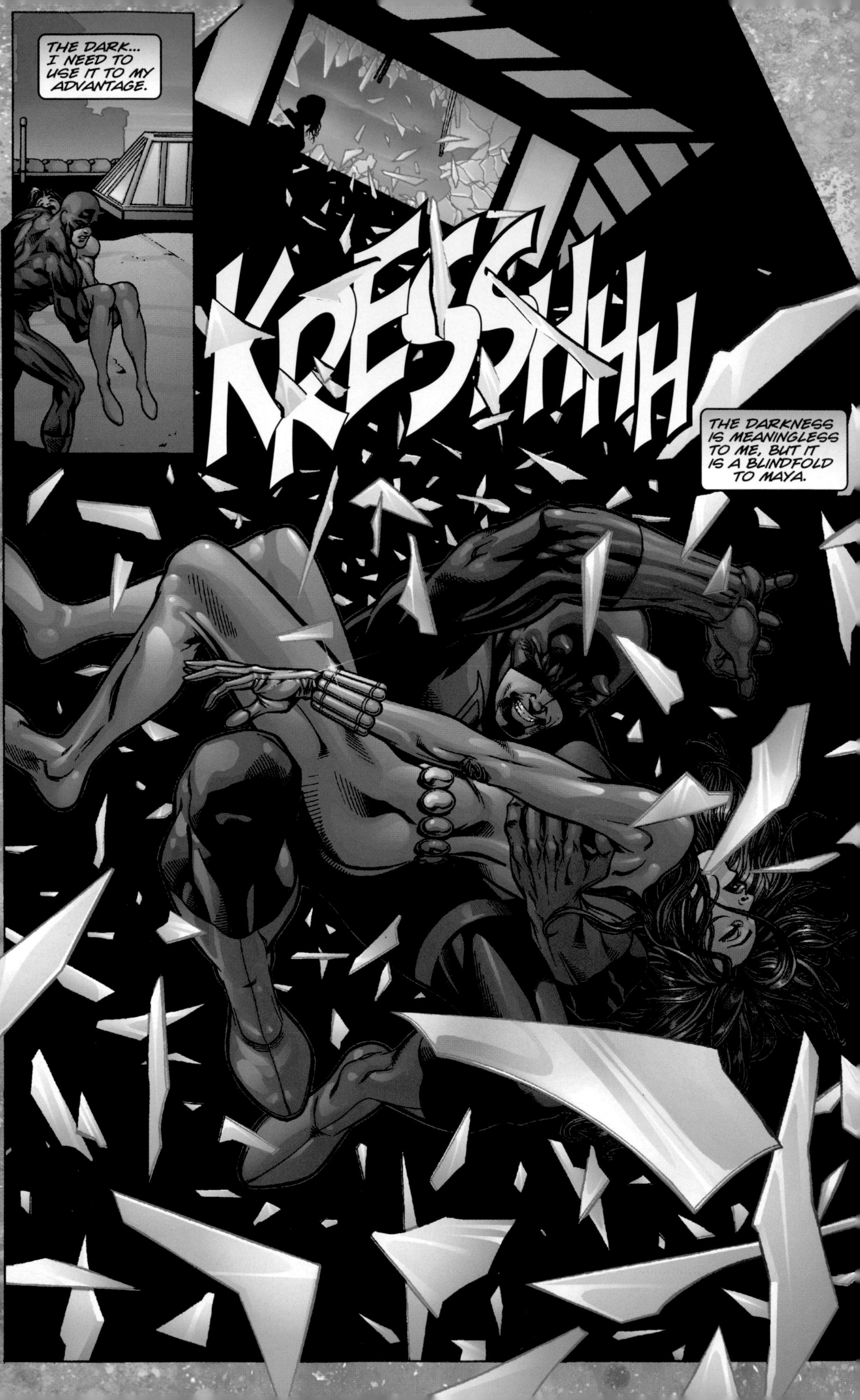
THE DARK... I NEED TO USE IT TO MY ADVANTAGE.
KRESSHHH
THE DARKNESS IS MEANINGLESS TO ME, BUT IT IS A BLINDFOLD TO MAYA.

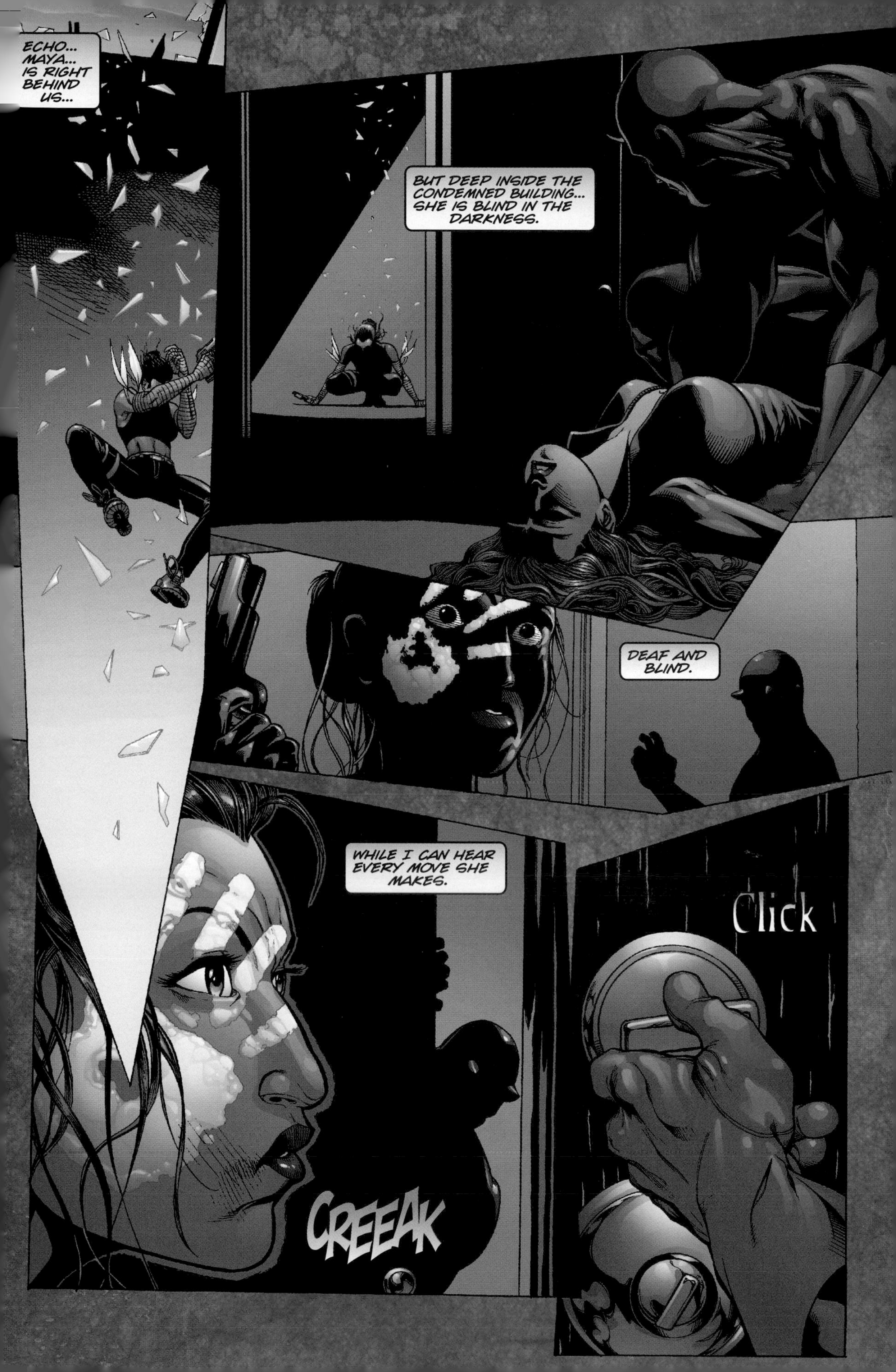
ECHO... MAYA... IS RIGHT BEHIND US...
BUT DEEP INSIDE THE CONDEMNED BUILDING... SHE IS BLIND IN THE DARKNESS.
DEAF AND BLIND.
WHILE I CAN HEAR EVERY MOVE SHE MAKES.
Click
CREEAK

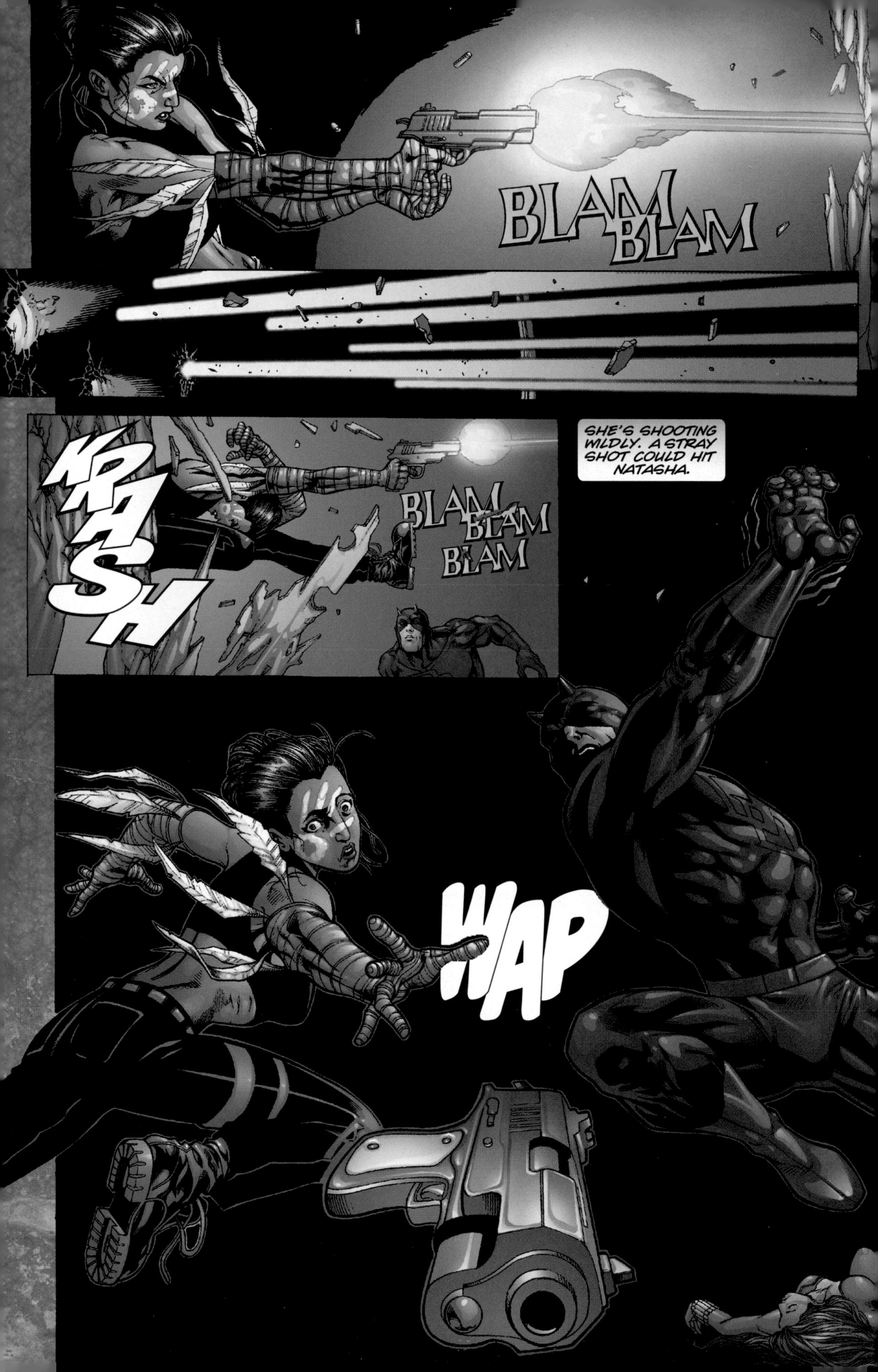
BLAM BLAM
KRASH
BLAM BLAM BLAM
SHE'S SHOOTING WILDLY. A STRAY SHOT COULD HIT NATASHA.
WAP

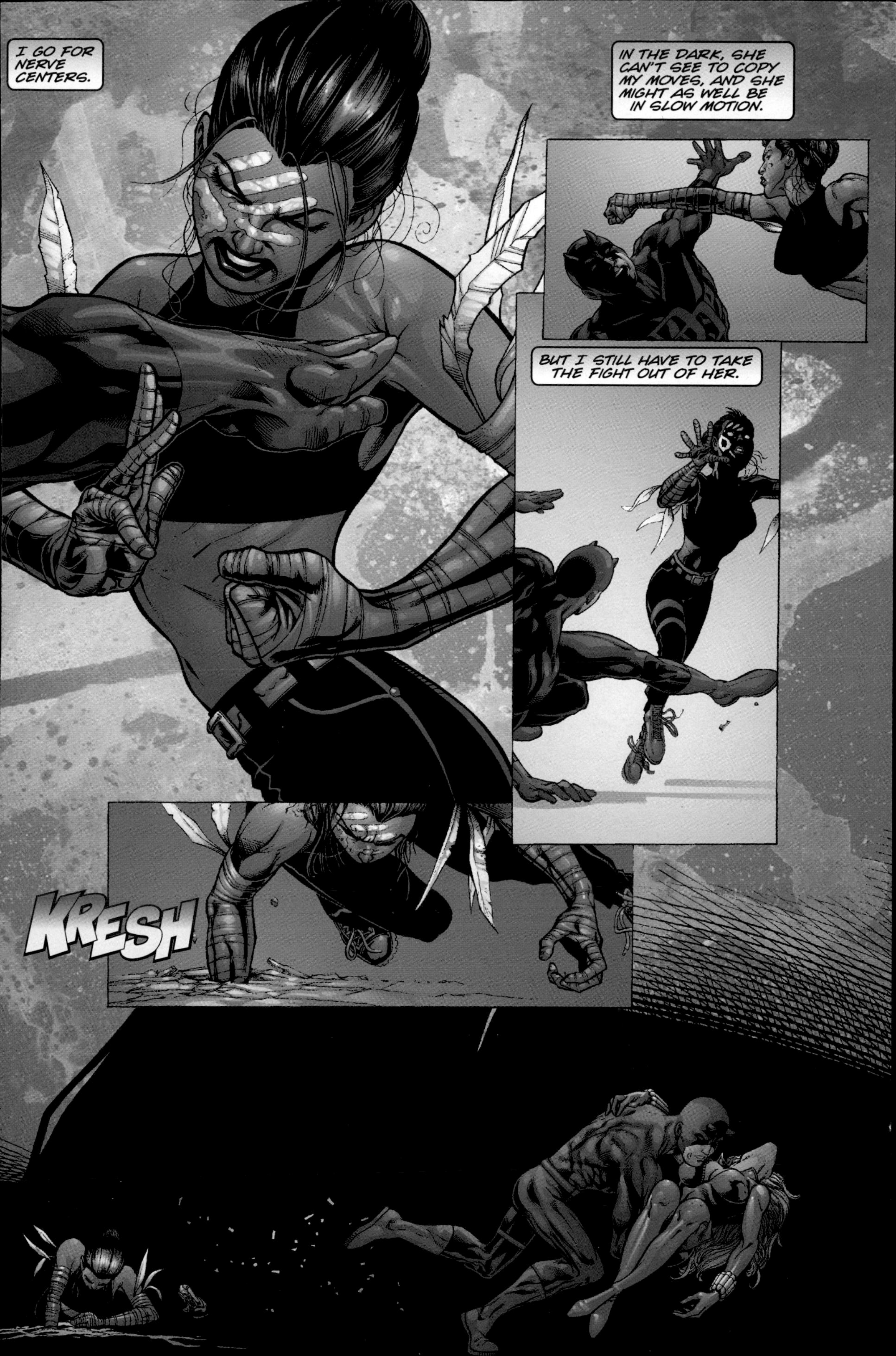

I GO FOR NERVE CENTERS.
IN THE DARK, SHE CAN'T SEE TO COPY MY MOVES, AND SHE MIGHT AS WELL BE IN SLOW MOTION.
BUT I STILL HAVE TO TAKE THE FIGHT OUT OF HER.
KRESH

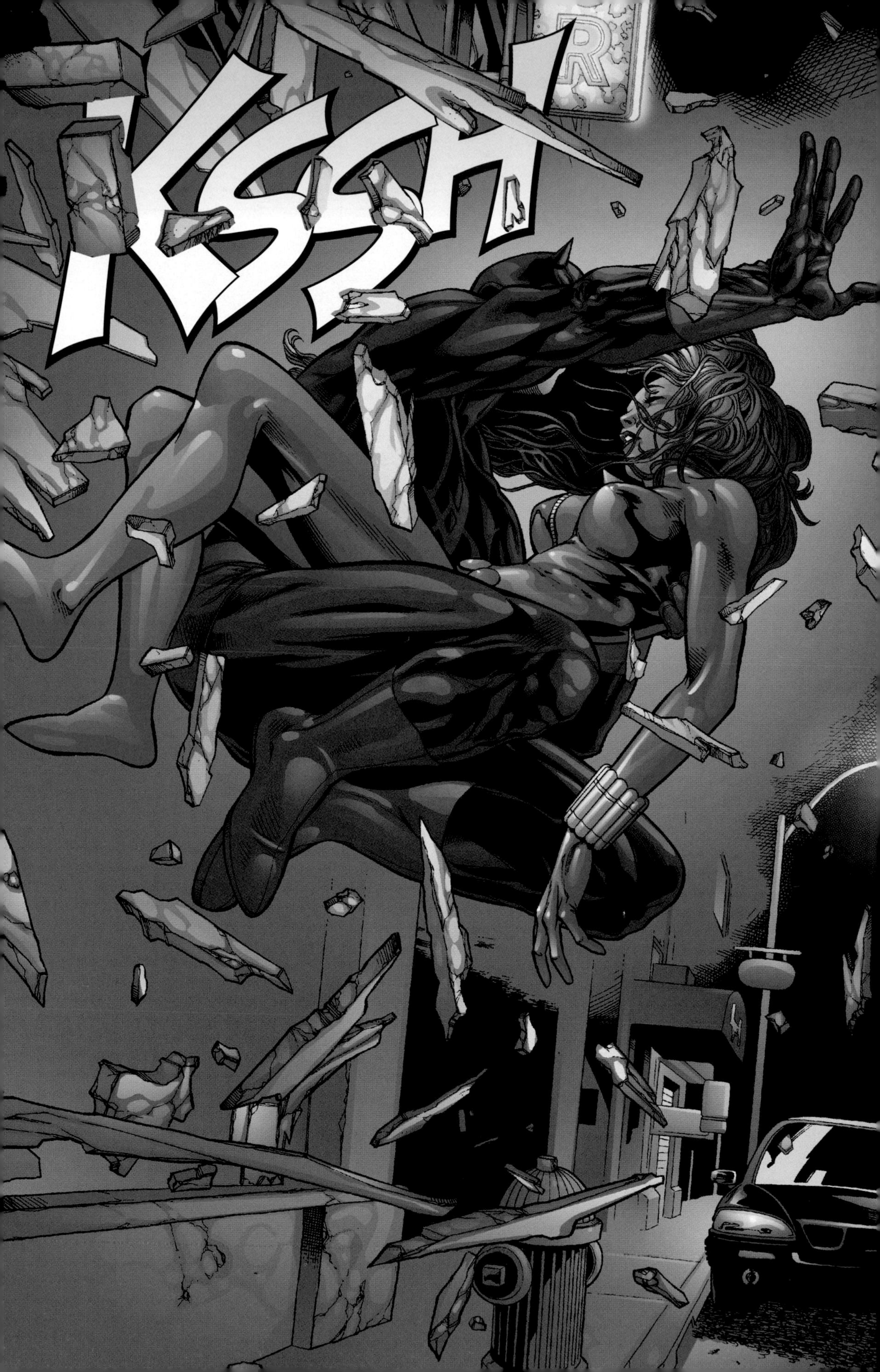
KSSH

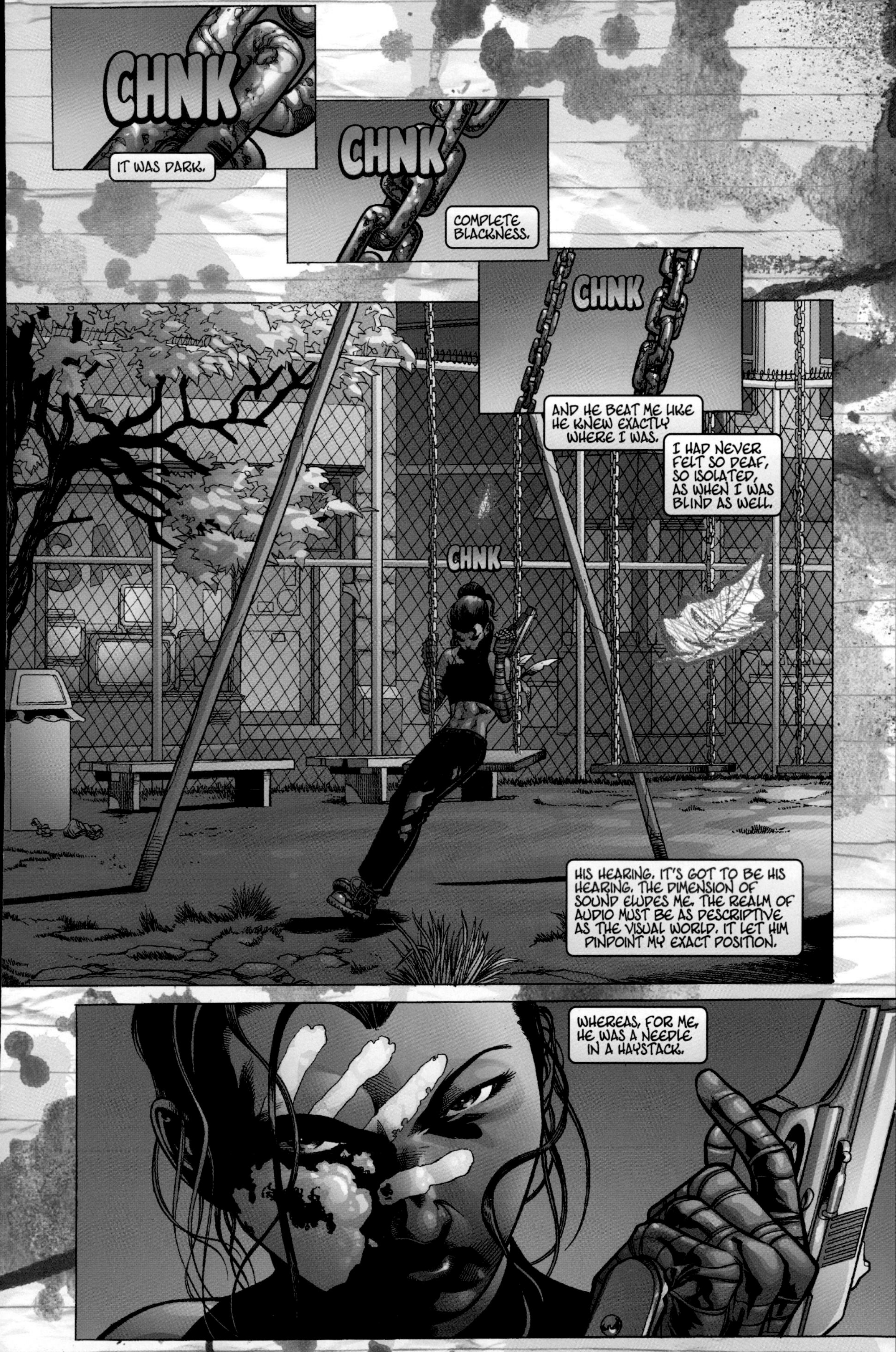
CHNK
IT WAS DARK.
CHNK
COMPLETE BLACKNESS.
CHNK
AND HE BEAT ME LIKE HE KNEW EXACTLY WHERE I WAS.
I HAD NEVER FELT SO DEAF, SO ISOLATED, AS WHEN I WAS BLIND AS WELL.
CHNK
HIS HEARING. IT'S GOT TO BE HIS HEARING. THE DIMENSION OF SOUND ELUDES ME. THE REALM OF AUDIO MUST BE AS DESCRIPTIVE AS THE VISUAL WORLD. IT LET HIM PINPOINT MY EXACT POSITION.
WHEREAS, FOR ME, HE WAS A NEEDLE IN A HAYSTACK.

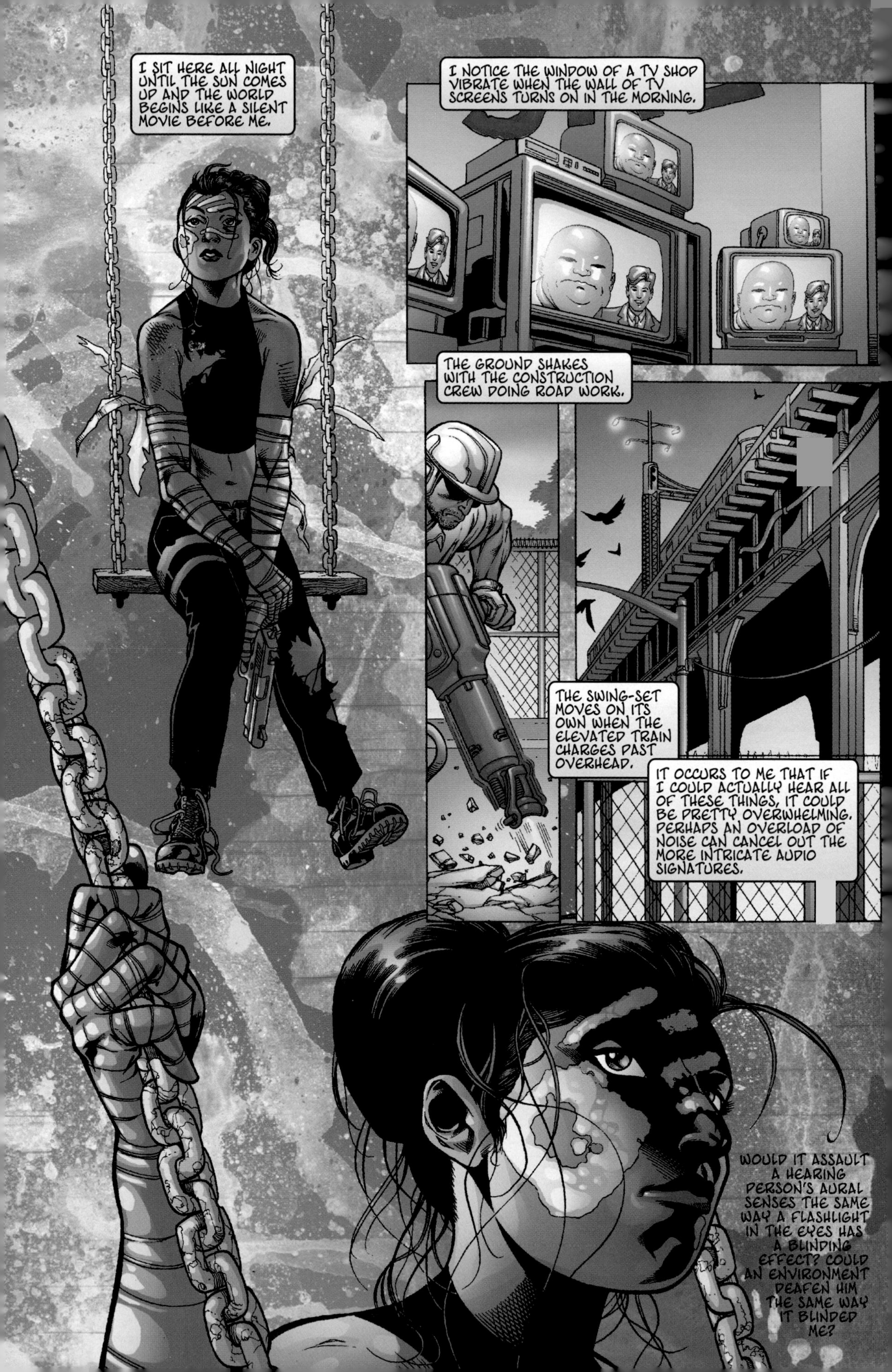
I SIT HERE ALL NIGHT UNTIL THE SUN COMES UP AND THE WORLD BEGINS LIKE A SILENT MOVIE BEFORE ME.
I NOTICE THE WINDOW OF A TV SHOP VIBRATE WHEN THE WALL OF TV SCREENS TURNS ON IN THE MORNING.
THE GROUND SHAKES WITH THE CONSTRUCTION CREW DOING ROAD WORK.
THE SWING-SET MOVES ON ITS OWN WHEN THE ELEVATED TRAIN CHARGES PAST OVERHEAD.
IT OCCURS TO ME THAT IF I COULD ACTUALLY HEAR ALL OF THESE THINGS, IT COULD BE PRETTY OVERWHELMING. PERHAPS AN OVERLOAD OF NOISE CAN CANCEL OUT THE MORE INTRICATE AUDIO SIGNATURES.
WOULD IT ASSAULT A HEARING PERSON'S AURAL SENSES THE SAME WAY A FLASHLIGHT IN THE EYES HAS A BLINDING EFFECT? COULD AN ENVIRONMENT DEAFEN HIM THE SAME WAY IT BLINDED ME?

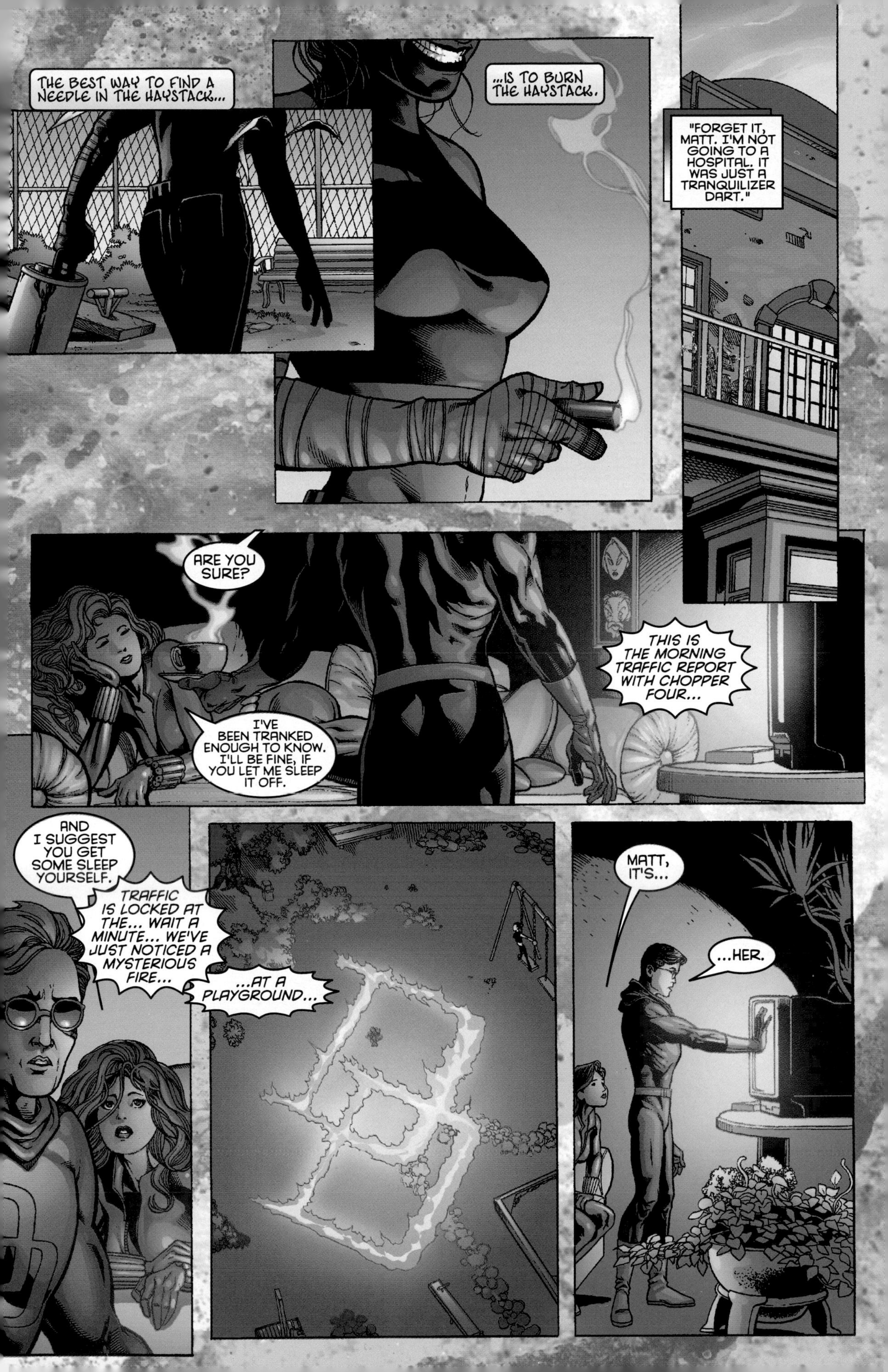
THE BEST WAY TO FIND A NEEDLE IN THE HAYSTACK...
...IS TO BURN THE HAYSTACK.
"FORGET IT, MATT. I'M NOT GOING TO A HOSPITAL. IT WAS JUST A TRANQUILIZER DART."
ARE YOU SURE?
I'VE BEEN TRANKED ENOUGH TO KNOW. I'LL BE FINE, IF YOU LET ME SLEEP IT OFF.
THIS IS THE MORNING TRAFFIC REPORT WITH CHOPPER FOUR...
AND I SUGGEST YOU GET SOME SLEEP YOURSELF.
TRAFFIC IS LOCKED AT THE... WAIT A MINUTE... WE'VE JUST NOTICED A MYSTERIOUS FIRE...
...AT A PLAYGROUND...
MATT, IT'S...
...HER.

HELICOPTER, TRAIN, TELEVISION, RADIO,
JACKHAMMER, GAZOLINE, SMOKE, FIRE,
IT'S JUST A LIGHT SHOW TO ME.
BUT IT SHOULD OVERWHELM HIS SENSES.
THE DARKNESS WAS HIS ELEMENT.
NOW LET HIM FACE MINE.

UNCLE WILSO

THE KINGPIN.

ON PAPER HE WAS A
SHADOW. A BUSINESSMAN.
HE WAS CAREFUL
NOT TO LEAVE A TRAIL...

HE WAS METICULOUS ENOUGH TO AVOID
THE HEAT. MANIPULATIVE ENOUGH TO
HAVE OTHERS DO HIS BIDDING.

HE HAD AN UNDERGROUND EMPIRE...

...IN WHICH AN ARMY OF RATS DID HIS DIRTY WORK.

HE WAS THE MAN BEHIND THE CURTAIN.
HE WAS A PROBLEM SOLVER.
THIS IS JUST ANOTHER SIMPLE PROBLEM.
IT IS NOTHING I CAN'T FIX...

...WITH MY HANDS.

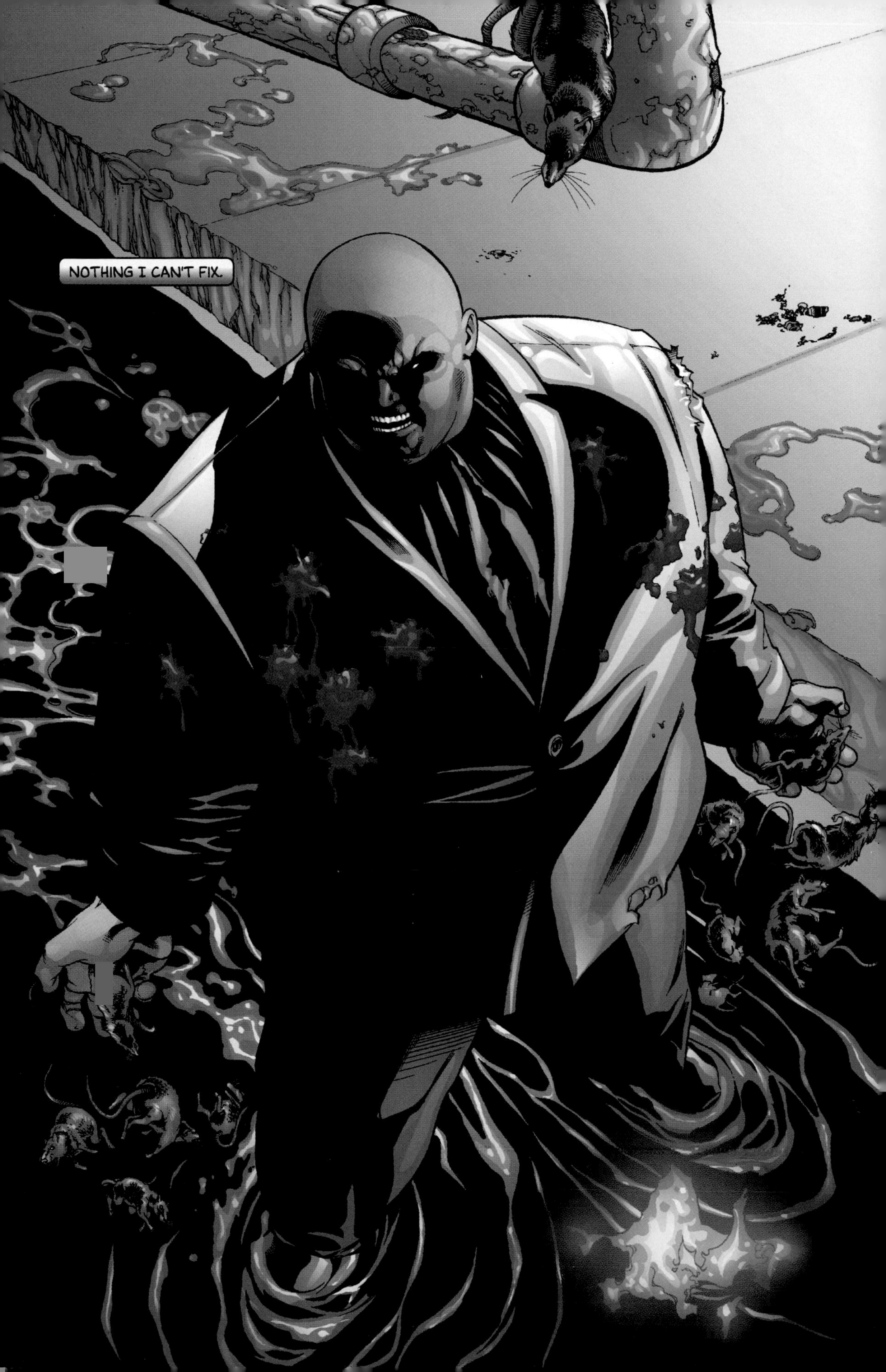
NOTHING I CAN'T FIX.

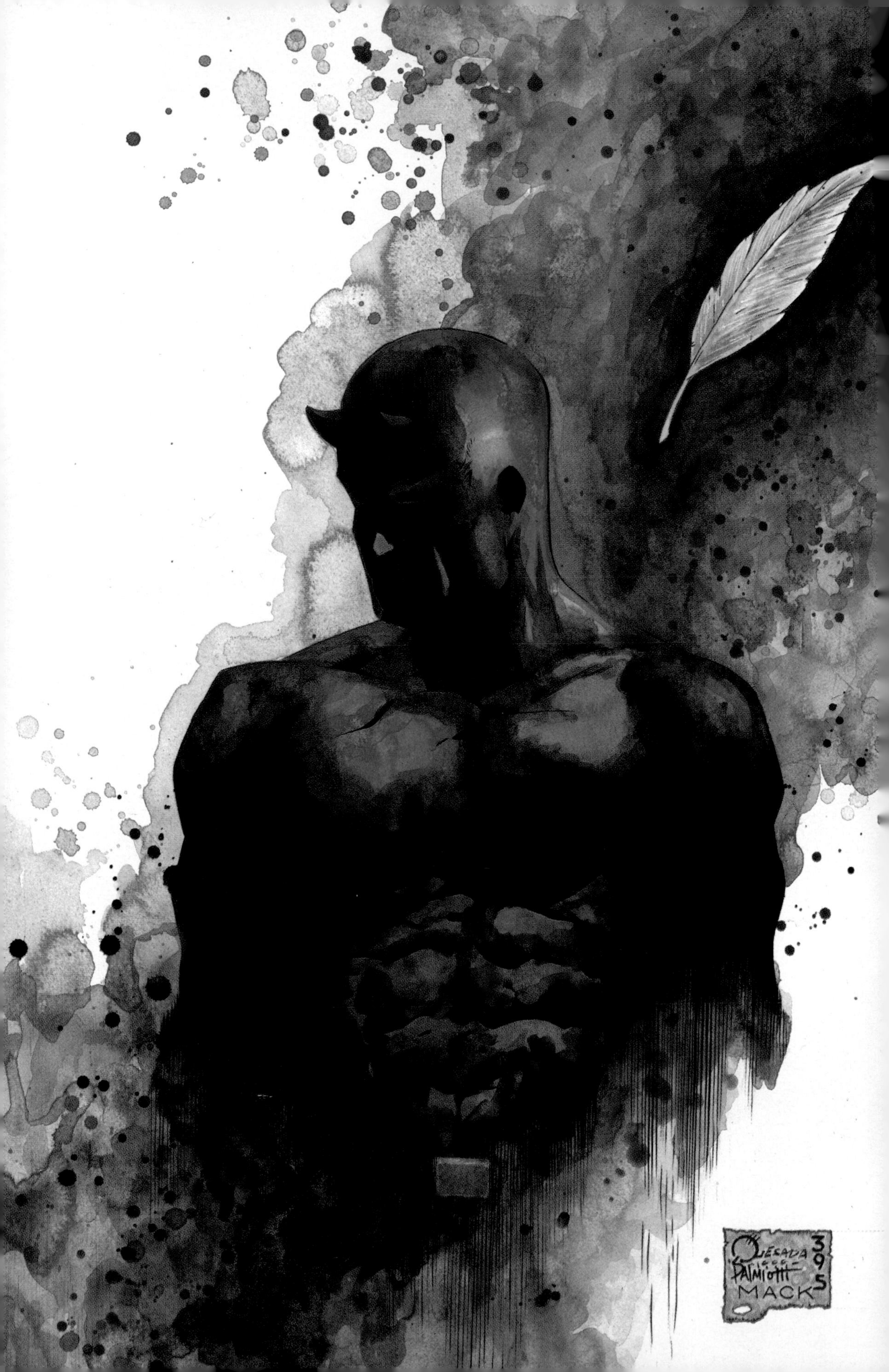
QUESADA
PALMIOTTI
MACK
395

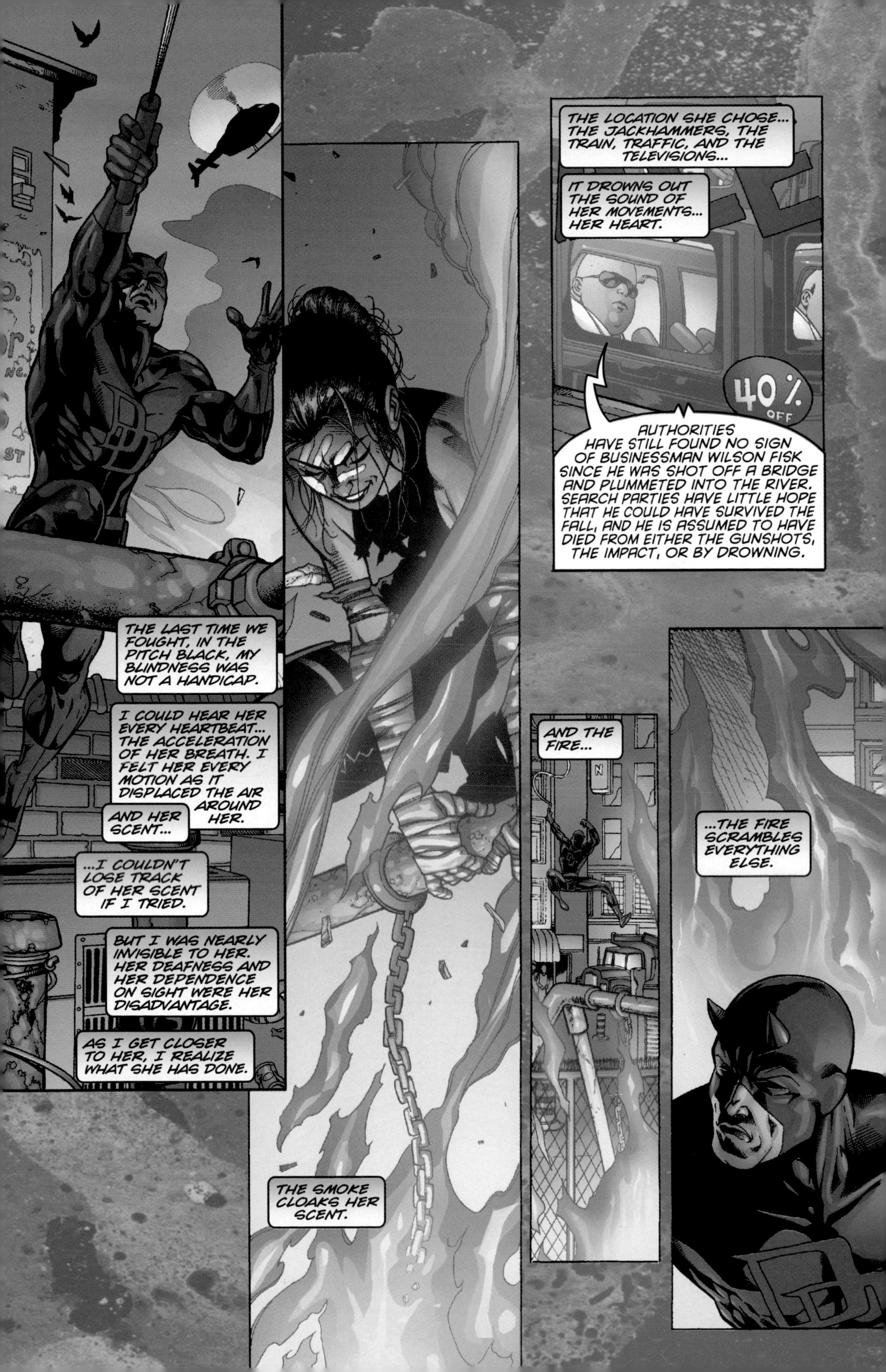
THE LAST TIME WE FOUGHT, IN THE PITCH BLACK, MY BLINDNESS WAS NOT A HANDICAP.
I COULD HEAR HER EVERY HEARTBEAT... THE ACCELERATION OF HER BREATH. I FELT HER EVERY MOTION AS IT DISPLACED THE AIR AROUND HER.
AND HER SCENT...
...I COULDN'T LOSE TRACK OF HER SCENT IF I TRIED.
BUT I WAS NEARLY INVISIBLE TO HER. HER DEAFNESS AND HER DEPENDENCE ON SIGHT WERE HER DISADVANTAGE.
AS I GET CLOSER TO HER, I REALIZE WHAT SHE HAS DONE.
THE SMOKE CLOAKS HER SCENT.
THE LOCATION SHE CHOSE... THE JACKHAMMERS, THE TRAIN, TRAFFIC, AND THE TELEVISIONS...
IT DROWNS OUT THE SOUND OF HER MOVEMENTS... HER HEART.
40% OFF
AUTHORITIES HAVE STILL FOUND NO SIGN OF BUSINESSMAN WILSON FISK SINCE HE WAS SHOT OFF A BRIDGE AND PLUMMETED INTO THE RIVER. SEARCH PARTIES HAVE LITTLE HOPE THAT HE COULD HAVE SURVIVED THE FALL, AND HE IS ASSUMED TO HAVE DIED FROM EITHER THE GUNSHOTS, THE IMPACT, OR BY DROWNING.
AND THE FIRE...
...THE FIRE SCRAMBLES EVERYTHING ELSE.

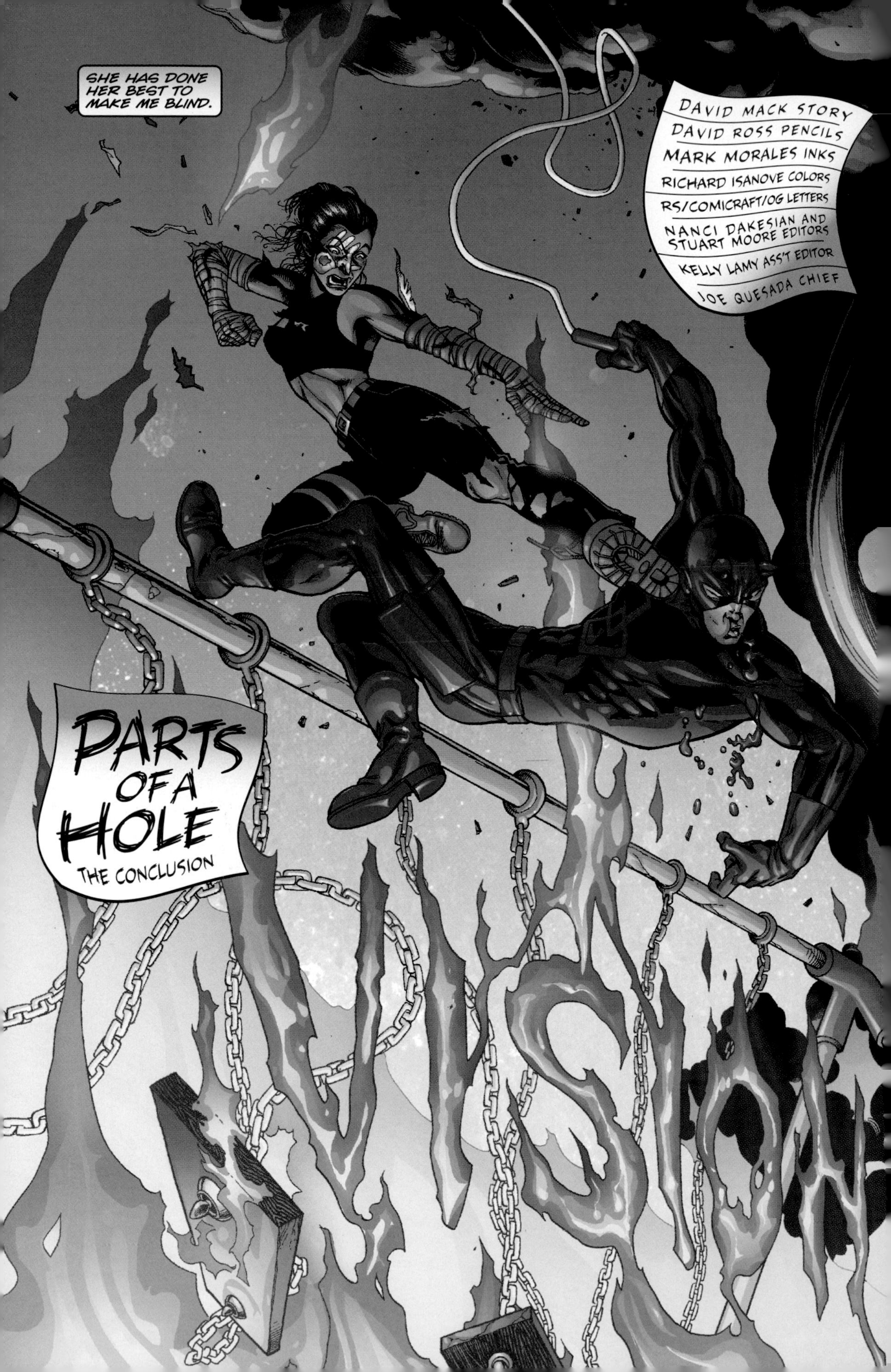
SHE HAS DONE HER BEST TO MAKE ME BLIND.
DAVID MACK STORY
DAVID ROSS PENCILS
MARK MORALES INKS
RICHARD ISANOVE COLORS
RS/COMICRAFT/OG LETTERS
NANCI DAKESIAN AND STUART MOORE EDITORS
KELLY LAMY ASS'T EDITOR
JOE QUESADA CHIEF
PARTS OF A HOLE
THE CONCLUSION

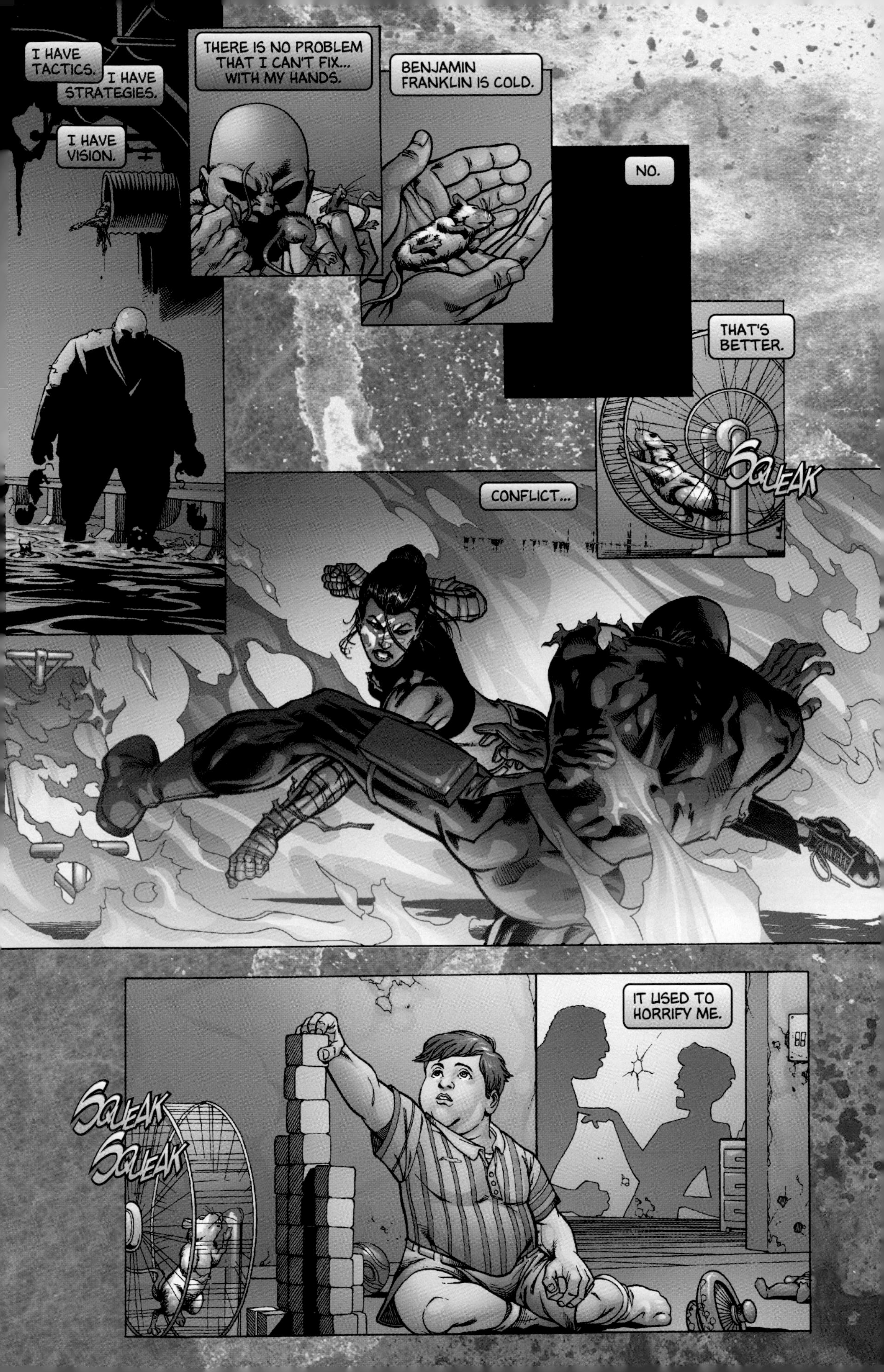
I HAVE TACTICS.
I HAVE STRATEGIES.
I HAVE VISION.
THERE IS NO PROBLEM THAT I CAN'T FIX... WITH MY HANDS.
BENJAMIN FRANKLIN IS COLD.
NO.
THAT'S BETTER.
SQUEAK
CONFLICT...
SQUEAK SQUEAK
IT USED TO HORRIFY ME.

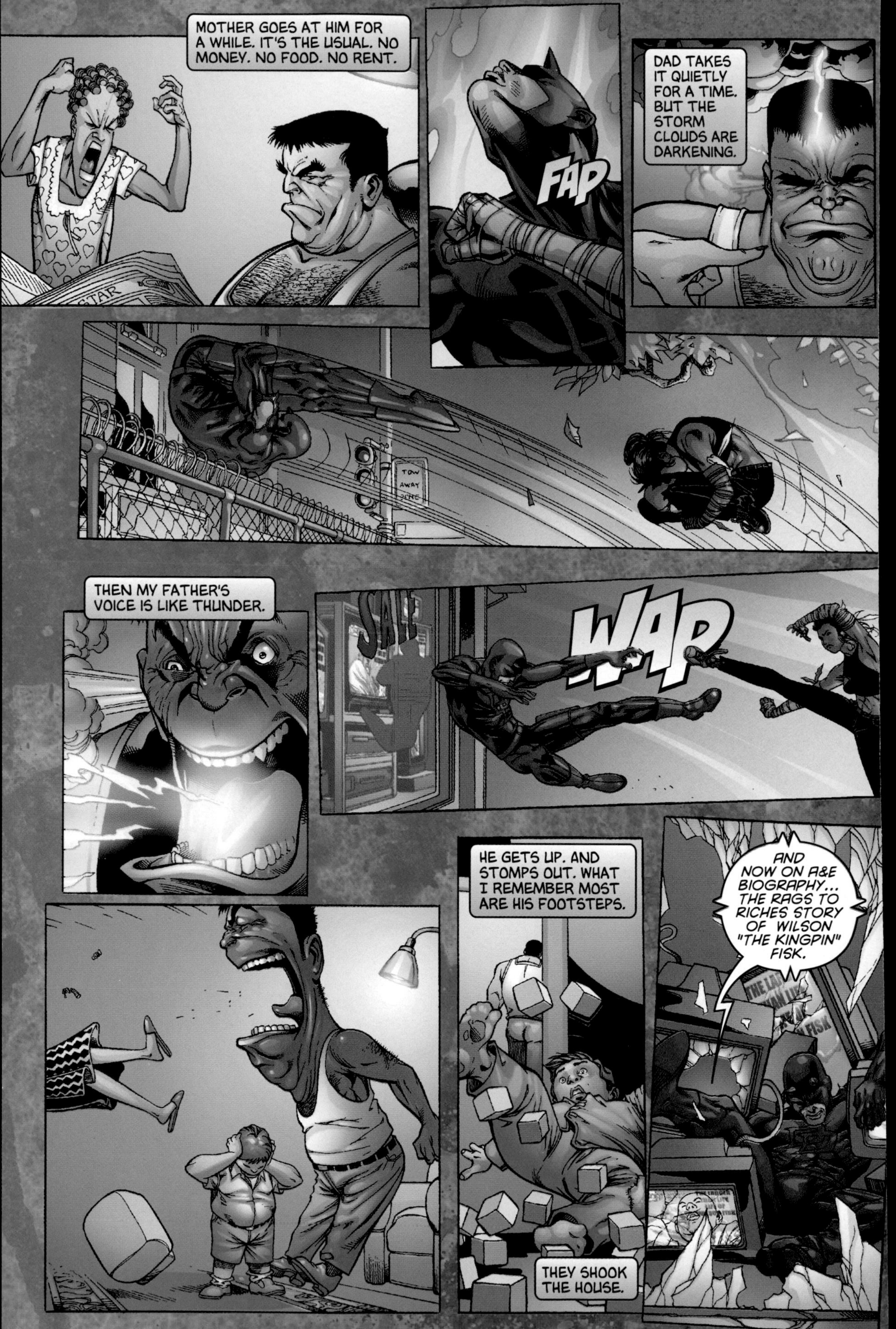
MOTHER GOES AT HIM FOR A WHILE. IT'S THE USUAL. NO MONEY. NO FOOD. NO RENT.
STAR
FAP
DAD TAKES IT QUIETLY FOR A TIME. BUT THE STORM CLOUDS ARE DARKENING.
TOW AWAY
THEN MY FATHER'S VOICE IS LIKE THUNDER.
WAP
HE GETS UP. AND STOMPS OUT. WHAT I REMEMBER MOST ARE HIS FOOTSTEPS.
THEY SHOOK THE HOUSE.
AND NOW ON A&E BIOGRAPHY... THE RAGS TO RICHES STORY OF WILSON "THE KINGPIN" FISK.

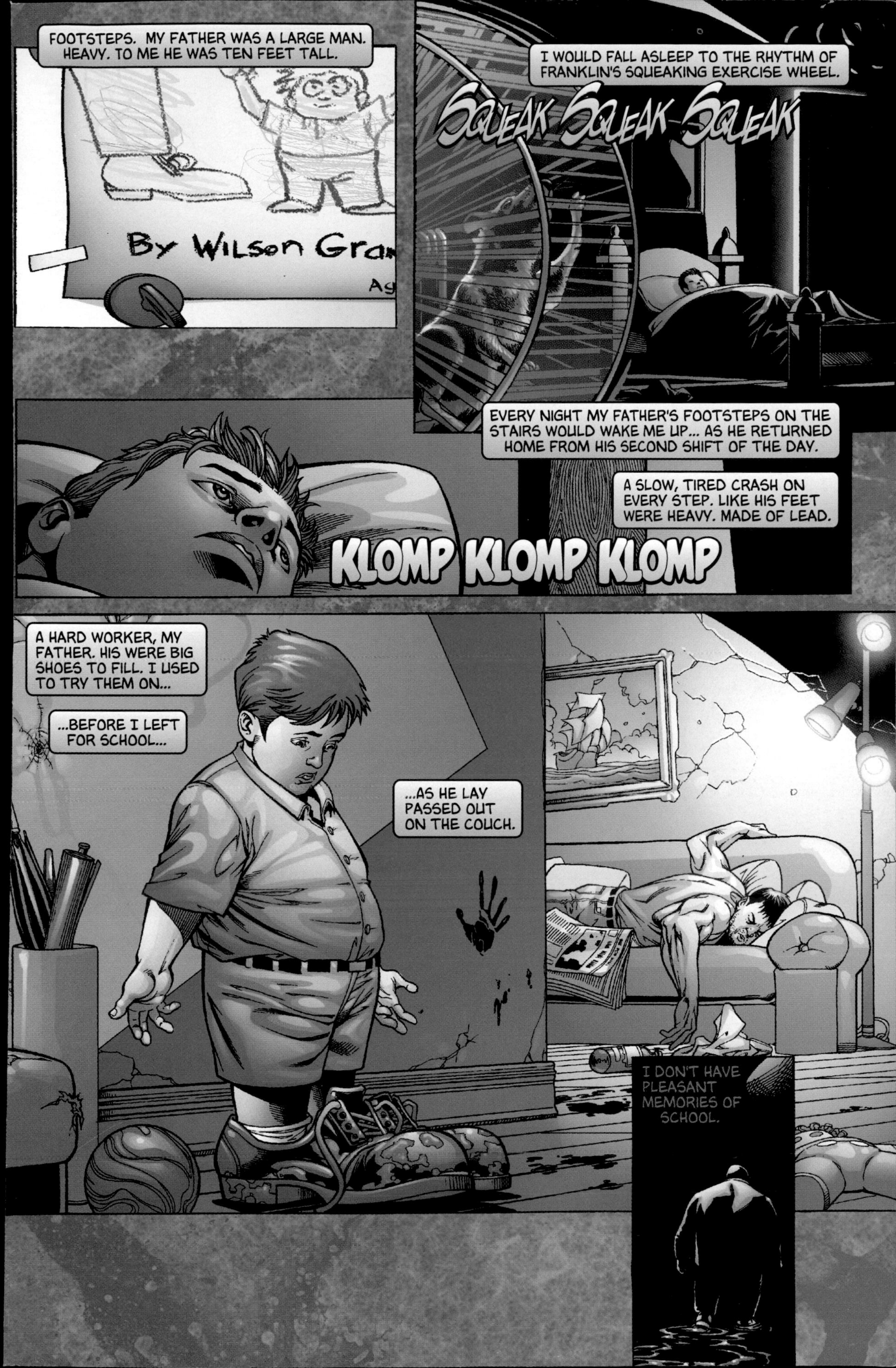

FOOTSTEPS. MY FATHER WAS A LARGE MAN. HEAVY. TO ME HE WAS TEN FEET TALL.
By Wilson Gra
I WOULD FALL ASLEEP TO THE RHYTHM OF FRANKLIN'S SQUEAKING EXERCISE WHEEL.
SQUEAK SQUEAK SQUEAK
EVERY NIGHT MY FATHER'S FOOTSTEPS ON THE STAIRS WOULD WAKE ME UP... AS HE RETURNED HOME FROM HIS SECOND SHIFT OF THE DAY.
A SLOW, TIRED CRASH ON EVERY STEP. LIKE HIS FEET WERE HEAVY. MADE OF LEAD.
KLOMP KLOMP KLOMP
A HARD WORKER, MY FATHER. HIS WERE BIG SHOES TO FILL. I USED TO TRY THEM ON...
...BEFORE I LEFT FOR SCHOOL...
...AS HE LAY PASSED OUT ON THE COUCH.
I DON'T HAVE PLEASANT MEMORIES OF SCHOOL.

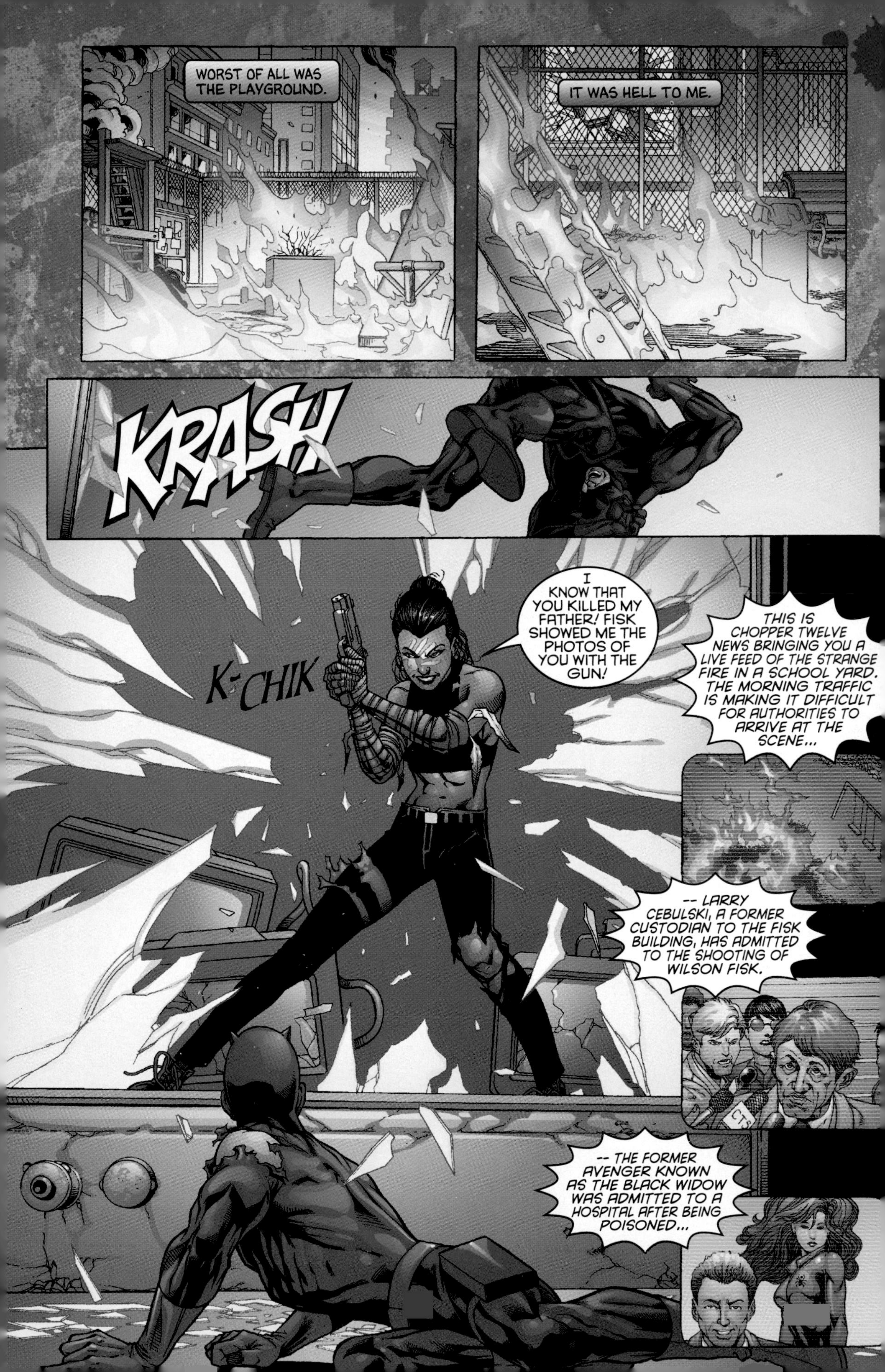
WORST OF ALL WAS THE PLAYGROUND.
IT WAS HELL TO ME.
KRASH
K-CHIK
I KNOW THAT YOU KILLED MY FATHER! FISK SHOWED ME THE PHOTOS OF YOU WITH THE GUN!
THIS IS CHOPPER TWELVE NEWS BRINGING YOU A LIVE FEED OF THE STRANGE FIRE IN A SCHOOL YARD. THE MORNING TRAFFIC IS MAKING IT DIFFICULT FOR AUTHORITIES TO ARRIVE AT THE SCENE...
-- LARRY CEBULSKI, A FORMER CUSTODIAN TO THE FISK BUILDING, HAS ADMITTED TO THE SHOOTING OF WILSON FISK.
CTS
-- THE FORMER AVENGER KNOWN AS THE BLACK WIDOW WAS ADMITTED TO A HOSPITAL AFTER BEING POISONED...

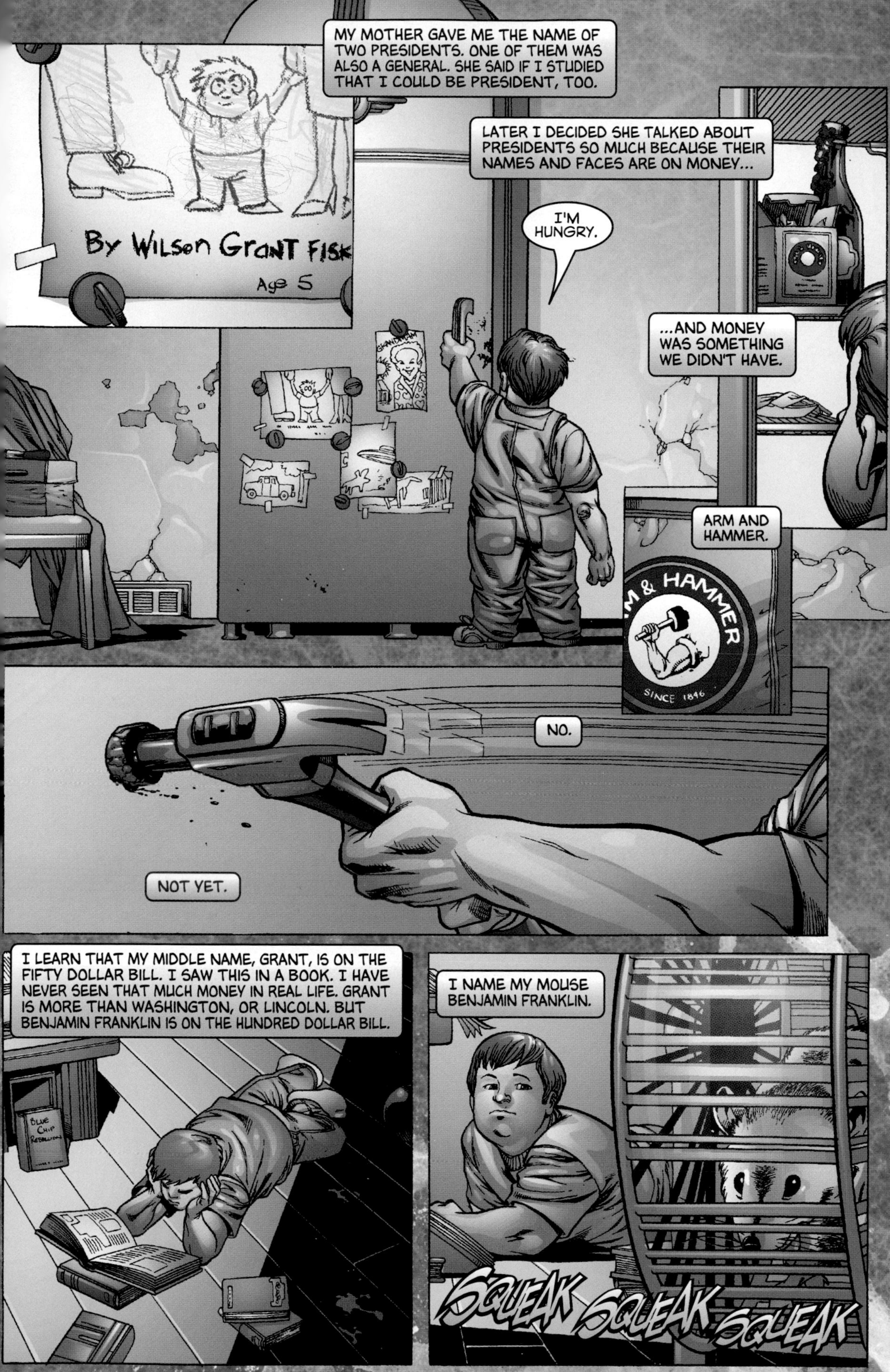
MY MOTHER GAVE ME THE NAME OF TWO PRESIDENTS. ONE OF THEM WAS ALSO A GENERAL. SHE SAID IF I STUDIED THAT I COULD BE PRESIDENT, TOO.
By Wilson Grant Fisk
Age 5
LATER I DECIDED SHE TALKED ABOUT PRESIDENTS SO MUCH BECAUSE THEIR NAMES AND FACES ARE ON MONEY...
I'M HUNGRY.
...AND MONEY WAS SOMETHING WE DIDN'T HAVE.
ARM AND HAMMER.
M & HAMMER
SINCE 1846
NO.
NOT YET.
I LEARN THAT MY MIDDLE NAME, GRANT, IS ON THE FIFTY DOLLAR BILL. I SAW THIS IN A BOOK. I HAVE NEVER SEEN THAT MUCH MONEY IN REAL LIFE. GRANT IS MORE THAN WASHINGTON, OR LINCOLN. BUT BENJAMIN FRANKLIN IS ON THE HUNDRED DOLLAR BILL.
BLUE CHIP REBELLION
I NAME MY MOUSE BENJAMIN FRANKLIN.
SQUEAK SQUEAK SQUEAK

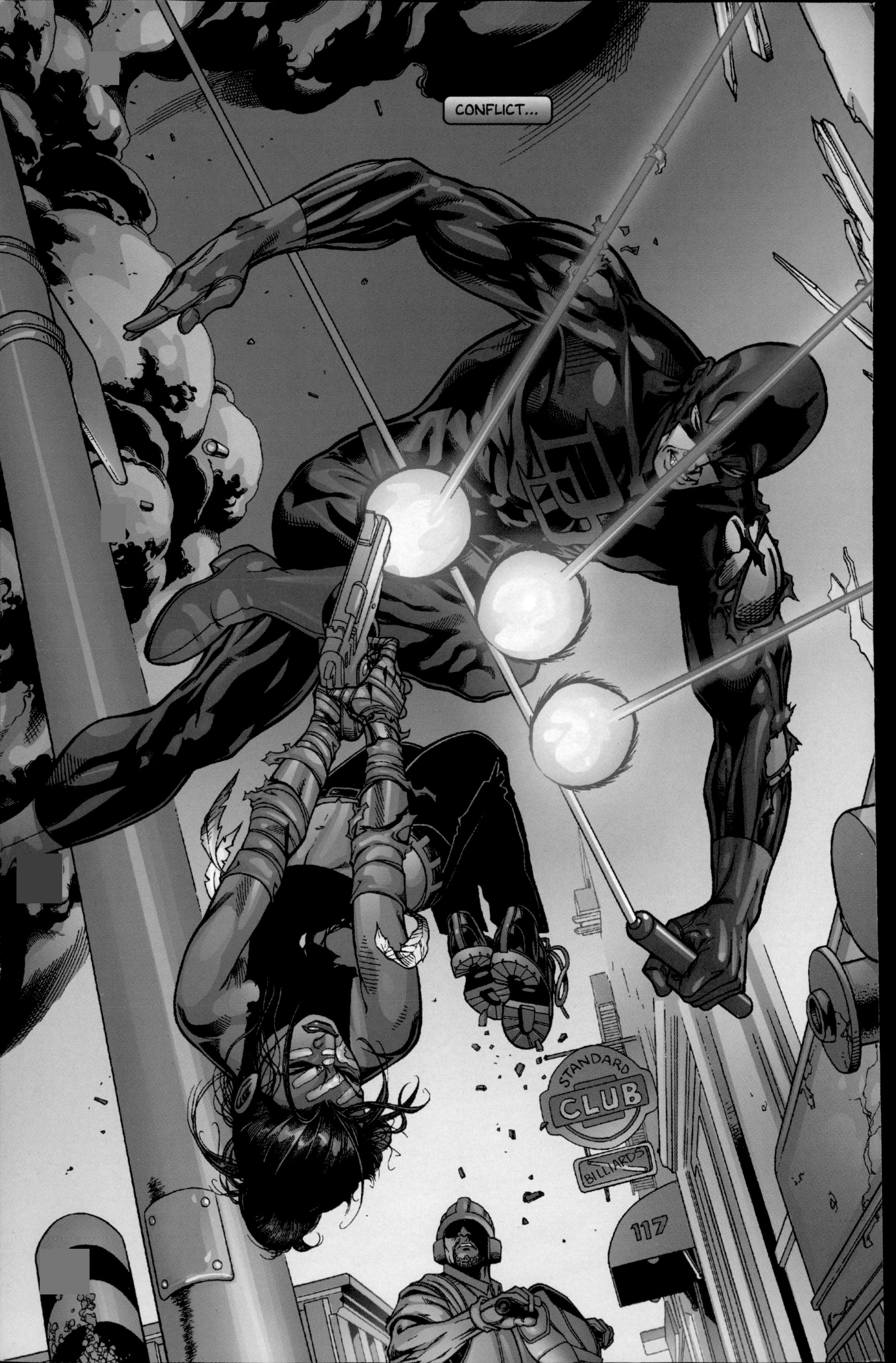
CONFLICT...
STANDARD
CLUB
BILLIARDS
117

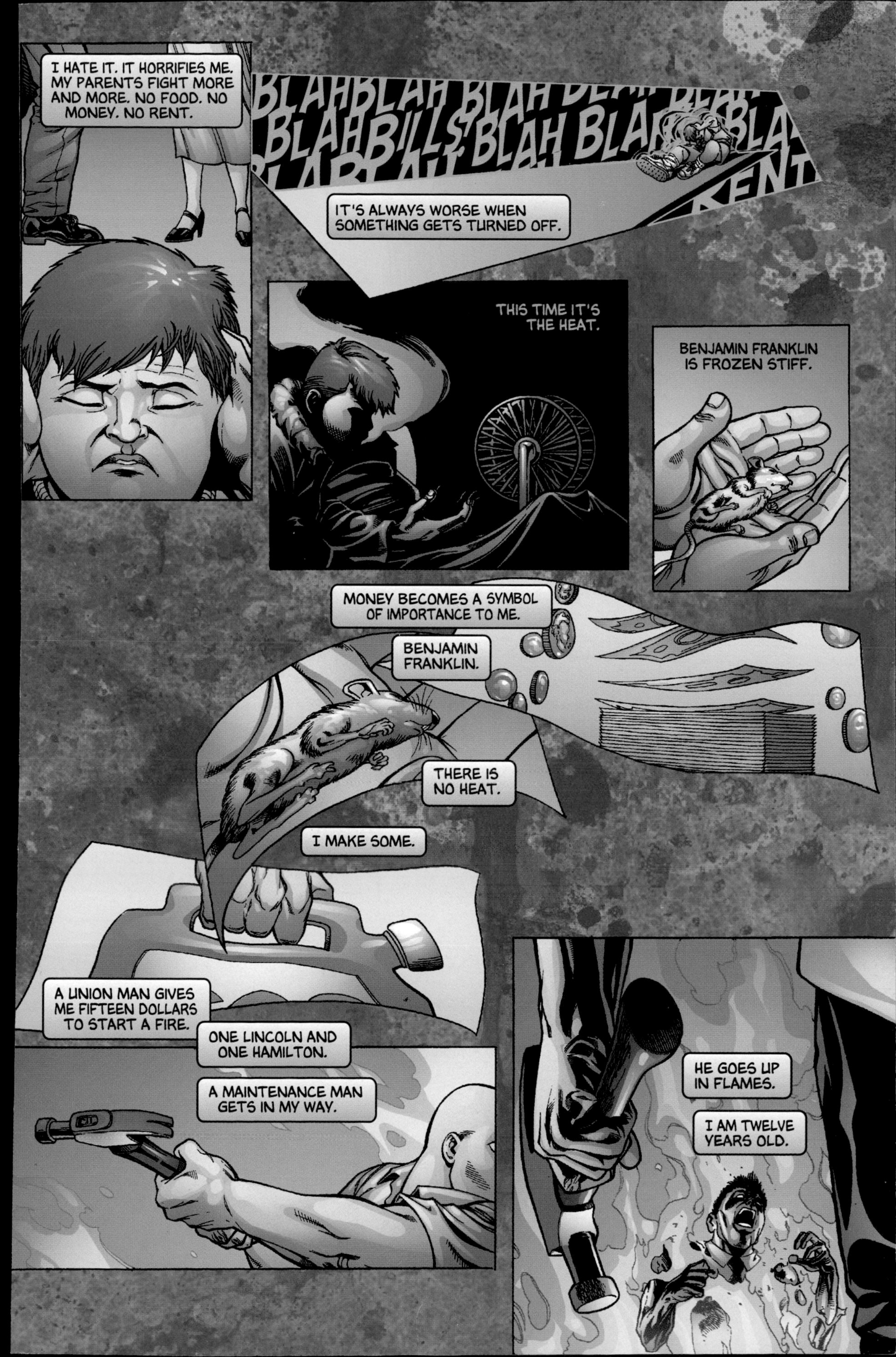
I HATE IT. IT HORRIFIES ME. MY PARENTS FIGHT MORE AND MORE. NO FOOD. NO MONEY. NO RENT.
BLAH BLAH BLAH BILLS BLAH BLAH BLAH
RENT
IT'S ALWAYS WORSE WHEN SOMETHING GETS TURNED OFF.
THIS TIME IT'S THE HEAT.
BENJAMIN FRANKLIN IS FROZEN STIFF.
MONEY BECOMES A SYMBOL OF IMPORTANCE TO ME.
BENJAMIN FRANKLIN.
THERE IS NO HEAT.
I MAKE SOME.
A UNION MAN GIVES ME FIFTEEN DOLLARS TO START A FIRE.
ONE LINCOLN AND ONE HAMILTON.
A MAINTENANCE MAN GETS IN MY WAY.
HE GOES UP IN FLAMES.
I AM TWELVE YEARS OLD.

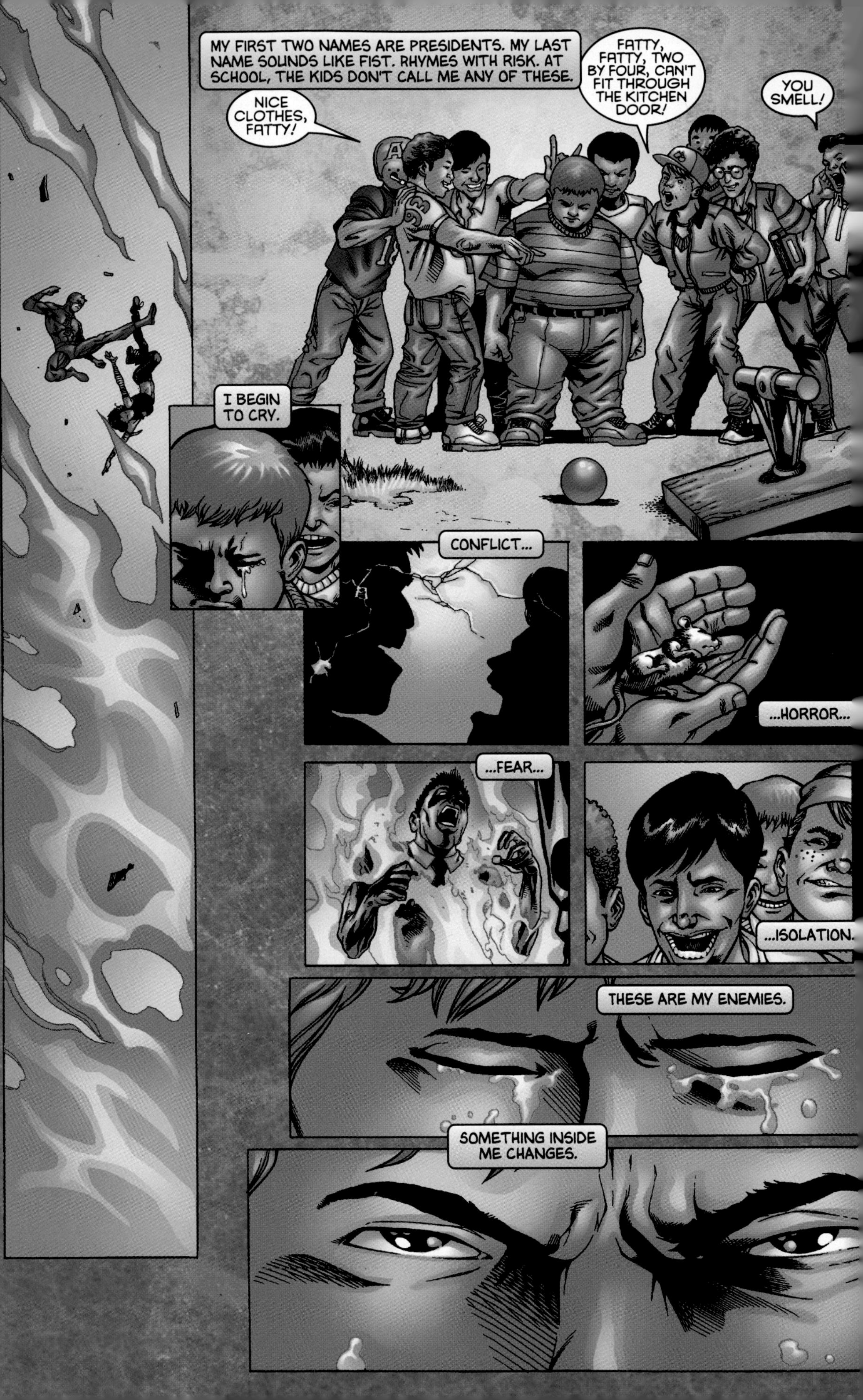
MY FIRST TWO NAMES ARE PRESIDENTS. MY LAST NAME SOUNDS LIKE FIST. RHYMES WITH RISK. AT SCHOOL, THE KIDS DON'T CALL ME ANY OF THESE.
NICE CLOTHES, FATTY!
FATTY, FATTY, TWO BY FOUR, CAN'T FIT THROUGH THE KITCHEN DOOR!
YOU SMELL!
I BEGIN TO CRY.
CONFLICT...
...HORROR...
...FEAR...
...ISOLATION.
THESE ARE MY ENEMIES.
SOMETHING INSIDE ME CHANGES.

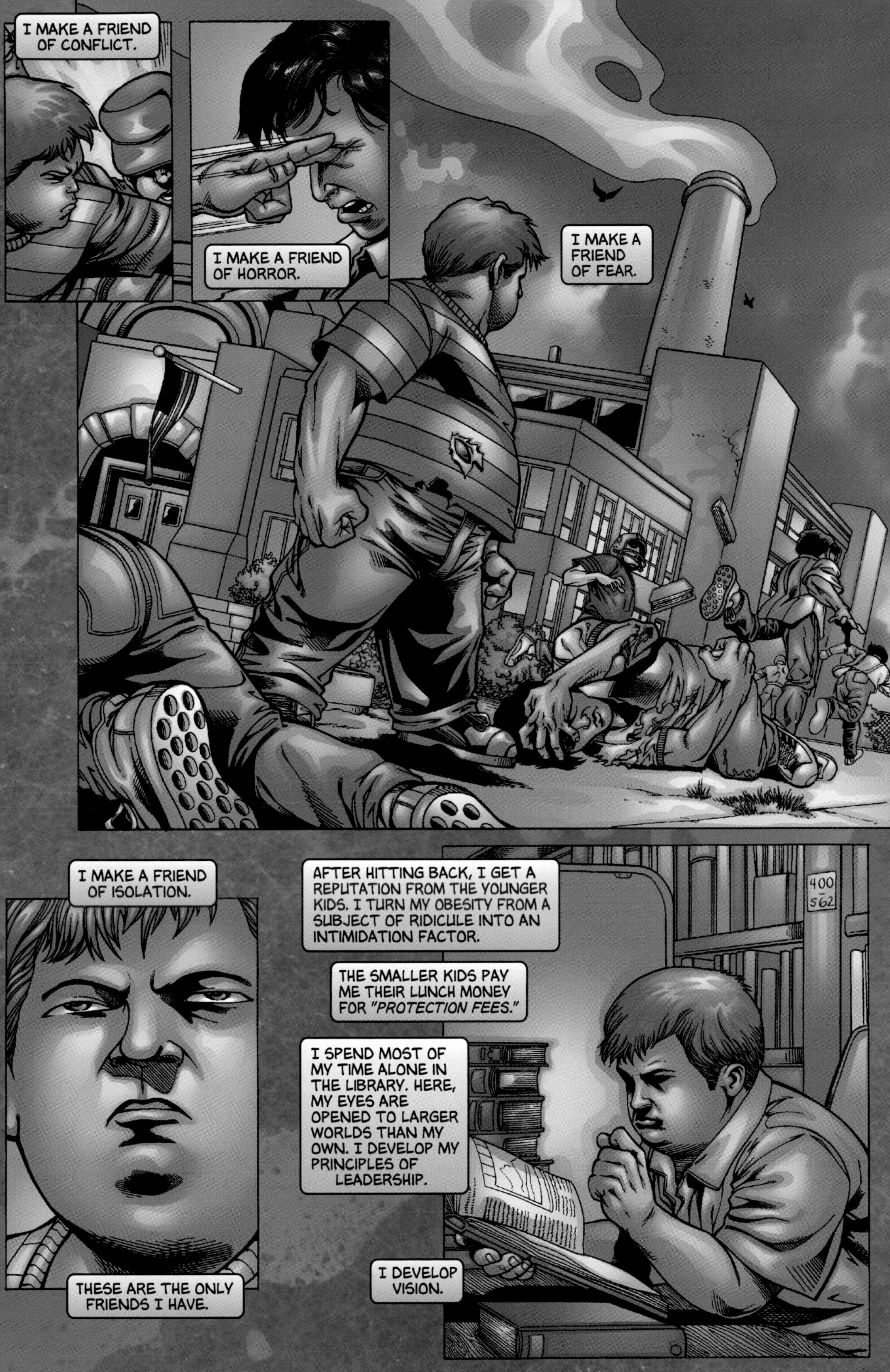
I MAKE A FRIEND OF CONFLICT.
I MAKE A FRIEND OF HORROR.
I MAKE A FRIEND OF FEAR.
I MAKE A FRIEND OF ISOLATION.
THESE ARE THE ONLY FRIENDS I HAVE.
AFTER HITTING BACK, I GET A REPUTATION FROM THE YOUNGER KIDS. I TURN MY OBESITY FROM A SUBJECT OF RIDICULE INTO AN INTIMIDATION FACTOR.
THE SMALLER KIDS PAY ME THEIR LUNCH MONEY FOR "PROTECTION FEES."
I SPEND MOST OF MY TIME ALONE IN THE LIBRARY. HERE, MY EYES ARE OPENED TO LARGER WORLDS THAN MY OWN. I DEVELOP MY PRINCIPLES OF LEADERSHIP.
400
562
I DEVELOP VISION.

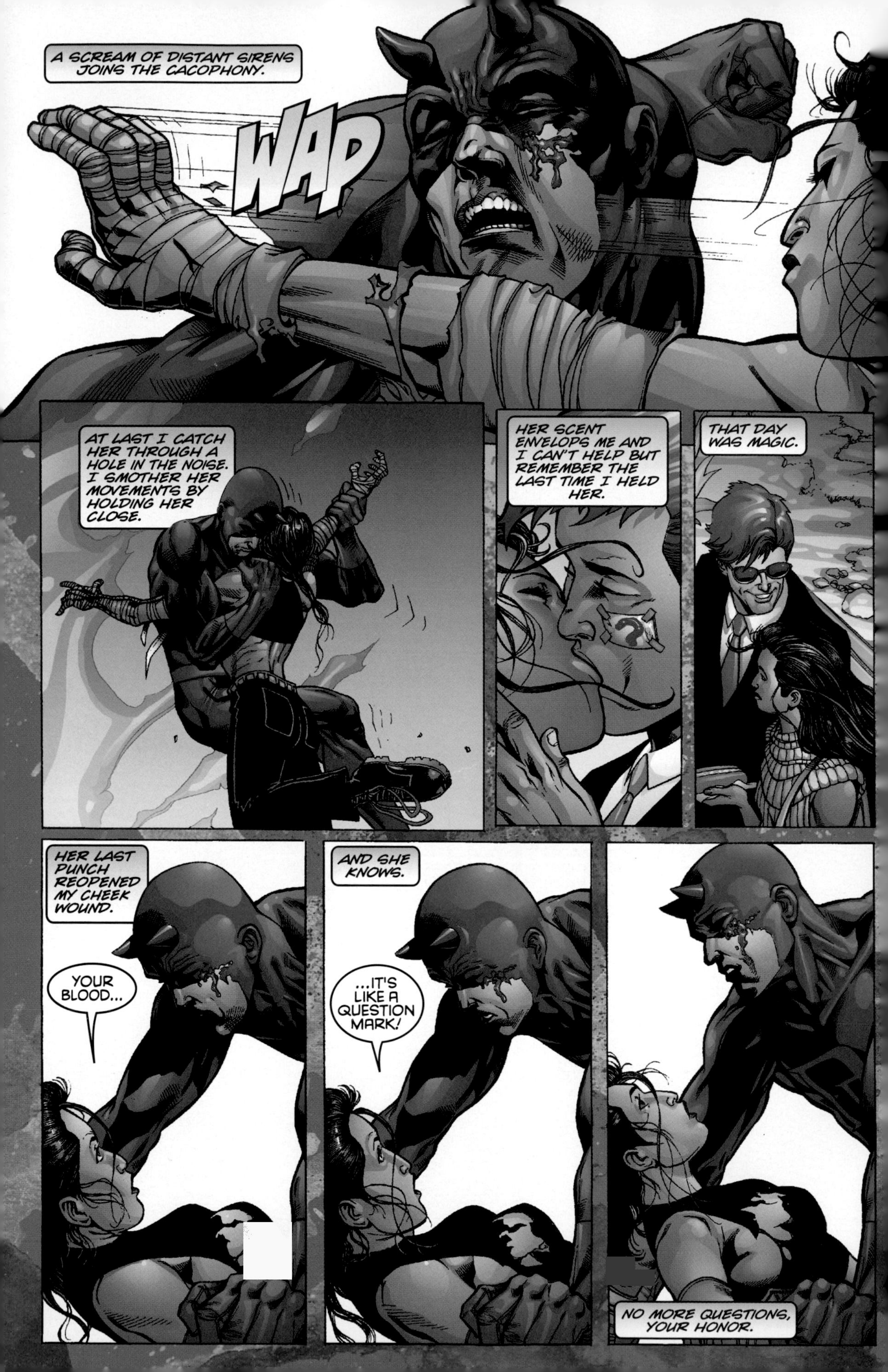
A SCREAM OF DISTANT SIRENS JOINS THE CACOPHONY.
WAP
AT LAST I CATCH HER THROUGH A HOLE IN THE NOISE. I SMOTHER HER MOVEMENTS BY HOLDING HER CLOSE.
HER SCENT ENVELOPS ME AND I CAN'T HELP BUT REMEMBER THE LAST TIME I HELD HER.
THAT DAY WAS MAGIC.
HER LAST PUNCH REOPENED MY CHEEK WOUND.
YOUR BLOOD...
AND SHE KNOWS.
...IT'S LIKE A QUESTION MARK!
NO MORE QUESTIONS, YOUR HONOR.

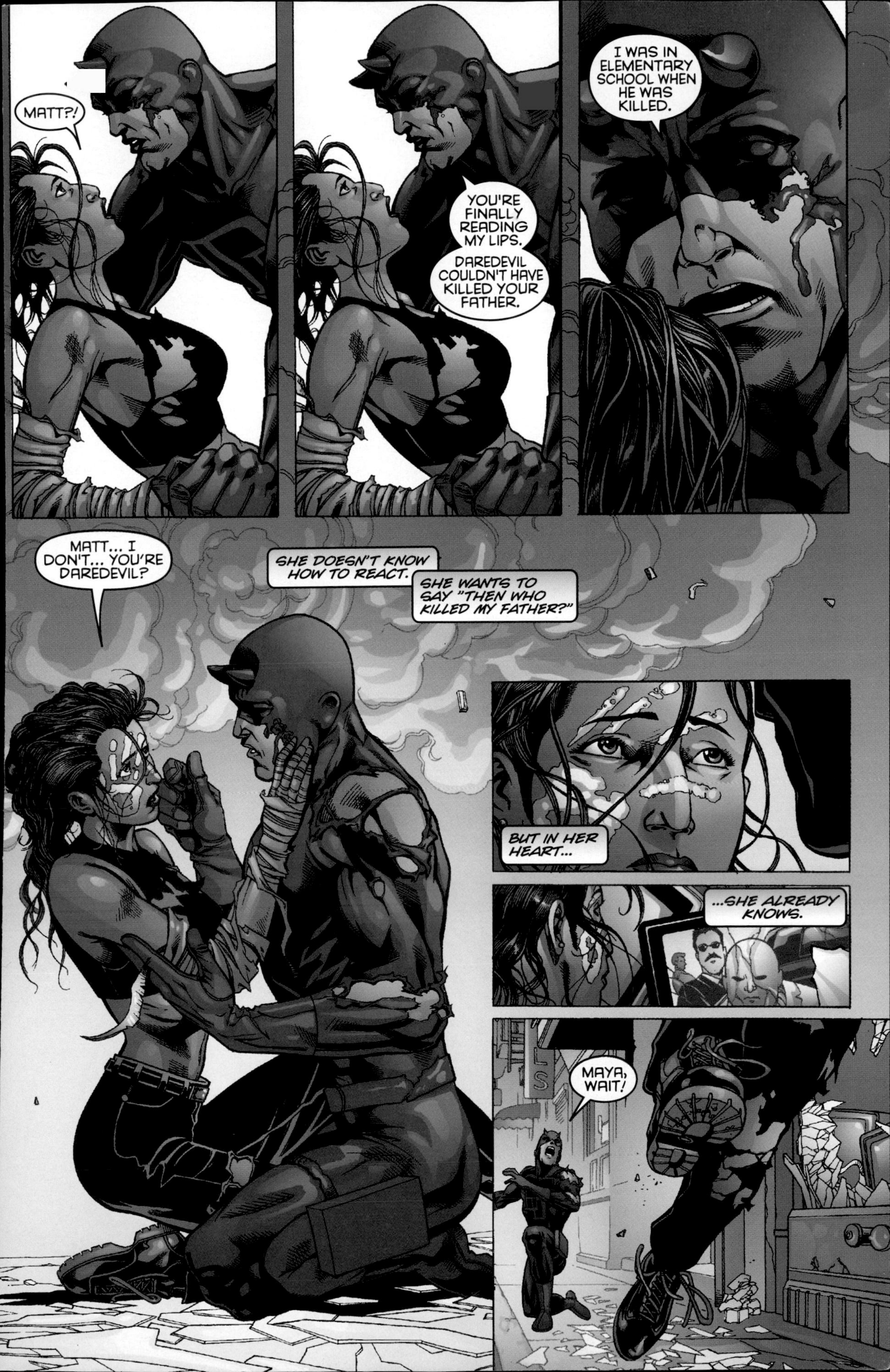

MATT?!
YOU'RE FINALLY READING MY LIPS.
DAREDEVIL COULDN'T HAVE KILLED YOUR FATHER.
I WAS IN ELEMENTARY SCHOOL WHEN HE WAS KILLED.
MATT... I DON'T... YOU'RE DAREDEVIL?
SHE DOESN'T KNOW HOW TO REACT.
SHE WANTS TO SAY "THEN WHO KILLED MY FATHER?"
BUT IN HER HEART...
...SHE ALREADY KNOWS.
MAYA, WAIT!

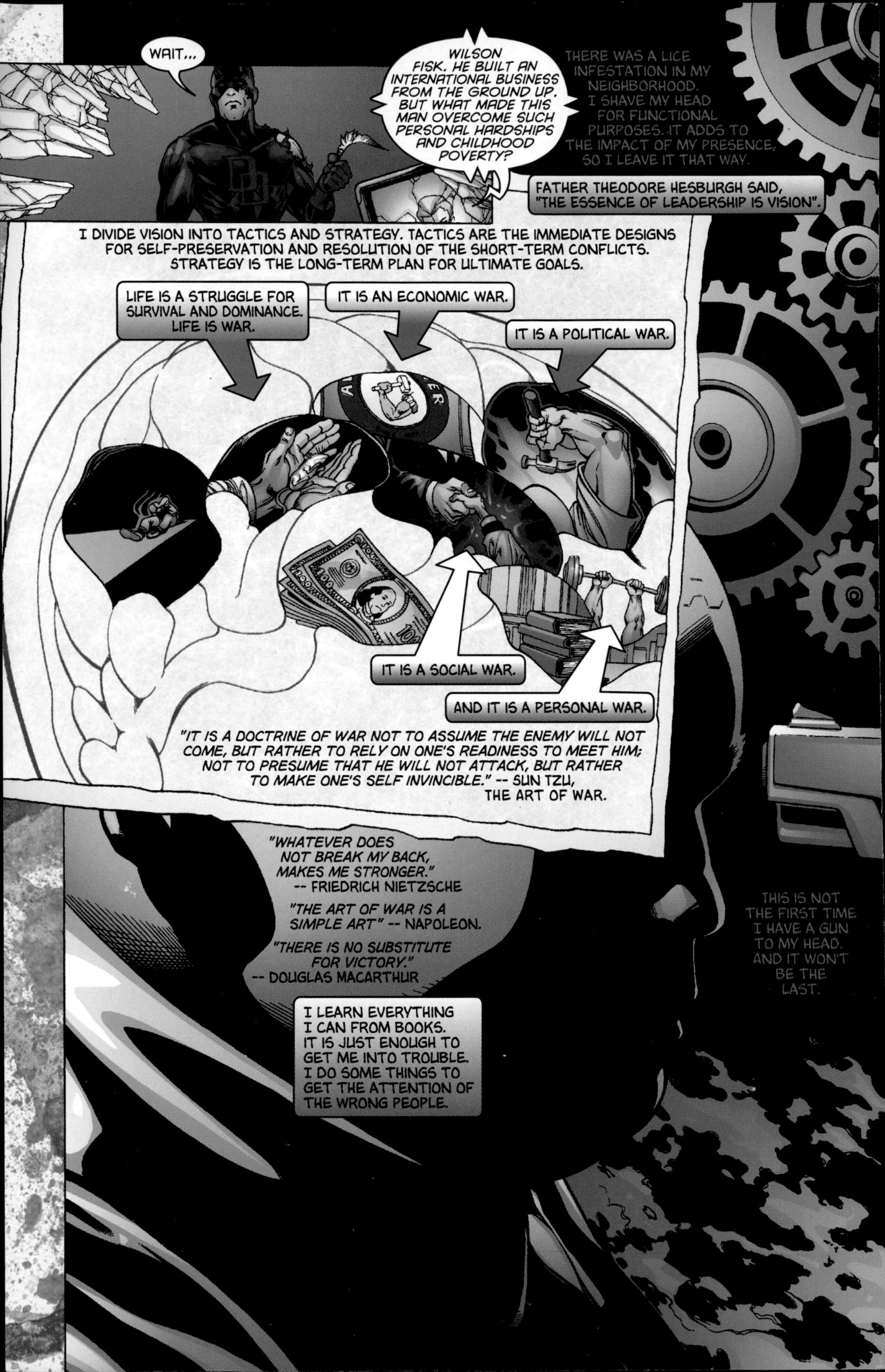
WAIT...
WILSON FISK. HE BUILT AN INTERNATIONAL BUSINESS FROM THE GROUND UP. BUT WHAT MADE THIS MAN OVERCOME SUCH PERSONAL HARDSHIPS AND CHILDHOOD POVERTY?
THERE WAS A LICE INFESTATION IN MY NEIGHBORHOOD. I SHAVE MY HEAD FOR FUNCTIONAL PURPOSES. IT ADDS TO THE IMPACT OF MY PRESENCE, SO I LEAVE IT THAT WAY.
FATHER THEODORE HESBURGH SAID, "THE ESSENCE OF LEADERSHIP IS VISION".
I DIVIDE VISION INTO TACTICS AND STRATEGY. TACTICS ARE THE IMMEDIATE DESIGNS FOR SELF-PRESERVATION AND RESOLUTION OF THE SHORT-TERM CONFLICTS. STRATEGY IS THE LONG-TERM PLAN FOR ULTIMATE GOALS.
LIFE IS A STRUGGLE FOR SURVIVAL AND DOMINANCE. LIFE IS WAR.
IT IS AN ECONOMIC WAR.
IT IS A POLITICAL WAR.
IT IS A SOCIAL WAR.
AND IT IS A PERSONAL WAR.
"IT IS A DOCTRINE OF WAR NOT TO ASSUME THE ENEMY WILL NOT COME, BUT RATHER TO RELY ON ONE'S READINESS TO MEET HIM; NOT TO PRESUME THAT HE WILL NOT ATTACK, BUT RATHER TO MAKE ONE'S SELF INVINCIBLE." -- SUN TZU, THE ART OF WAR.
"WHATEVER DOES NOT BREAK MY BACK, MAKES ME STRONGER." -- FRIEDRICH NIETZSCHE
"THE ART OF WAR IS A SIMPLE ART" -- NAPOLEON.
"THERE IS NO SUBSTITUTE FOR VICTORY." -- DOUGLAS MACARTHUR
I LEARN EVERYTHING I CAN FROM BOOKS. IT IS JUST ENOUGH TO GET ME INTO TROUBLE. I DO SOME THINGS TO GET THE ATTENTION OF THE WRONG PEOPLE.
THIS IS NOT THE FIRST TIME I HAVE A GUN TO MY HEAD. AND IT WON'T BE THE LAST.

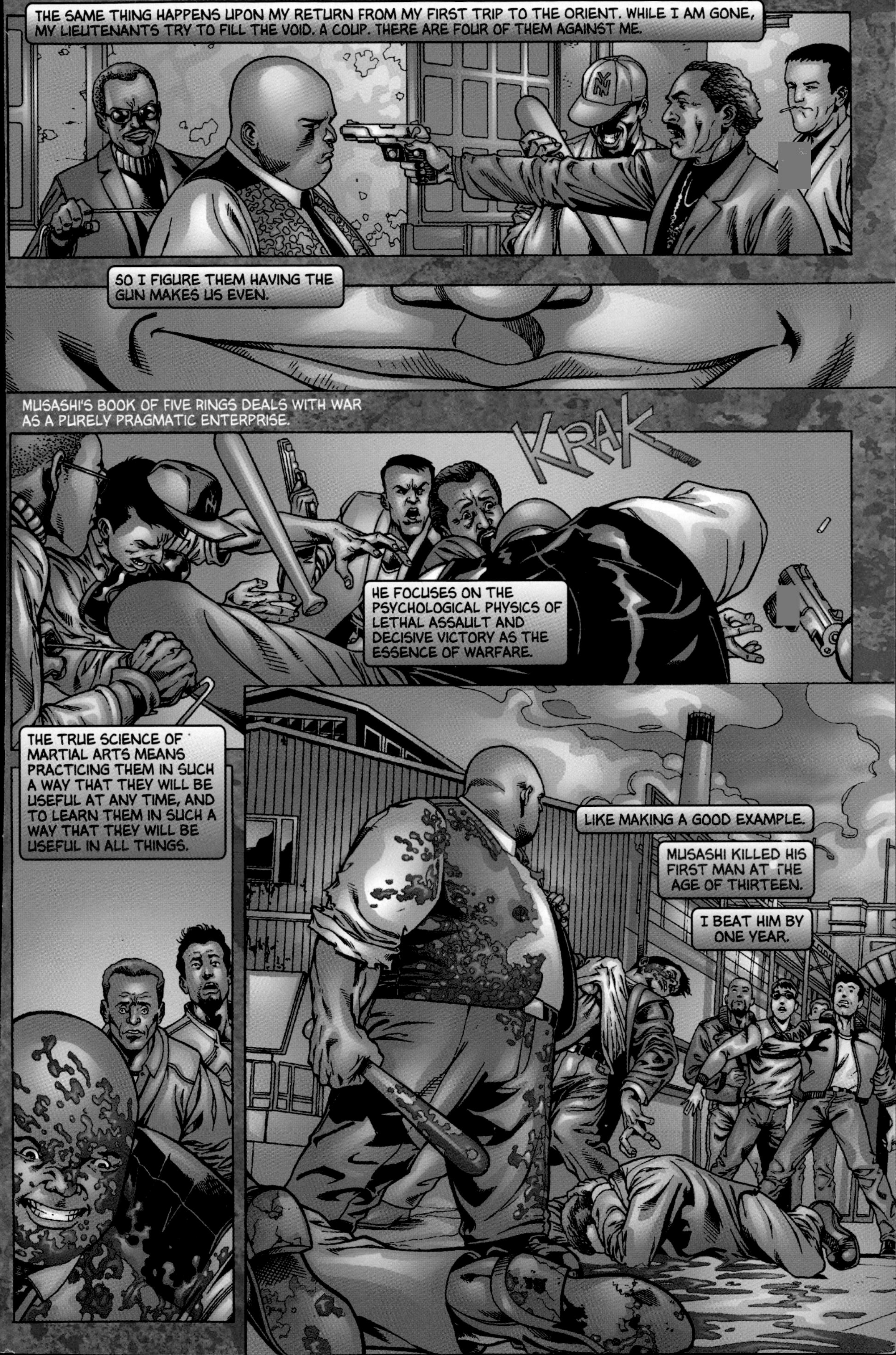
THE SAME THING HAPPENS UPON MY RETURN FROM MY FIRST TRIP TO THE ORIENT. WHILE I AM GONE, MY LIEUTENANTS TRY TO FILL THE VOID. A COUP. THERE ARE FOUR OF THEM AGAINST ME.
SO I FIGURE THEM HAVING THE GUN MAKES US EVEN.
MUSASHI'S BOOK OF FIVE RINGS DEALS WITH WAR AS A PURELY PRAGMATIC ENTERPRISE.
KRAK
HE FOCUSES ON THE PSYCHOLOGICAL PHYSICS OF LETHAL ASSAULT AND DECISIVE VICTORY AS THE ESSENCE OF WARFARE.
THE TRUE SCIENCE OF MARTIAL ARTS MEANS PRACTICING THEM IN SUCH A WAY THAT THEY WILL BE USEFUL AT ANY TIME, AND TO LEARN THEM IN SUCH A WAY THAT THEY WILL BE USEFUL IN ALL THINGS.
LIKE MAKING A GOOD EXAMPLE.
MUSASHI KILLED HIS FIRST MAN AT THE AGE OF THIRTEEN.
I BEAT HIM BY ONE YEAR.

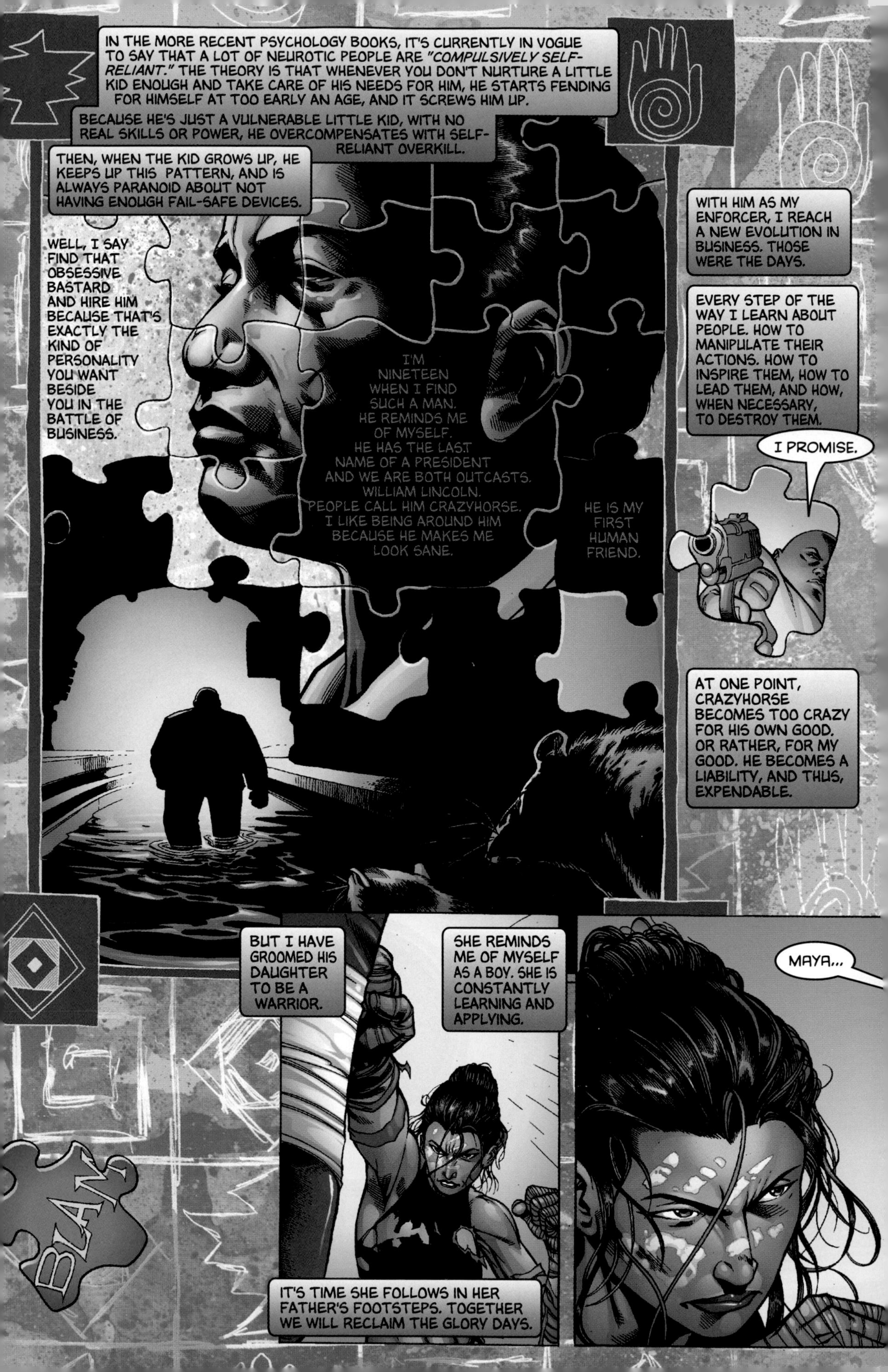
IN THE MORE RECENT PSYCHOLOGY BOOKS, IT'S CURRENTLY IN VOGUE TO SAY THAT A LOT OF NEUROTIC PEOPLE ARE "COMPULSIVELY SELF-RELIANT." THE THEORY IS THAT WHENEVER YOU DON'T NURTURE A LITTLE KID ENOUGH AND TAKE CARE OF HIS NEEDS FOR HIM, HE STARTS FENDING FOR HIMSELF AT TOO EARLY AN AGE, AND IT SCREWS HIM UP.
BECAUSE HE'S JUST A VULNERABLE LITTLE KID, WITH NO REAL SKILLS OR POWER, HE OVERCOMPENSATES WITH SELF-RELIANT OVERKILL.
THEN, WHEN THE KID GROWS UP, HE KEEPS UP THIS PATTERN, AND IS ALWAYS PARANOID ABOUT NOT HAVING ENOUGH FAIL-SAFE DEVICES.
WELL, I SAY FIND THAT OBSESSIVE BASTARD AND HIRE HIM BECAUSE THAT'S EXACTLY THE KIND OF PERSONALITY YOU WANT BESIDE YOU IN THE BATTLE OF BUSINESS.
I'M NINETEEN WHEN I FIND SUCH A MAN. HE REMINDS ME OF MYSELF. HE HAS THE LAST NAME OF A PRESIDENT AND WE ARE BOTH OUTCASTS. WILLIAM LINCOLN. PEOPLE CALL HIM CRAZYHORSE. I LIKE BEING AROUND HIM BECAUSE HE MAKES ME LOOK SANE.
HE IS MY FIRST HUMAN FRIEND.
WITH HIM AS MY ENFORCER, I REACH A NEW EVOLUTION IN BUSINESS. THOSE WERE THE DAYS.
EVERY STEP OF THE WAY I LEARN ABOUT PEOPLE. HOW TO MANIPULATE THEIR ACTIONS. HOW TO INSPIRE THEM, HOW TO LEAD THEM, AND HOW, WHEN NECESSARY, TO DESTROY THEM.
I PROMISE.
AT ONE POINT, CRAZYHORSE BECOMES TOO CRAZY FOR HIS OWN GOOD, OR RATHER, FOR MY GOOD. HE BECOMES A LIABILITY, AND THUS, EXPENDABLE.
BLAM
BUT I HAVE GROOMED HIS DAUGHTER TO BE A WARRIOR.
SHE REMINDS ME OF MYSELF AS A BOY. SHE IS CONSTANTLY LEARNING AND APPLYING.
IT'S TIME SHE FOLLOWS IN HER FATHER'S FOOTSTEPS. TOGETHER WE WILL RECLAIM THE GLORY DAYS.
MAYA...

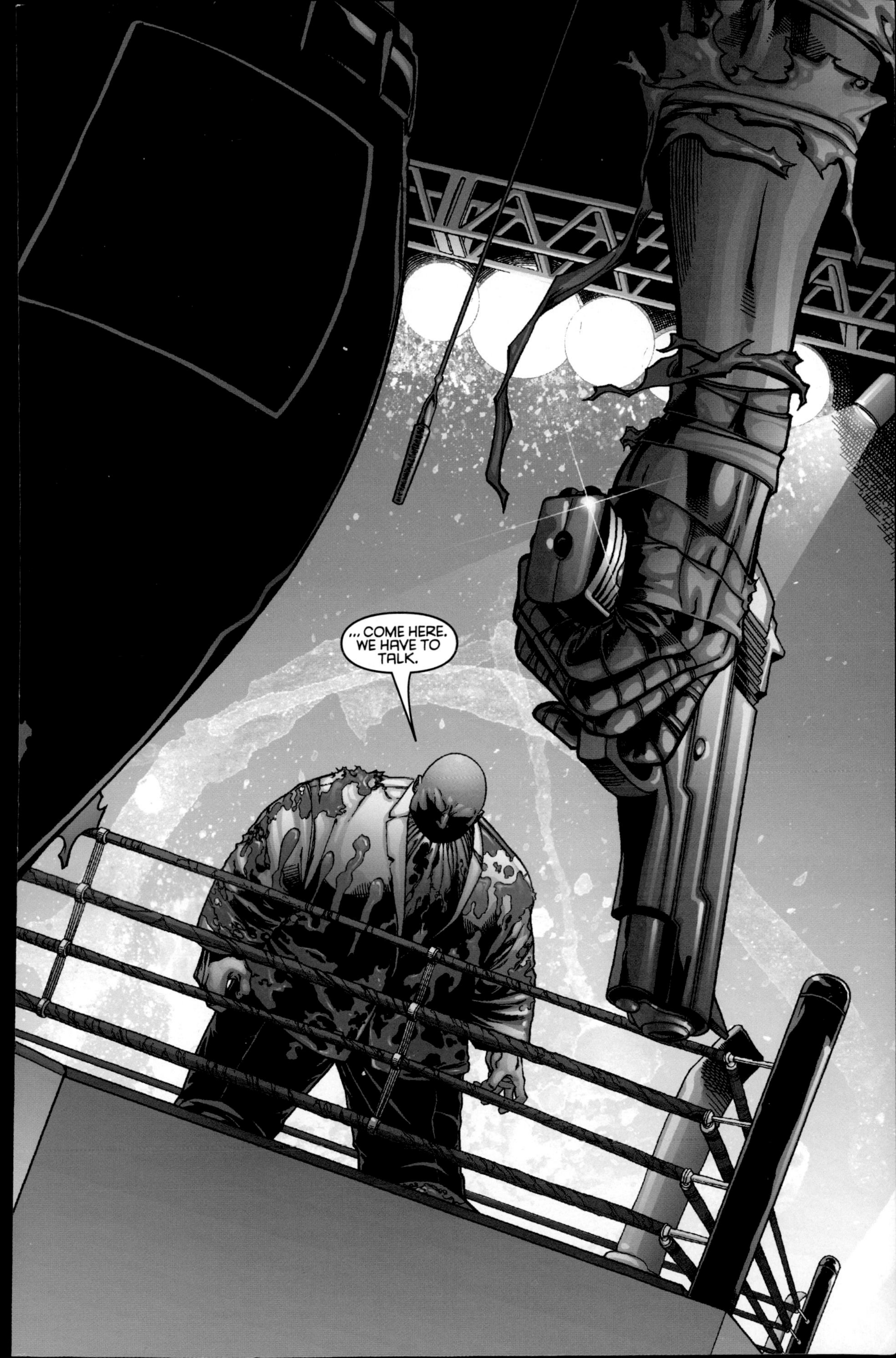
...COME HERE. WE HAVE TO TALK.

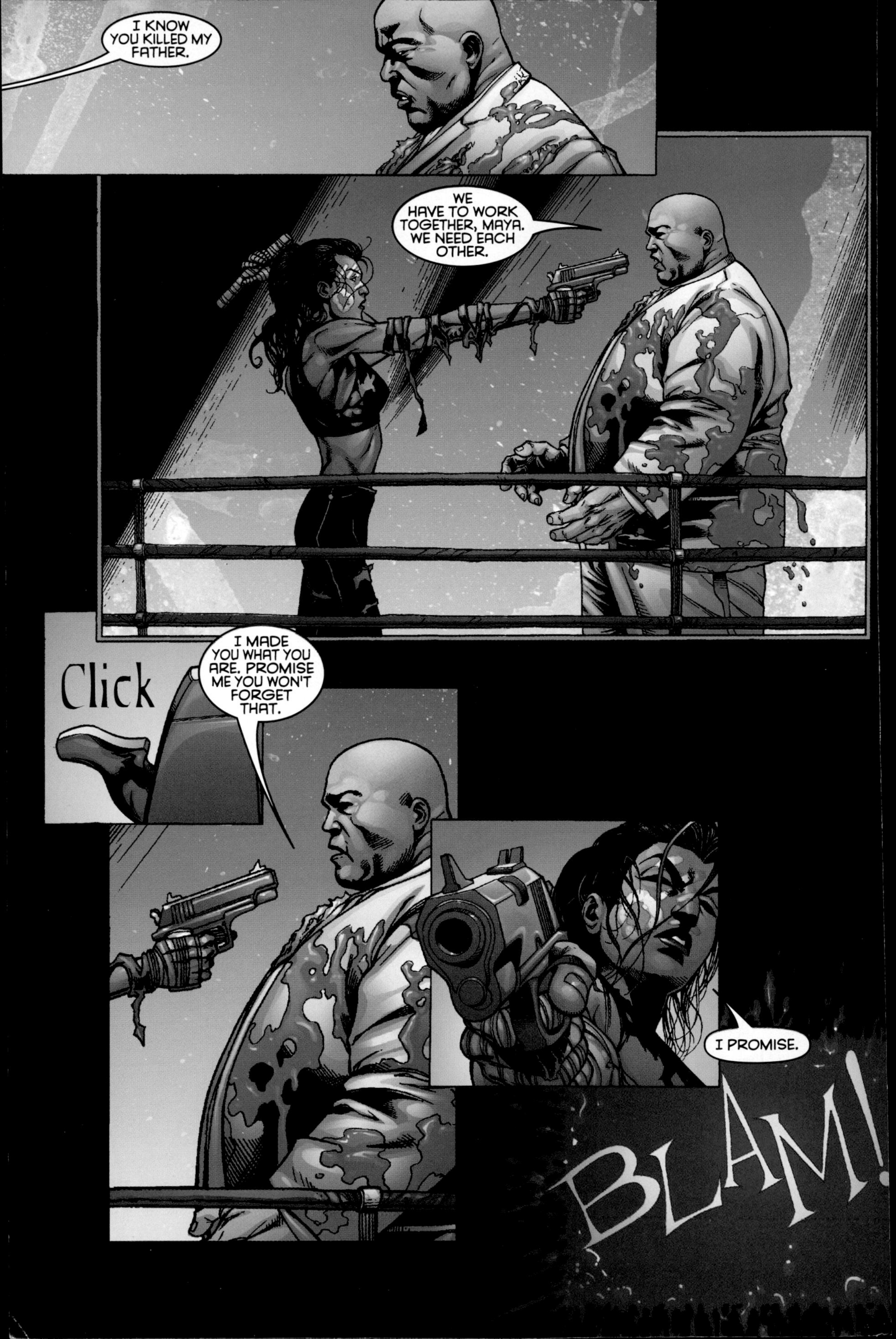
I KNOW YOU KILLED MY FATHER.
WE HAVE TO WORK TOGETHER, MAYA. WE NEED EACH OTHER.
Click
I MADE YOU WHAT YOU ARE. PROMISE ME YOU WON'T FORGET THAT.
I PROMISE.
BLAM!

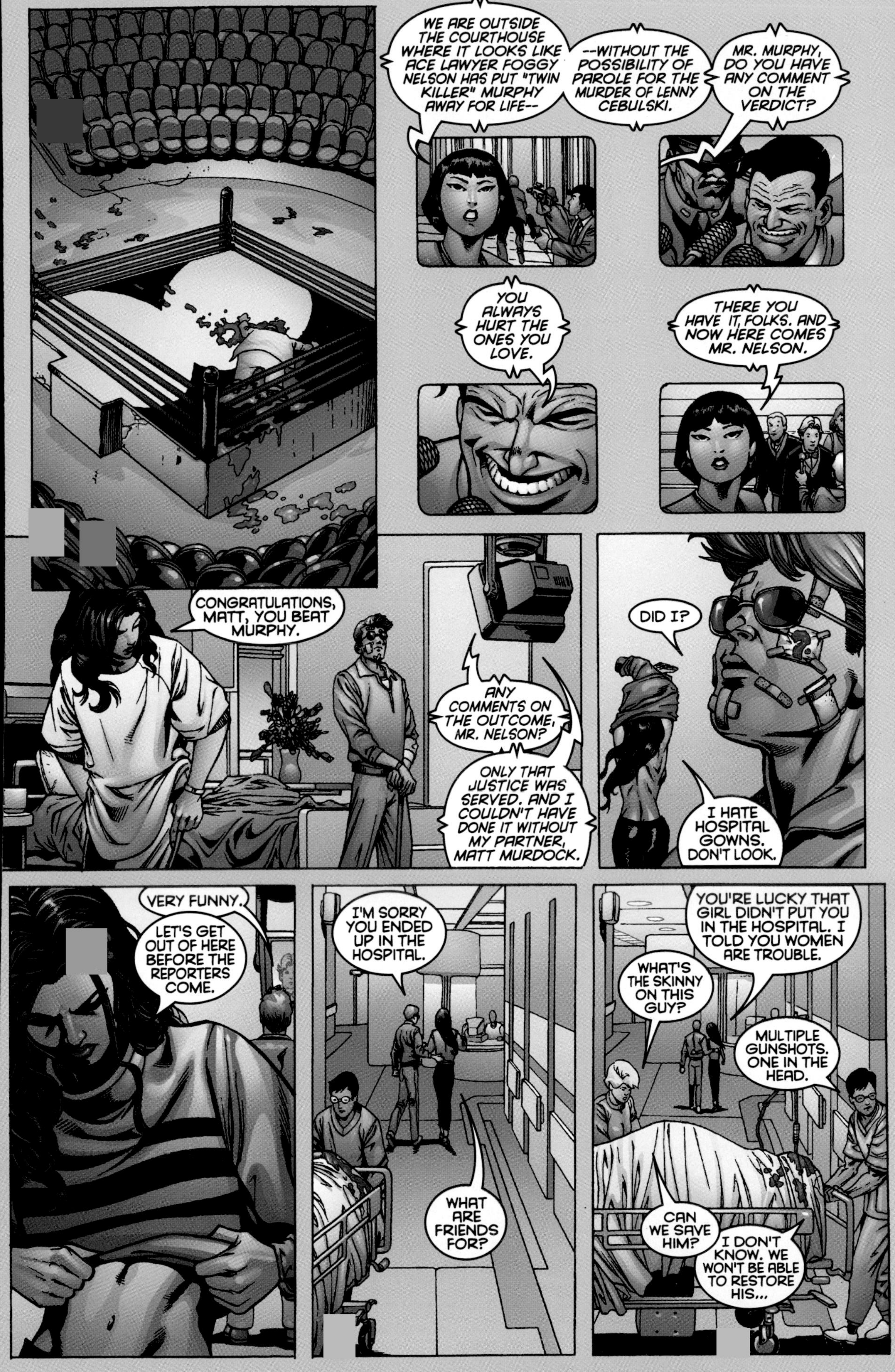
WE ARE OUTSIDE THE COURTHOUSE WHERE IT LOOKS LIKE ACE LAWYER FOGGY NELSON HAS PUT "TWIN KILLER" MURPHY AWAY FOR LIFE--
--WITHOUT THE POSSIBILITY OF PAROLE FOR THE MURDER OF LENNY CEBULSKI.
MR. MURPHY, DO YOU HAVE ANY COMMENT ON THE VERDICT?
YOU ALWAYS HURT THE ONES YOU LOVE.
THERE YOU HAVE IT, FOLKS. AND NOW HERE COMES MR. NELSON.
CONGRATULATIONS, MATT, YOU BEAT MURPHY.
ANY COMMENTS ON THE OUTCOME, MR. NELSON?
ONLY THAT JUSTICE WAS SERVED. AND I COULDN'T HAVE DONE IT WITHOUT MY PARTNER, MATT MURDOCK.
DID I?
I HATE HOSPITAL GOWNS. DON'T LOOK.
VERY FUNNY.
LET'S GET OUT OF HERE BEFORE THE REPORTERS COME.
I'M SORRY YOU ENDED UP IN THE HOSPITAL.
WHAT ARE FRIENDS FOR?
YOU'RE LUCKY THAT GIRL DIDN'T PUT YOU IN THE HOSPITAL. I TOLD YOU WOMEN ARE TROUBLE.
WHAT'S THE SKINNY ON THIS GUY?
MULTIPLE GUNSHOTS. ONE IN THE HEAD.
CAN WE SAVE HIM?
I DON'T KNOW. WE WON'T BE ABLE TO RESTORE HIS...

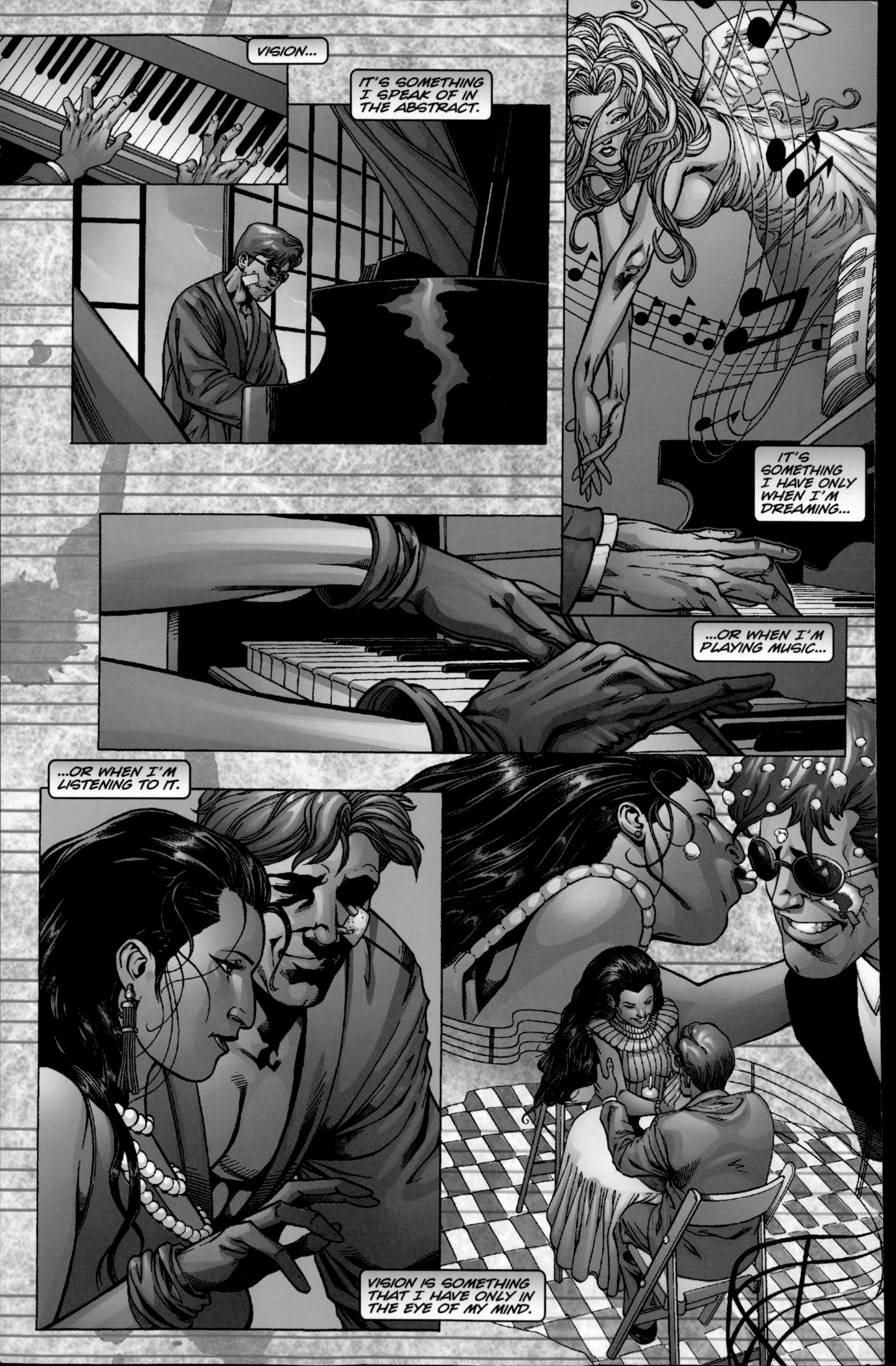
VISION...
IT'S SOMETHING I SPEAK OF IN THE ABSTRACT.
IT'S SOMETHING I HAVE ONLY WHEN I'M DREAMING...
...OR WHEN I'M PLAYING MUSIC...
...OR WHEN I'M LISTENING TO IT.
VISION IS SOMETHING THAT I HAVE ONLY IN THE EYE OF MY MIND.

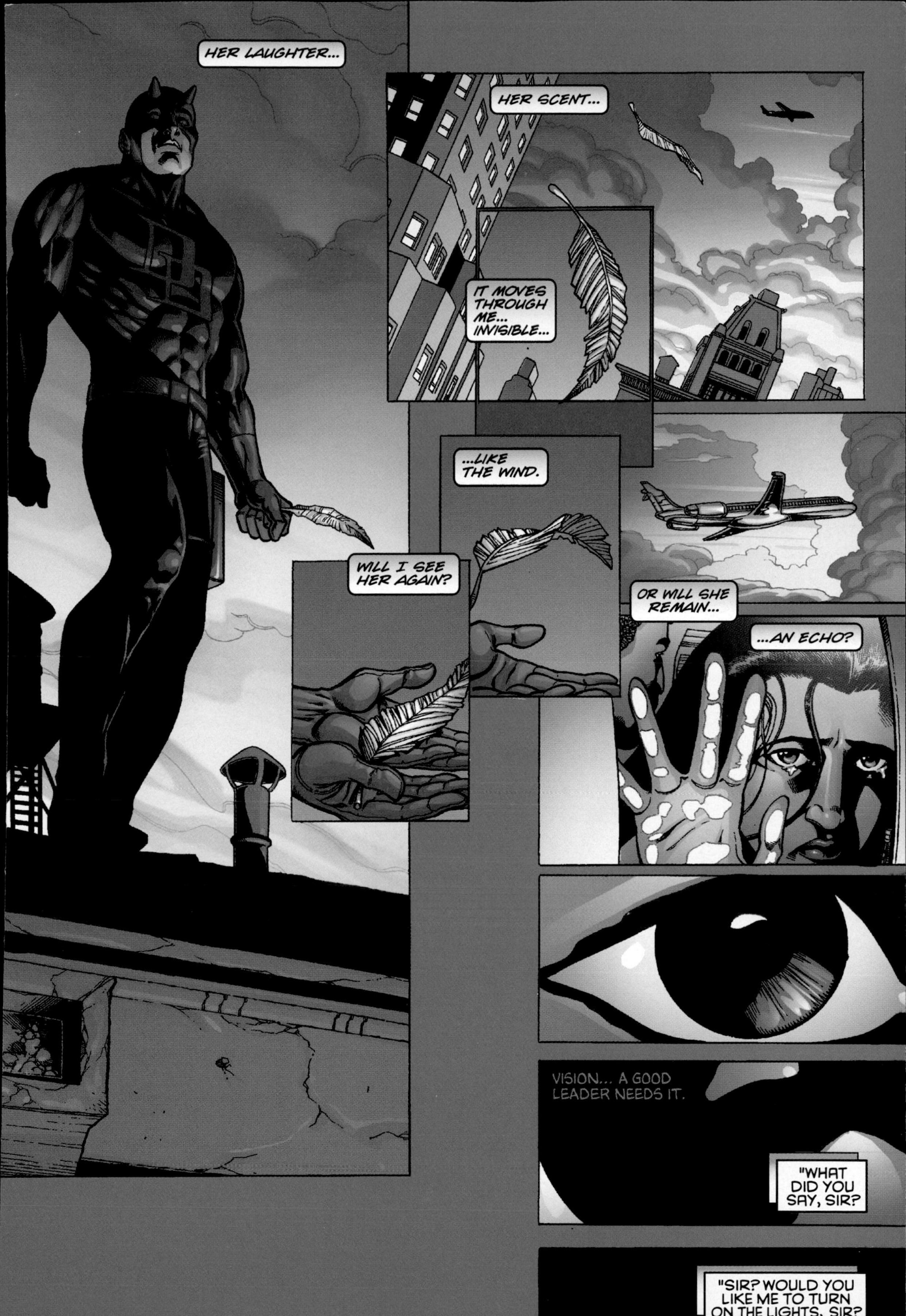
HER LAUGHTER...
HER SCENT...
IT MOVES THROUGH ME... INVISIBLE...
...LIKE THE WIND.
WILL I SEE HER AGAIN?
OR WILL SHE REMAIN...
...AN ECHO?
VISION... A GOOD LEADER NEEDS IT.
"WHAT DID YOU SAY, SIR?
"SIR? WOULD YOU LIKE ME TO TURN ON THE LIGHTS, SIR?

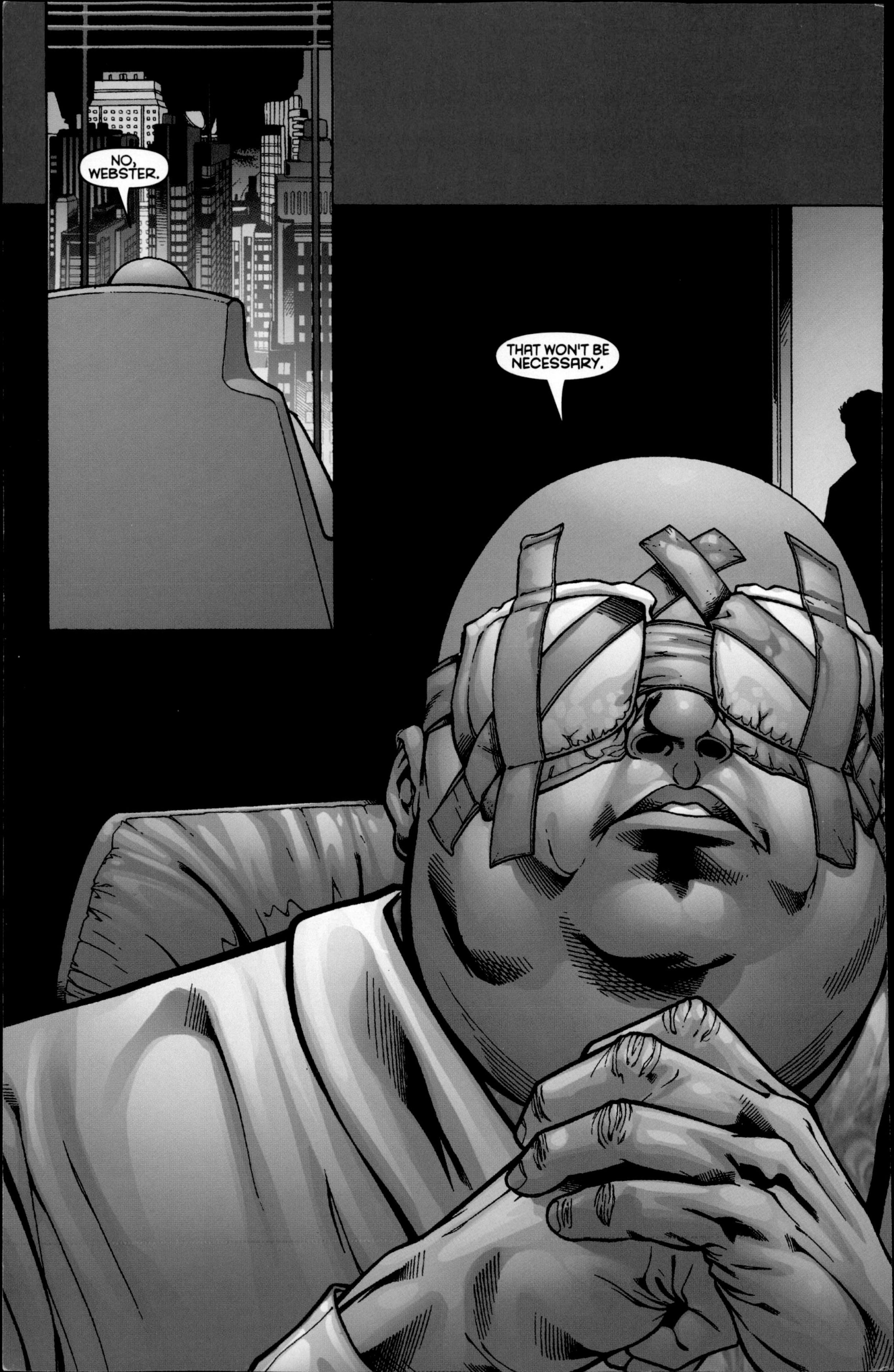
NO, WEBSTER.
THAT WON'T BE NECESSARY.

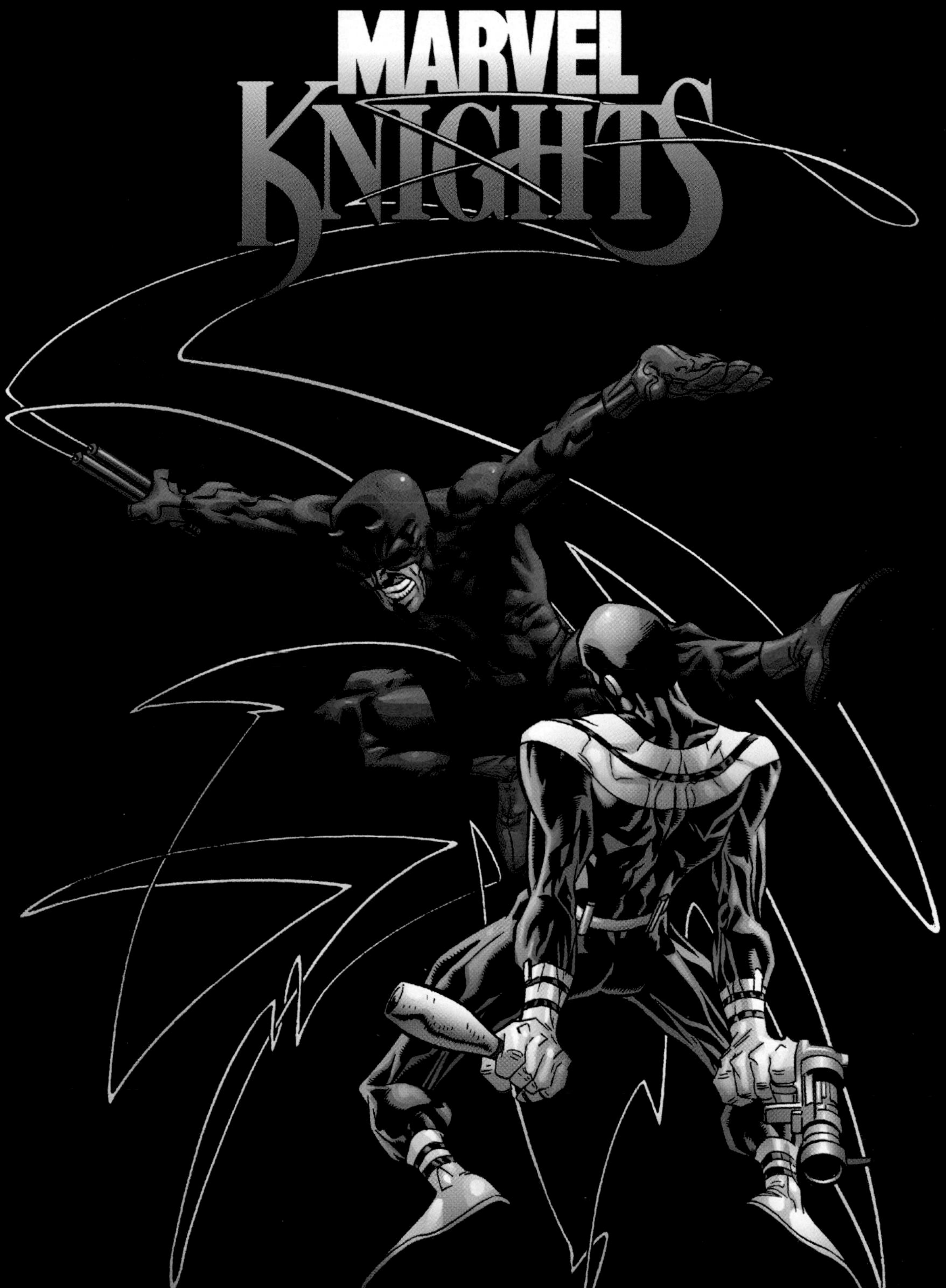
MARVEL
KNIGHTS

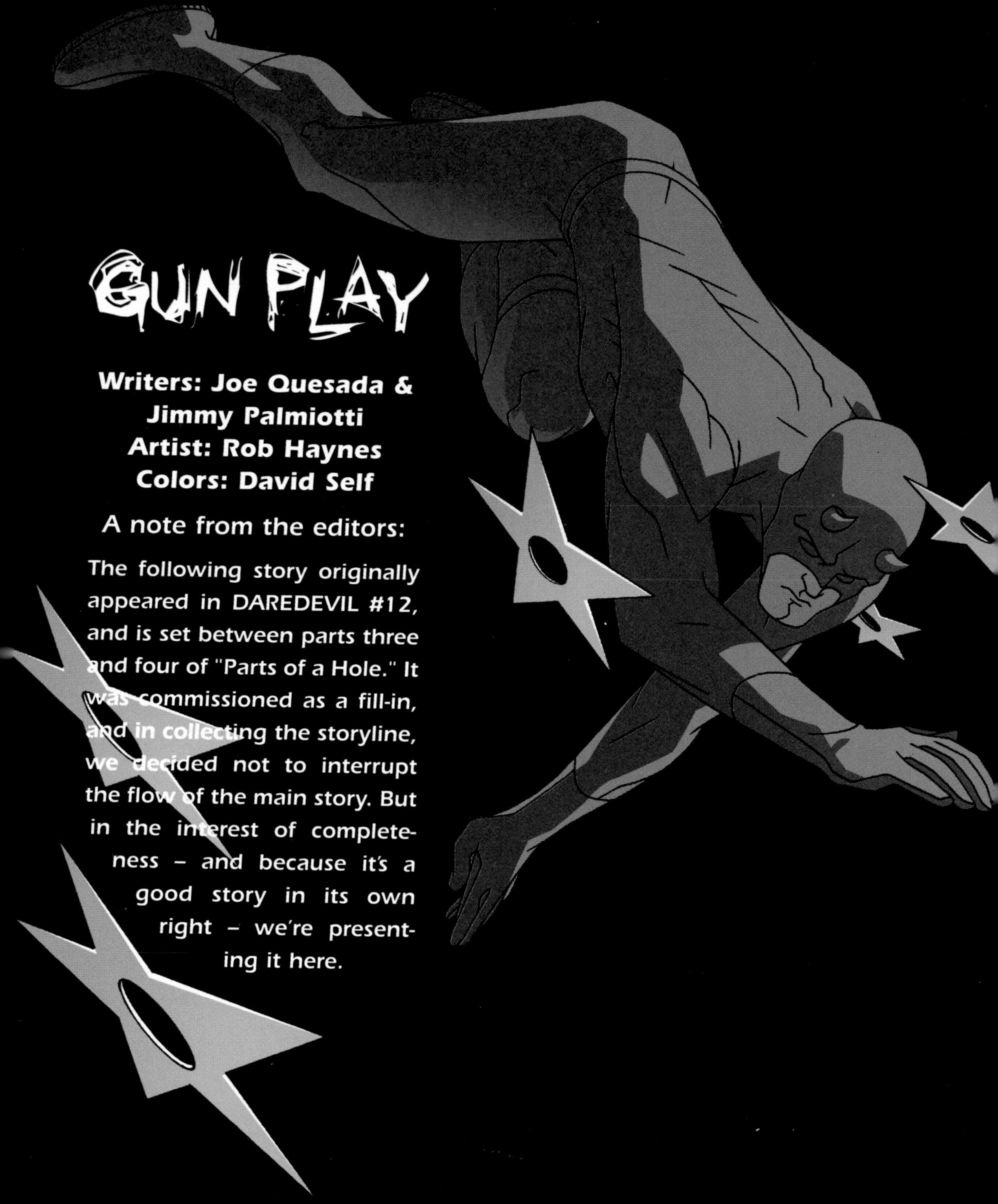

GUN PLAY

Writers: Joe Quesada & Jimmy Palmiotti
Artist: Rob Haynes
Colors: David Self

A note from the editors:

The following story originally appeared in DAREDEVIL #12, and is set between parts three and four of "Parts of a Hole." It was commissioned as a fill-in, and in collecting the storyline, we decided not to interrupt the flow of the main story. But in the interest of completeness – and because it's a good story in its own right – we're presenting it here.

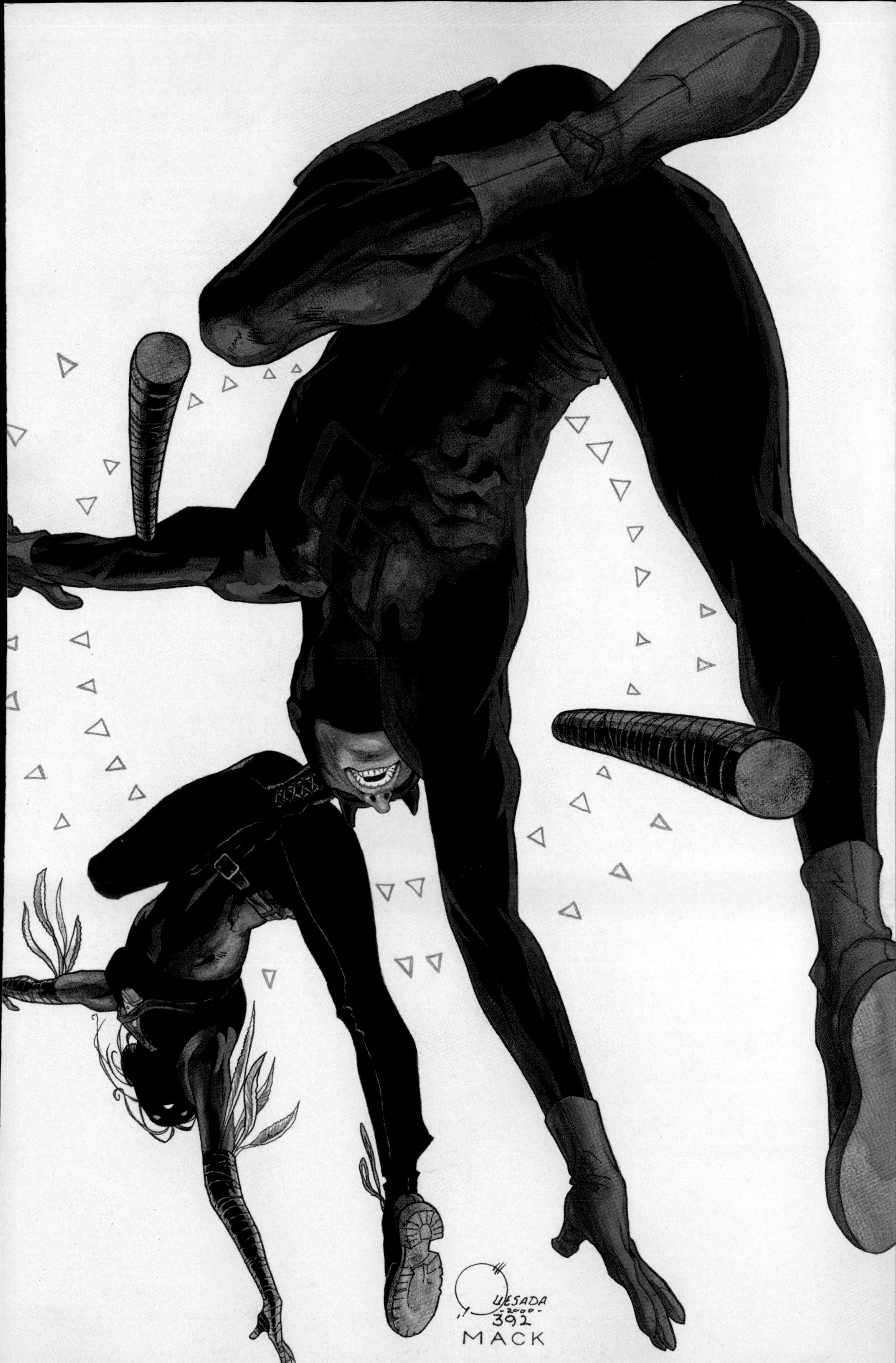
QUESADA
-2000-
392
MACK

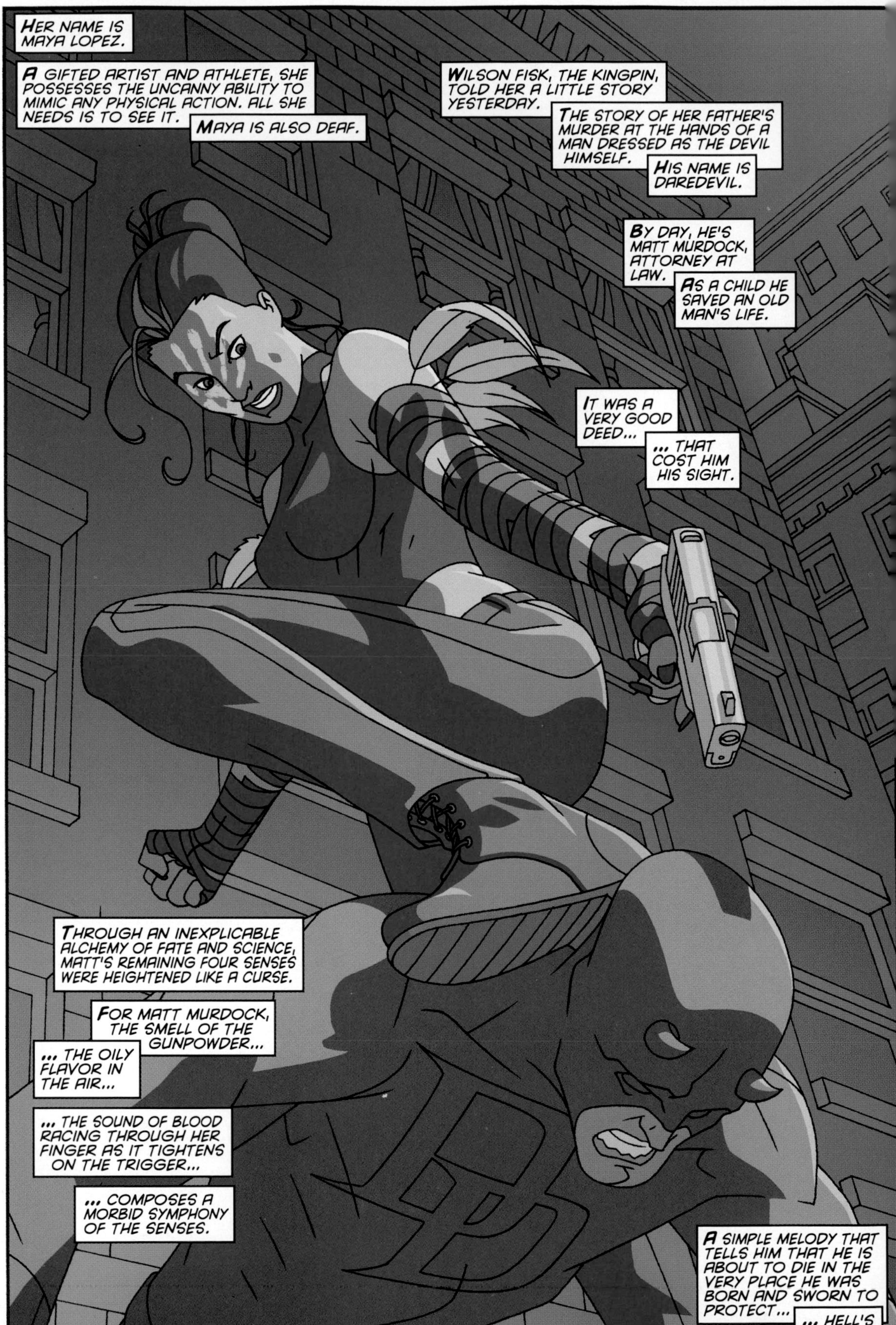
HER NAME IS MAYA LOPEZ.
A GIFTED ARTIST AND ATHLETE, SHE POSSESSES THE UNCANNY ABILITY TO MIMIC ANY PHYSICAL ACTION. ALL SHE NEEDS IS TO SEE IT.
MAYA IS ALSO DEAF.
WILSON FISK, THE KINGPIN, TOLD HER A LITTLE STORY YESTERDAY.
THE STORY OF HER FATHER'S MURDER AT THE HANDS OF A MAN DRESSED AS THE DEVIL HIMSELF.
HIS NAME IS DAREDEVIL.
BY DAY, HE'S MATT MURDOCK, ATTORNEY AT LAW.
AS A CHILD HE SAVED AN OLD MAN'S LIFE.
IT WAS A VERY GOOD DEED...
...THAT COST HIM HIS SIGHT.
THROUGH AN INEXPLICABLE ALCHEMY OF FATE AND SCIENCE, MATT'S REMAINING FOUR SENSES WERE HEIGHTENED LIKE A CURSE.
FOR MATT MURDOCK, THE SMELL OF THE GUNPOWDER...
...THE OILY FLAVOR IN THE AIR...
...THE SOUND OF BLOOD RACING THROUGH HER FINGER AS IT TIGHTENS ON THE TRIGGER...
...COMPOSES A MORBID SYMPHONY OF THE SENSES.
A SIMPLE MELODY THAT TELLS HIM THAT HE IS ABOUT TO DIE IN THE VERY PLACE HE WAS BORN AND SWORN TO PROTECT...
...HELL'S KITCHEN.

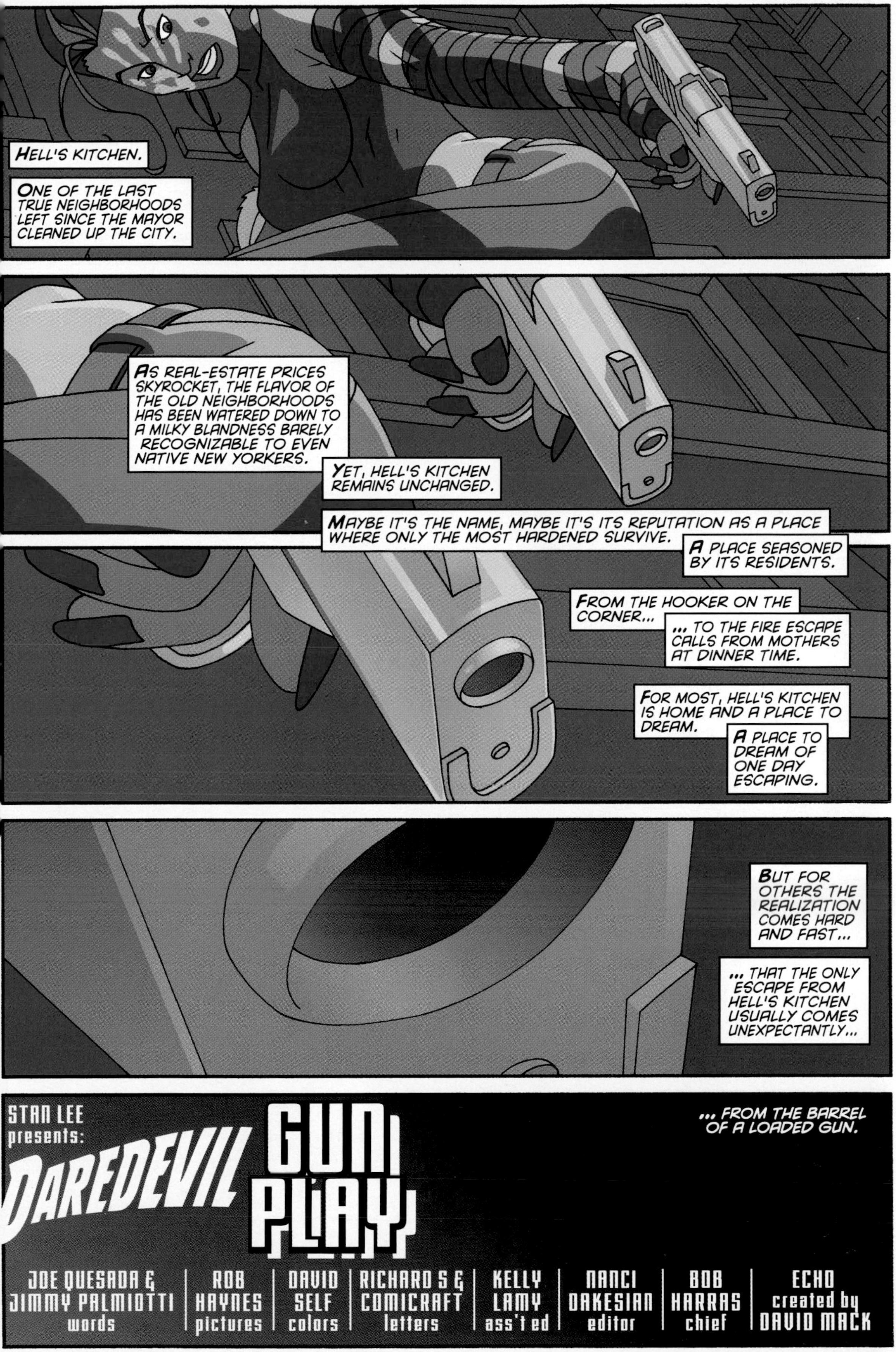
HELL'S KITCHEN.
ONE OF THE LAST TRUE NEIGHBORHOODS LEFT SINCE THE MAYOR CLEANED UP THE CITY.
AS REAL-ESTATE PRICES SKYROCKET, THE FLAVOR OF THE OLD NEIGHBORHOODS HAS BEEN WATERED DOWN TO A MILKY BLANDNESS BARELY RECOGNIZABLE TO EVEN NATIVE NEW YORKERS.
YET, HELL'S KITCHEN REMAINS UNCHANGED.
MAYBE IT'S THE NAME, MAYBE IT'S ITS REPUTATION AS A PLACE WHERE ONLY THE MOST HARDENED SURVIVE.
A PLACE SEASONED BY ITS RESIDENTS.
FROM THE HOOKER ON THE CORNER...
...TO THE FIRE ESCAPE CALLS FROM MOTHERS AT DINNER TIME.
FOR MOST, HELL'S KITCHEN IS HOME AND A PLACE TO DREAM.
A PLACE TO DREAM OF ONE DAY ESCAPING.
BUT FOR OTHERS THE REALIZATION COMES HARD AND FAST...
...THAT THE ONLY ESCAPE FROM HELL'S KITCHEN USUALLY COMES UNEXPECTANTLY...
STAN LEE presents:
DAREDEVIL
GUN PLAY
...FROM THE BARREL OF A LOADED GUN.
JOE QUESADA & JIMMY PALMIOTTI words
ROB HAYNES pictures
DAVID SELF colors
RICHARD S & COMICRAFT letters
KELLY LAMY ass't ed
NANCI DAKESIAN editor
BOB HARRAS chief
ECHO created by DAVID MACK

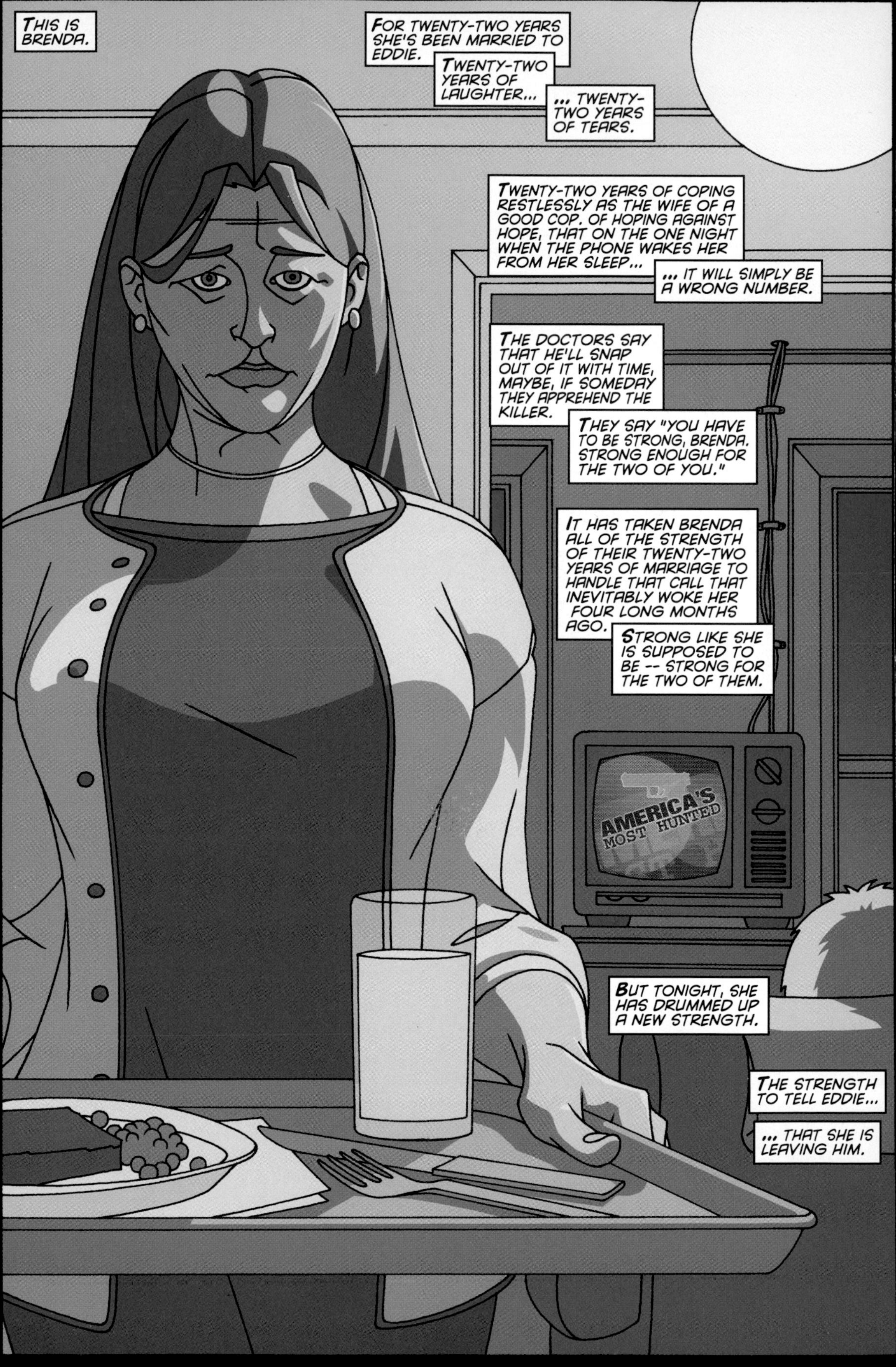
THIS IS BRENDA.
FOR TWENTY-TWO YEARS SHE'S BEEN MARRIED TO EDDIE.
TWENTY-TWO YEARS OF LAUGHTER...
... TWENTY-TWO YEARS OF TEARS.
TWENTY-TWO YEARS OF COPING RESTLESSLY AS THE WIFE OF A GOOD COP. OF HOPING AGAINST HOPE, THAT ON THE ONE NIGHT WHEN THE PHONE WAKES HER FROM HER SLEEP...
... IT WILL SIMPLY BE A WRONG NUMBER.
THE DOCTORS SAY THAT HE'LL SNAP OUT OF IT WITH TIME, MAYBE, IF SOMEDAY THEY APPREHEND THE KILLER.
THEY SAY "YOU HAVE TO BE STRONG, BRENDA. STRONG ENOUGH FOR THE TWO OF YOU."
IT HAS TAKEN BRENDA ALL OF THE STRENGTH OF THEIR TWENTY-TWO YEARS OF MARRIAGE TO HANDLE THAT CALL THAT INEVITABLY WOKE HER FOUR LONG MONTHS AGO.
STRONG LIKE SHE IS SUPPOSED TO BE -- STRONG FOR THE TWO OF THEM.
AMERICA'S MOST HUNTED
BUT TONIGHT, SHE HAS DRUMMED UP A NEW STRENGTH.
THE STRENGTH TO TELL EDDIE...
... THAT SHE IS LEAVING HIM.

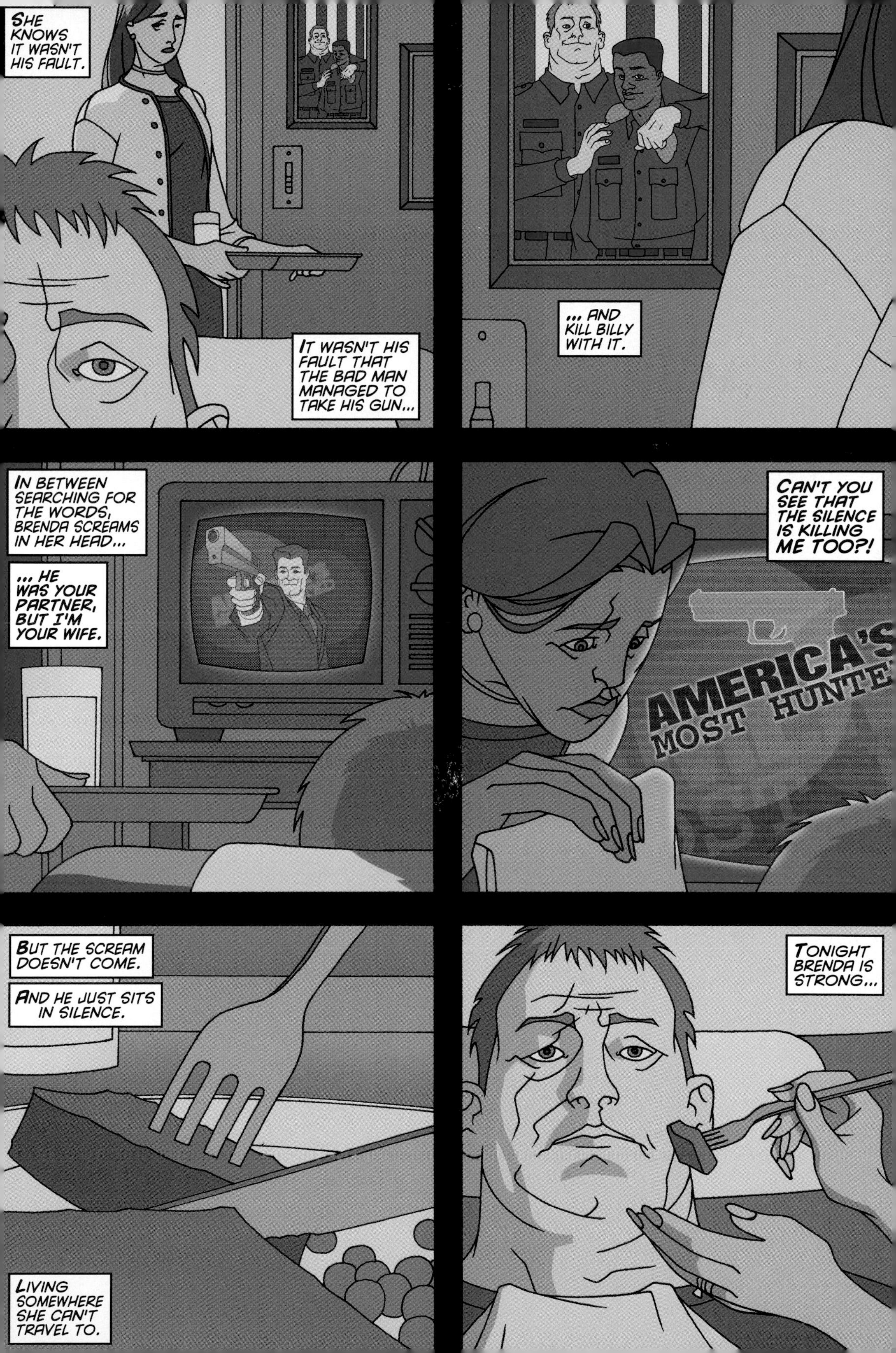
SHE KNOWS IT WASN'T HIS FAULT.
IT WASN'T HIS FAULT THAT THE BAD MAN MANAGED TO TAKE HIS GUN...
... AND KILL BILLY WITH IT.
IN BETWEEN SEARCHING FOR THE WORDS, BRENDA SCREAMS IN HER HEAD...
... HE WAS YOUR PARTNER, BUT I'M YOUR WIFE.
CAN'T YOU SEE THAT THE SILENCE IS KILLING ME TOO?!
AMERICA'S MOST HUNTE
BUT THE SCREAM DOESN'T COME.
AND HE JUST SITS IN SILENCE.
LIVING SOMEWHERE SHE CAN'T TRAVEL TO.
TONIGHT BRENDA IS STRONG...

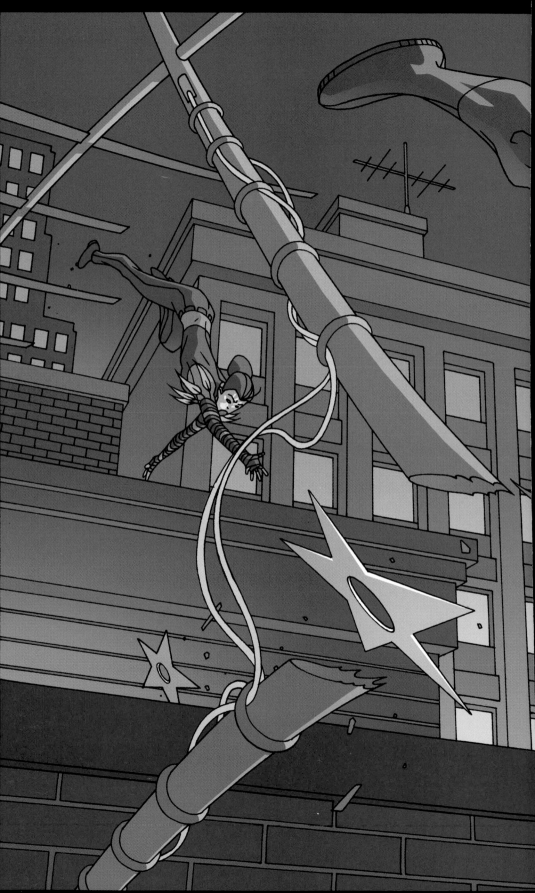

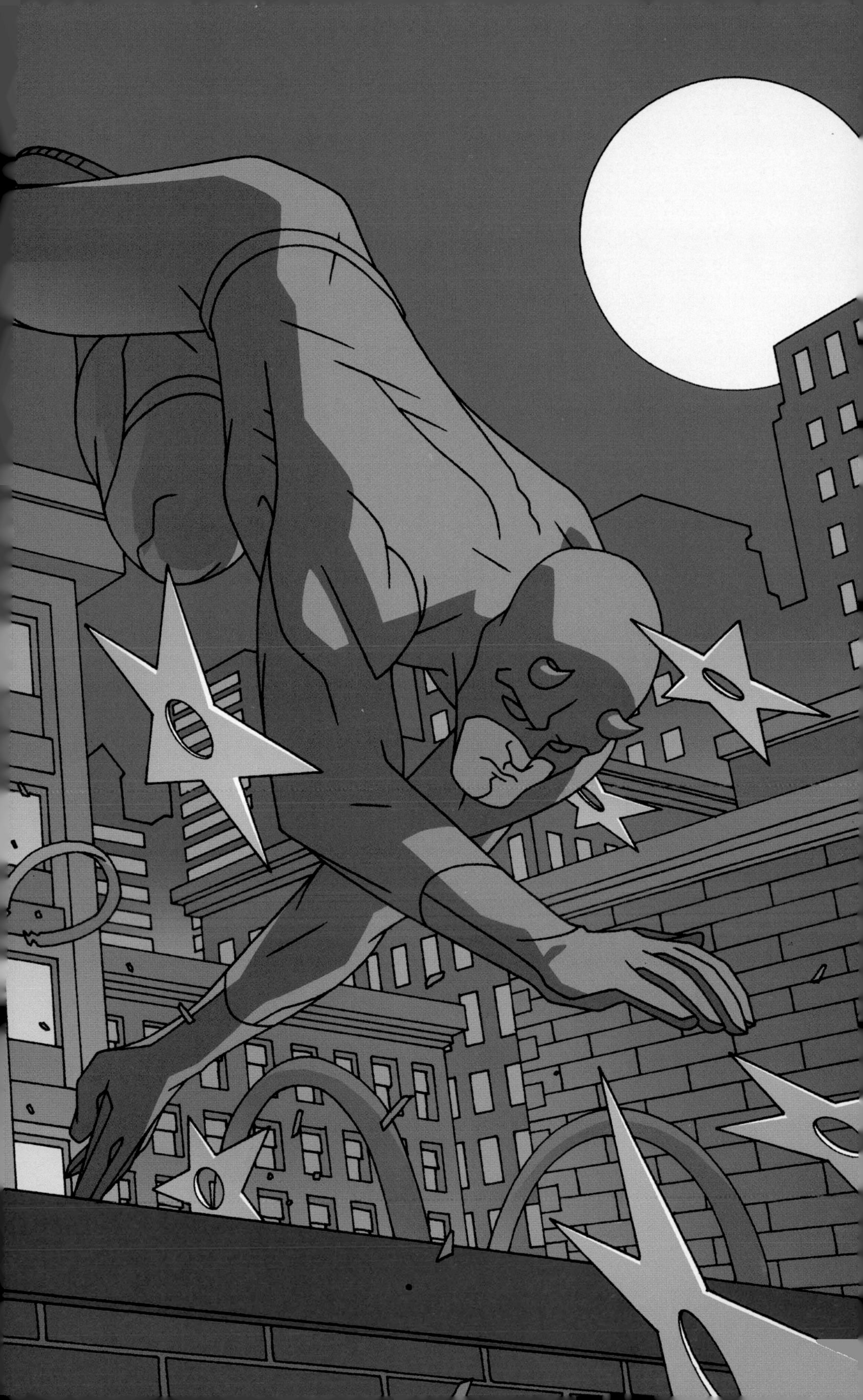

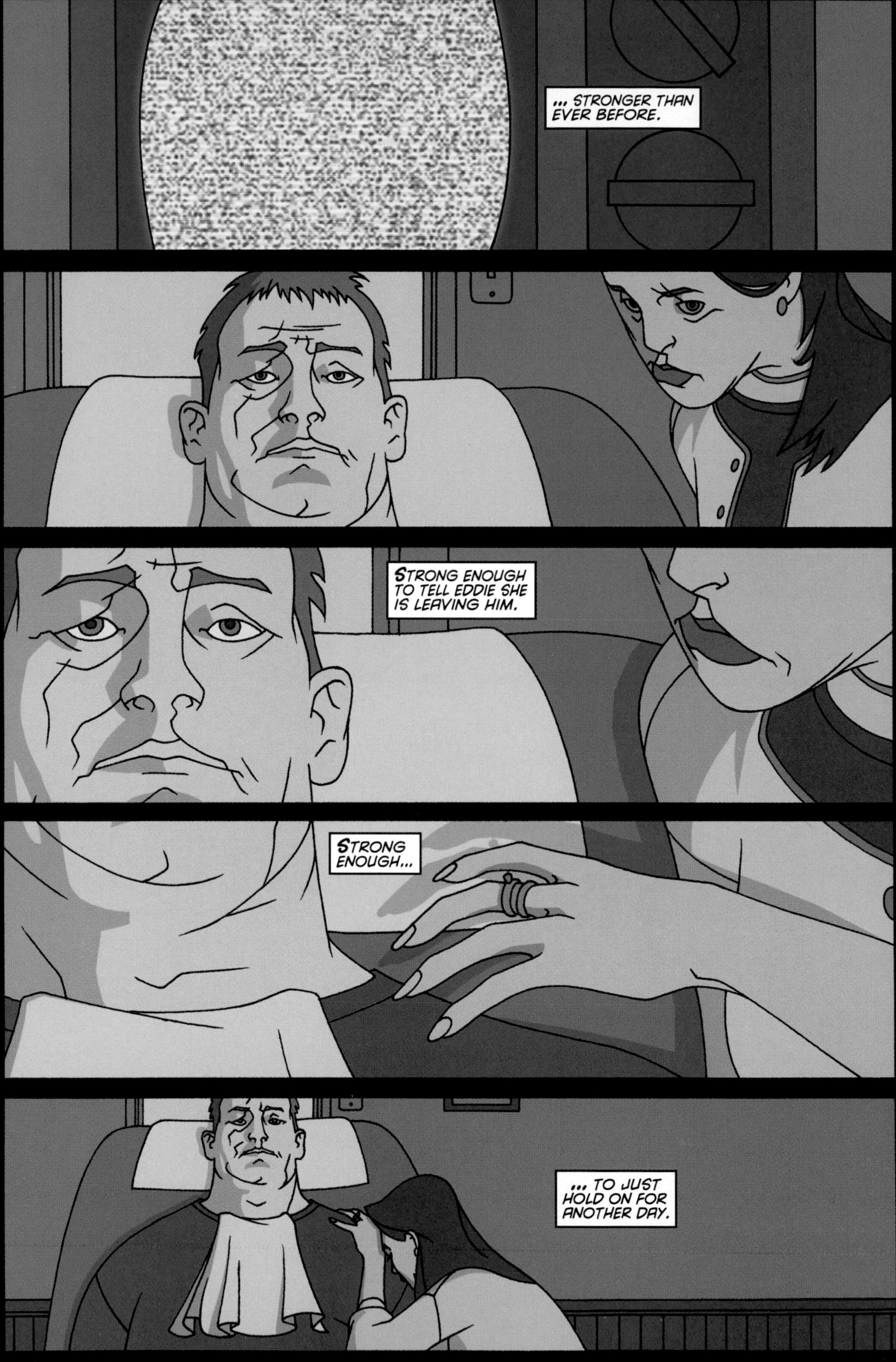
... STRONGER THAN EVER BEFORE.
STRONG ENOUGH TO TELL EDDIE SHE IS LEAVING HIM.
STRONG ENOUGH...
... TO JUST HOLD ON FOR ANOTHER DAY.

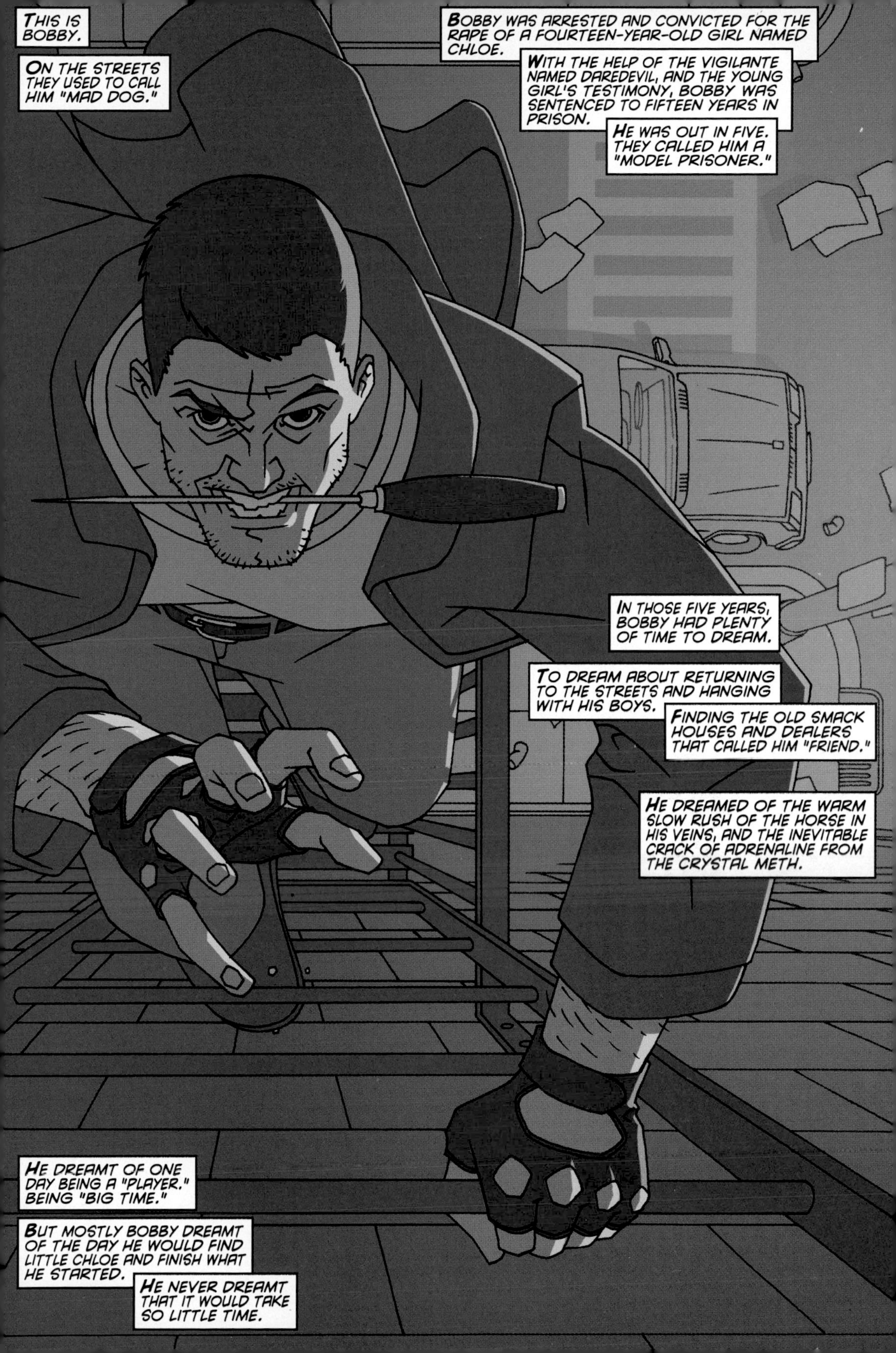
THIS IS BOBBY.
ON THE STREETS THEY USED TO CALL HIM "MAD DOG."
BOBBY WAS ARRESTED AND CONVICTED FOR THE RAPE OF A FOURTEEN-YEAR-OLD GIRL NAMED CHLOE.
WITH THE HELP OF THE VIGILANTE NAMED DAREDEVIL, AND THE YOUNG GIRL'S TESTIMONY, BOBBY WAS SENTENCED TO FIFTEEN YEARS IN PRISON.
HE WAS OUT IN FIVE. THEY CALLED HIM A "MODEL PRISONER."
IN THOSE FIVE YEARS, BOBBY HAD PLENTY OF TIME TO DREAM.
TO DREAM ABOUT RETURNING TO THE STREETS AND HANGING WITH HIS BOYS.
FINDING THE OLD SMACK HOUSES AND DEALERS THAT CALLED HIM "FRIEND."
HE DREAMED OF THE WARM SLOW RUSH OF THE HORSE IN HIS VEINS, AND THE INEVITABLE CRACK OF ADRENALINE FROM THE CRYSTAL METH.
HE DREAMT OF ONE DAY BEING A "PLAYER." BEING "BIG TIME."
BUT MOSTLY BOBBY DREAMT OF THE DAY HE WOULD FIND LITTLE CHLOE AND FINISH WHAT HE STARTED.
HE NEVER DREAMT THAT IT WOULD TAKE SO LITTLE TIME.

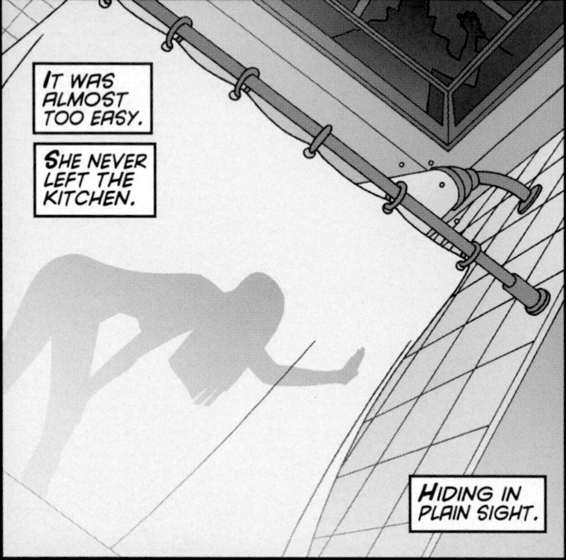
IT WAS ALMOST TOO EASY.
SHE NEVER LEFT THE KITCHEN.
HIDING IN PLAIN SIGHT.

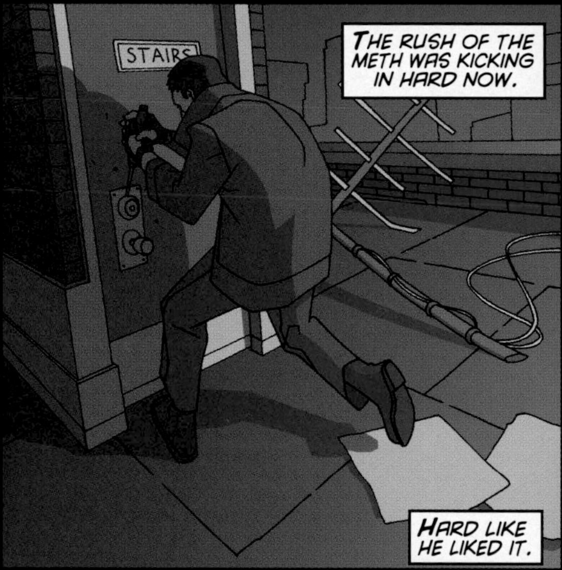
THE RUSH OF THE METH WAS KICKING IN HARD NOW.
STAIRS
HARD LIKE HE LIKED IT.

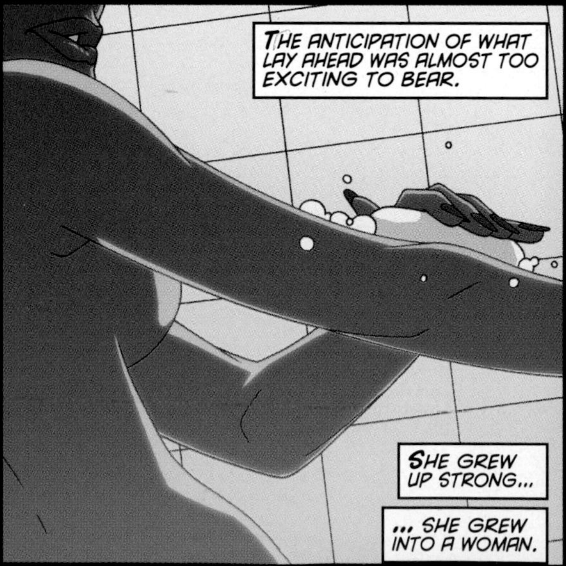
THE ANTICIPATION OF WHAT LAY AHEAD WAS ALMOST TOO EXCITING TO BEAR.
SHE GREW UP STRONG...
... SHE GREW INTO A WOMAN.

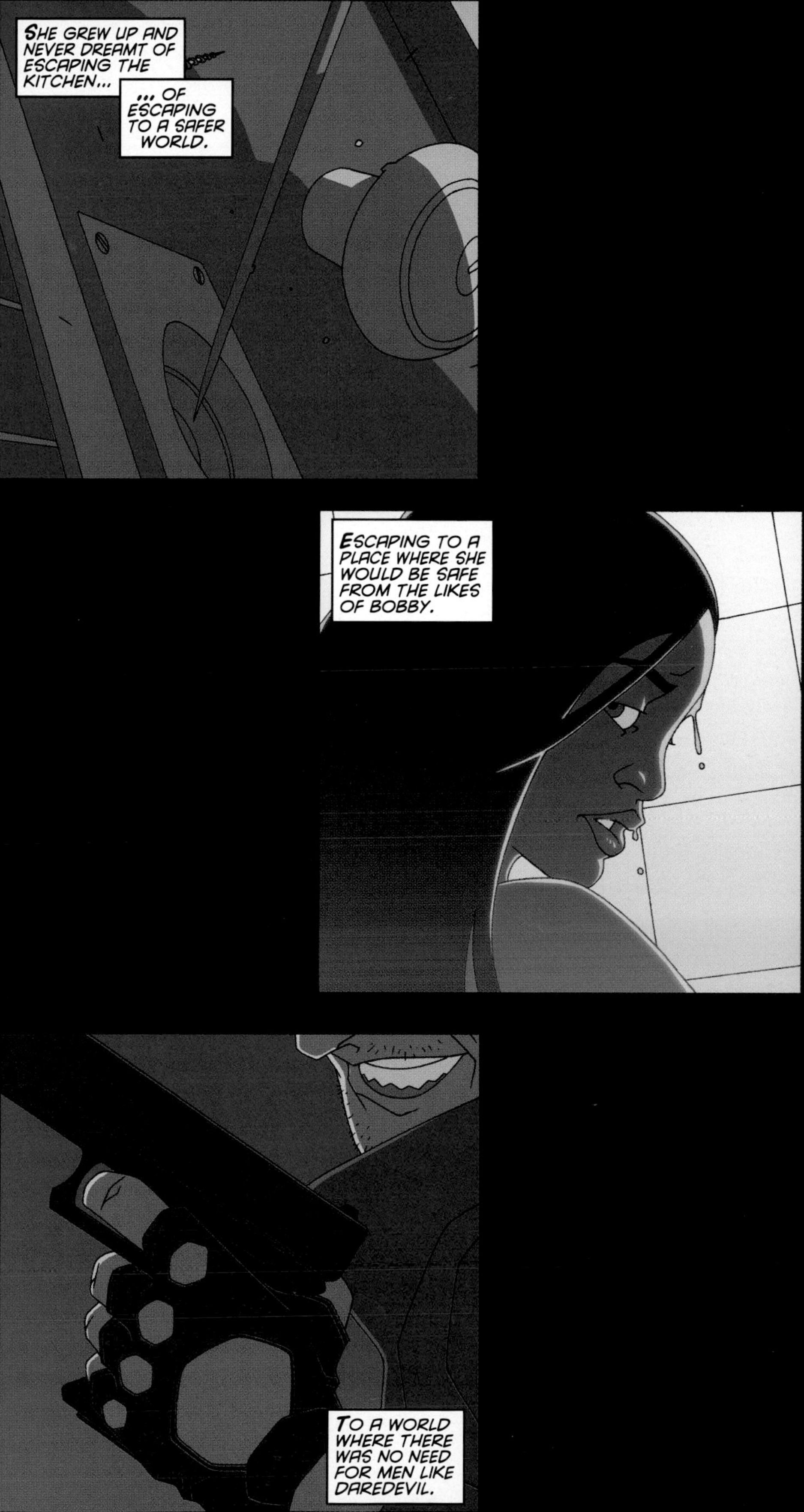
SHE GREW UP AND NEVER DREAMT OF ESCAPING THE KITCHEN...
... OF ESCAPING TO A SAFER WORLD.
ESCAPING TO A PLACE WHERE SHE WOULD BE SAFE FROM THE LIKES OF BOBBY.
TO A WORLD WHERE THERE WAS NO NEED FOR MEN LIKE DAREDEVIL.

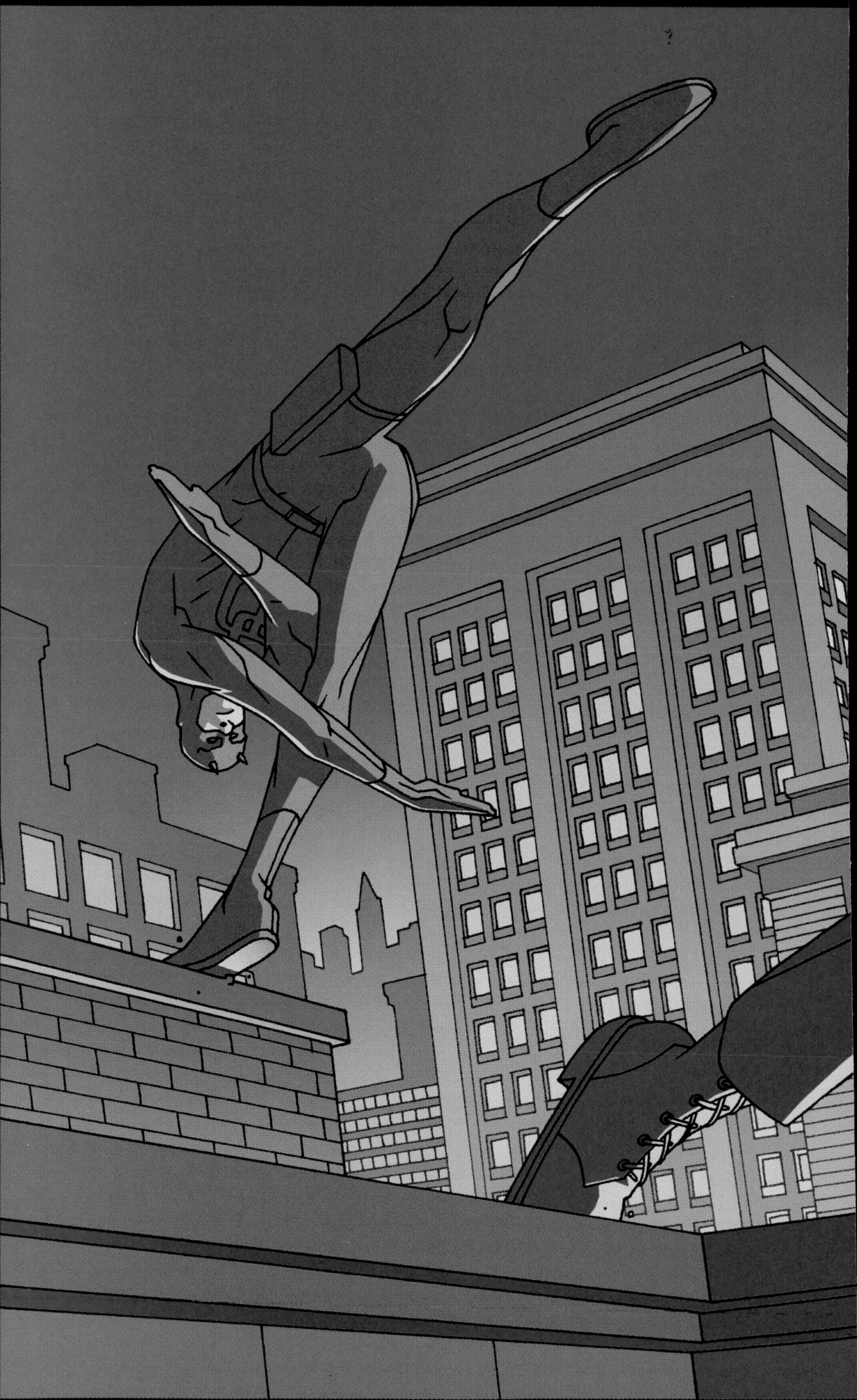

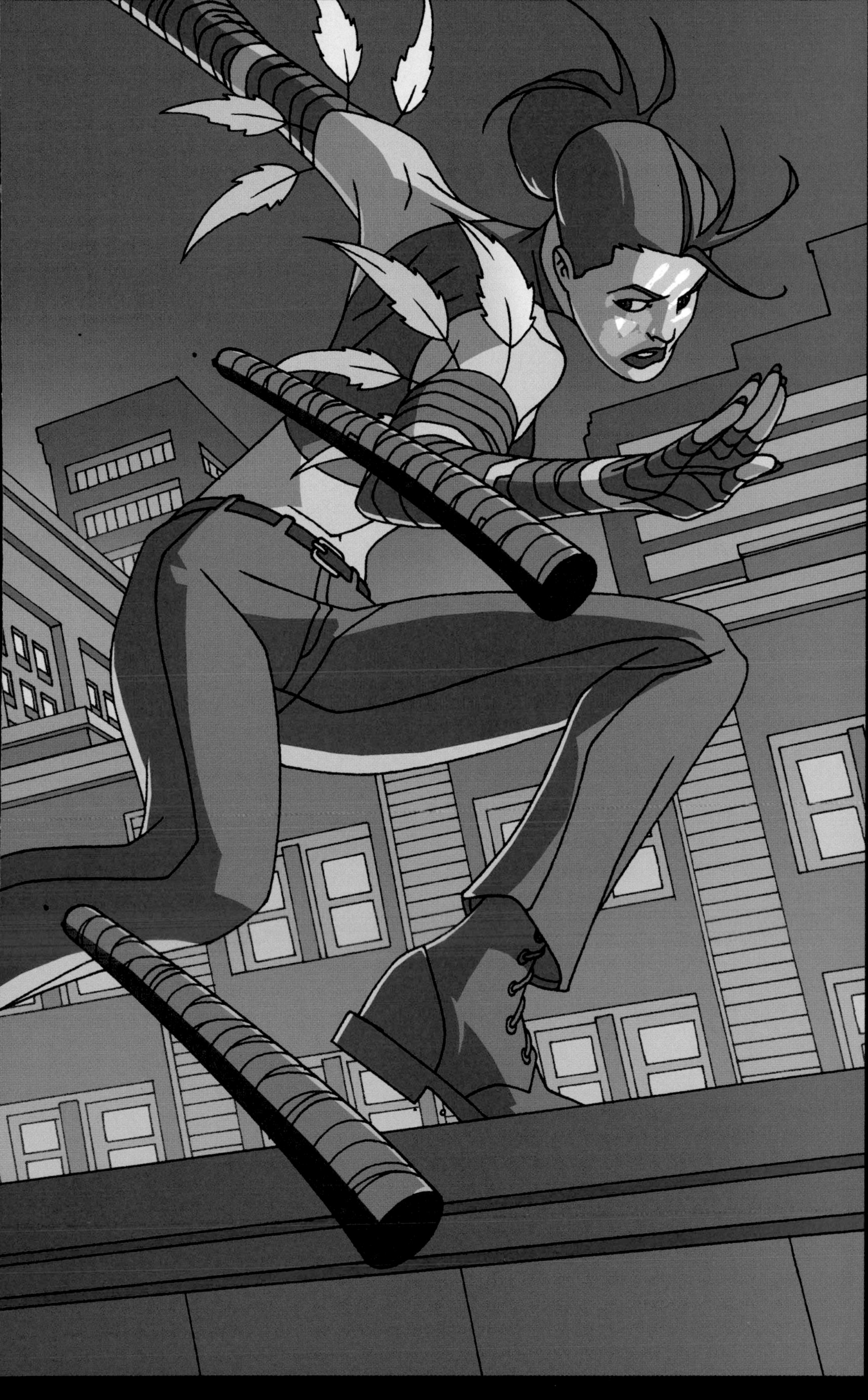

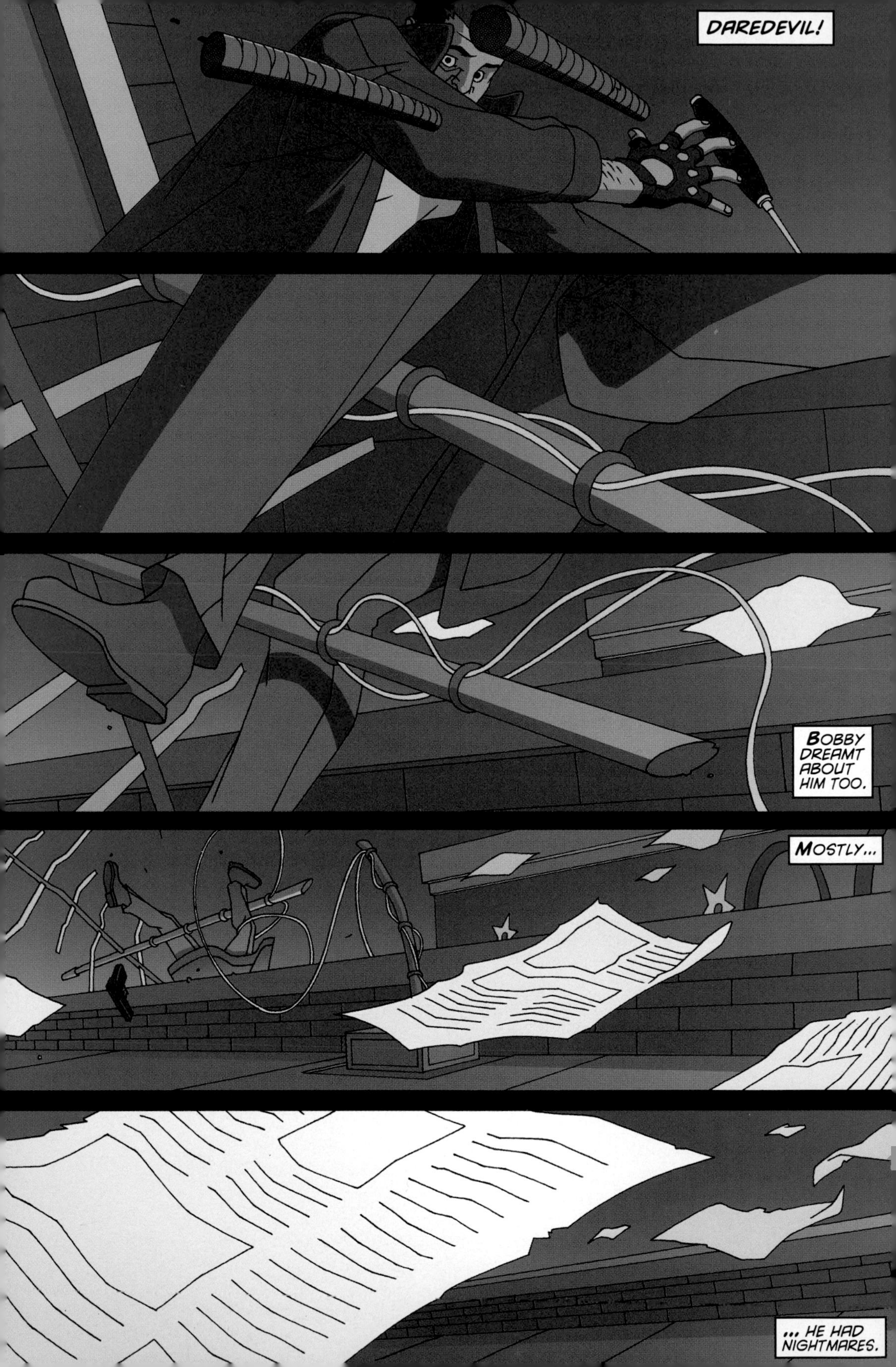
DAREDEVIL!
BOBBY DREAMT ABOUT HIM TOO.
MOSTLY...
... HE HAD NIGHTMARES.

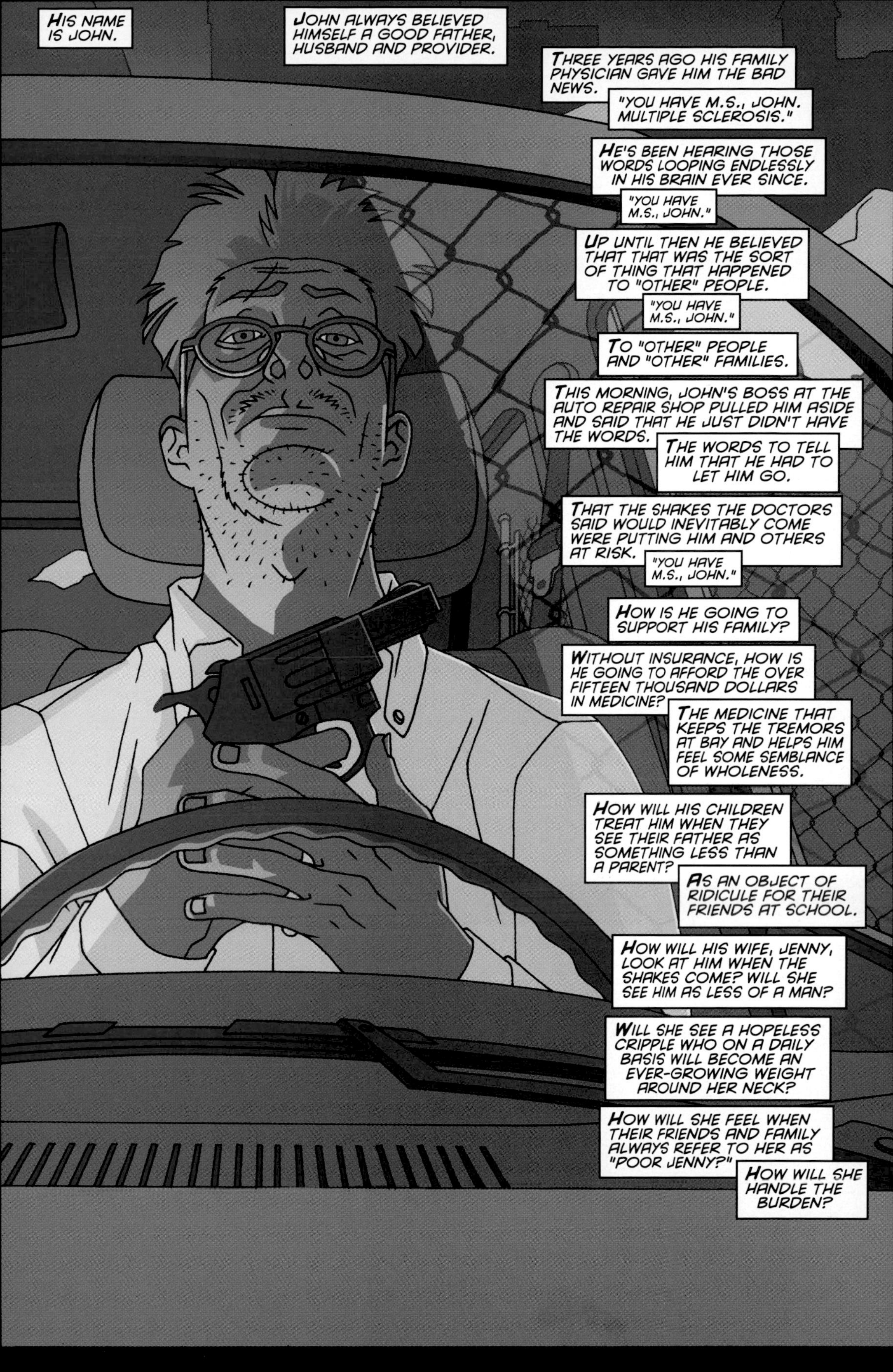
HIS NAME IS JOHN.
JOHN ALWAYS BELIEVED HIMSELF A GOOD FATHER, HUSBAND AND PROVIDER.
THREE YEARS AGO HIS FAMILY PHYSICIAN GAVE HIM THE BAD NEWS.
"YOU HAVE M.S., JOHN. MULTIPLE SCLEROSIS."
HE'S BEEN HEARING THOSE WORDS LOOPING ENDLESSLY IN HIS BRAIN EVER SINCE.
"YOU HAVE M.S., JOHN."
UP UNTIL THEN HE BELIEVED THAT THAT WAS THE SORT OF THING THAT HAPPENED TO "OTHER" PEOPLE.
"YOU HAVE M.S., JOHN."
TO "OTHER" PEOPLE AND "OTHER" FAMILIES.
THIS MORNING, JOHN'S BOSS AT THE AUTO REPAIR SHOP PULLED HIM ASIDE AND SAID THAT HE JUST DIDN'T HAVE THE WORDS.
THE WORDS TO TELL HIM THAT HE HAD TO LET HIM GO.
THAT THE SHAKES THE DOCTORS SAID WOULD INEVITABLY COME WERE PUTTING HIM AND OTHERS AT RISK.
"YOU HAVE M.S., JOHN."
HOW IS HE GOING TO SUPPORT HIS FAMILY?
WITHOUT INSURANCE, HOW IS HE GOING TO AFFORD THE OVER FIFTEEN THOUSAND DOLLARS IN MEDICINE?
THE MEDICINE THAT KEEPS THE TREMORS AT BAY AND HELPS HIM FEEL SOME SEMBLANCE OF WHOLENESS.
HOW WILL HIS CHILDREN TREAT HIM WHEN THEY SEE THEIR FATHER AS SOMETHING LESS THAN A PARENT?
AS AN OBJECT OF RIDICULE FOR THEIR FRIENDS AT SCHOOL.
HOW WILL HIS WIFE, JENNY, LOOK AT HIM WHEN THE SHAKES COME? WILL SHE SEE HIM AS LESS OF A MAN?
WILL SHE SEE A HOPELESS CRIPPLE WHO ON A DAILY BASIS WILL BECOME AN EVER-GROWING WEIGHT AROUND HER NECK?
HOW WILL SHE FEEL WHEN THEIR FRIENDS AND FAMILY ALWAYS REFER TO HER AS "POOR JENNY?"
HOW WILL SHE HANDLE THE BURDEN?

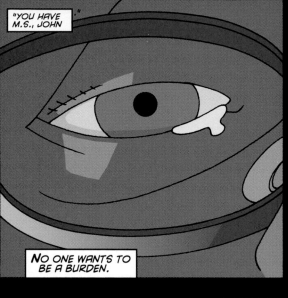

"YOU HAVE M.S., JOHN "

NO ONE WANTS TO BE A BURDEN.

"YOU HAVE M.S., JOHN."

JOHN USED TO BELIEVE ONE SHOULD NEVER QUESTION GOD.

"YOU HAVE M.S., JOHN."

FOR HE GIVES US NO MORE THAN HE FEELS WE ARE CAPABLE OF HANDLING.

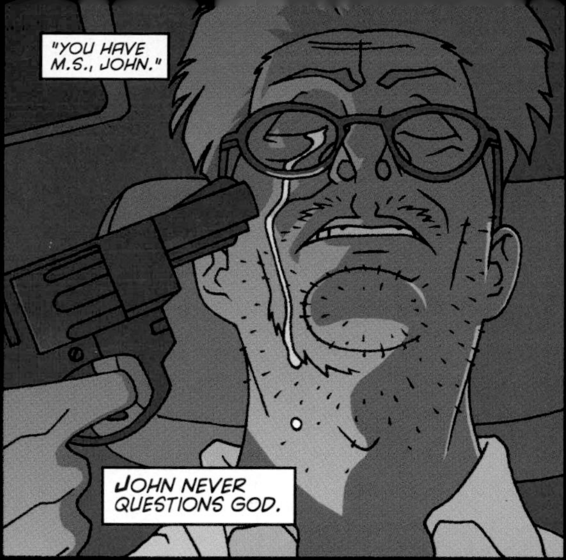
"YOU HAVE M.S., JOHN."
JOHN NEVER QUESTIONS GOD.
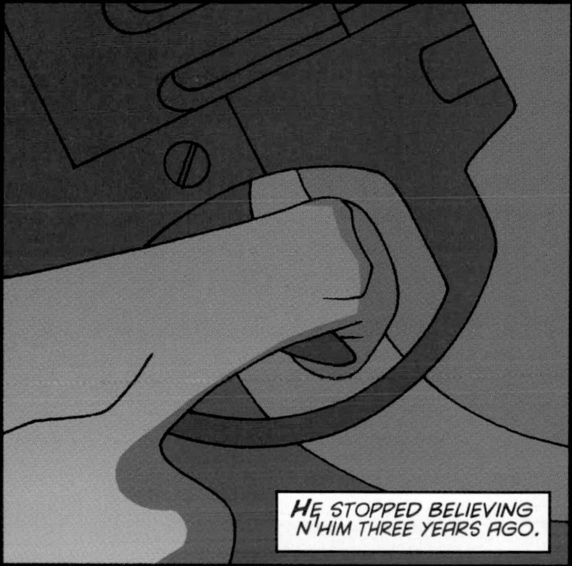
HE STOPPED BELIEVING N'HIM THREE YEARS AGO.
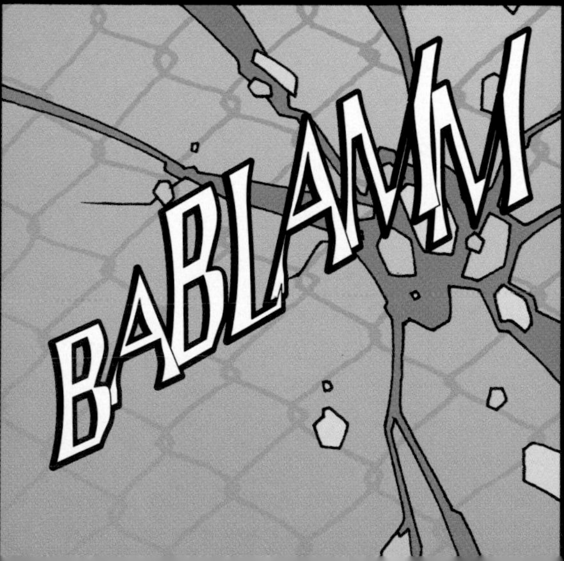
BABLAMM

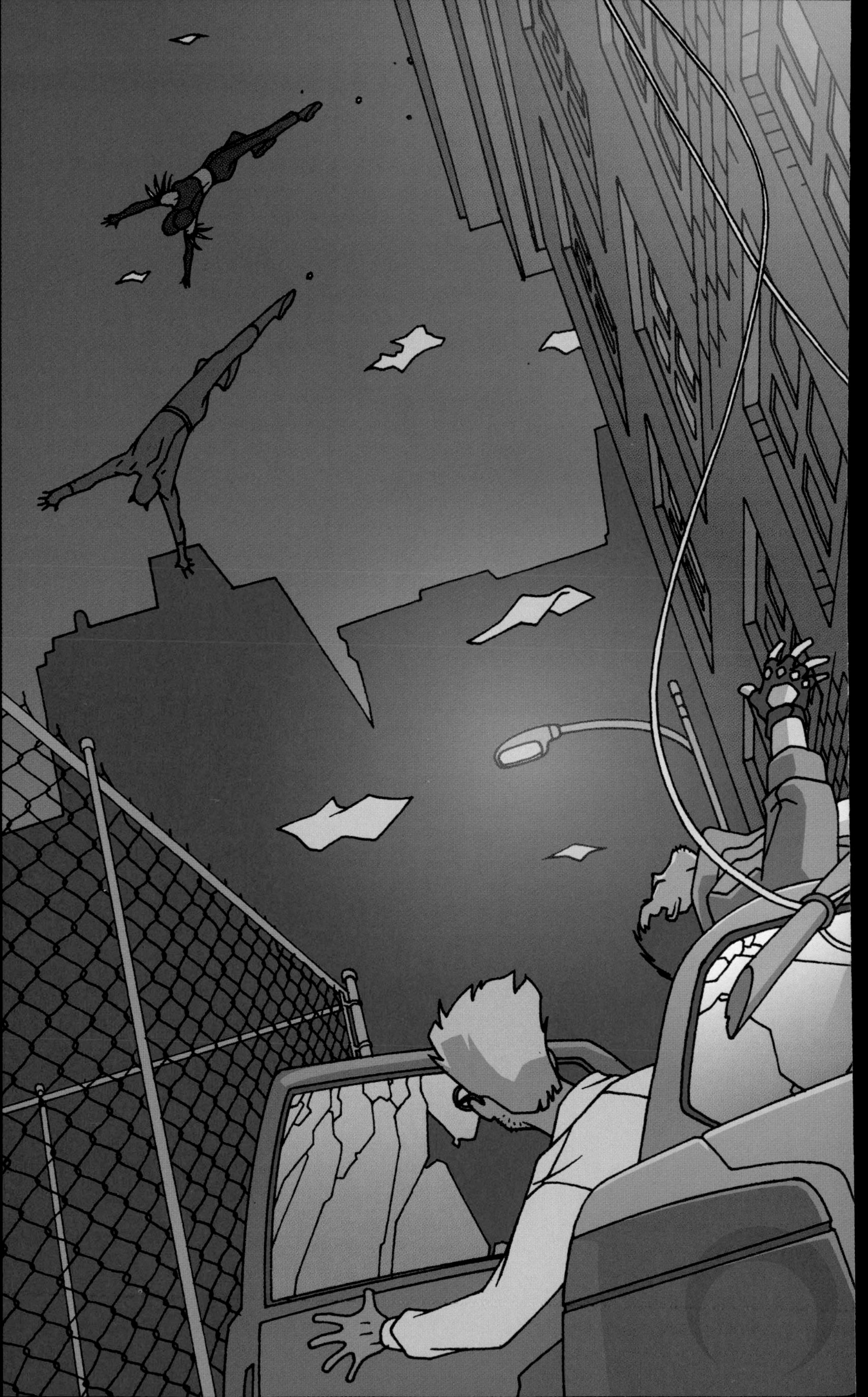

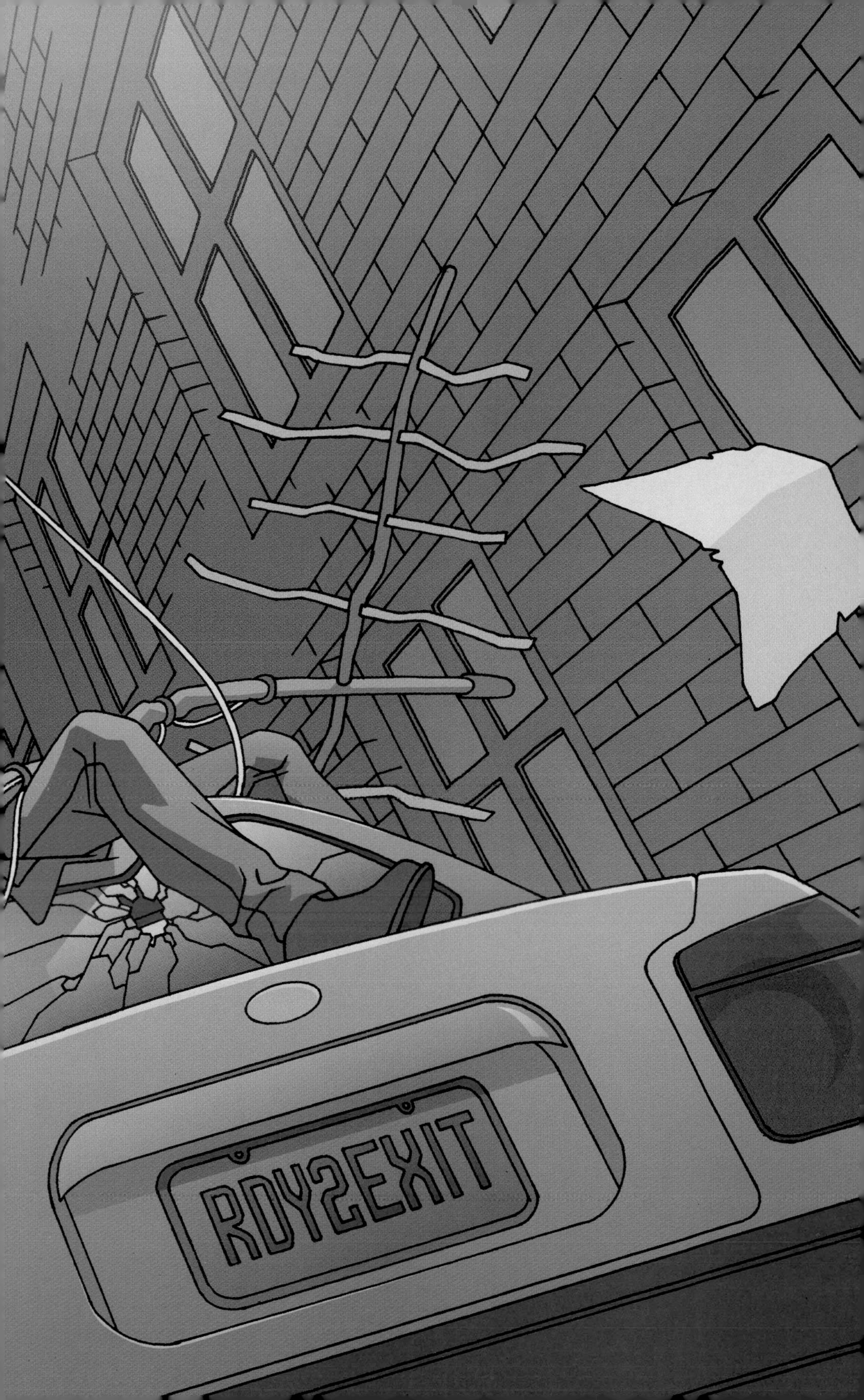
RDY2EXIT

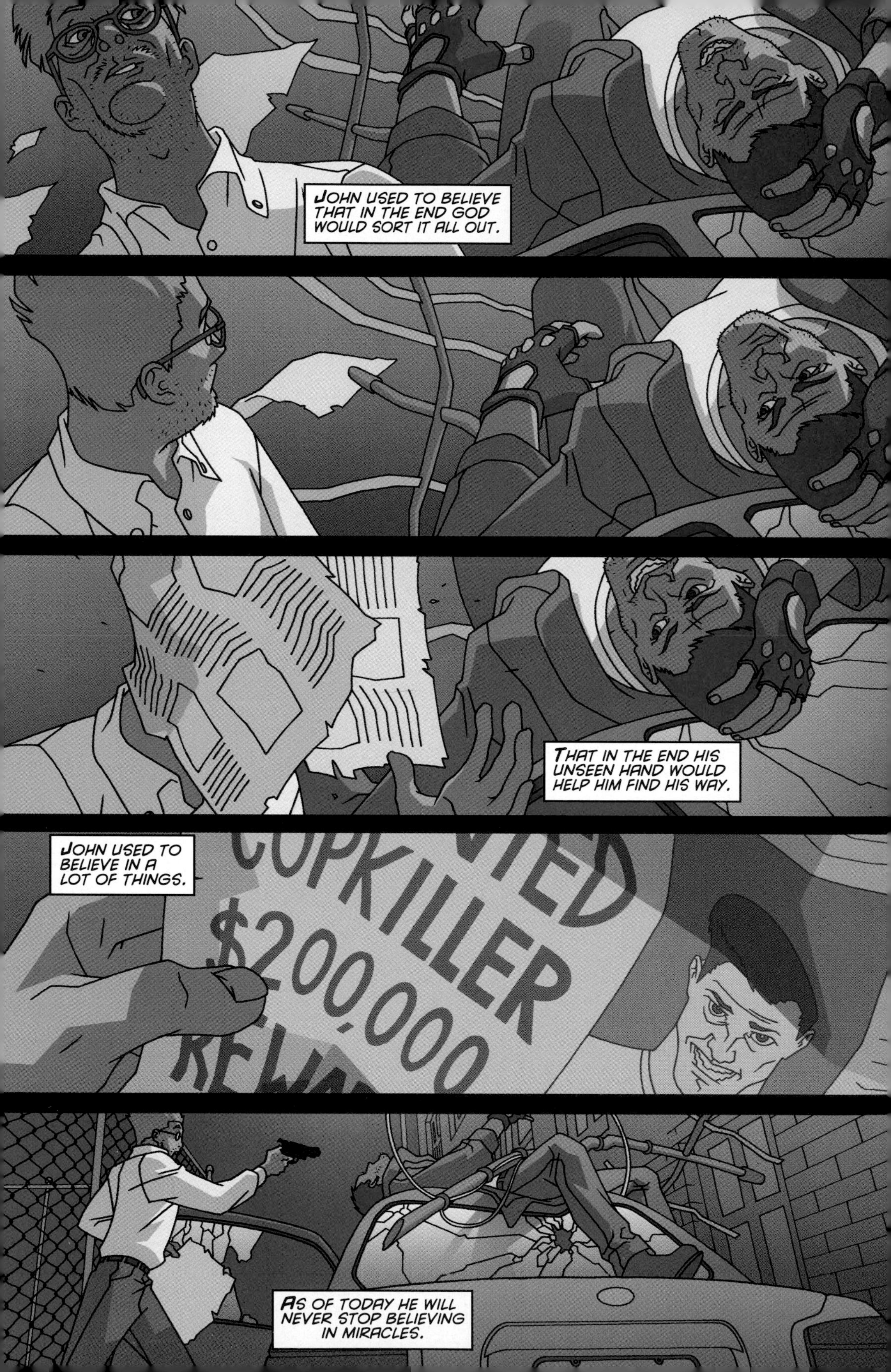
JOHN USED TO BELIEVE THAT IN THE END GOD WOULD SORT IT ALL OUT.
THAT IN THE END HIS UNSEEN HAND WOULD HELP HIM FIND HIS WAY.
JOHN USED TO BELIEVE IN A LOT OF THINGS.
COPKILLER
$200,000
AS OF TODAY HE WILL NEVER STOP BELIEVING IN MIRACLES.

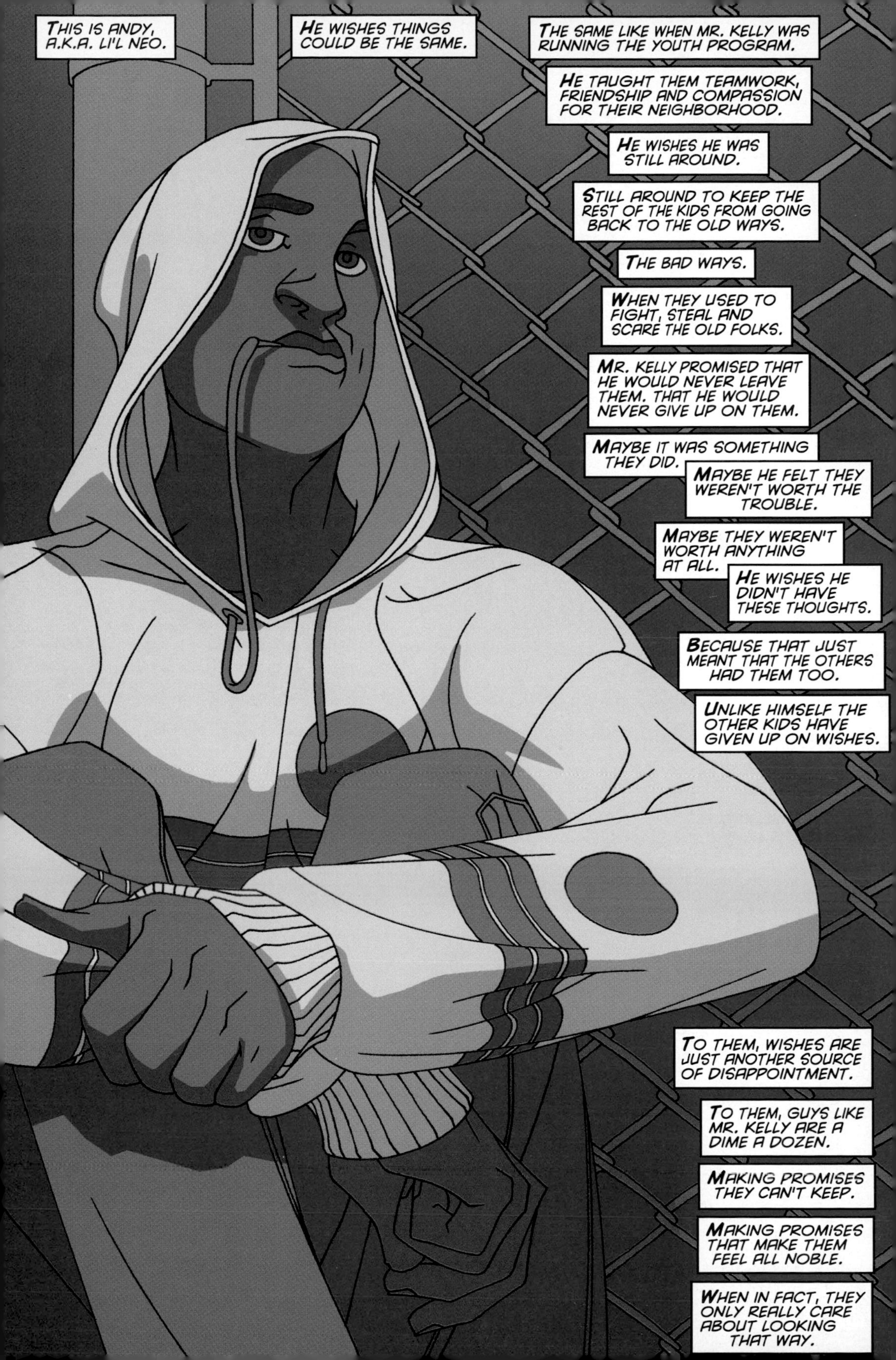
THIS IS ANDY, A.K.A. LI'L NEO.
HE WISHES THINGS COULD BE THE SAME.
THE SAME LIKE WHEN MR. KELLY WAS RUNNING THE YOUTH PROGRAM.
HE TAUGHT THEM TEAMWORK, FRIENDSHIP AND COMPASSION FOR THEIR NEIGHBORHOOD.
HE WISHES HE WAS STILL AROUND.
STILL AROUND TO KEEP THE REST OF THE KIDS FROM GOING BACK TO THE OLD WAYS.
THE BAD WAYS.
WHEN THEY USED TO FIGHT, STEAL AND SCARE THE OLD FOLKS.
MR. KELLY PROMISED THAT HE WOULD NEVER LEAVE THEM. THAT HE WOULD NEVER GIVE UP ON THEM.
MAYBE IT WAS SOMETHING THEY DID.
MAYBE HE FELT THEY WEREN'T WORTH THE TROUBLE.
MAYBE THEY WEREN'T WORTH ANYTHING AT ALL.
HE WISHES HE DIDN'T HAVE THESE THOUGHTS.
BECAUSE THAT JUST MEANT THAT THE OTHERS HAD THEM TOO.
UNLIKE HIMSELF THE OTHER KIDS HAVE GIVEN UP ON WISHES.
TO THEM, WISHES ARE JUST ANOTHER SOURCE OF DISAPPOINTMENT.
TO THEM, GUYS LIKE MR. KELLY ARE A DIME A DOZEN.
MAKING PROMISES THEY CAN'T KEEP.
MAKING PROMISES THAT MAKE THEM FEEL ALL NOBLE.
WHEN IN FACT, THEY ONLY REALLY CARE ABOUT LOOKING THAT WAY.

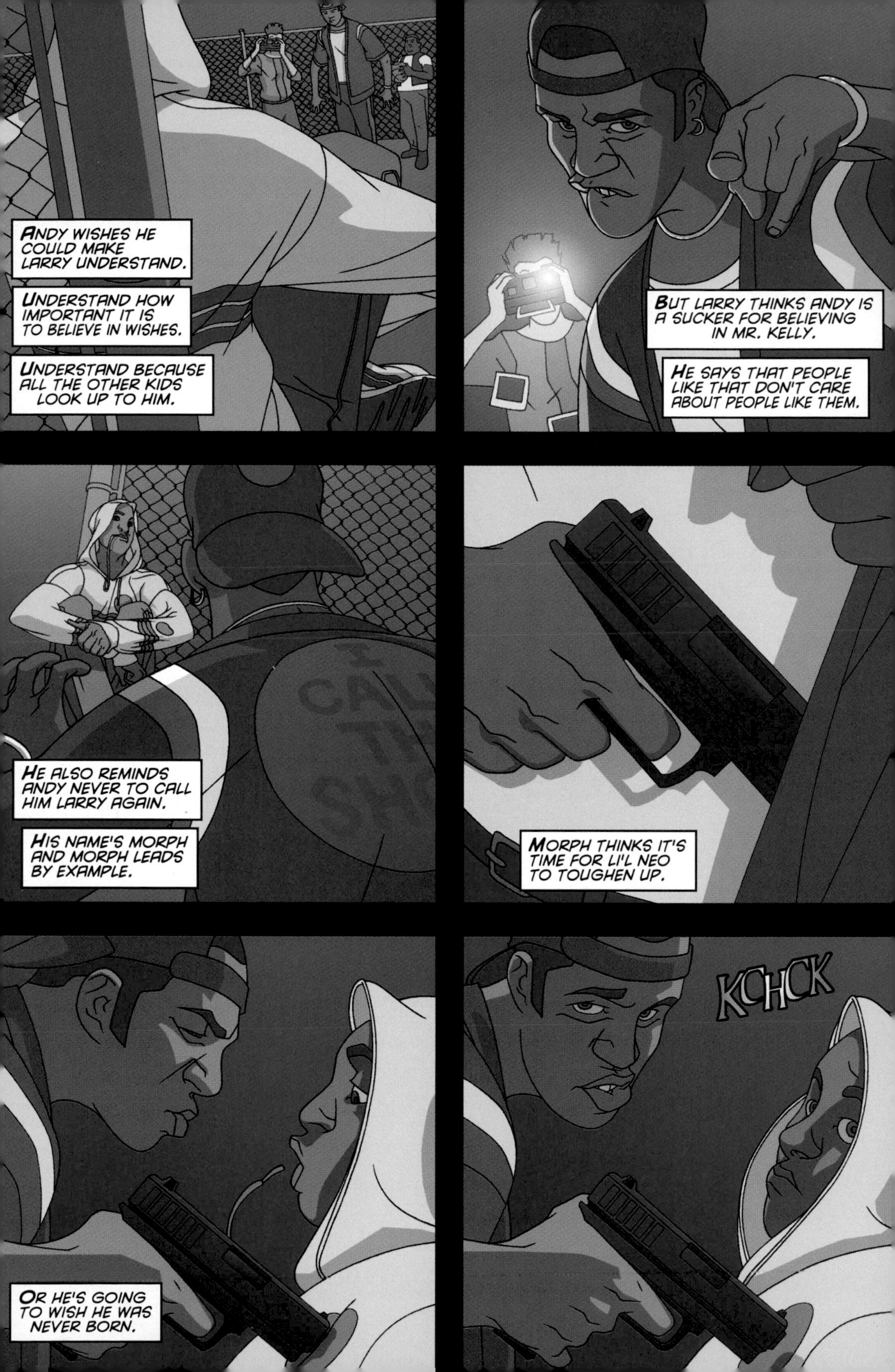
ANDY WISHES HE COULD MAKE LARRY UNDERSTAND.
UNDERSTAND HOW IMPORTANT IT IS TO BELIEVE IN WISHES.
UNDERSTAND BECAUSE ALL THE OTHER KIDS LOOK UP TO HIM.
BUT LARRY THINKS ANDY IS A SUCKER FOR BELIEVING IN MR. KELLY.
HE SAYS THAT PEOPLE LIKE THAT DON'T CARE ABOUT PEOPLE LIKE THEM.
HE ALSO REMINDS ANDY NEVER TO CALL HIM LARRY AGAIN.
HIS NAME'S MORPH AND MORPH LEADS BY EXAMPLE.
MORPH THINKS IT'S TIME FOR LI'L NEO TO TOUGHEN UP.
OR HE'S GOING TO WISH HE WAS NEVER BORN.
KCHCK

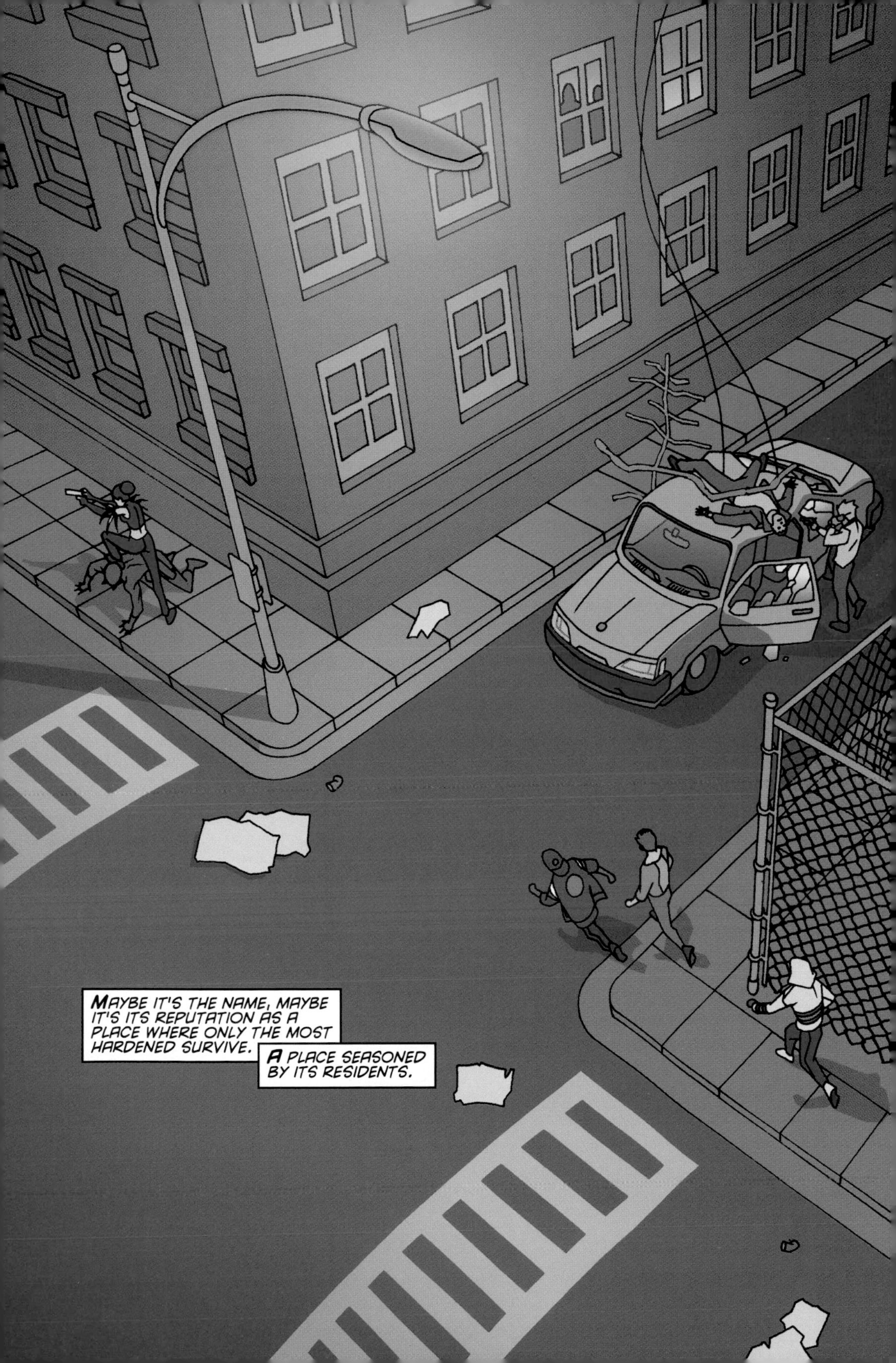
MAYBE IT'S THE NAME, MAYBE IT'S ITS REPUTATION AS A PLACE WHERE ONLY THE MOST HARDENED SURVIVE.
A PLACE SEASONED BY ITS RESIDENTS.

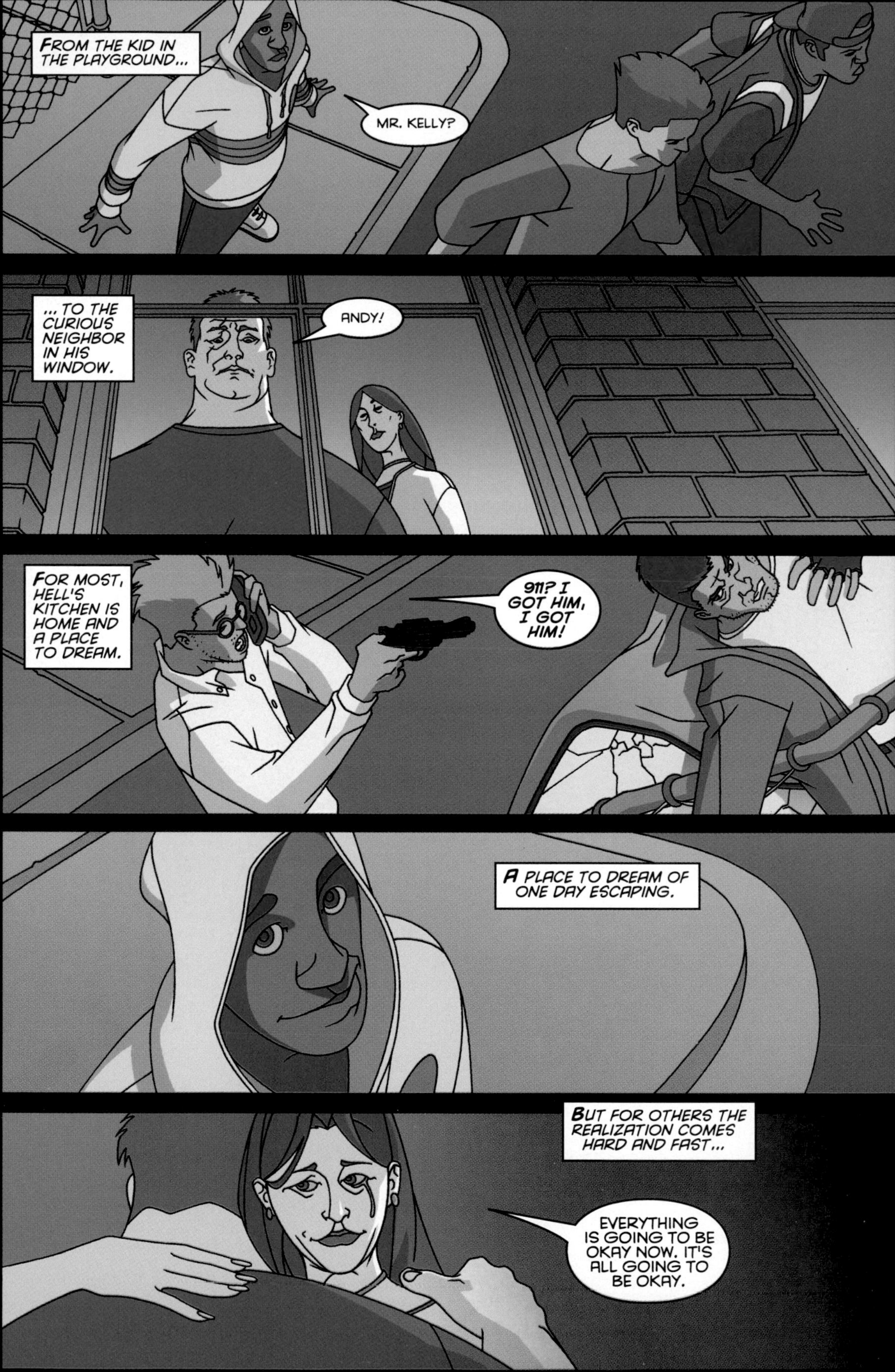
FROM THE KID IN THE PLAYGROUND...
MR. KELLY?
...TO THE CURIOUS NEIGHBOR IN HIS WINDOW.
ANDY!
FOR MOST, HELL'S KITCHEN IS HOME AND A PLACE TO DREAM.
911? I GOT HIM, I GOT HIM!
A PLACE TO DREAM OF ONE DAY ESCAPING.
BUT FOR OTHERS THE REALIZATION COMES HARD AND FAST...
EVERYTHING IS GOING TO BE OKAY NOW. IT'S ALL GOING TO BE OKAY.

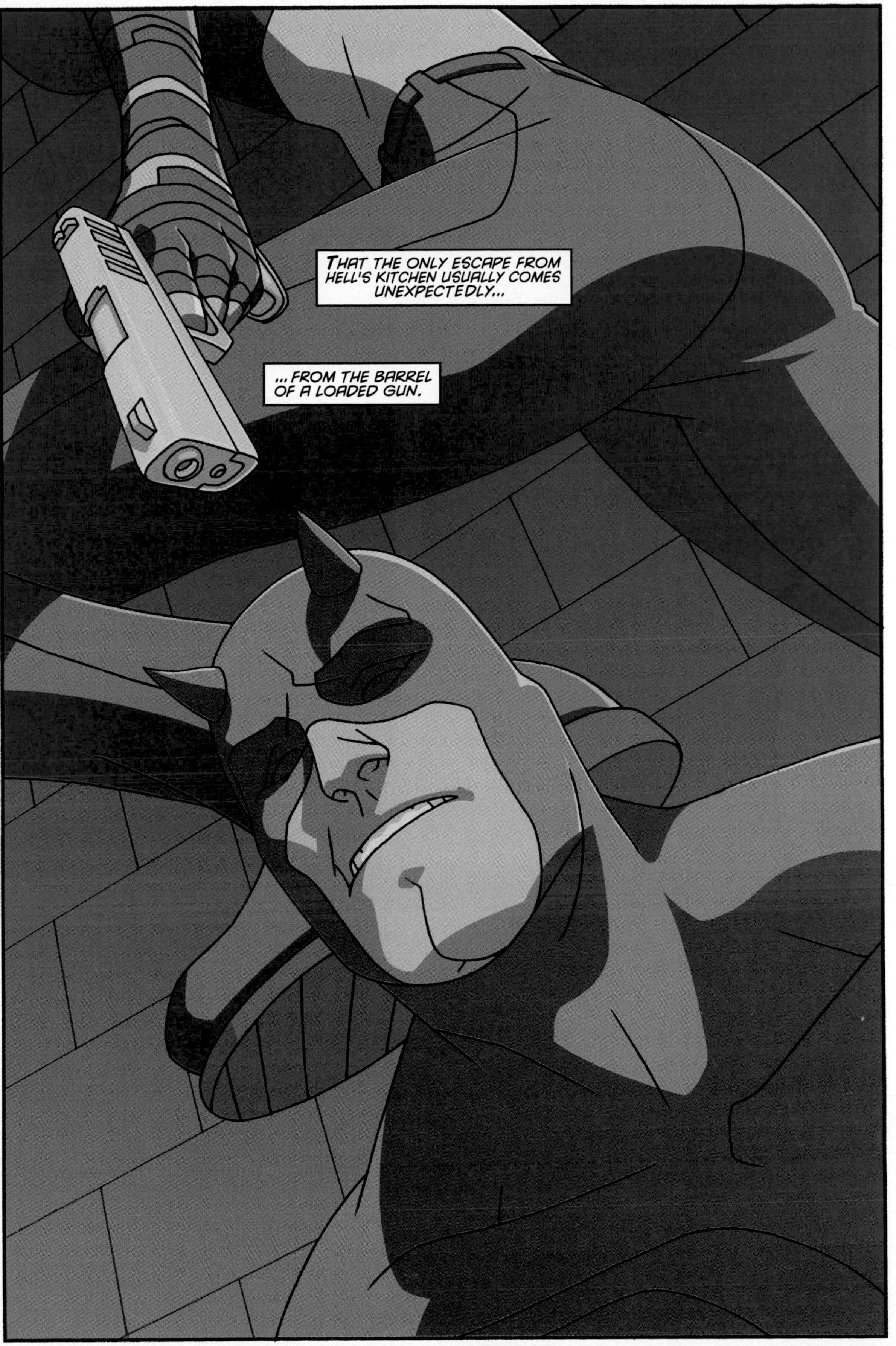
THAT THE ONLY ESCAPE FROM HELL'S KITCHEN USUALLY COMES UNEXPECTEDLY...
...FROM THE BARREL OF A LOADED GUN.

Sketchbook

David Mack

Character Design:
Echo

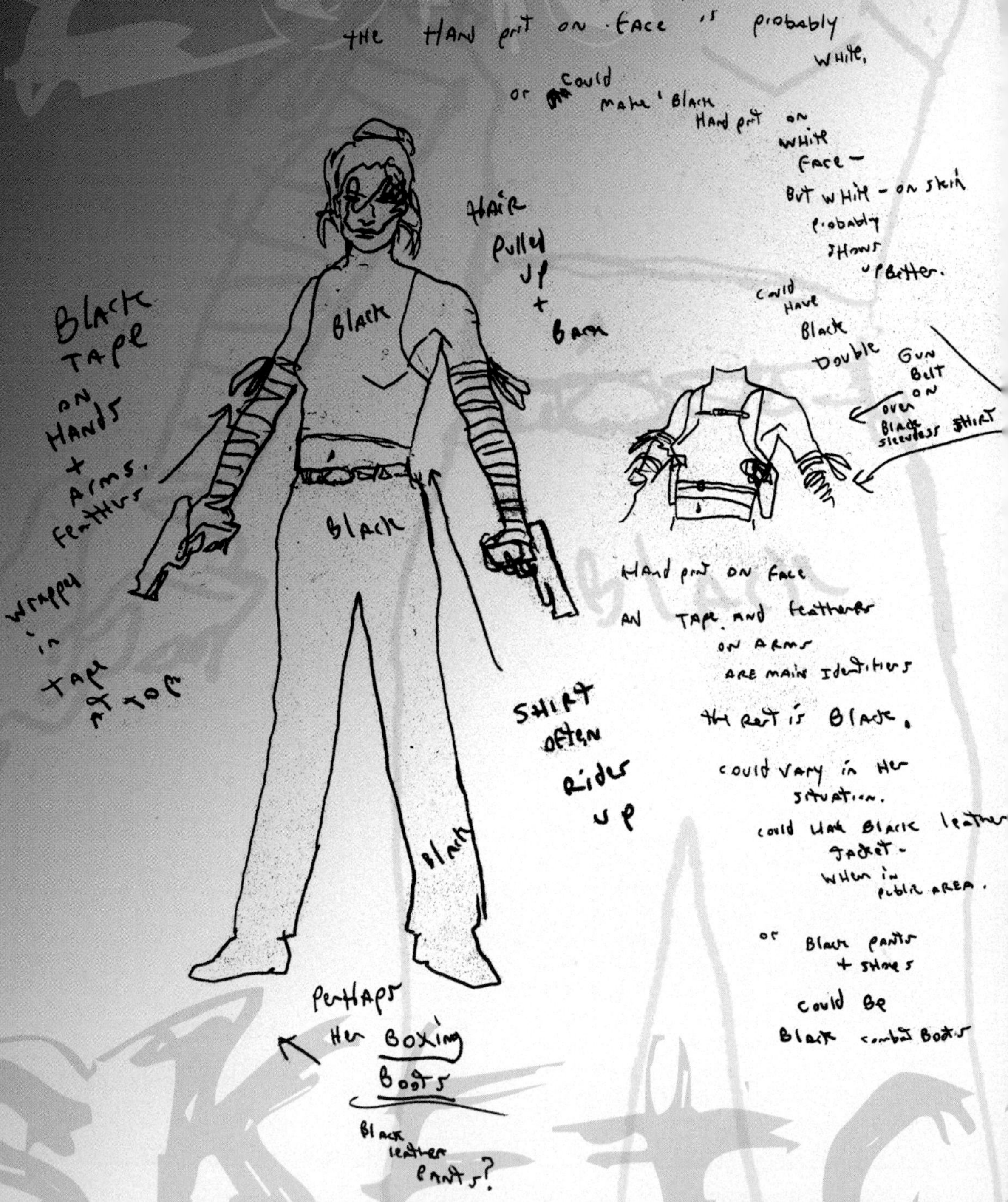
the HAND print on face is probably white.
or could make Black Hand print on white face — But white — on skin probably shows up better.
Hair pulled up + back
Black
Black tape on Hands + arms. feathers
wrapped in tape at top
Black
Black
could have Black double gun belt on over Black sleeveless shirt
Hand print on face an tape and feathers on arms are main identifiers
the rest is Black.
could vary in her situation.
could have Black leather jacket — when in public area.
or Black pants + shoes
could be Black combat Boots
Shirt often rides up
Perhaps her Boxing Boots
Black leather pants?

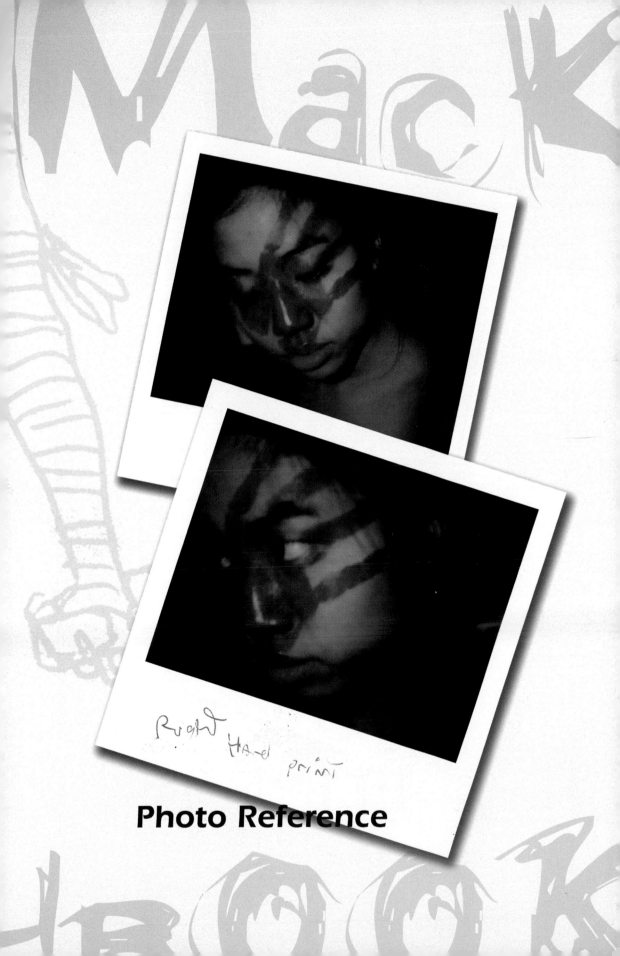

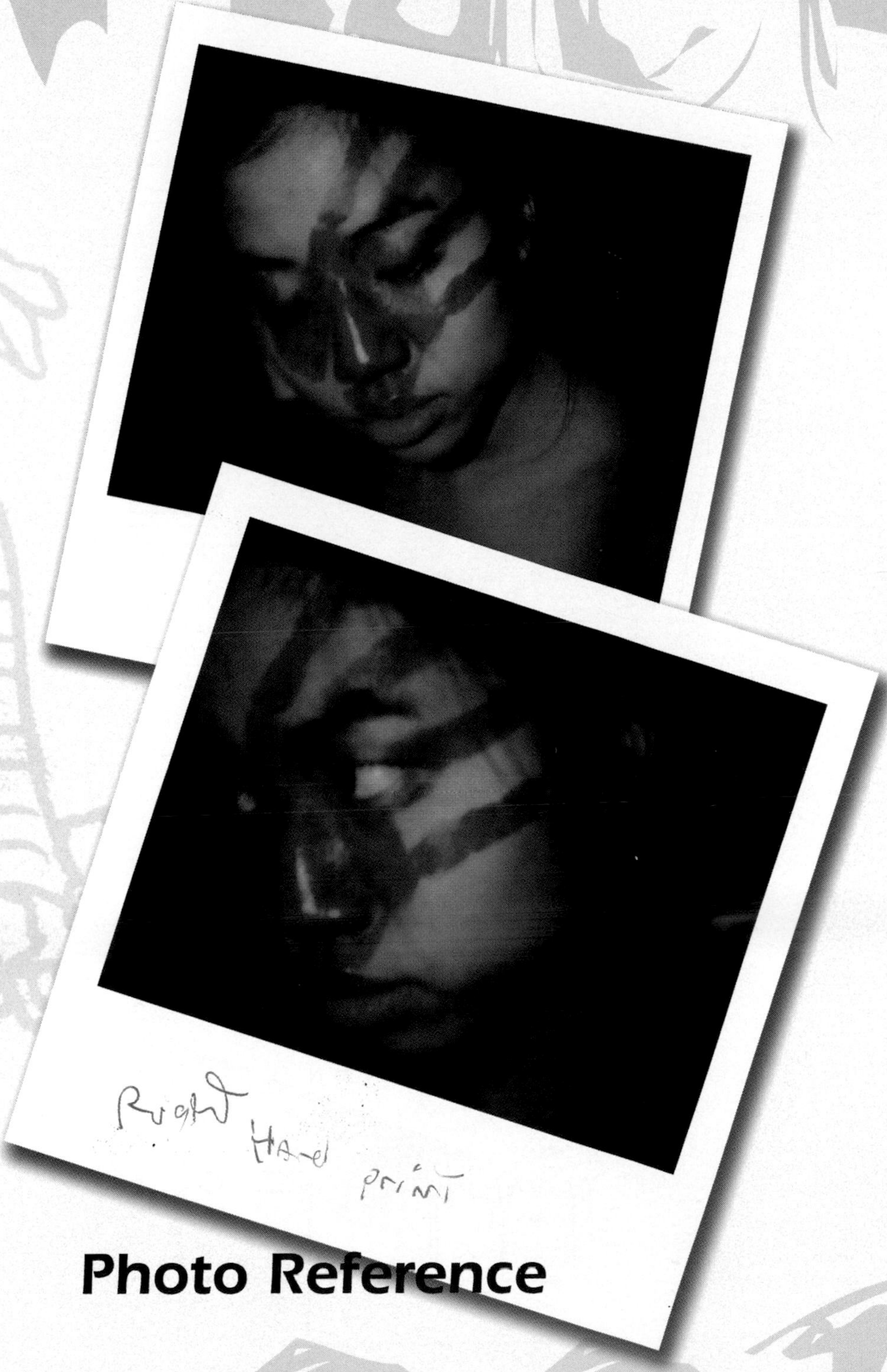
Right Hand print

Photo Reference

Layout Sketches

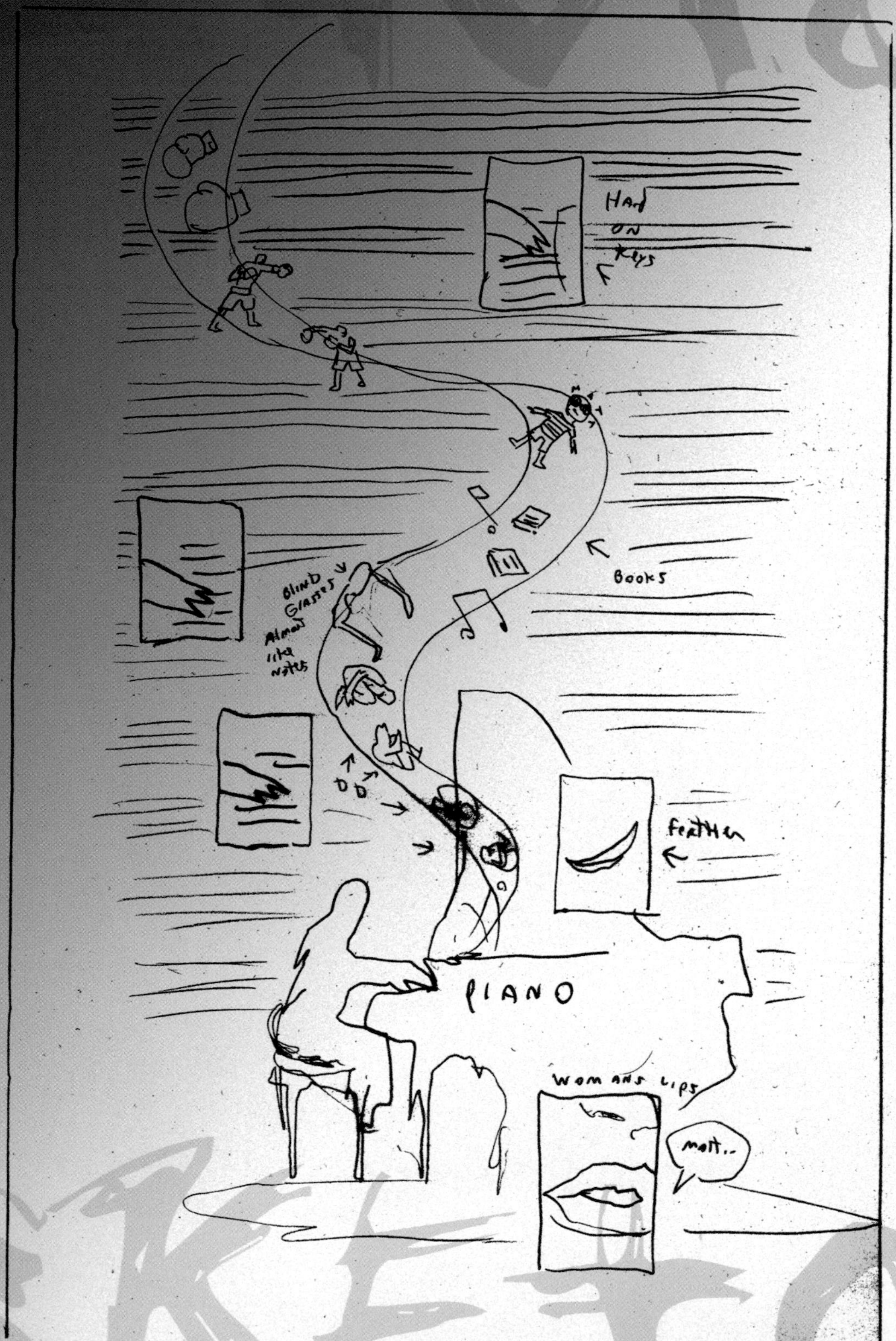

Hard on keys
Books
Blind Glasses
Almost like notes
feather
PIANO
Womans lips
matt..

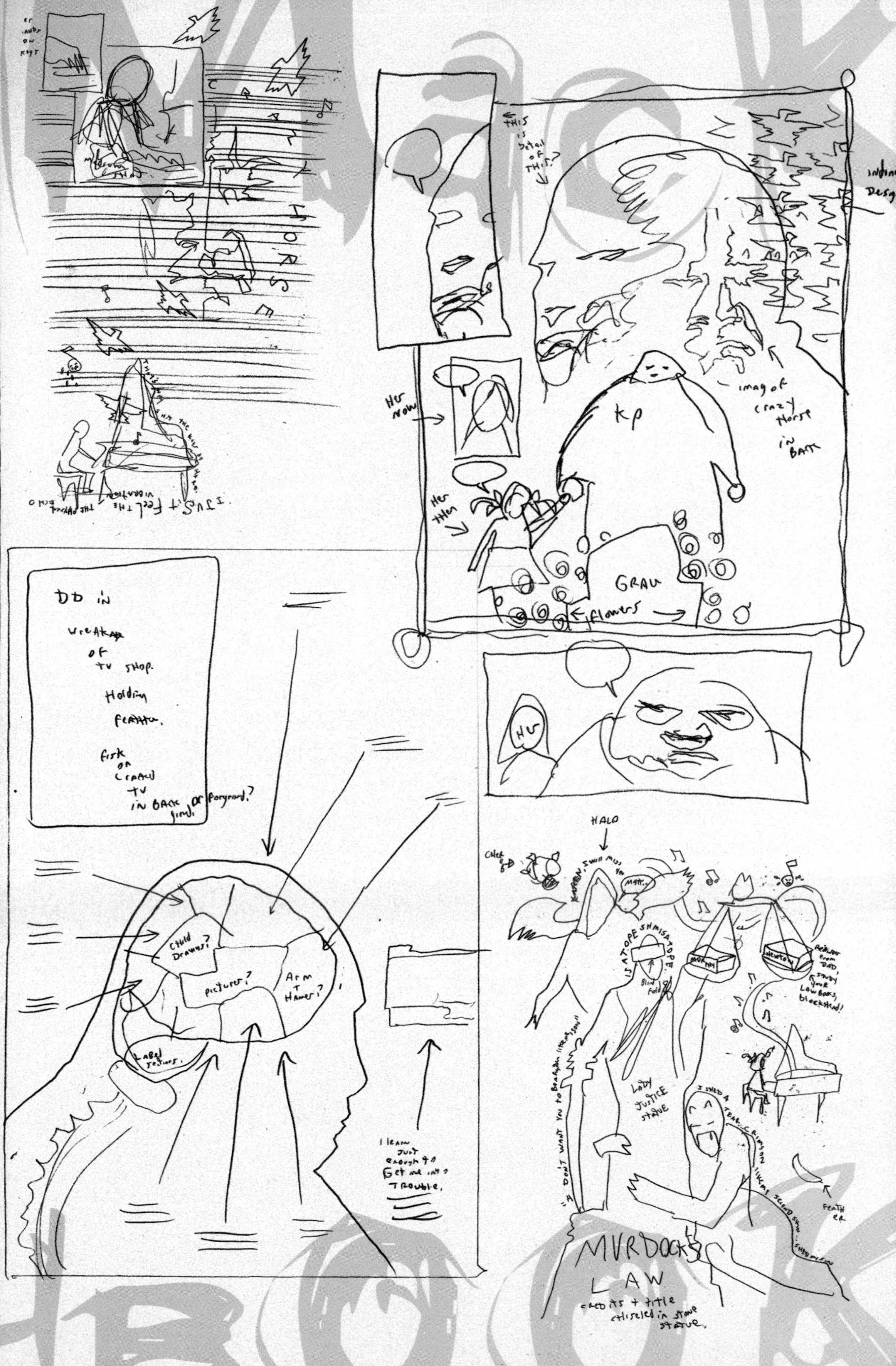
THIS is detail of THIS?
Indian Designs
image of crazy horse in BATH
Her now
Her then
KP
GRAU
flowers
DD in wreckage of TV shop. Holding feather.
fist or crack TV in BACK or graveyard?
Child Drawings?
pictures?
Arm + Hammer?
I learn just enough to get me into trouble.
HALO
Newton
Reminder from Dad, study your law books, blockhead!
Blind fold
Lady Justice statue
FEATH ER
MURDOCK'S LAW
credits + title chiseled in stone statue.

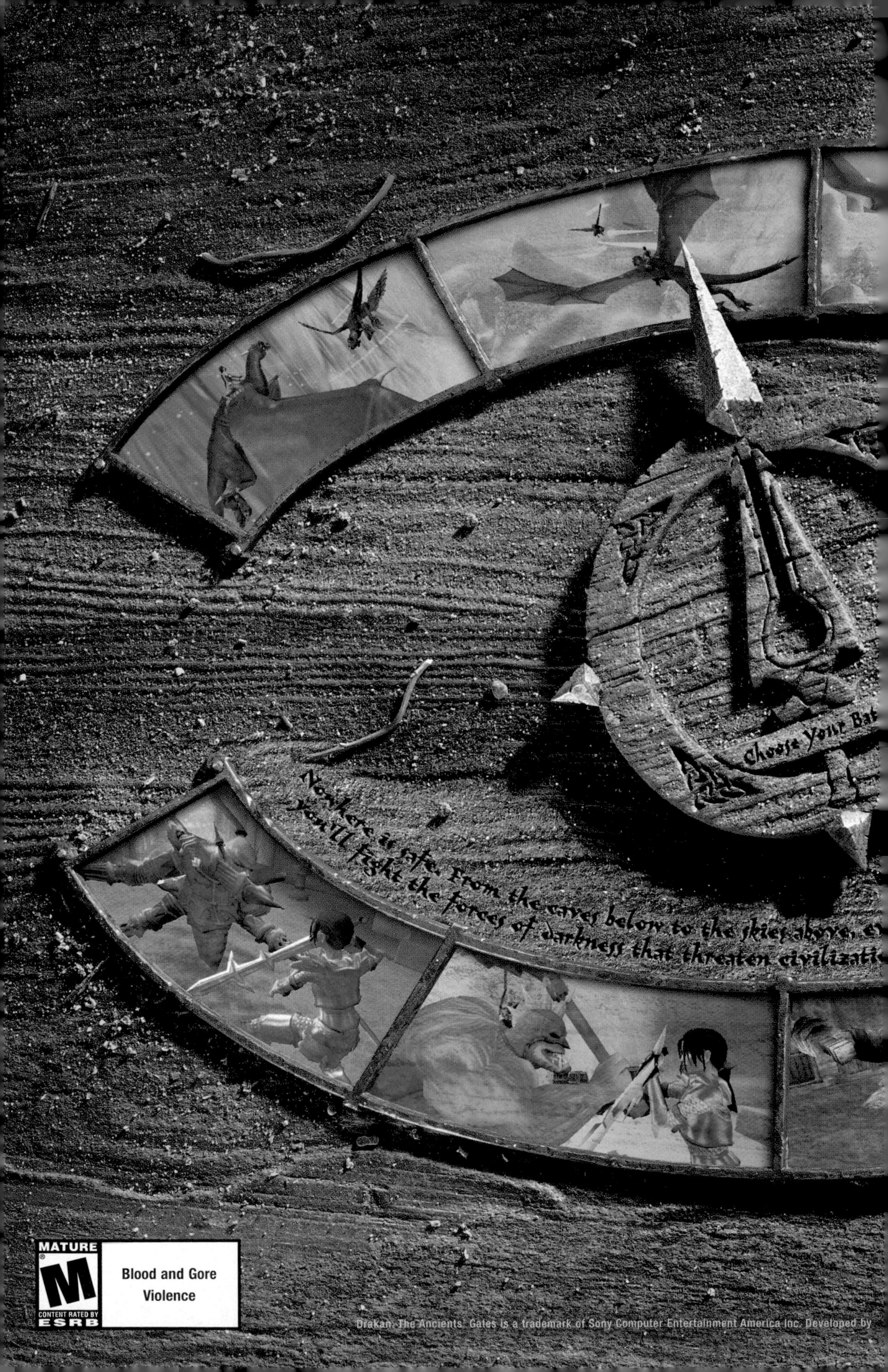
Choose Your Bat
Nowhere is safe. From the caves below to the skies above, ev
you'll fight the forces of darkness that threaten civilizati
MATURE
M
CONTENT RATED BY ESRB
Blood and Gore
Violence
Drakan: The Ancients' Gates is a trademark of Sony Computer Entertainment America Inc. Developed by

www.scea.com

DRAKAN
THE ANCIENTS' GATES

attack from all sides as Rynn and Arokh sharpen your swords and prepare for battle.

PlayStation 2

SUBSCRIBERS... ASSEMBLE!

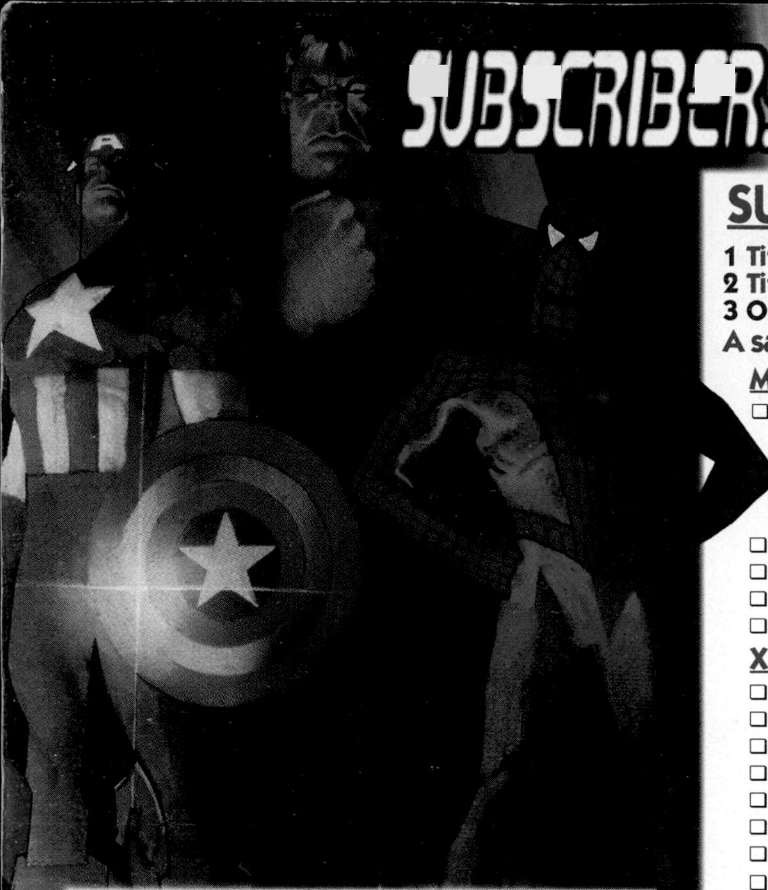

SUBSCRIBE AND SAVE!

1 Title For $23.97- A savings of $3!
2 Titles For $22.97- A savings of $8!
3 Or More Titles For $21.97 each- A savings of $15 or more!

MARVEL HEROES

- ❑ AVE — Avengers
- ❑ BPR — Black Panther
- ❑ CAM — Captain America
- ❑ CMV — Captain Marvel
- ❑ FAN — Fantastic Four
- ❑ INC — Hulk
- ❑ IRM — Iron Man
- ❑ THO — Thor
- ❑ BLT — Thunderbolts

X-MEN

- ❑ CAB — Cable
- ❑ DDP — Deadpool
- ❑ EXL — Exiles
- ❑ XME — Uncanny X-Men
- ❑ WOL — Wolverine
- ❑ XFO — X-Force
- ❑ MEN — New X-Men
- ❑ XTR — X-Treme X-Men

SPIDER-MAN

- ❑ AMZ — Amazing Spider-Man
- ❑ SPI — Peter Parker, Spider-Man
- ❑ TAW — Spider-Man: Tangled Web
- ❑ SPG — Spider-Girl

MARVEL ULTIMATES

- ❑ ULA — The Ultimates
- ❑ USP — Ultimate Spider-Man
- ❑ UXM — Ultimate X-Men
- ❑ UMT — Ultimate Marvel Team-Up

MARVEL KNIGHTS

- ❑ DDV — Daredevil
- ❑ ELK — Elektra (Mature Readers)
- ❑ PUN — Punisher (Mature Readers)

LIMITED TIME HEROES OFFER

❑ Yes! I want both Avengers and Incredible Hulk for just $37.94

A Savings of $16.00!

Exclusive Subscriber Savings and Services

Your satisfaction guaranteed or your money back on all remaining issues!

IMPROVED PACKAGING!

All issues are mailed with cardboard backing in new weather resistant cellophane bags!

Ordering is fast and easy!

❑ **Yes! Sign me up for home delivery of the comics I've checked. I deserve the most in savings, convenience, service, and selection!**

My satisfaction is guaranteed!

Check off the subscriptions you want delivered to your home (12 issues each) and return this page or a copy to:

MARVEL ENTERTAINMENT GROUP, INC.
P.O. BOX 32 NEWBURGH, NY 12551.

Please provide credit card information or make your check or money order payable to "Marvel Entertainment Group, Inc."

Or order Toll Free at 800-217-9158.

OFFER GOOD UNTIL 3/31/2002.
YES, YOU CAN PHOTOCOPY THIS AD!

Please print:

NAME OF READER ____ DATE OF BIRTH (M/D/Y) ____

STREET ADDRESS ____ E-MAIL ____

CITY ____ STATE ____ ZIP ____

# of subscriptions ____ **Amount enclosed: $** ____

Charge my: ☐ **VISA** ☐ **MasterCard**

CREDIT CARD # ____ EXPIRATION DATE ____

NAME OF CREDIT CARD HOLDER (IF DIFFERENT FROM NAME ABOVE) ____

SIGNATURE FOR CREDIT CARD ORDERS ____

Canada, add $10.00 per title (in U.S. funds only, includes GST#R127032852). Foreign, add $12 per title in U.S. funds only. Allow 6 to 10 weeks for delivery of your first issue.

H21MD2

WWW.MARVEL.COM

For a comic store near you call 1-888-comicbook

MARVEL

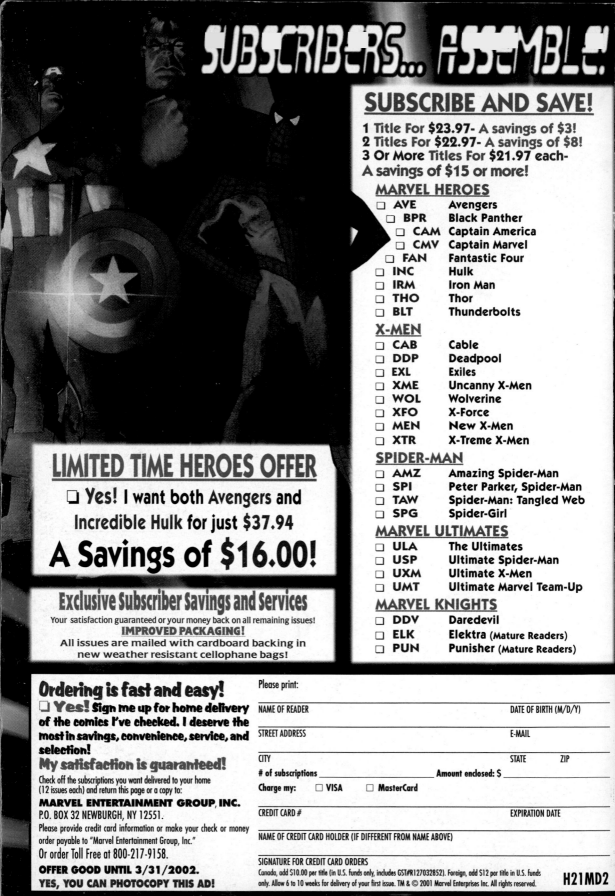